JO ANN BROWN-SCOTT

EPIPHANY AND HER FRIENDS

INTUITIVE REALIZATIONS THAT HAVE CHANGED WOMEN'S LIVES

2007

Epiphany and Her Friends

TABLE OF CONTENTS

At age sixteen, rape's aftermath builds the foundation for
a woman's life-long personal strength. The healing powers
of a self-imposed exile to the woods, then witnessing primal
struggles for survival by man and beast in a trip to Africa, leave
a lasting impression of the beauty and brutality of life. A story
told with stunning honesty by a strong woman not afraid to
reveal undertones of deep sensitivity and fragile vulnerability.
A story about *learning how to love, nurture and heal yourself,* while
falling in love with wild country.
<u>by Christine Mahree Fowler, age 44</u>

How a horrific house fire was the catalyst for a series of difficult
challenges, both mental and physical; ultimately providing self-
discoveries for both husband and wife and their two children.
Positive changes, including greater marital solidarity and career
success, were the admirable end results for a brave family in a
classic story of "what does not kill us makes us stronger." A
message, offered with straightforward clarity, that accidental
tragedy does not necessarily result in shattered lives; *and how
not to remain a victim.*
<u>by Patricia D. Brewster, age 64</u>

A woman gifted with many of life's blessings reveals her early
development of bulimia, and the "perfect storm" of circumstances
that enabled it to get a grip and take control of her life. She

documents the horrific repercussions of struggling since the age of twelve years with body/self image issues resulting in the disorder; then gradually fighting her way back to balanced eating, while gaining the understanding that the best way to feed her *self* is to feed her *soul*. She finally experiences the ultimate empowerment of realizing who she *now* wants to be, for the rest of her life. A story about *taking back control of your life*.

by Jessica K. Rivers, age 42

A true-life travel adventure of mind, body and soul takes you to Peru and back, offering food for thought and vivid visual description. How leaving the USA opens one woman's eyes to the automatic advantages of American citizenship by witnessing first-hand the disparity of living conditions in another part of the world; then her stunning re-entry into the surreal culture of Silicon Valley in its "hey-day" after seeing the simple joy on the faces of the poverty-stricken people of Peru. *A realization about awareness of life's inequities, having compassion and sharing life's fortunes.*

by Kelly K. Heapy, age 37

How being a doormat only gets you mud. A humorous account of a daughter-in-law's refusal to accept, for one minute longer, the constantly accumulating insults of her mother-in-law. How the daughter-in-law snaps, suddenly exploding into a mind- cleansing and air-clearing loss of temper; followed by a firm insistence on some changes in the family. This universal theme, all too familiar, will bring thoughts of *"Oh I wish I had done that!"*

by Christine Anne Speranza, age 53

During some volunteer time in Africa, a young woman understands exactly what had been missing in her life; lessons learned about the gift of your time, the gift of your love and

the gift of caring enough to act. Realizing that skills will save the youth of the world from a life of poverty; a mother and daughter found a charitable organization that sells imported pillows, donating funds to teach skills to children in Thailand, Viet Nam and Africa, thus keeping them off the streets. *A story for anyone who does not know how to begin to make a difference.*
by Laura Rietmeijer, age 23

A story of basic survival disguised as normal living—a young woman's courageous *agreement* to accept the difficult challenges of just staying alive, without having the proper tools to cope. After years of self-destructive behavior born of deep internal sadness, and hitting rock bottom, she finally reaches out for help with a call to one particular person and a critical change of direction is accomplished through her inability to lie to a child. This woman bravely offers you a private glimpse into her *almost* invisible, and nearly fatal, personal pain; told with intelligence and even humor. *An insight into a courageous, uphill climb out of personal suffering.*
by Leela Kaisa Sundquist, age 31

A busy woman learns how ignoring one's health and becoming over-extended in the midst of everyday chaos can lead to a dangerous meltdown. Being stressed out and unable to jump off a treadmill of activity ultimately results in a case of shingles that stops her in her tracks and threatens serious and potentially permanent damage. A story that picks up speed as it unfolds, leaving you hanging on for the ride and wondering how it will stop. *A realization for self-less women who must learn to be the "good" kind of selfish.*
by Vicki Rossiter Hand, age 58

A story about a rough cut stone who becomes a diamond of a woman in the painful growing up process of a young girl. A parent's suffocating over-protectiveness results in a daughter's difficult struggle to overcome insecurity, gain confidence, define herself as a person separate and unique from her mother and finally grasp the meaning of her life. This life-long quest for self-knowledge ultimately leads to her spiritual awakening and transformation, away from severe religiosity to joyful spirituality, and an acute awareness of a loving, forgiving God and *His noble purpose for her life*—that of finding ideal parents for adoptive children.

<u>**by Dae Helena Leckie, age 68**</u>

This story is a reminder about the importance of providing our children with validation for being extraordinary, unique human beings, worthy of love and respect. A woman, reared in a simpler place and time, received the most priceless yet least expensive gift a parent can give to a child—the confidence that she was loved and treasured. Later in life, as an educator of children with special needs, she passed to a new generation of challenged youngsters this gift of self-esteem. Parents, friends, family members and neighbors all comprise the village of people required to raise children who are healthy in mind and body. *The bright future of our children depends upon their validation.*

<u>**by Lorelei Ann Hoxie, age 66**</u>

One of life's mysteries is solved in this story about a woman's awakening to the basic law of attraction. A savvy and practical, no-nonsense type of woman, on a day when she was truly listening, was given a spiritual message that changed the way she viewed herself and the particular struggle that had shadowed her life and hampered her happiness. In an instant

she understood that her personal belief that she had been a *victim* of the struggle was a convenient and incorrect perception; she had in fact *drawn herself* to the struggle. Clear insight is given into the deeper meaning inherent in experiencing life's biggest challenges; and finally understanding the answer to the universal question, *"WHY ME?"*
<u>by Denise Diana Imansepahi, age 40</u>

Endnotes for Chapter Twenty-Two

ACKNOWLEDGMENTS

In the process of compiling this anthology and crafting its style and content there were many people who contributed ideas and inspiration without ever realizing it. I am grateful for "chance" meetings and seemingly random conversations with treasured friends, dear family and casual acquaintances, who offered valuable insights and comments about their own life experiences. Creative additions and alterations in the book resulted from these chats, along the journey to its completion. These people were unaware, and yet I thank them.

Particular friends and family who have given me constant support and encouragement in this labor of love include, first and foremost, my daughter Kelly, who has been my consultant in the book's creation and development, offering excellent advice and unique insight. She has kept me balanced and sane. She alone could recognize when I was nearly at the end of my project-management rope, and would quickly tie a knot of irreverent humor, preventing me from losing my grip and slipping off the end. Her graphic design expertise is evident in the book's cover; accurately capturing the essence and character of the book just as she envisioned it. I thank her for the unique brilliance and perspective she has consistently cast on the entire project; from the encouragement she offered me at the first glimmer of my idea all the way to the final decisions. I thank her for her patience, dedication and love.

My son Tom, a fine author, will discuss written pages, both his and mine, over countless pleasurable lunches. His keen literary mind, his extraordinary vocabulary and his high standard for excellence in the basic skill of crafting word arrangements on the printed page have proved to be priceless resources in my decisions for this book. I thank him for his love, his time, his interest and his support.

My husband, Ed, has been my in-house, tech-support, computer-wizard and saved me from running screaming from the computer on many occasions. He created a monster many years ago by insisting that I could write more efficiently on the computer than in a yellow chief tablet.

He is the only one who has lived up close and personal, day and night, with my book-birthing experience, for well over a year. His early evening inquiry, "What did you do today?" was almost always answered in the same way…"Breathed. Ate something. Worked on the book…." He is cautiously asking me now if I have plans for another book. Yes. Please watch for the Epiphany Series to continue.

The friends of epiphany I have gathered together for this book are women of great wisdom and depth, who provided me with my raw material—fascinating stories with simple but powerful themes that we pored over and polished into finished chapters. Their friendship, humor, honesty and patience with my constant emails and calls and deadlines, and their loyalty to the project and to each other, kept this little epiphany ship not only afloat, but sailing. These remarkable women were my constant inspiration and our journey together became my almost daily purpose. I know I have used a mixed metaphor—first it was a book *birthing* and now it is a book *ship*. But the similarities are numerous and I am conflicted. It has seemed like both to me—painful labor one moment and blissful sailing the next; resulting in the final destination—a creation of unique beauty—after a long and arduous journey.

Now we have finally come into port. I am grateful to all of these caring human beings for being exactly the kind of common yet extraordinary women I needed for the project. Some have labored with me for well over a year; others came to me running, full speed, at the very last minute before it was too late to contribute. Instinct and intuitive realization drew me to each of them. It might have seemed like a random compilation to some, but it was *so* not. Each perfect one led me to another. Some people were found, interviewed, invited to write, brought into the circle, and then did not continue for a variety of agonizing reasons. But they led me to others who filled the void the first had left. Additional friends who were living *inside the chaos* of some life-changing epiphany could not be asked to write because their current situations were too grueling and intense—they were busy just surviving. You know who you are. I am glad you made it through the storms.

Once we all started writing, we were still in constant flux. The chapters grew in number, size and intensity, then, dwindled again. We ebbed and we flowed. Behind the scenes, all of our busy lives continued to unfold with a mix and match of tragic and happy events occurring to virtually every single one of us, often at breakneck and frightening speed; yet ultimately awarding us the gift of additional perspectives and insights. Life is never dull; with this many vital, active women there will always be layers upon layers of happenings—new epiphany stories within the "old" epiphany stories—and so it will go from now forward. I had faith that things would eventually settle down for a second or two so that we could go to print, in some narrow window of time between one event and another. The labyrinth of our connections to each other and the way the "map of us" was charted is nothing short of amazing, and it all worked out beautifully as it was meant to.

The memoirs of this book are subjective in nature and written from the exclusive perspectives and recollections of our authors, however we believe these memoirs to be true and accurate in their content and written to portray real life events as they actually occurred. Out of respect for the unique expression of each contributing writer we have chosen to honor a range of individual preferences in grammar, punctuation and style within acceptable parameters.

I would like to thank my mother who, although she has passed on, was with me every step of the way, clearly having infused me with her own love for the printed page, the perfect word, correct grammar and the economical use of descriptive text. She was a fine English teacher. I often asked myself, "What would Mom do?" as I edited and composed. She lives in these pages and she would be proud to be there.

The world is in turmoil as we finish this special project. I am continually humbled and saddened by what occurs to other less fortunate people and animals of the world every day as I sit at my computer, comfortable in my home, and compose. I am feeling the weight of concerns for the future of our beautiful blue planet. Our small and simple book will still contribute, I know, to the collective wisdom of the world. It has a humanitarian purpose, a message of hope and a beating heart. We are all in this together, carrying the world's problems shoulder to shoulder. Friends of epiphany, everywhere, must offer whatever fine bits of enlightenment we are able to contribute in the brief time we are here. We owe it to the universe.

Jo Ann Brown-Scott

This Book Is Dedicated
To
My Entire Family
And
My Extended Family Of Friends.

"There is in every woman's heart a spark of heavenly fire,
which lies dormant in the broad daylight of prosperity;
but which kindles up and beams and blazes
in the dark hour of adversity."
Washington Irving

INTRODUCTION

What is an Epiphany?

A comprehension or perception of reality
by means of sudden intuitive realization.

An abrupt manifestation of the essence or the meaning
of something.

"A spiritual flash that changed the way I view myself."

Truth revealed, as if a light was turned on.

I see Epiphany as a beautiful, mysterious woman,
who sends tinkling, wind-chime chills up your spine
at her first tapping on your mind's door.
If you decide to let her in,
shafts of white light will open your mind,
clearing away the cobwebs of previous perceptions;
offering you the fresh, clear dawn of intuitive realization,
as she comes gliding into your consciousness
and enters the rooms of your soul.
She is a forceful yet gentle woman, demanding your attention;
singing the truth to you
in melodies you have never heard before.
She is dressed in the colors of her message—
hot coral with intensity;
cool Mediterranean blue with determination—
finally the lily white gown of truth.
You must listen.
You must open your heart and soul to her,
or she will arrive again and again
with louder knocking and brighter, deeper colors
until you cannot deny her brilliant entrance.
Listen willingly to her once,
hear her wisdom;
she will return faithfully every time you need her.

Everyone's struggle is to become who they really are in life. We all feel a need to know ourselves; to define ourselves. At the core of our being and in the nucleus of our soul we are *somebody*. It all boils down to that. Genes determine some of it. The rest is the result of circumstance and desire.

The search for who we are is our life-long journey. A few people never consciously get it, bobbing around in the sea of life like a cork, going wherever the next wave takes them. They look back on their lives and see no patterns, no lessons, no inspirational moments and no choices in it all. They have not looked hard enough.

Some people misinterpret the person they truly are. They temporarily get it wrong. They might choose a direction in life that does not accurately represent their authenticity and so they have somehow missed becoming who they actually wanted to be. They took the path of least resistance. But they can re-direct.

Others believe that life unfolds like a vast network of delicious choices and opportunities for making positive differences in the world. The struggle lies in the difference we each choose to make and that difference becomes the definition of who we are. In this process, potential is limitless, rewards boundless and the journey is meant to be savored. Although mistakes are made and disappointments and tragedies are experienced along the way, we recover and move forward. We constantly search for answers, we welcome healing and we continue to strive for goodness.

We all have choices, every single day to the end, about who we want to be. That is the beauty of life; each dawning day is a fresh chance for reinvention.

In our journey of life, as we pay attention, we experience *occasions in time when startling truth is revealed to us*, and we put the discovery to good use by adding it to the basic knowledge of who we are. Truth may come suddenly, even violently, in a single illuminating flash of thought, hitting us squarely between the eyes, any time of the day or night. Or a quieter realization may finally occur to us after a long, agonizing unfolding of events when no solutions could be found. Years might go by, then quite abruptly, a wise, new insight percolates and bubbles up from the depths and erupts peacefully through our consciousness, providing a lesson or a plan or an alternative, solving everything. Gaining time—gaining perspective—is critical to this process. They say that life keeps sending us its big lessons until we learn them, repeating familiar themes with increasing impact until finally our full attention is captured and we are completely aware; we absorb the wisdom thrown repeatedly at us and we finally begin to live and breathe it. As Gandhi said, "Be the change you wish to see in the world."

When we suddenly "get it"—when we receive the truth—*the vehicle by which it arrives varies* from person to person and epiphany to epiphany. The energy that carried it might have been an audible inner voice from our soul, or it might have come to our attention in a powerful, rumbling shudder of realization that pushed up from the depths of our intuition like a slow earthquake with no voice, or it might have hit us like a bright hot bolt of lightening contradicted by cold chills. In whatever language it comes to us, this is the experience of the epiphany. Some believe it is communication direct from a higher power. Some believe it is simply our own higher self; our soul. Some believe those to be one and the same.

To those of you who claim you have never had one, I say that you most assuredly have. You have just not been in tune with the signs. You must be living in the moment to experience one. You must be honest. You must know yourself. You cannot be off in neverland; wishing for free miracles to bail you out of your dark little hole. You must be in the *here* and *now*. You must be alert and eager to receive the messages of the universe. You must be "present" to win one—the prized epiphany. You must be listening to your heart.

When the idea for this book came to me I was on an adrenaline high for days. I knew that my friends had lived remarkable lives, ripe with epiphanies. I had heard many of their stories in conversations over dinner and a couple of glasses of wine. I knew that the most difficult part for each of us would be to choose just one epiphany to write about. In addition to the twenty main chapters, we have included some "epipha-minis," as we affectionately call them, (mini-epiphanies) for quick reading and instant insights; meant to be enjoyed in moments when you might like to cheer up a friend or illustrate a point about a life issue.

The larger stories we have chosen to tell are stunning and relevant. They are stories where the bottom line is hope. These stories needed to be told. I like to believe that more often than not, epiphanies are inspirational rather than disturbing, but inspiration can result from disturbing incidents. They can also be side-splittingly funny, loud, quietly moving, lengthy, nanosecond quick, ugly or beautiful. Epiphanies come in many packages and sometimes wear a disguise so, as that first goose-bump begins to rise to attention and then progresses to full-blown body chills, we still might not recognize their significance. But the next time you get chills, stop and think. I always heard wise people say that when you experience chills, the truth has been revealed to you.

Epiphanies can also be brutal. An epiphany can nearly kill you with its clarity. An epiphany can singe your soul with the humbling and embarrassing fire of realization that you have screwed up, or reduce you to shivers with an instant discovery of betrayal by someone you love, revealing a truth too painful to bear. You suddenly understand the signals you had been missing. As they say, "What doesn't kill you makes you stronger."

When children have an epiphany it is a beautiful thing to witness— the look of pure wonder on a little face when the realization dawns that bravery is often rewarded, or kindness to another makes you feel good or even perhaps that Grandma's voice can be heard on the phone when she is far away. I remember the epiphany I had, very young, looking in a full length mirror and seeing my raw self with the astounding realization that I was a part of the human race, not just a mere kid, and the thoughts I was having at that moment were inside that head that I saw in the mirror. No one knew those thoughts except me. I could tell them to people or keep them secret. It gave me confidence. I felt empowered; the light turned on for me at that very point in time.

When older people have an epiphany it is an acknowledgment that they are continuing to learn about life. They have remained open to possibility. They have not yet seen it all. Think of the elderly Caucasian woman in the nursing home, having lived most of her life during a time when prejudice thrived; then finding that her new best friend and/or possibly even her roommate is an Afro-American woman who she grows to love and respect through long and honest conversations about life. An open heart attracts profound life lessons, to the very last breath, and in the process of taking that last breath, one can experience a final epiphany.

A coincidence can bring about an epiphany but an epiphany is rarely a coincidence. An epiphany happens as the result of a series of events, or one simple occurrence that has brought about a powerful insight...thus revealing the truth of a situation. It is not as random as coincidence seems to be—although many of us do not actually believe in the randomness of coincidence.

Allow us to tell you some stories, not of the rich and famous, not of any people whose names you will recognize, but of women who have led spectacular lives, nonetheless. We have chosen to include women who are not worse for the wear from their often gritty experiences, but who are instead wiser, kinder, funnier, smarter about life and more beautiful of spirit as a result of their epiphanies. If you enjoy learning from the experiences of others, no matter what age you are, you will find guidance, insight and strength within these pages. Age is irrelevant to the process of having an epiphany, but it is fascinating to know the time in life that these women received their translucent messages of truth, and we represent a variety of ages within these selections. Our younger writers have already lived a lifetime's worth of epiphanies.

Humankind is being led along an evolving course;
Through this migration of intelligences,
And though we seem to be sleeping,
There is an inner wakefulness
That directs the dream,
And that will eventually startle us back
To the truth of who we are.
Rumi, 13ᵗʰ century poet from ancient Persia

You will meet the lonely, the lost, the attacked, the betrayed, the recovering, the grieving, the enlightened, the gifted, the giving, the poor and the privileged. Critical in the women of our collection is their awakened awareness as human beings—now unafraid to live a life truly engaged, involved, in action, in tune and in step with the universe. We include courageous women who would rather make a mistake in life than feel nothing at all. Strong women, who know that good seldom comes without struggle, will reveal their struggles. Compassionate women will explain how to *begin* to make a humanitarian impact in the world. Witty women, who know that humor can grease the way through many a tough situation, tell stories of shocking challenges still told with humor. Gutsy women will graphically illustrate that making an intuitive, last minute decision toward a deeper human connection can stop violence in its tracks; thus saving their own lives and the lives of others.

All of us who are friends of epiphany wish we had been given a book like this a long time ago. It is a user's guide for living your authentic life. Like exchanging stories on the back porch, in the coolness of a summer evening with friends, this book reinforces the value of hearing other women's experiences. It awakens our hearts and minds to the simple truth that listening to the inner voice of our higher selves, in moments of quiet concentration, is an infallible guide for life. You will recognize your own epiphanies more easily after you read this book and you will observe epiphanies happening to others.

Epiphanies are all around us like angels in frenzy, revealing truth.
Jo Ann Brown-Scott

All the women writers of our book can be reached at this email address epiphs20@yahoo.com. Please specify individual author's names on the subject line if you choose to email a specific person.

Watch for the website www.epiphanysfriends.com. This is where you can contribute your own epiphany experience.

CHAPTER ONE
WILDNESS
Christine Mahree Fowler

We need the tonic of wildness...
at the same time that we are earnest to explore
and learn all things,
we require that all things be mysterious and unexplorable,
that land and sea be infinitely wild, unsurveyed
and unfathomed by us because unfathomable.
We can never have enough of nature...
We need to witness our own limits transgressed,
and some life pasturing freely where we never wander.
Henry David Thoreau

Just off my balcony, a cocoon of some sort is shaking and twirling violently from a twig. Some mysterious creature, maybe a butterfly or a moth is trying to break free from its clay-like prison. The eight year old inside of me would like to reach out and break him free—help the little guy out. But my forty-two year old self, in all of her wisdom, knows that by struggling he is building up the wing-strength he will need to fly with the big boys. He is transforming. Nature, in her wisdom, would not allow him to crawl around like a worm even if he wanted to. There have been a few times in my life I have felt like I was in a cocoon. This is one of them.

Part of me still feels like the sixteen year old who left home with nothing but a carton of cigarettes and a poncho. She was wild-eyed, uncontrollable, and reckless. But middle age has gifted me with perhaps a little more control. If I ran away today I'd surely pack some hiking boots and a pair of killer stilettos. There is however, still an impulsive spirit that rises up in my chest from time to time. It has frightened family, husbands, and friends. But age has a way of putting the reins on wild impulses, as does motherhood.

Children came early, two of them—a boy and a girl. I adapted to my role like a mother lion; hunting, fighting, protecting and caring for them with a primal fierceness. After their arrival each and every decision I made would revolve around them. As all mothers understand, your life is never again your own. Their successes would become my successes and their failures would become my failures. Motherhood opens one's heart but sometimes in a way that feels as if it's being opened surgically without anesthesia. If it's hard not to bust a moth free from its struggle out of a cocoon, that is no comparison to watching your child struggle as he or she tries to find wings in this tough mother of a world. In addition to these children, I lost my twin boys before they were born. I still carry the scars of their memory on my body and my heart. They linger with me like a gift I never got to open or a poem I never got to read. But by my age, I know there are many things in life like that.

While motherhood seemed to come naturally, monogamy did not. Maybe that's because in nature monogamy doesn't occur that often. I have had two husbands and a couple of love affairs that have been epic. Unlike the beasts of the field, I never took lovers for the sake of the act itself. I became truly attached—for decades. I haven't had as many lovers as most women I know. I just couldn't seem to part with any of the ones I had. You know how you're out there fishing and you're supposed to catch and release? Well I just caught and kept. I had a little pile of fish at the bottom of my boat; barracudas, minnows, big-mouth bass and sharks—all of them flopping around and gasping for breath as I lovingly poked at them, unable to let any of them go. Yes it's been hard for me to settle down. This can present problems; broken hearts, dishes and homes. I've told myself that maybe I'm a naturalist at heart. It has been exciting—wild but not always happy. Someone recently said to me that maybe I was being greedy with the universe and I should let some *things* go. This reminded me of a Buddhist saying, that one cannot receive the next gifts of life if his hands are full. With these bits of wisdom I have let some fish back into the sea.

I am in the roller coaster business of art dealing—a career choice that has placed me among the creative and the eccentric, keeping things precariously interesting. I have walked the razor blade's edge of feast or famine for as long as I can remember. As a teenager, I was once so poor and hungry I had to rely on the charity of canned food from a church. I was worth over a million dollars by the time I was thirty-five. And then, I lost it.

I have a penchant for the beautiful. I am surrounded by beauty. Even now, at a time when I am nowhere close to the top of my game, I manage to live in decadent style. My home is a luxurious Victorian flat built at the turn of the century. The entrance to the building has been noted as one of the three grandest entrances of any building in the city. A birdcage elevator carries me to the top floor where a stained glass dome portraying three angels peers down on me each day. I open the door to rooms that could be from another time in some exotic place. They are filled with paintings and Persian rugs, African artifacts, stone fireplaces and hand-carved mahogany moldings. My iron balcony looks over the trees and rooftops. I am surrounded by beauty. The closet is host to Chanel, Prada, Escada and plenty of cashmere. My social life often takes me to some of the finest resorts in the world. Thousand dollar dinners, luxury suites, celebrities, backstage passes, ringside seats and more.

I am certainly not a "kept" woman. Remember, I mentioned, I'm pretty broke. I somehow manage to sell a painting or an artifact just in time to make a house payment. I'm also lucky—with generous friends who pass down their designer clothing and my ability to magically attract amazing experiences like a magnet.

My mother once described me as a little wild horse, hard to break or fence in. One of my best friends describes me as a cross between Albert Einstein and Mick Jagger. I certainly hope I don't look it. I don't. I'm blonde, blue-eyed and if I don't watch how I dress I can look porn-star-ish. But I'm getting a little older now and my laugh lines are showing. As for laughing, I laugh a lot. I've always said that my greatest blessing and sometimes curse is that I think everything is funny. I also cry a lot. Everything is funny, everything is sad. Everything to me is intense. I'm passionate. It's exhausting.

I grew up in a small town in Colorado. I rode horses, climbed around on rocks, skied and always had skinned up knees and messed up hair. I collected animals including snakes and lizards, a duck named "Fukky" and a cat named "Humpty." I had three boyfriends in kindergarten and was teaching them how to kiss behind the school while collecting treasured gifts of petrified wood and marbles from my runny-nosed admirers. Yes, I started "fishing" at an early age and lovin' my boys. I was busy; busy and happy in my little town. I had one brother until my parents divorced. My father's next marriage would bring me two more brothers. My life has been filled with boys and men, all of whom I have cherished and adored. I took Shop in high school instead of Home Ed because I figured there would be more boys. I'm sure by now you get the point.

My family was torn to pieces with my parent's divorce. My mother went to bed for weeks and ate nothing but soup. When she finally got up, she moved my brother and me out of our little town and into the city. As an eleven year old I learned about depression, infidelity, violence and other grown up things. It's the year I first remember being truly unhappy. We all were.

About a year into our hellish, foggy existence something magical happened. We went to Africa. I had no way of knowing then that this would be the first of many journeys there that would change my life forever. My mother decided to take us to visit her brother who had already lived in Africa for some time. He had, at one time, been a pilot in Viet Nam. His training and a series of events had led him to fly helicopters for the great Kruger Park, the largest game reserve in all of Africa.

Within hours of landing on this mysterious continent, my uncle had me back in the air—this time in his helicopter. We flew over the Limpopo River as crocodiles scurried away from us into the murky water. We hovered over herds of elephant, buffalo, and zebra; everything I could have ever imagined. I was a bird in the biggest sky I'd ever seen. We spent our days exploring the vast African bush, walking, driving and flying over miles of territory. I had every vantage point to view this new and amazing land. We traveled to sights not accessible by any other vehicle but helicopter and set up our camp. Lying in my tent at night I listened to the low rhythmic calls of the lions, the haunting shrill cry of the hyenas and the hippos splashing and snorting in the river below. I was immersed in the wild and something passionate and wild awoke in me. I felt strangely at home.

My uncle taught me many things concerning the creatures of the bush. One odd thing that occasionally occurs is that an animal is sometimes separated from his own species and joins another group of animals thinking he is one of them. For example, a zebra may suddenly join a herd of wildebeest and become part of the herd in the ultimate identity crisis. Something in that story struck me to the core as a child, as I felt that I belonged in Africa, in the bush, more than I belonged in my own habitat. I was connecting to something very powerful there that would prove not to be just a fleeting childhood whim but a love affair that has lasted for thirty years.

In the days that followed, my soul woke up. The colors, smells and flavors of Africa washed over me and healed my wounds. I felt like a little girl being rocked in her mother's arms. Everything seemed better.

At the same time I was well aware of the turmoil in Africa. Apartheid was in full swing. I had journeyed from the most painful, unjust time I had ever experienced to a land where nothing I had experienced at home compared to the pain or the injustice I was witnessing. I saw a brutality in both nature and in man.

I befriended a beautiful black woman who worked as a maid. She worked for approximately $9.00 a month and saw her husband and child only a few times a year. They lived in a shantytown outside of Johannesburg. Before I left she asked me to take her photograph in hopes that part of her soul would travel with me to America. The irony of that moment haunts me to this day. She wanted to send her soul with me; I wanted to leave my soul with her. That strange connection we shared, all in one click of a twelve year old's camera. I still carry her image in the photograph. I remember traveling past those shantytowns wondering how anyone could live in those little tin and barbed wire shacks. I was a little American girl riding in the backseat peering out of the window. What I remember most is how these people, who didn't seem to have anything to be happy about, always smiled and waved. I fell in love with their smiling faces. I fell in love with Africa.

Even when you're wide-awake, sometimes you have to emerge from a dream. Wake up and smell that damned coffee. I smelled that coffee all the way home on the plane. Not likely to be adopted by a herd of wildebeest or a tribe of Zulus, I stared forlornly out of the window. I saw the hazy outline of JFK come into view.

We returned to Colorado, back to the city, and the three of us scattered. Over the next few years my mother, due to her work, began traveling for extended lengths of time leaving my brother and I to our own devices. The three of us were probably all lonely and searching; my brother and I growing up confused and afraid. I developed a kind of wildness, a feral independence. I always wanted to go back to Africa and talked about it way too much. More and more I withdrew from my family. In the pre-teen years I spent much of my time alone but by the age of sixteen I began seeking out the company of others. With the house dark, I searched for and found a tribe, a tribe of equally lost, lonely teenagers. We clung to one another in rebellious unity. I adopted a uniform that would make my parents wince; beaded African chokers, long skirts, knee high moccasins, Indian blouses. I refused to wear a bra. Our rituals included plenty of drugs, alcohol and sex. I felt a lot better.

The days melted into one another. This was a different kind of dream and I was sure I was managing. I tried to go to school when I wasn't busy with tribal affairs. I even got a job in a diner. I was sixteen years old and balancing school, work, my tribe and my dark house. Boys came and went. Most of them I hardly remember. One of them I do.

One cold afternoon I walked into the diner. The cook, looking up from the fryer, with bandanna on head, stated as usual, "I love you."

"Love you too," I said.

A strange voice called from somewhere in the back, "*Why* don't you *ever* say that to *me?*" Making my way toward the voice, I saw him emerge from behind the enormous dishwasher—a beautiful man as strange as his voice. He had long, wavy, blonde hair all the way to his waist, bright blue eyes and a crooked smile.

"I love you," I said.

He smiled his crooked smile and said, "I love you too."

He was riding his bicycle from Texas to Alaska. A twist of fate had separated him from his riding partner who was holding all of their money. Out of necessity, he stopped at my diner to try and earn a little cash until they could be reunited.

It was the dead of winter so I decided to sneak him in and out of my bedroom window at night so that he didn't have to sleep in his tent. Neither the tribe nor my family met him. He was my secret. One day he rode away. I wouldn't call it love although those were my first words to him. He left me with nothing but some memories and directions to his remote cabin in the woods. They were scribbled on a napkin. Not in a million years would I have imagined that this stranger would eventually become the father of my children.

There are pivotal moments in everyone's lives that just change everything. We are caught in motion, circling around and around in the same cycle like a feather in front of a fan. And then it's like someone pulls the plug and the swirling suddenly stops.

The tribe was at a party way up in the mountains. It was one of those out of control under-age affairs where everyone drinks too much, gets too high and regrets who they slept with the next day. The sky was beautiful that night—one of those cloudless, moonless, Colorado nights where the stars overwhelm the sky. The sound of the river washing over the rocks and broken trees couldn't be heard very well over the howling, laughing adolescents—like human wolves calling from the woods. The coolness of the mountains on a summer night is blissful. The river seems to flow right into the air and then over your skin along with the scent of the pines. It was a seemingly perfect night. I don't know why I didn't want to stay. I'd just had enough. Wandering around the river just a little tipsy in my moccasins and skirt, I felt sleepy and content. I wanted to go home.

About fifty teenagers per Volkswagen made their way up the steep canyon to attend this event. No way was anyone taking me home. Campfires were burning, tents were pitched; but I was still determined. I was asking everyone I knew.

"Come on baby. We're having fun," was pretty much the response.

I was just about to climb up to the main road to start hitchhiking when I spotted a guy I'd met a couple of times. He was much older than any of us and I always wondered why he hung out at these things. As a last resort I approached him and asked if he was by any chance going down the mountain.

"Yeah, I have to. I need to be at work in the morning." I had my ride.

No matter how hard I might try, I could never begin to identify this man. The features of his face have become a mystery to me. My mind has locked those details away somewhere or maybe chucked them out like yesterday's garbage. I remember his dark, rough hair, his smell and I remember his body but I do not remember his face. There was a moment of hesitation before I slammed the passenger door. The inside of the car smelled of alcohol and sealed off the breeze, the pines, the stars and my tribe.

Heading down the canyon I felt myself wishing I had stayed by the river. We weren't talking at all which I found weird and then weirder still, he turned onto the wrong road. Immediately I pointed this out to him but he drove faster down the dusty dirt road.

"I know where I'm going," he said. He drove farther, faster. I panicked.

"Where are you going?" No answers. Finally he came to a stop. We were back to the river but this time very far from anyone. I didn't know where we were but I knew why we were there.

As he reached for me, all I said was, "This is not going to happen." He tried to talk me into it at first and when he was convinced this was not going to work, he just lunged like some kind of animal. Instinctively, I kicked, and flew out of the car door toward the river. Running as fast as I could, I heard him behind me and I could feel him before he was even there.

My face went into the sand as I felt the weight of his body push all of the air out of my lungs. For some reason he stood up for a moment and I tried to run again. This time he grabbed my arm and dragged me into the river. My jewelry broke, falling off of my arms. I imagined the beads sinking down to the bottom of the riverbed. Shiny little African beads in the water. Then he dragged me out. That's when I began negotiating. I knew I had to get home so I pleaded with him to just get me there, and then I would give him sex. I don't know why this worked. He could have easily overpowered me there and then. I'm sure he sensed I was beaten, broken and tired and he had probably grown tired of fighting me. Finally he agreed to drive me. Down the winding mountain roads I sat next to him shivering, wet, bleeding and bruised. Again, we did not talk except for my directions. I looked for places to jump from the car and get help. Fear was caving in on me and I never jumped.

Somewhere near the dark house I told him he could let me out but he had not forgotten my terrible promise. I felt weak and beaten. Shaking, I knew there was no way out. He took me a little further to an abandoned lot and pulled me from the car. I wasn't fighting now. I just lay down in the gravel. He lifted up my skirt as I stared into his featureless face. I didn't move a muscle and I didn't cry. When he entered me, my sixteen-year-old spirit bled into the gravel beneath me. She evacuated, and then she rose up over my body, watching everything from above. My body couldn't move. My spirit had left. After she watched, she drifted away. When he was finished he got up and left without saying a word.

I heard his car pull away, leaving me lying in the dirt. Without tears, I pulled myself together, ran my fingers through my hair and began to walk toward the dark house. My spirit slowly returned but she was to be forever so very much older.

Out of damp and gloomy days, out of solitude, out of loveless words directed at us, conclusions grow up in us like fungus: one morning they are there, we know not how, and they gaze upon us, morose and gray. Woe to the thinker who is not the gardener but only the soil of the plants that grow in him.

Friedrich Nietzsche

In the United States someone is sexually assaulted every two and a half minutes.

Forty-four percent are under the age of eighteen.

Eighty-four percent of rape victims do not report these offenses to the police.

In South Africa there is a rape approximately every thirty-eight seconds.

More than sixty children are raped per day.

Only one in twenty offences is reported to the police.

Of course I knew nothing of these statistics then and you don't really give a rat's ass about statistics when something like that happens to you. It's personal. I'm well aware of them now and I care.

No one ever mentioned my bruises or cuts but of course I did my best to hide them. I told my best friend what had happened but no one else. I'm sure what was noticed was my new seriousness. There was someone older and wounded who had taken up residence in my skin. She didn't like hanging out with the tribe as much as I did. She really didn't want to go to school and nothing seemed to make her feel any better. She was an unpleasant roommate.

If I could have magically transported myself to Africa, that is where I would have gone. I just wanted to hear the sound of elephants and I wanted to walk around the bush by myself looking at insects and birds all day. It was a strange craving from somewhere deep inside but it was impossible to fulfill. I wanted to climb around on rocks and ride horses like a little girl but the "old lady" inside of me could not even imagine doing that. It was as if I was a wounded animal. My natural wild spirit was nowhere to be found. I felt confused, lost and unable to move forward.

Fighting with myself every day and with my parents every other day, my desire to bolt overcame me. I pulled the rumpled napkin from inside my dresser drawer.

I left at night with my poncho, my cigarettes and about $60.00. I inspected the napkin the strange man had given me. There was no phone number, no way to tell if he was there and no way to know how I would be received. All I knew was that my destination was out of state, it was remote and that I'd have many hours to think as I drove.

Well past midnight I pulled onto the final dirt road of my journey. From here there was only an X marking the position of the cabin, nothing as civilized as an address, just an X. I must have driven up and down the same five mile stretch of road a hundred times looking for that evasive X and saw nothing but pine trees. Exhausted and frightened, I finally stopped the car and stepped out into the night. I screamed his name as loud as I could and after just a moment I heard through the pine trees "What?!"

I would stay for a year.

If I was looking for remote, I'd found it. In the winter, I hiked down the side of a mountain, across the log, over the stream and then up the side of the hill—all in deep snow. The cabin itself was simple, nestled among the trees with a tiny porch. There were three small rooms and a sleeping loft in the rafters. There was no electricity, no running water, only one simple wood stove to stay warm and another to do the cooking. Kerosene lanterns and candles were our only source of light. During the day you could see the snow through the floorboards.

Comfort had to be earned. Every day there was wood to be chopped. I had to cut the logs into manageable pieces with a chainsaw and then hack them with an axe for the unending fire. I learned to cook over the woodstove, burning everything at first and then eventually mastering the art of baking bread with twigs. Taking a bath was a monumental effort that took half of my day. It required hauling buckets of water from the stream and then heating them on the stove before pouring them into the tiny metal washtub. It hardly seemed worth the effort. Surviving was an all day event—every day. Nothing I had experienced had prepared me for this.

My home had always had a television, telephone, refrigerator and a shower. I was isolated from all I had known. Nature became my everything. When I wasn't busy surviving I walked for miles through the woods. I studied the birds, the trees, and the fish in the stream. In the meadow I watched and listened to the elk. I walked over the fields of snow when the moon was full and there were no footprints; I watched for hours as the fog moved down the canyon. I was alone.

The man I lived with was away working most of the time. He worked during the day in a nearby town and worked the night shift at a ski area leaving me alone at night. For company and protection we acquired two St. Bernards, one for me and one for him. They became my companions day and night, as the human variety was hard to come by. There was one exception.

Just as a woman had deeply affected me while I was in Africa, so was another strong woman to reach out to me here. She was part Cherokee, confined to a wheelchair from the age of three. Her face was incredibly beautiful—chiseled perfection. Her brown eyes were as striking and strong as her shoulders and arms. The rest of her body tapered down to tiny withered legs that could not move. In wilder times she had been married to the president of a notorious motorcycle gang in San Francisco. One of their rituals that she had witnessed was that of gang rape and in a rebellious move she had chosen to prevent one such attack. She had snuck an intended victim out of a window and had then taken her to the airport and put the woman on a plane. Then she fled with her daughter, changing her life forever, and landing close to me in the wilderness. The same brutal act had touched both of our lives. I had to heal and she had to hide, but really we were both hiding and healing. We never really spoke of the tragic coincidence of our past. It just wasn't necessary. We were girlfriends who talked and laughed when we were together but we needed to spend most of our time alone in nature. It's what we had come for.

There were a few others I did meet who also seemed to be touched by something tragic; Viet Nam vets, widows, and people who just seemed odd—people who needed to be alone or embraced by the arms of nature. Maybe they just needed the peace and quiet or they needed to work all day just to survive. Whatever it was that pulled these people, and me, was very primal and very strong.

It is a rite of passage in many indigenous cultures for young adults to take a solitary journey into nature. The Aboriginal adolescent is sent on Walkabout. He is sent alone to wander the Australian bush until he discovers his strengths and weaknesses and truly understands his character. The American Indian was sent in search of the Vision Quest, yet another sole journey into the wilderness, which involved fasting and soul searching. Clarity and adulthood would eventually arrive, often accompanied by a vision and a message in the form of an animal spirit.

Many African tribes also initiated their youth in a similar fashion sending young adults into the bush with nothing but a spear and a knife for long periods of time. These experiences obviously were to build character, strength and courage but beyond this there was something that was supposed to occur through nature that was spiritual and supernatural.

Although I was far from wandering alone with a spear through the bush, I did experience a transformation. Something happened about a year into my wilderness retreat. I had listened to the woods, to the river, the wind in the trees and finally I heard something else. I heard my own voice. My epiphany was that I had a voice— an inner voice that had been speaking all along. It was there the night I got into the car. For a brief moment it told me not to get in. I didn't listen. It told me to leave my dark house, my tribe and be alone in the wilderness. It told me to get back to myself. I had to come to the most primitive place to find my stripped down self—the primal, wild self, the strong self, the self that has pure instinct. I proved to myself that I could live without electricity, running water, heat. Yes, I can live without a lot of things but I cannot live without my inner voice.

Nature is all at once beautiful and brutal—unapologetic— manifested in birth, death, the seasons, predators, scavengers, the balance of life, instinct and intuition. In that year I would not necessarily say that I came to peace, but I came to a place of strength, and I found myself feeling that I do belong. I am part of this unapologetic earth; it's brutality as well as its beauty. I had found something in myself that has never left me.

Trust your instinct to the end, though you can render no reason.
Ralph Waldo Emerson

One winter day I knew it was time for me to leave. My wilderness cocoon had done its job. The cabin, the canyon and the woods were confining—lonely. I'd had enough. I left a goodbye note on the kitchen table, loaded my St. Bernard into my Volkswagen and drove toward the future. It had been twelve months of introspection, struggle, healing and ultimately birth to a new self. The woman who left that day had a renewal of strength and a resolve to go forward based upon a fresh sense of fearlessness. Although she had been hurt, she had not been destroyed. She had been knocked down but had gotten up. Instead of running away from life, she would run towards it with senses heightened and intuition intact.

The next five years took me back to school and then led me into the rewarding and always interesting career that I still hold today. I had gone from catching and cooking my own fish over an open fire to selling Picassos on Rodeo Drive. My wilderness lover chose to follow me, as I seemed to change gears from first to fifth, which was hard for him. He married me and tagged along as I moved over three states while following *my* heart. Ultimately my husband and I would part and he would return to the very place I found him—in the woods. He remains near there today. We had gifted each other in many ways, most of all with our children. I will never forget the gift of my year of solitude that he helped to give me in the wilderness.

I find myself continually drawn back into the wild especially during times of crisis. It is Africa that has rescued me so many times that I feel I owe her a debt. I run to her when I am afraid, wounded and need to connect again with my inner self. Maybe it is because this is where we all came from, maybe it is because it is the wildest place I can find, or maybe it is because it is where I first experienced great healing through nature. I am not sure why, but she has never failed me. It was into the heart of Africa I ran when I lost my twin boys. I immersed myself there again after I lost my business and my marriage. To be in Africa is to witness the ultimate struggle for survival on so many different levels. It is in this wild place that I see our vulnerability and our power; our ability to hurt or to help one another. It is the surest way for me to break free of self-absorption, to find my passion and my compassion, and to reconnect with something much larger than myself.

Today as I watch a cocoon spinning and twirling over the city streets I hear nature speaking to me and telling me the story of us. We are one with all things; we are part of the stars, the rivers, the seas. We are interconnected with everyone and everything. We are divine.

You do not have to be good
You do not have to walk on your knees
for a hundred miles through the desert, repenting.
You only have to let the soft animal of your body

love what it loves.
Tell me about despair, yours, and I will tell you mine.
Meanwhile the world goes on.
Meanwhile the sun and the clear pebbles of the rain
are moving across the landscapes,
over the prairies and the deep trees,
the mountains and the rivers.
Meanwhile the wild geese, high in the clean blue air,
are heading home again.
Whoever you are, no matter how lonely,
the world offers itself to the imagination,
calls to you like the wild geese, harsh and exciting -
over and over announcing your place
in the family of things.
Mary Oliver

CHAPTER TWO
THE FIERY ROAD TO SUCCESS
Patricia D. Brewster

The real voyage of discovery is not seeking new landscapes
but in having new eyes.
Marcel Proust

It all began in a small town in Northern New Jersey. Just on the other side of the George Washington Bridge in a bedroom community of New York City, families likes ours enjoyed the innocence of the late 1940's and the 1950's. Our home along the edge of woods provided the playground for many. We ran along maple tree-lined streets, attended steeple churches and walked to school. This is the place I learned to ride a bike, run with a gang of other kids and play jacks for hours. I learned my love of nature and the outdoors from those years and the need to soak in both the warmth and coolness of each day remains with me still.

A long standing passion of gardening, cooking and reading is attributed to my mother, a stay at home mom during those early years. My father, a self-made man, born in the U.S. but raised in Eastern Europe, had worked his way back to the United States before the age of twenty-one in order to retain his citizenship. Despite speaking no English when he arrived, he built a successful business, flourished financially and retired at age fifty-two. He and my mother spent the remaining years of his life doing what he loved—namely traveling and fishing. I proudly attribute my drive, confidence, commitment and energy to him.

The first ten years in New Jersey ended abruptly when my father decided that we needed to get out of the rat race of commuting and the crowds of New York City. With that decision he also earmarked a move to the less crowded West. Eying the Northwest or Colorado, we landed in a tiny mountainous area called Deckers, Colorado, and "vacationed" for three months in my eleventh summer. My father, an adventurous and domineering man, had clearly made up his mind. My mother, who was a good deal more cautious, was very nervous. Her worst expectations came true as we unpacked in a three-room log cabin, no running water, dirt roads and free roaming animals. While the outhouse might be quaint, it was unbelievable for us!

Three months later, as we began the long road trip back to the East coast, I assumed a second round of investigation to the Northwest was in store. Yet, a short nine months later, Dad flew to Denver to investigate business locations. Lo and behold, when school was out, we were uprooted to Colorado, a place so far away and foreign from what any of us were used to. Our neighbors told us there were still "Indians running wild."

David Brinkley once said that, *"A successful man is one who can lay a firm foundation with the bricks others have thrown at him."* I, too, have had plenty of bricks thrown my way and I've picked up my share along the way. When I was twenty, I was convinced I'd have "it" all together by the time I was forty. By the time I was in my forties, I certainly hadn't figured it all out. However, I found myself well into self-examination of my life, values, roles and future. For the first time in my life I was beginning to see that much of how I lived was a response to early upbringing.

What a surprise! I finally figured out I had been (and still was) the daughter who pleased her parents and had figured out that achievements were valued over everything else. Unfortunately, feelings had not been given much attention; and that internal perspective shaped how I approached my life. Seeing with different eyes during that midlife growth changed how I perceived myself, others, and how I was perceived.

"Just do it," exclaims Nike. The cheer of the Generation X could be aimed at me. In other words, I might be called a pragmatist. Nonetheless, I believe I have demonstrated a knack for knowing how to take a practical approach to make things happen and then doing what it takes to make them work. My life and work have been about having stated goals, doing whatever I need to do and accomplishing them. Positive thinking and the business technique of management by objective have been and are the fabric of my approach to life.

Like everyone, I have a characteristic agenda and operate within a particular decision-making framework. From those early life experiences I became the achiever, the producer or the leader. Eager, talkative, responsible, goal-oriented and persistent—these were my descriptors.

Today, among other things, I am wife, mom, grandma, gardener, volunteer, and caretaker of my now elderly mother. She continues to live alone at the remarkable age of ninety-three, but that's a whole other story. While my dominant style is extroverted, I have learned to meander introspectively in the second half of my life. I have learned to appreciate the need to be a bit private and not talk as much. Seeing things with that different eye has also broadened my scope of what others have to say.

Today, after nearly twenty-five years in the business world, I chose retirement a year or so ago. At what I prefer to think is a young sixty-two, I relish the freedom to do "whatever." All those meetings, appointments, emails, responsibilities, personnel issues and business trips have gone by the wayside. All of that, along with the realities of life as we all experience, shaped me into who I am today. That translates into a generally satisfied woman whose days are now filled with many activities like family, golf, gardening, volunteering, travel and friends. Overall, I'm pretty sure I have all I need. Well, okay, I'm sure there are always a few things I could ask for.

We all experience special personal relationships and role models in our lives. Some of the sweetest aspects of my life are our sons and their families; for without them, all that I have gone through, sought and achieved would be for naught. And, more importantly, I treasure and bask in a solid and loving marriage to an incredible man, one who has been a stabilizing force since the age of eighteen, the staunchest supporter one could ask for. In addition to the positive legacies given to me by my father and husband, a unique influence on my life and attitude grew through a relationship with my husband's mother, a lovely and refined Bostonian lady. From her I gleaned a deep appreciation of many cultural areas including classical music and the art world. She also left me with a sense of style that has served me well.

I graduated from a private college in Colorado Springs, after studying abroad in Southern France for a semester. In the mid-sixties, fresh from college and newly married, I felt I had the world by the tail. I taught secondary junior high for nearly five years, serving also as chair of the English department. Those years spent with bustling, hormone-exploding young teens were an unforgettable education for me and I loved it. Teaching educates the teacher, maybe as much as the student. Spit wads, challenges, disruptive noises, wisecracks and general teenage know-it-all attitudes are quick to teach you patience.

With the arrival of our first son, I embarked on another special time in my life, which was the role of a stay-at-home mom. After the arrival of son number two, we relocated to a beautiful area west of Denver in the foothills—Evergreen, Colorado. Again the love of nature, the free roaming wildlife and space were a huge part of our life with two youngsters. Spectacular views, fresh fallen snow, brilliant golden aspen in the fall and wildflowers became my landmarks for the seasons.

One of the most precious benefits of time spent at home with children as they matured was the development of close girlfriends. And, to this day a small cadre of couples from those years remains as best friends, able to share in memories, children rearing stories, and laughter. But just as importantly, during that period I was gathering valuable experience by starting my own business, volunteering extensively with two symphony orchestras and dabbling again in substitute teaching.

However, restlessness also set in my late thirties and I yearned for something more. Little did I know that a horrific fire would rock our world and serve as a catalyst for enormous self-examination and growth. The next five years, until I had reached the age of forty-five, I would see the loss of everything and the chaotic effects on my husband and our children. I'd also experience the slow rebuilding of confidence and trust to move forward and achieve personal and professional success beyond my wildest expectations.

In *The Road Less Traveled*, author Scott Peck, tells his readers that, *"Life is difficult. This is great truth, one of the greatest truths. It is a great truth because once we truly see this truth, we transcend it. Once we truly know that life is difficult—once we truly understand and accept it—then life is no longer difficult...that life is difficult no longer matters."*

Despite reading this book, years after tragic events had occurred, it was nonetheless eye-opening for me. It stated so well what I had learned through devastating circumstances. I went from the feeling that I had lived in a bubble of prosperity to plunging to the depths of despair with the losses I experienced. Letting go of the old, living in the confusion of "nowhere" and once again growing in a new situation are tough places to be. Yet once I accepted that hard times are part of the package deal of life, it just didn't matter. The fears that came with loss and the need to move forward were actually more easily met. In a funny way it became a challenge to conquer. If I had kept on wishing I had been dealt different cards, I would never have been motivated to figure out the best way to deal with the situation. I could never have known how devastating my next life transition would be.

I remember the day well. It was Tuesday, December 6, 1983, just weeks before Christmas. The ground was heavy with an early Thanksgiving snow of eighteen to twenty inches. The light of day was nearly gone and all of us had arrived home after I had picked up the boys from the school bus stop in town. It wasn't unusual for people living at 7000' above sea level to use space heaters to take the chill off rooms in their homes. We used a popular variety my parents had given us, a free standing kerosene heater. While I began to assemble dinner, one of our sons turned the heater on. Calling into the kitchen from a library/TV area to his father that it didn't look "right." My husband left to check it out. Moments later, I heard what I recall as the most chilling and frightened scream I had ever heard. I ran to the TV area and there were flames everywhere. He had turned the heater off and then restarted it, only to have it flare into a terrible column of fire. Nudging it with his foot to activate the turn-off mechanism, it turned over and spilled kerosene on the wood floors.

In a split second attempt to save his family and home, he grabbed the flaming device and shouted for me to open the door in the adjacent room facing the outside. Hoping to get it tossed through the door, it smashed into the wall and ignited that room.

We screamed to our children to take our two Golden Retrievers, get out and run through the deep snow on our property to the neighbors. They tore out of the house. In the few minutes that followed we fumbled through toxic smoke and flames, produced instantly. To this day I don't know how we communicated so clearly. Somehow we simultaneously ran for the lower level garage in order to remove the cars, both of which held full tanks of gas. Our thoughts were that we could avert an even greater explosion. Little did we know that fire burns up and over, not down; the garage remained virtually intact, the only area not really affected.

It was dinnertime for many and luckily our neighbors to the south were in their kitchen and observed the flash of fire. They called the fire department immediately for dispatch to our home. Other neighbors nearby also miraculously showed up. As my husband asked me to look at his hands in that nearly dark early evening, I viewed shreds of skin hanging from each. His clothes were burned and his hair scorched. The sound of his voice wasn't what I knew so well. What a godsend when one neighbor wisely put him in our car and came around to speed him into the emergency room. The irony of this act was that our two Goldens were not going to let a stranger get into the car! Quieting them down, they took off.

Fire dispatch received the call and phoned it in. Little did we know at the time that it was called into the wrong district. When the trucks finally arrived, to the wild chagrin of those helping us, they refused to fight the fire! In reality, the correct response department had to authorize a secondary department. I watched in horror from the living room of a neighbor's home as the flames licked and swallowed the house for a full forty-five minutes before the correct department arrived. Five hours later at midnight, the fire was deemed out, although fire personnel remained through the early hours to prevent flare-ups. My husband was in route to the hospital and burn center in downtown Denver and various ER/ trauma doctors and plastic surgeons were dispatched.

In those hours, I watched as my world as I knew it literally evaporated. The safety of our home was violated, the "stuff" of our eighteen year history together gone. My husband was burned over twenty percent of his body with a smoke-damaged throat, burned lips and hands so damaged it would be two years before they functioned well with scarring minimized. Our sons, aged ten and thirteen, lost part of their childhoods that night. Loved pet cats perished in the inferno as well. We had run for our lives and left with the clothes on our back and I with mismatched shoes, one mine and the other my husband's!

The days that immediately followed are still a blur. I remember the unbelievable sense of community that enveloped us. I don't know what we would have done without them. Neighbors carted what little was left, but damaged with smoke and water, from the house into storage. I can still feel the emotions of watching the boarding up of the house within twenty-four hours and remember walking through the awful black darkness of my home, stepping on broken and burned remains of our life. The recovery of my husband was excruciating. Indescribable pain from the burn therapy, a broken leg, and surgery were now the critical pathways. Psychological trauma and fear for all of us were the stuff of life for weeks and the year to come. The only other times I heard that horrible frightened scream again were during the burn therapy treatments. My heart felt as if it was gouged from me during those long, wrenching days at the hospital watching someone you love suffer, unable to do anything for him.

Yet there were hints of hope that emerged. Miraculously our many photo albums, each encased in a slide and tightly packed on the bottom shelving of bookcases, survived somehow. So little oxygen was able to penetrate the spaces that fire did not consume them. Our pictorial history was saved! Several boxes full of childhood toys, matchbox cars, Lego blocks and baseball cards remained. Smoky and blackened, the cars and building blocks became usable once again, and are now played with by the next generation, our grandchildren. And, miraculously, one cat was carried from the charred remains, in shock, but alive. She was nursed through her trauma and rejoined our family once we were settled again, several months later.

Last, but not least, in a larger sense, others in that mountain area were spared the possibility of experiencing our frustration and loss due to incorrect referral and response criteria. Our foothills community was designated a mutual response area. No longer would an administrative error add insult to injury and loss.

We lived temporarily in three houses until we were able to locate a more permanent rental house. It proved to be a completely disorienting time. At times it felt as though I were watching someone else go through this ordeal. We lived out of bags of clothes for those first few days, gradually accumulating what we needed to survive. After razing and rebuilding the house, we finally moved back into our redesigned home nine months later. We lasted about another year in that location and then moved on to another foothill community for a fresh start.

The smell of fire remains with me still, but in a much diminished way. We can talk about it, sometimes without getting teary. Yet we react quickly if we smell smoke. To this day we are extremely sensitive to open flames. I prefer to live close to fire hydrants and occasionally awaken at night, sure that I can smell smoke.

I experienced many dark nights in those first years after the fire.

Dante expressed in *The Divine Comedy*, *"In the middle of the journey of our life, I came to myself in a dark wood."*

That was me emotionally and physically. Incredibly, my father who had been such a mainstay in my life was on the edge of dying from a debilitating form of dementia. Between the struggles of holding our family together through both physical and mental healing, I was now the main support to my mother. I watched and cried with Dad as his mind slowly slipped away. In the two years following our worst nightmare, Dad died, bringing more loss and grieving.

Yet time does heal. Time heals faster if you find someone to help you. It heals faster if you look to the support you have in life, even if that support sometimes waivers.

I'm happy to say that life is good again, but it took a mighty rough road getting there. And it's been good for many years now. True to the saying, there was good that came from that awful tragedy. And there was learning. Lots of it.

We realized that the comfort of our routines before the fire was destroyed. Yet that fire served as a catalyst for me, and ultimately my husband as well, to take a hard look at who we were and what we wanted from life. It took periods of solitude, separation and sorrow. In a funny way I had to disengage in order to engage again. Interestingly, children are resilient and in many ways they fared better. I like to think we did well by them and they adjusted fairly well, with the help of school, friends, and family. I, however, began the long road to understanding the restlessness and need for "something more" that I had experienced those many years before. So the learning and exploring began again.

It's a funny thing about lessons learned. Some of them seep into your being without your being aware of them. All of sudden, or it seems, you see things through different eyes, and it makes sense. Others jump out at you. Some you fight. You don't necessarily want to see it differently, because you know how to deal with life seeing everything with the old eyes.

For me, the sudden learning, my epiphany, came in the shape of Scott Peck's words. Life is difficult and once you accept that with your heart, you are able to do what you need to do. Again it's the hand of cards. If you stop wishing for another hand, you can play out the ones you have, however difficult it may be. You muster your strength, find the resources you need and "Just do it!" Wishful thinking serves us all well. It certainly served me ably. I could recite a litany of reasons why I hadn't been able to move forward and do what I needed to do to fulfill my own destiny—my parents did thus and so, I have children to take care of, the fire, fear of failure and the best one—maybe someone else would solve it for me!

Another realization came later through the rebuilding of my life after fire, injury and grief. Each time I committed to take on and complete something really overwhelming, it bolstered my feelings of confidence to go on. The loss of things was not important. It's people and relationships that counted. Yes, I grieved for all we lost. We all did. Yet at the end of the dark tunnel I looked back on all that I had done well—teaching, raising children, volunteering, coping with a horrendous tragedy, rebuilding a house and a life, working outside the home. I knew I could go for the dream I wanted.

Ever since I had stopped working professionally, I felt I had given up parts of me to be someone else. I lived in the shadow of my husband's professional success. I loved being the "home mom," but it was time for more.

Too often in the past I realized I had mistrusted my own intuitive sense. As I mentioned, feelings weren't talked about in my growing years. Therefore, it was hard to admit or, for that matter, trust the emotions I felt. Yet I was also an optimist and that helped me focus on what I have, not what I lacked. Along those paths of childhood I had developed determination, persistence and an ability to get things done. It's said that women possess great intuitive sense. And as I relied more on those "gut" feelings, instead of the fears and wishful thinking of the past, I found the strength to redouble my efforts. I had finally learned to listen to and heed the voice inside of me.

So life is difficult. Accept it and just do it. I applied for and was hired as an educational coordinator in a living history museum, serving as the volunteer coordinator for a county-wide educational program in the school district's curriculum. Everything I did in this role was a challenge. Yet since I had gleaned the skills earlier in my life, I had the confidence to go for it. I just had not tapped those skills before. Yet with the wonderful spark of successfully handling the hard times, I knew I could do more. The first thing I needed was a road map.

Upgrading my education and seeking a greater challenge were my next agenda items. Enrolling into a graduate management program, I also left the museum world and moved into healthcare. Going to school on a full-time schedule and working part-time in the new job were exciting, stimulating and the future rewards became real motivators. The comfort of my part-time status disappeared when the job became full time after six months. Commuting daily, taking care of teenagers, attending classes three nights per week, studying and papers, housework and a husband filled a thirty-six hour day.

To think that in four years, with one graduate degree and the recognition of opportunities, I managed to become President and CEO of a regional not-for-profit tissue bank! The challenge was huge and I flourished in it. Admitting that I was really "juiced" by the pressure, growth, education, and professional environment just made it all the more exciting. As the organization engaged in strategic planning, the ultimate goal became a merger with the region's organ donor bank. The scope of a merged entity serving the community would be much greater as an organ and tissue procurement organization. It would be now federally designated by the Department of Health and Human Services and regulated by the Federal Drug Administration, as well as serving a two state area. With five offices and a staff that more than tripled, I knew I was the right person for the job.

That merger process proved to be a slow and tedious investigation by a joint group of board of director members with the two CEO's of the separate organizations assisting. At that time, in a niche healthcare industry with a preponderance of men at the top, the prospect of how it would shake out was daunting. Was I working towards a lesser position or, more fearfully, no position at all?

Oddly enough, after all that I and my family had been through made me just that much stronger, resilient and determined. In a way it was simply a way of taking a risk. Surely it would have been easier to run away from the challenge, to give in. Yet intuitively I knew that not taking this risk and not going for it all would be a regret of a lifetime. Nothing ventured, nothing gained. If I didn't put everything into the race, then I stood no chance of winning the trophy at the end.

At the end of an agonizing year and a final decision to merge the two organizations, the competitive aspect of who would be declared the President/CEO was finally upon me. In reality, a year-long interview process had been taking place, yet there was still the last interview by the search committee for the final decision. Two sides each wanted "their" candidate. A day that seemed to never end finally did with the job offer. I felt a sense of pride and accomplishment that I had never experienced before. In the organ donor world, it was a stunning decision as I replaced a long time individual in that arena. That's not to say that many unbelievably difficult and frustrating days would not be upon me.

The changes that occurred as a result of this opportunity were tremendous. I learned volumes about healthcare, death and dying, compassion, caring and people. Lots of mini-epiphanies dawned. I learned new respect for every talent that we possess, as well for the varied talents of others. For without those talented players in the orchestra of life, we would end up with much less interesting songs. I learned to trust myself and to listen to my heart and intuition more. As a woman who lives in her head, this was not an easy task.

I learned that there are special people who are there for you all the time, no matter what, no matter when. I treasure those folks for they have enriched my life beyond words. I believe there is a soul mate for us, probably more than one, in this world and I was lucky to have found mine. I learned that I was fortunate to have struggled through darkness, aloneness and unhappiness to emerge on the other side in a better place than where I started. I felt success. After nearly ten years in the top role of an organization, I was ready and willing to step down, still intact, stronger and confident about the next phase of my life. The sense of restlessness was gone. And, most of the time now, a sense of peace prevails.

I survived it all and, yes, as the old saying goes, what does not kill you makes you stronger.

We cannot tell what may happen to us in the strange medley of life. But we can decide what happens in us—how we can take it, what we do with it—and that is what really counts in the end. How to take the raw stuff of life and make a thing of worth and beauty— that is the test of living. Life is an adventure of faith if we are to be victors over it, not victims of it.

Anonymous, *Seasons of the Heart*—Paul C. Brownlow

CHAPTER THREE
FEEDING MYSELF
Jessica K. Rivers

One cannot think well, love well, sleep well,
if one has not dined well.
Virginia Woolf

I am a recovered bulimic. I spent nearly eighteen years, almost half of my life, gorging on obscene amounts of food that I then regurgitated in a variety of self-induced purging behaviors. I have never been happy with my body. No matter what I weighed, I would look into the mirror and see an amorphous blob of fat. I forever wanted to be someone other than who I was. A thinner person. A prettier person. A cute girl with a straight nose. Someone skinny who could fit into size six designer jeans with a snake belt draped over her flat stomach. I was always trying to lose ten, fifteen, twenty pounds. I believed that some magical three digit number on the scale would instantly transport me to happiness and perfection. I never saw beyond my perceived flaws: the bump on my nose, my thin, flat hair, my fat thighs, my enormous breasts, my inability to fit into any of the current fashions. I never saw what I had; only what I didn't. I wanted a nose job. I wanted long straight hair. I wanted that effortless knowledge other girls seemed to have when putting together an outfit. Nothing I did was right. Everything I did or had or thought was slightly off. I had no idea how to be me. I had no idea who "me" was. So when I headed into the emotionally turbulent years of high school, I didn't just go through the usual teen angst. I somehow got severely sidetracked by a debilitating illness that sabotaged a bright, beautiful young girl who only wanted to fit in and feel "normal."

Of course, looking back now I can see the reality of who I was and what I looked like. There was nothing wrong with me. I wasn't fat. I definitely had more of a curvy figure then most of the girls my age and for sure an outsized bust for my age but overall I looked fine.

Looking back at my high school photos you'd see an engaging young girl with sparkling hazel eyes, flawless white skin without one blemish and an amazing smile. Yeah, OK, the nose was a bit large but definitely not anything you'd notice first. You'd see charm, vivaciousness, energy. Certainly nothing that would indicate an inner inventory of pain and anger. Each photo shows me surrounded by friends and laughing or enjoying myself. You'd see someone experimenting with her clothes and hair, never looking like anyone else but obviously comfortable doing her own thing, establishing her own style. You'd see a maverick, an icon, a leader, someone paving her own way in the world regardless of what others thought. You'd want to meet this interesting character and listen to what was going on inside her head. You'd think she was comfortable in her skin. But she/I wasn't.

It's still baffling to me (and to my mother) why I developed such a negative self-portrait of myself. I was a planned child as my mother never ceases to inform me. Despite my parents divorce at the tender age of five, I remember nothing but love and encouragement throughout my upbringing. Creativity was encouraged. Play-acting was embraced. My sisters and I always had costumes and props to play with and woods and fields to play in. Life was fun and stimulating. Each day brought a new adventure of discovery. I grew up in small town that was host to many of the teachers and artisans who worked at the local regional junior/senior high school. Many of these people were part of my mother's circle of friends and since they worked at the school we had access to many of the creative programs during the summer session. My mother played the recorder and I was part of her ensemble. I joined the summer orchestra one year and each child was asked to pick up an instrument they had never tried but were curious about. I chose the oboe. An early indication of my tendency to over-achieve. But whatever I did, I was good at. I danced. I performed in plays. I sang solo in the school chorus. I was always center stage, not because I craved it, but because I naturally came to be there. It wasn't something anyone expected or demanded of me. It was just what I wanted to do. I was also very physically blessed with strength and agility and I was often taken out of my regular elementary school classes to assist the gym teacher and act as a junior coach/demonstrator. Again, I was naturally in the spotlight and doing something special and different from everyone else but never seeing it as anything but ordinary.

I continued to grow socially in this manner until age twelve. I was a favored student, popular playground friend and totally confident in myself. I was happy and content and looking forward to entering junior high where I would finally be an official part of the curriculum and not dependent on what classes my mother's friends could get me into. I was ready to begin making my own choices. At the same time, my mother began dating seriously and eventually met the man who was to become my current step-father. News of Joe and my mother's imminent marriage became the prime focus in all of our lives. Junior high wasn't so important now because I would be leaving to start elsewhere the next year. After the wedding, we were all going to move to Joe's hometown to set up a household there. We were moving from a small country town to a large affluent suburb of Boston where everything would be different. I was thrilled! I couldn't wait to start this new adventure. We sold our house, had a big yard sale and packed up for our new life.

Initially, I was entranced with the novelty of the move. Our house was a block away from the town business center and for the first time I was able to walk to the shops and explore at my leisure. I was amazed at the food choices. I had never seen a 7-11 store and walking into a shop with a whole aisle dedicated to candy amazed me. There was also a bakery, a deli and two pizza parlors. Having spent all of my life in a small town, I was only accustomed to food either purchased weekly at the supermarket or cooked in our own kitchen. I was overwhelmed by this new, instant accessibility to "gourmet" food. Coupled with this discovery was my new weekly allowance that began soon after we had all set up our household. Prior to my mother's second marriage we had done household chores out of necessity. Now those same chores were rewarded with a five dollar a week allowance. A fortune in my eyes! So now I had money and access to new food outlets and a whole summer to explore this new experience. With my mother focusing on her new house and husband, and my sisters back in our hometown with friends (they wanted to prolong their stay; not as eager as I to move) I was free to indulge myself as I wanted to. Let the games begin.

I spent the next three summer months eating my way through every shop on the street. I was so excited to have the newly discovered experience of walking into a shop and ordering a submarine sandwich with exactly the toppings and filling that I wanted. I never realized there were so many choices! My mother and my step-father, accustomed to my independent behavior, allowed me to spend my time doing what I wanted. I am sure it never occurred to them that I was spending all that time eating. I also discovered the local library during this time and fell into the habit during those tranquil summer months of buying my lunch, taking out a book and going out into their garden to eat and read for hours. Soon, I was bringing more than just lunch. Since I had moved to town in the summer, I had no access to meeting kids my age. It didn't bother me at first since I was fine with my own company but as we grew closer to the beginning of the school year, I was both excited and apprehensive. My pristine, controlled afternoons of self-indulgence would soon be coming to an end. I was ready for company but also much attached to my private rituals that had grown to fill all my free time.

A week before school began, my sisters joined us in our new house and mother took us all shopping for school clothes. Again, the sheer enormity of the choices in the department store impressed me yet overwhelmed me. I had no idea where to begin. Somehow, I had had no problem deciding between sausage or pepperoni pizza, but I was lost when trying to decide which outfit would look right on me. Where to begin? I seriously had no real idea what size I was, having recently passed from kids to "juniors" sizes. I was a medium before so I started there. I grabbed some things off a rack and went to try them on and was shocked when I couldn't get the pants up over my hips. What had happened? I looked at myself in the mirror for the first time in months and saw that I was no longer the slim-hipped athletic girl I'd known from before. My butt was really rounded, my breasts were spilling out of the training bra I had stolen out of my older sister's bureau and my thighs looked HUGE! I was looking at a stranger. I really didn't know what to do. Any other time when I needed anything, I would call my mom, but this need, this call for support, seemed alien to me. How do you ask anyone to explain the monster you had become? I felt instant shame and the need to hide. My embarrassment was crippling and for the first time in my life, I experienced a blinding blow to my confidence.

This was the beginning of it all for me. I had eagerly awaited my new life in this town but had spent the summer in solitude. I had wanted to embrace big-city style with a new wardrobe for school but instead discovered that I had morphed into an unrecognizable being (when in reality I had just gone through puberty). For the first time ever in my life, things were not happening the way I expected them to. I felt as if I had no control. And so the school year began. It was tough. The school was so much bigger. It was difficult to know who to make friends with. There were obvious cliques, identifiable groups. Which one did I belong to? I didn't have any of the right clothes having finally selected what I thought were "elegant" outfits for the city but they were in fact far too old for me and made me stand out. A new sensation hit me: I didn't like being singled out anymore because this selection of being labeled "different" wasn't a compliment or something as desirable in high school as it had been when I was little. Everything I did seemed somehow "off." I tried out for the school band, having always been so musical, only to discover that I had to demonstrate that I knew all of the scales. I never had to do that before! I just played by ear and was first chair. Another blow to my sensitive ego. And all along, I never talked to my mom about it. I was too embarrassed to admit that I needed help in figuring things out.

By my sophomore year, I had come to find a group of friends that I could relate to; the Performing Arts students who were the creative, honor student, classically "geeky" kids. But even though I had found my peers, I still felt that I didn't quite belong. I was in the band but I wasn't studying privately after school as many of the other students were. I was on the swim team, but only as an alternate because I didn't have qualifying times. I was in the school play but only as an extra. I was starting to fall behind in my honors classes because the work was increasingly difficult and again, for some reason, I couldn't admit that I needed help. To admit that I couldn't conquer something on my own, with my own internal resources, represented failure to me. The self-deprecating attitude was becoming more prevalent in my personality and I began really truly disliking myself because I didn't know this new person who existed on the fringes and wasn't the star performer any longer. I felt that I was a mediocre, insecure, confused loser. That's how I saw myself in my mind's eye. So I retaliated. I created an external persona of a confident, carefree, eccentric chick who didn't care what anyone thought of me. I came to school in outrageous outfits. Embraced the punk look and chopped my hair off. I was friends with everyone from every clique because everyone thought I was so cool. But no one really knew me. I didn't even know myself. I had created a space where I could deflect all question of self-doubt. I just skated along the surface of all these external personality traits and never let on to anyone how scared and lonely I was inside. I was hungry for love and acceptance.

Over the summer after my sophomore year, I decided to go on a diet. I felt that if I returned to school thin, I could be the person I truly wanted to be and could stop all of the charades. Again, I didn't ask for any guidance on this from my parents; I simply stopped eating. I became completely engrossed in diet foods and sugar-free items basically eating just Jell-O, diet soda, and coffee yogurt. I spent long hours reading and listening to my Walkman, returning to the safe, solitary rituals I had developed that first summer of moving. I didn't want to see friends because that would mean eating. I didn't want to go out because I might run into someone I knew before my personal transformation was complete. I retreated into myself and my fantasies of being thin and beautiful and perfect. After about a month, I couldn't take the restrictive eating so I tried something new. I horded all the "forbidden" foods that I wanted to eat over a period of three days, continuing on my diet. On the third day I binged on all the goodies I had saved. I didn't purge them at this point but the hording and binging continued on, and became my new obsession. What could I buy or bake or steal from the houses I babysat at to save for my binge? Gathering this food became my time-filler. Needless to say, I didn't lose any weight that summer since I was consuming basically the same calories as before, despite my "diet days."

I went back to school and the character I had assumed from the previous year continued. I was still play-acting at who I was and desperately trying to find the right me. In addition to this charade, I had the added misery of loathing myself for having failed to loose any weight over the summer. One of my friends had. I asked her about it. She was pretty dismissive and weird but her sister, also a friend, told me the secret: making herself throw-up after meals. Well, needless to say, this caught my attention. I was desperate to try anything. It would also connect me in a bizarre way to these two slim beautiful girls. And so it began. I had the binge part down pat but the purging was foreign. And it hurt! But I picked up tricks and tips from my girlfriend, like eating ice-cream or a milkshake with your meal to help the regurgitation. It didn't take long before I was purging each meal. I was hooked. Finally, something I was good at again. I became the Master Bulimic. Over the course of the year, I spent all my waking hours planning my binges. What I would eat, where I would get the food, how I would hide the evidence. I attacked this illness as I had attacked learning the oboe as a girl with an obsessive, direct, relentless drive. It was all-consuming. I managed to lose some weight but nothing overly obvious so my parents never noticed any difference in my appearance. I was always off by myself and my parents never questioned why I spent so much time alone. I was starting to go out more to parties with my group of friends but no one realized that I was raiding the pantries of their parents for supplies rather than making out with boys as my friends were doing. My sham of a life continued, only I was hiding a deeper secret.

This behavior continued on through high school, getting worse and worse. I was now binging six to eight times a day. My mother caught me once and yelled at me for my stupidity but I convinced her I had only tried it a few times and I would stop. I took to sneaking outside and vomiting in the bushes so that I could continue my routine. I couldn't stop because I was now so hooked on the behavior. It filled up my time so that I didn't have to think about friends or grades or relationships. It consumed my energy so I had the illusion of having a rich, fulfilled social life. I was also addicted to that calm, sedated, numbed feeling I got after a purge when my potassium level was so low from vomiting. I was so lonely, so scared, so angry—but unable to express any of these emotions so I ate them away, stuffed them into the empty shell of myself, then barfed them up and dealt with everything that way. My emotions were so scary and unfamiliar that my binging rituals became the only perceived place of stability, control and safety. No wonder I didn't want to give this up.

On I went to college, each year growing more tragically engrossed in the disorder. I was still succeeding at hiding it from everyone but I was growing tired from the strain of the constant lies. I decided to get help in my senior year, not wanting to enter the adult world with this horrible problem. But I was now eight years into the behaviors of the illness and it wasn't easy to extricate myself from the tangled layers I had incorporated into my daily life. I graduated, got a good first job and entered into the trappings of the young adult world. I was seeing a therapist and really trying to work on my problem but it was tough. I had some major stepping stones, the first being able to come clean to my mother. She was shocked, but for the first time, supportive, and I made some headway. But I still didn't know how to function normally, how to actually sit down and eat off a plate instead of shoving food directly from bag into mouth. I still didn't feel comfortable admitting I needed help. I still couldn't express my feelings very easily. You see, I had spent all of the years that normal girls spend learning and perfecting these skills with my head in the toilet. At age twenty-four I was still the shy, uncertain girl of sixteen. I needed more help growing up and I needed to be able to both ask for and accept it. But I still wasn't completely sure of how to do that. The behavior continued.

The turning point in my battle with bulimia came when I joined a women's self-help group. Having been through years of individual therapy with little success, I was willing to try anything to overcome my problem. By now, I was no longer getting off on my binges. I was deeply tired of the process but so entrenched in the behavior that I didn't know what else to do. I saw an ad in the weekly lifestyle newspaper that was looking for female volunteers to participate in a study about women with eating disorders. It was run by the reputable local university and as a perk, all participants in the study were entitled to free access to a women's support group run by a post-grad student of psychology. It seemed like a good deal, and as I said, I had reached the end of my tether and was ready to try anything. I promptly called the number listed and I was asked a number of questions over the phone to determine if I was a viable candidate—my age, my occupation, my marital status, the number of years I'd been binging/purging and what kind of treatment I had had in the past. Apparently, my answers convinced them that my years of self-abuse would be worth cataloging so I was asked in for a more in-depth interview. I hung up feeling relieved and for the first time, hopeful. Someone, finally, had a plan of action and all I needed to do was follow their lead. I couldn't wait to begin. I was ready for a change.

The following week I went to the university for my first session. I learned about the program in more detail. Basically, I would be asked each week for six weeks to come to the lab and fill out a questionnaire about my moods, my binge history that week, any exercise I had done, any emotional issues that had come up; things of that sort. After filling out the questionnaire, I was shown into a room that had a table full of various foods. A mixture of healthy things like pretzels and fruit as well as the classic "binge-foods" like potato chips, Twinkies, candy, etc. The woman running the test explained that I would stay in the room for half an hour to choose any food I wanted to eat in any combination. She showed me a private bathroom adjacent to the room and explained that I should feel free to use it to purge in if I needed to. It was all so bizarre to me. I couldn't figure out what they were trying to figure out. Were they going to watch me through a one-way mirror? Was there a camera in the bathroom? Was I going to be lectured on my disgusting behavior if I chose all the binge foods? I was really nervous and uncomfortable. So I sat in the room as directed and waited for her to leave. There was no way I was going to binge in front of anyone. No way that I was going to reveal my secret behavior. Being the commensurate pleaser, I wanted to be helpful and do as they asked, but all of a sudden, I balked.

It was so bizarre to me to have everyone talking so calmly and matter-of-factly about what I did. Even in therapy, I never talked about what I did; just discussed my emotions and my frustrations. No one ever said "purge," let alone show me a private toilet where I could do it in peace. I was freaked out; uncomfortable. So I reacted the way I always did when I felt out of control. I took control and planned a binge. I proceeded to stuff half a box of Ding-Dong cakes and a canister of Pringles into my backpack then calmly nibbled at a portion of the generic salad on the table. I couldn't bring myself to binge in front of anyone, let alone these nice people. After a time, the woman returned and she asked me if I was ready to go. Honestly, I can't exactly remember what I had to do next, whether or not I had to tell her what I did, but there was obviously food gone from the table and I figured they would make their own conclusions. I couldn't wait to get the hell out of there. I was asked to return the following week when I would be given more information about the group treatment. I guess they wanted to see if you were going to live up to your end of the bargain before doling out free therapy.

I smiled and thanked her but all I could think about was the stash of food in my pack and how soon I could get home to the safety of my apartment to binge in peace. Once again, I chose the secret comfort zone of my ritual to negate my feelings of unease and uncertainty. These people were trying to help me but I didn't know how to accept it. My first reaction was to steal, hide, and pretend. My second reaction was to binge. The third step of the process was to purge, to attain a state of calm from the "K-level" (the term I had coined that referred to the potassium depletion from vomiting that induced a sense of emotional and physical numbness). This had become my only reliable, calming fix for discomfort and uncertainty.

I debated whether to return the following week. I was so confused by the process and didn't really understand what they were doing. In addition, I was slightly embarrassed about the food I had stolen. But something made me get on the bus and head back over to the lab for another session. I filled out my questionnaire again and was then given some more information. This study was trying to determine if there was a direct correlation between the foods consumed by a bulimic and the bulimic's subsequent desire to binge. Did eating junk food result in a binge while eating healthy things did not? This, again, was another novelty for me. I had never actually stopped to think about that. Of course, fatty, fried, high caloric food was a primary player in my binges but I had also spent plenty of time puking up "healthy" food as well. Hell, I could binge on anything. It really didn't matter what the food was. It only mattered how I was going to fill up the hole inside of me. I felt that I should share this information with them—it seemed significant. But again, I wasn't ready to reveal so much of myself yet. I just wanted to do the exercise and go home to my private space and not think about it. When was the group going to start? How was this helping me?

The room this time had an addition to the table: a thick chocolate milkshake. Again, there was the mixture of junk foods and healthy foods and this time I approached the table with a different mindset. They wanted to see a binge, so I would show it to them. I quickly turned to the Ding-Dongs and ate my way through the whole box. A large bag of Cheetos followed and that familiar feeling of fullness began. The robotic routine of transferring food into my mouth without tasting it brought me into a trance-like state. It was about finishing the box, emptying the bag, cleaning the plate. I was very methodical, never mixing things up. I would eat my way entirely through the chosen food before moving on to the next. I knew when I had almost reached my limit and I saved this last bit of space in my stomach for the finishing touch: the milkshake. The smooth liquid was the perfect element in creating an easy purge. Everything came up easier when there was ice-cream involved and I typically ended a binge with it to facilitate the regurgitation. I moved into the bathroom and quickly finished the routine, making sure to carefully clean any spatters of vomit off the toilet seat so that no one could tell what I had done. I went back into the room and waited for the woman to return. I filled out my questionnaire then quickly left without engaging in any conversation. I was slightly mortified at what I had done since it was obvious what was missing from the table. Last week had been different since I hadn't purged in front of them—taking the food away kept me in control of the situation. But letting go in front of other people was slightly terrifying. But also, a slight relief as well. My "secret" was out.

Although I was in this study, my binging behavior continued. I didn't stop just because I was in this test. I figured I would address it when the group started. But something was changing. I wasn't so focused on the daily binge anymore. I didn't focus all my energy into binges. The binges were diminishing in their intensity. I was getting tired of them. I actually began looking forward to the next session the following week. I was curious to know what would happen. And even though I was still doing this very destructive thing, I was for the first time allowing others a glimpse into my secret world and it didn't seem all that bizarre and terrible anymore. There was a safe space and people were trying to help me and this was new and comforting for me. Plus, I had all this free binge food at my disposal. I didn't have to spend time gathering it or waste my energy stealing it. I didn't have to worry if my roommate came home early. I could binge in peace.

I binged and purged again the next two weeks, dutifully logging in my emotions, my binges, my self-analysis. I was getting comfortable with this routine and the directors of the study. I actually started looking forward to going. I was routinely eating my way through the junk food but adding the salad in too. But then something happened in week five. I came in fully expecting to binge/purge when suddenly the sight of that milkshake triggered something new in me. **I didn't want to binge.** I didn't want to go through the routine. I didn't want to have to hide my actions. I didn't want to have to once again bend over that toilet, stick my finger down my throat, and heave up the contents of my stomach coated in chocolate milkshake, then check around the bowl to make sure every bit of evidence of the act was gone. I didn't want to do it anymore. I sat down quietly and looked at the contents of the table. It no longer had the same appeal. Instead of seeing a bottomless spread of goodies, I saw junk.

I began to really look at what was on the table. Stuff I didn't even really like and never really binged on before this study. I hated Italian dressing and iceberg lettuce. Hostess products never really caught my eye in the market: I preferred zucchini bread. And then the milkshake. It disgusted me. It became the iconic symbol to my nasty behavior. That thick liquid suddenly became synonymous with puke. I couldn't touch it.

The director sensed something was wrong. Usually animated and cooperative, I was quiet and subdued. She asked what was wrong and I explained that I didn't want to binge. I was horrified of putting anything on that table in my mouth because I knew where it would take me. The director studied my face and told me that I didn't have to binge. That I didn't have to do anything I didn't want to. She explained that she still needed to go through the routine of leaving me in the room and she would check back as usual. After she left, I just sat there, bewildered, defeated, deflated. I don't remember feeling good or triumphant. I simply remember feeling sad. What now? What do I do with all the food now? Should I resort to my first week's trick of stealing the goods and bringing it home for later in case I changed my mind? Do I just eat the "good" stuff to show that I am capable of eating "normally?" Do I just go ahead and binge anyway? I sat there for twenty minutes doing nothing. I didn't touch anything. I didn't take anything. I didn't eat anything. I waited, waited for the next step. The director returned with my check-out questionnaire which I filled out quickly, forgoing my usually thorough answers. I just wanted to get away from that room.

My last session came the next week and I went with mixed emotions: anticipation because today I was going to get the information about the group and trepidation because I didn't want to be trapped in that room again with all that food. I didn't want to have to be in the position of deciding whether or not to empty the table. I didn't want to look at that damn chocolate shake. I said hello to the staff and was told I would get the meeting info after the last session. I went into the room and as soon as I saw the usual spread, I just started crying. I felt so angry, so frustrated. Why did I have to be in this damn study? Why couldn't they just help me? Why did food trigger such an intense response in me? What had happened to put me here? Why was I sitting in a room full of junk food instead of being out on a date? What was wrong with me? I continued to cry but it was a definite catharsis. A purge of a different kind. I cried for the years I had lost, wasted; I cried for my current situation of helplessness. I cried and cried. I just let it all out. It stopped as abruptly as it had started and in some weird way, it felt similar to the feeling I had after purging. A calm, resigned feeling. I looked at the table of food again and my eye stopped at the milkshake. Without thinking, I went over to it, picked it up and brought it into the bathroom. I turned the glass over, dumped it in the toilet bowl and flushed. I returned to the other room to wait for the session to conclude.

In my exit questionnaire I attempted to explain my feelings but it seemed too much, too raw, too confusing to put down on paper. The director could see that I had been crying but didn't push it. She asked if I was OK and I replied that I was more than ready to finish the study and get started with group. She glanced at my questionnaire and saw that I had checked the "didn't binge" box. She looked at me and smiled and for the first time in so long I felt the satisfaction of having pleased someone by doing something that pleased me. I had experienced a pure emotion of pride and was sharing it with another human being. She gave me a brochure entitled "Feeding Ourselves." It was the program I would be participating in; a new approach to treating women with eating disorders. It took a multi-dimensional approach to bulimia and anorexia, focusing on cognitive behavioral therapy techniques. We'd be meeting once a week and go through different tasks related to eating. We'd have a chance to talk about our feelings but the emphasis was to be on the exercise and how we related to it. I couldn't wait to get started. And there again, a new feeling: a desire to be with other people and not hide.

The group met the following week. Six women "patients" suffering from either anorexia or bulimia, under the tutelage of our team leader from the university. The first moments were a bit uncomfortable as we all waited expectantly to be told what to do and how we would be cured. But all we ended up doing was talking. Talking about ourselves, our specific issues with food, and our history with our illnesses. Instead of feeling embarrassed, I was comforted by the camaraderie our bizarre group had. I wasn't so alone in my head with my struggle. I wasn't as grotesque as I thought I was. I had peers who were suffering as much as I was. It was another breakthrough for me. I could see for the first time that I wasn't alone and I didn't need to keep viewing myself as a messed-up, disgusting pig. I could talk instead of binging and people would listen and reply. Thus began the slow exchange of food for human contact.

The weeks passed and we were led through various exercises. We talked about body image and spent time drawing pictures of what we thought we looked like while simultaneously, the others in the group sketched how they saw each other. The results were unbelievable. Not one self-portrait matched a "real" sketch from another teammate. Inevitably, the self-portrait would be totally disconnected from reality, with bodies drawn hugely fat and facial features absent while the other portraits showed an array of smiling, wide-eyed young women with normal proportions. I really, then, started to see myself in a different light. I was finally becoming tuned in to what I felt on the inside vs. what I actually looked like to others. The discrepancy was huge and I was seeing it. I was finally coming to grips with reality.

One evening's activity was the ultimate connecting experience for me, the night that I really turned the corner and came out of my lonely place, my self-imposed prison that had held me in a state of delusional madness and pain for so many years. The weeks in the group had opened my eyes to self-perception, opened my heart to accepting feedback and opened my mind to the hope of releasing myself from my disgusting habits. The night's activity was teaching us how to tune into what we really wanted to eat rather than just mindlessly bingeing. We were to state to the group exactly what we felt like eating at that moment and then go out into the neighborhood restaurants and purchase that exact food to bring back and eat with the team. To normal eaters, this may seem like a ridiculously easy task. But for those of us with eating disorders, it was unfamiliar territory. To first actually take the time to examine a feeling, a desire for a meal was alien. Before, we hadn't cared what we ate; we had just filled up an empty hole inside with whatever was available. And then to be asked to actually go out and request this perfect meal, again, was not something we were familiar with. All-you-can-eat buffets, half-price bakery goods or forgotten leftovers were the typical binge foods we were accustomed to. But this was the point of the whole exercise, to become attuned to what we were really craving.

We went out in pairs and I knew exactly what I wanted: Joyce Chen's Chicken and Broccoli in Black Bean Sauce. Why this? I couldn't tell you except that it represented to me a simple, tasty, wholesome meal with an exotic twist. A food version of myself? I couldn't say at the time but in retrospect, it could be that I was personifying myself through a food choice. My teammate was just as specific. A tiny, waif-like woman with glasses, she confidently stated that she wanted a big juicy hamburger. We set out for our meals. Mine came first and as I received the take-out bag from the cashier, the delicious aroma of soy and sesame drifting out of the package. Normally, I would have gone straight home to devour whatever food I had, then throw it up before I had a chance to even enjoy it or think about it, but tonight I had to wait. We set off to find the hamburger. We deliberately passed by McDonalds and Burger King knowing that it was a grill-cooked thick burger that we wanted. But we couldn't find a shop. Time was running out so we finally went into a pizza place that offered burgers on the menu. My friend placed her order and then we watched the cook take a frozen, thin patty out of the freezer and plop it down on a greasy flat cooking stove. This was not right. This was not what she wanted and I turned to her and saw panic in her face. She wasn't getting her perfect burger but she had no idea how to extract herself from the order. And then I felt it. A feeling that had been dormant in me for so many years. Confidence and control and self-possession surfaced in me in defense for my suffering colleague. She couldn't speak up, but I could and I would. I could help her. So I called out to the chef to cancel the order and grabbed her arm and ran out of the shop. We went on for a few more blocks until we saw a bar and grill and the tantalizing smell of barbeque assured us that this burger was what we were looking for. And so we ordered and quickly got back to the group to finish the evening.

Without going into too much detail about the rest of the evening, I can simply say that I was well fed that night. I enjoyed my meal but even more so, I enjoyed seeing the slight smile on my friend's face as she unwrapped her burger and took her first juicy bite. I knew she was eating what she wanted and more importantly, I had helped her to get it. This was a true change for me. I had gotten out of my own headspace in order to help someone. And by helping someone else, I realized that I was feeding something inside of me. I was nurturing my natural human instinct to reach out and to connect. This realization brought tears of joy to my eyes and I knew then that I was on my way to recovering. I had come out of my dark place of self-imposed solitude to finally see how to connect with others, to help others and to ultimately help myself. I now saw food and people as conduits to positive emotions and interactions. I was finally learning how to feed myself.

Today, anyone who knows me would find it difficult to believe that I had spent so many years stuck in such an intense battle with food. They would find it incredible to learn that I had voluntarily consumed so much junk food. They would find it incomprehensible that there was a time in my life when I didn't really know how to eat properly. I say this because I now live with an incredibly healthy appreciation for food and for how it nourishes my body, feeds my senses and cultivates my sense of well-being. I celebrate food. I revere it. I appreciate it. I have chosen San Francisco, a food connoisseur's Mecca as my adopted home. I thrive on all of the varieties of local and ethnic foods available to me. I am a regular at farmer's markets and can happily spend fifteen minutes deciding upon just the right bunch of golden baby carrots to purchase. Most importantly, the rituals I now have attached to food involve celebration and joy both of food and the experience of eating. I now take great pleasure in feeding myself.

CHAPTER FOUR
AN EPIPHA-MINI

A GIFT OF GREEN
Ann Thomas Hamilton

When the world focused on the tragic events of September 11, 2001, I endured my own personal "9/11" just eight days after the planes hit the twin towers, the Pentagon and the field in Pennsylvania.

On September 19, 2001, I received a call from my primary physician's nurse with news that every woman dreads. I had breast cancer.

The diagnosis suggested that it was a stage one, likely hormone-induced, malignancy which would require a lumpectomy followed by a few radiation treatments. After finding the right surgeon, I entered into the surgery with a positive attitude having been told that it had been caught early, the lump was very small and therefore the prognosis looked very good. There was a lingering concern that, because the lump was on the far left side of my left breast, the cancer cells might have spread into my lymph glands. As my very supportive sister, Evelyn, said at the time: *You don't have breast cancer, you have armpit cancer!* Humor has always been a real source of comfort in our family.

The surgery went well, but the lingering concern became reality. The cells had spread into the lymph glands which meant more aggressive treatment—chemotherapy for six months, followed by another surgery to ensure "clean margins" around the site, followed by five weeks of radiation, followed by five years of preventive medication. WOW! So much to absorb!!! All my cancer survivor friends advised me to take a year of my life and focus on getting well. Good advice.

This is the backdrop for my story of acceptance and generosity.

In February, 2000, I moved into my wonderful little bungalow in Section One of Garden Oaks just north of Houston Heights. It had been remodeled by another resident of the neighborhood who has since passed away. John did an incredible job of transforming what had been a very small, degraded, unoccupied house into a warm, cozy, colorful place that I could finally call home, having rented since my arrival in Houston in 1985. The large yard was standard St. Augustine grass, some old unpruned trees, and a few new shrubs planted around the house's perimeter. The Asakuras, my new neighbors to the east, were a family of four—a landscape architect, his wife and their two young daughters. We became fast friends. I greatly admired their beautiful yard and told Keiji, the architect, that I wanted my yard to meld into theirs and create a greater green space to attract more birds, butterflies and wildlife.

Over the next several months, Keiji and I put together a conceptual plan, added topsoil, visited a local, organic nursery, and planted a few low-maintenance native plants. Occasionally, he would bring left-over plants from his various client sites and either leave them for me to plant or just do it himself. I kept asking to pay him, but never received a bill. Slowly, my yard began "melding" with the Asakura's as intended, but it was a "work in progress" when cancer struck.

After my surgery and hospitalization, I spent ten days of recovery with my sister and brother-in-law in their home across town. Having boarded my dogs, the house remained empty save for my housekeepers who picked up the mail and fed the cats daily. The day finally arrived for me to go home for a visit and begin getting my life back. Evelyn drove me and I felt such joy being back in the neighborhood with its lovely little homes, large lawns, big old trees, cool green spaces, and narrow streets. When we pulled into my driveway, we were astounded at the change that had taken place during my absence. The front yard had been transformed from a "work in progress" to a beautiful, serpentine garden of wonder—full of a rainbow of diverse grasses, flowering ground cover, and shrubs of every shape and variety. We were speechless!!! I just broke into tears knowing that my gentle, generous neighbor had undertaken this task of love and kindness as his gift to a worried, sick neighbor. What a gift.

One of the most important lessons I learned during that year of treatment and recovery was to accept the kindness of others and, when needing something, not to be shy in asking for help. Keiji's gift was the start of a personal change, from being a fiercely independent woman to one who could seek and accept help from others. After five years, my garden continues to thrive and bloom with fragrance and color. Birds and butterflies abound. Unfortunately, Keiji is no longer my neighbor, but his essence and life force remain in the garden he gave me. I think of him every day as I walk past this garden so full of life and love, grace and gratitude. It continually nurtures my soul and brings me joy and peace. Thank you, dear Keiji, for this gift of green.

CHAPTER FIVE
WANDERLUST
Kelly K. Heapy

Be not the slave of your own past—plunge into the sublime seas,
dive deep and swim far, so you shall come back with self-respect,
with new power, with an advanced experience
that shall explain and overlook the old.
Ralph Waldo Emerson

In August of 1999 I left the U.S. on a ten-day journey to hike the Inca Trail to Machu Picchu. Peru had never been on my "someday" wish list of places to go. At the time my list was filled with more common destinations like New York City, Hawaii and the Bahamas. But Peru found its way to the top of my list when the travel section of my local newspaper featured the hilltop fortress of Machu Picchu. Aside from its natural beauty, Machu Picchu's architectural history and mysterious demise compelled me to go.

Machu Picchu was established in the mid-1400s, strategically located on an 8,000-foot peak in the Andes Mountains where the Inca Trail terminates at Intipunku, or Gate of the Sun. Machu Picchu is a compact village that once accommodated about 1,000 Incas, the majority of whom were women. Its remarkable granite structures (which had thatched roofs at the time) were formed with hundreds of stones exactingly fitted together so that not even a piece of paper can slide between them, like corn-on-the-cob at a gargantuan scale. Additionally, its ceremonial sites were precisely aligned with directional and celestial bearings, indicating the advanced scientific knowledge with which Machu Picchu was plotted. According to research, the entire site was abandoned by the mid-1500s. It was around this time that Spanish explorers came ashore and conquered much of Peru, giving partial cause to some of the many unproven theories as to why Machu Picchu's inhabitants deserted the site. The Spaniards, however, did not find Machu Picchu. The site remained overgrown and forgotten until 1911 when explorer Hiram Bingham, with the help of local residents, finally pinpointed this proverbial needle in the haystack of the Andes Mountains.

Never before had I dreamed of going to a place so far from home in terms of cultural and societal differences. Accordingly, most people I knew judged Peru and the Inca Trail to be uncharted and dangerous, probably with a warning on the State Department's website. They felt it was not a place a single woman should go without an insanely detailed itinerary from an experienced tour company guaranteeing her safety at every moment. This foreboding played on my conscience and I eventually booked my trip through a reputable company and reluctantly contemplated inviting someone to go with me. But I had lived in Northern California for less than a year. None of my newly found friends had a penchant for altitude sickness and iodine-treated water.

***

I moved to Northern California in 1998 after I received a prestigious job offer from a well-known animated feature film company in the Silicon Valley, just south of San Francisco. To get the job I had flown in from Arizona for an off-site interview that was followed by a second trip and formal interviews with twelve more people. The company's screening process was thorough, to say the least. I had shown up in a skirt, blazer, high heels, bun in my hair and portfolio in my hand. Looking back now I have to laugh. It's California. It's casual. I definitely was not. Luckily, my fashion faux pas was overlooked and I was offered a job based solely on the design work in my portfolio.

The company was typical of most in the Bay Area with exceptional fringe benefits like catered lunches, stocked kitchens, pets at work and flexible hours. But to me it wasn't typical...it was blissful. I had never worked for a company with such a basic approach to finding good people and making them happy. I loved my job and the tremendously creative people with whom I worked. It was a job that afforded me great opportunity inside and outside of the office.

I was twenty-eight, at a crucial point in forming my adult identity... just past the confusion and turbulence of early twenties while on the verge of the greater responsibility and self-awareness of early thirties. Up to this point my life had followed the first half of the formula for The American

Dream: grow up, go to school, graduate, go to college, get a degree, get a job, work hard, get married, make more money, buy a house, start a family, live happily ever after. I was at step number seven—work hard. I was single but hoping to move on soon to step number eight—get married. I never thought too deeply about this well-beaten path of life in America. I never questioned whether or not it was creating the life I really wanted to live, or if I was becoming the person I really wanted to be.

During this time I was renting a room from a peculiar man named Devin. He worked for an Internet start-up company and was obsessed with the "dot com" environment of Silicon Valley, continually telling me what obnoxious purchases he was going to make when his stock options finally vested. He moved from start-up to start-up in search of the most lucrative opportunity as a Director of User Experience, an ironically appropriate title.

Each evening when I returned home from work Devin was there like a live newscast spitting out stories of which companies had gone public and what was happening with tech stocks. Devin's fixation with money was hard to ignore and similar sentiment permeated the Silicon Valley like a virus. It was an intensely competitive environment with an overly stocked pond of highly educated and ambitious people, all working toward The Next Big Thing. Stock options and salaries were being dangled like huge carrots to anyone with an MBA, a great idea or a willingness to spend day and night in front of a computer. The houses, the cars, the explosion of wealth that could literally be seen on every street were enough to make anyone in the area clamber to keep up and feel passed up if they didn't measure up. It even made a person like me who loved her job (for a privately held company) occasionally wonder if there wasn't some other better opportunity to be had. Tired of the show, I was ecstatic to be escaping to Peru, a place that was primitive and unplugged by comparison.

***

With just three weeks until my departure for Peru I purchased the remaining gear I needed for the trip: daypack, convertible pants, hiking boots, mosquito repellent. I increased my usual workouts to prepare for full days of hiking through the Andes Mountains. I got my typhoid shot and tetanus booster. Still, however, I hadn't found a willing travel companion with a sense of adventure and, at this late date, a love of spontaneity. But as I biked to work one morning I stopped at a red light and glanced at the cyclist next to me. We said hello and introduced ourselves. An introduction like this was not uncommon for the area and the time—Silicon Valley in its heyday, when riding along in the morning you might encounter any number of CEOs or VIPs pedaling to work at companies like Google, Netscape, eBay or Apple. Talking to other cyclists wasn't just socializing, it was networking.

The cyclist's name was Michael and he worked at a local pharmaceutical company in business development. He also conducted lab experiments with future multimillion-dollar medications. He was part conversationalist, part scientist and as I came to find out he loved to travel. I invited Michael to Peru.

"That's Crazy!"

"You just met him!"

"What if you don't get along?"

"He probably thinks you're into him."

"Are you sure he's not a killer?"

Red flags assailed me from every direction when I told people I'd be traveling to Peru with The Stranger I Met On The Bike Path, but this was Silicon Valley and Michael had an enviable job, a love of good wine and a really expensive bike. He probably wasn't a killer, but he might be a snob. Besides, this trip was fraught with greater, potentially detrimental risks for me...a suburban middle-class woman who had only been to Paris and Puerto Vallarta with people I knew. A man I might not get along with was the least of my worries. That was one situation I knew I could deal with.

After some last-minute planning Michael and I left for Peru on a red-eye flight from San Francisco to Lima. I had never flown south of the equator. I felt as though we were diving below the surface of the world to its rough and mysterious underside. Our confined middle seats and the darkness through the far windows hid any hint of what lay below us. We landed in Lima just after sunrise, changed planes and took off again for Cusco, a red-roofed town tucked in the Andes at 12,000 feet where we would spend two nights adjusting to the altitude before starting our hike.

After collecting our bags we walked out of the airport into a barrage of locals offering taxis to town. Among the eager faces, we located the driver from our tour company who helped us with our bags and led us to an air-conditioned van. It was more youthful than the other cars on the road. Already I could see our tourist dollars at work, separating us from the real Peru.

As we drove away from the airport Cusco began to reveal itself. It was a surprisingly large city of three hundred thousand people with just a few paved roads leading to a wider maze of cobblestone streets. A mishmash of mud huts and stone shacks overlapped each other, with children spilling from the central courtyards into the streets. Most of the city was basic, unadorned and even a little dirty but charming in its simplicity. Arid mountains with pine and eucalyptus trees surrounded it, alluding to the journey ahead of us.

After a twenty-minute drive we arrived at our "three-star" hotel and were shown inside to a pair of chairs in the lobby. Exhausted and impatient, Michael and I wanted to get to our room to change our clothes and relax. Instead, we were served two slow cups of coca tea in true Peruvian fashion. What I didn't know that day but I do know now, after traveling extensively, is that serving tea is a traditional way for many cultures to welcome visitors, initiate conversation or negotiate a sale. This was my first cup in a foreign country. Many have been offered to me since and it's now a tradition I love, even though I prefer coffee. This simple gesture was one of the first differences I encountered that subtly introduced me to life and tradition outside of America.

After our tea Michael and I were shown upstairs to our room. It had two single beds and a stone-tiled bathroom. A window opened out to the main street below us. For what little I knew of Cusco it seemed almost fancy. I unpacked a few things and decided to take a shower. I shut myself in the bathroom and turned on the water. I waited. And waited. Hot water was a normal expectation in my part of the world, but this was the first of many expectations I'd have to reevaluate on this trip. A short cold shower was my only choice.

After an afternoon walk around town we returned to our room. We were jet lagged and thought it best to stay in and get some sleep so we could adjust to the time difference before we started hiking. We talked for an hour and then turned off the lights. At eleven o'clock that evening we were awakened by noise outside and got up to peek out the window. Our room was overlooking a bar across the street that hadn't been open during the day. The band had just arrived and started playing wildly, with people dancing and yelling. We rolled our eyes and got back in our beds expecting the bar to close down shortly after midnight. But yet again, this was an expectation based on a scheduled life back at home. The Peruvian party lasted all night with hours of people singing and banging on instruments. It wasn't until sunrise that the steel door was rolled down and everyone finally left to go home. Michael was incensed. I tried to laugh and eventually accepted it as a joyous part of Peruvian life we'd been lucky to overhear.

We spent the next day walking around Cusco taking endless photos of a place so unfamiliar to us. It was vastly different than the wide paved avenues, landscaped yards and perfectly constructed homes of my neighborhood, or just about any neighborhood in America. To me it was no less beautiful and far more embedded with history. Every street, every structure, every façade held remnants of Incan civilization. At the base of most buildings were several rows of stones from the original foundations laid first by the Incas and later rebuilt upon by the Spaniards. Two Spanish cathedrals in Cusco's central plaza, with exquisite domes and arches, stood in testimony to the city's conflicted past of imposed religious beliefs. Cusco told a tale of two cities built by two nations.

Most stunning to me were Peruvian women selling their wares on the streets. Their traditional dress was intensely colorful with stripes and patterns in vivid pinks and shades of teal green. They carried their items in shawls on their backs that wrapped their shoulders and tied in front with tidy knots. They wore flat shoes with knee-length socks, their hair was neatly kept in braids and their ensembles were topped with tall brimmed hats. They dressed for business, hoping to make a daily handful of Nuevo Sols to feed their families. Much like the tea tradition I had been introduced to the day before, this was the first time I had seen the traditional dress of a culture so different from my own. It was quirky and exquisite. By comparison my technically advanced, designed-for-travel clothing seemed completely uninspired.

Finally acclimatized, we checked out of our hotel and departed for the Inca Trail. There were six other people in our tour group, all of whom we met that morning. Our guide was Ian, a lanky English-speaking Argentine with an educated passion for the route. He couldn't wait to get us on the trail. We boarded a van and drove off, most of us having no true idea of what we were about to embark on. Having never hiked for five days at high altitude in a remote location without a bathroom or a shower, I felt slightly nauseous and apprehensive. I hoped I wouldn't be The Slow Hiker, The Whiny Hiker or The Hiker Who Had to Go Back.

After two hours bumping along a rutted dirt road the van stopped near Oyantaytambo in an open field at the base of the Andes Mountains. Standing there seeing these mountains for the first time I was dumbstruck. It seemed presumptuous to stand so small before something so insurmountable with the intent of making a successful five-day journey into the bowels of this visual labyrinth.

A large truck arrived with our porters crowded in the open bed. These Peruvian men, with their Alpaca hats and tattered sweaters, had been hired to carry the brunt of our individual loads in addition to the group's food and their own supplies. Some stood shorter than I and all, except one who was barefoot, wore plastic flip-flops on their feet. How they expected to get through the mountains so seemingly ill-equipped was beyond my comprehension. But they had made this trip before and I had not, so I figured there must be more ways than the way I had chosen to survive this five-day trek. Within an hour each porter had donned a massive load on his back and hurriedly set off down the Inca Trail…well ahead of the rest of us.

After a few hours of hiking we reached our first camp near Llactapata, nicely pitched within earshot of the Urubamba River. The Urubamba carves a deep gorge through the mountains and sustains a number of small communities along the trail. Camp was a scenic playground and we eagerly unpacked in our triangular tents. Dinner was sufficient— potatoes, rice and all the usual camping foods that carry easily and don't spoil. We slept early and waited for sunlight.

We began the second day with a big breakfast and a better idea of what the day would hold. We filled our bottles with boiled water, rubbed on sunscreen and began hiking at our own pace. Michael and I led the group for most of the day. Michael's competitive nature (from years of competitive cycling) propelled him to the forefront of nearly every situation in which he found himself. But in the afternoon I deliberately hung back from him and shifted my focus from getting to camp to just seeing, in the simplest sense, the journey I was making.

The Inca Trail was broad and smooth, paved by the Incas hundreds of years ago with large flat stones. A dirt trail would have sufficed but the Incas' masonry seemed to be limitless, stretching for mile after mile. Steep sections of the trail became stone staircases, relentless but efficient tools for getting to higher elevations. I stopped up on one such staircase and turned around to see the valley view behind me, crowded with cumulus clouds and serrated peaks. Magnificent. A few steps up from me were two of our group's porters. They had stopped to rest as well, struggling under their ponderous loads of tents, pots and pans and baggage. They were breathing and sweating heavily. We had no common language, no real means of communication, but the tired look in their eyes spoke universally.

Typical of most guided trips, there was an implied distance created between the paying tourists and the hired help. Until now I had followed this unspoken rule, but I really felt this hierarchy was creating an imbalance. I'd been taught by my parents to treat all people as equals.

I reached for my water bottle and walked up the steps to the two men. I motioned for them to share the bottle with me. Unsure if he understood me correctly, the first porter wearily took it in his hand. With a little more encouragement he held it above his lips and took a long drink. He handed it to his friend who did the same. Big smiles broke between us, eliminating the needless distance. We were all just thirsty people on a long hike. I pointed to myself and said my name and shook their hands. The three of us hiked together to our next campsite at Llullucha Pampa.

After this exchange I learned all the porters' names and tried to communicate with them, often unsuccessfully but with understandable laughter nonetheless. I had brought with me a few toys and pencils from the U.S. to give to children along the way. At camp I revealed a travel-sized Etch-A-Sketch to our cooks, Esteban and Carmelio, who enthusiastically took their turns writing their names, having never seen such a thing before. It was like magic to them and I gave the toy to Carmelio who would take it home to his two daughters. It was rewarding to further close the distance between myself and the crew.

On the third day we tackled two mountain passes between 12,000 and 14,000 feet. When we reached the top of the first pass we could clearly see the foreboding second pass and the Inca Trail snaking endlessly up to it. To get there would require a lengthy descent into a valley before this next uphill climb. Ian pointed to the second pass telling us it would be the location of our lunch break. A visual like this can be interpreted in two ways: challenge or defeat. Seven out of eight of us chose the former but Richard, the most uncooperative member of our group, chose the latter and was mentally defeated almost before he started. He made the descent to the bottom of the valley but then stopped and refused to go any further. For Ian this presented an inconvenient situation. We were two and a half days into the journey—exactly halfway, the worst place for a breakdown. If Richard defected Ian would have to escort him all the way back to the trailhead, then hike back to the group to resume leading us to Machu Picchu.

Ian deliberated with the porters, experienced hikers themselves, establishing who in their group would assume leadership responsibilities while he would be gone. In the midst of this an astonishing thing happened. One of the porters volunteered to disperse his own load to the others and carry Richard up the mountain. For the next twenty minutes we watched transfixed as this magnanimous porter worked with Richard to find the most comfortable position in which he could be carried. With Richard on his back, the porter slowly put one foot in front of the other and began the arduous journey of two men up the mountain. For the sake of the group this porter had offered his strength for no reward, except perhaps the hope of a good tip. At the top of the pass Richard was feeling better and able to slowly hike on after lunch.

By late afternoon our group was strung out across the distance of about two miles. The porters were leading the way, Ian and Richard were bringing up the rear and the rest of us were scattered in between. It was the longest day of hiking with the most elevation gain and we were tiring. Michael and I had run out of water with no idea how much farther we had to go. We stopped at a stream running down the backside of the mountain pass and filled our bottles and treated the water with iodine tablets. We resumed hiking and reached the cloud forest that foretold of our arrival at our highest campsite, above Puyupatamarca.

Fog crept up the mountainside on to the trail, blocking the sun for the first time since we'd started the trek. We hiked uphill in a long white corridor of dampness that hid any indication of our place in the world. Finally the trail emerged at a clear summit overlooking the entire vast mountain range. Saw-toothed cloudbanks moving slowly through the valleys below us were nearly indistinguishable from the jagged mountains themselves. Our camp awaited us on a precipitous ledge just down the trail. The reward of this long day was inimitable.

By the fourth day I was really enjoying life on the trail. Devoid of luxury or excess, it contained few choices. Which shirt would I wear of the three I had with me? Fleece or down vest? Eggs or oatmeal? That was about it.

There was no shower for the first four days. Instead we were given a shallow bowl of warm water to wash with in the morning and the evening. I wore a bandanna the entire trip, unable to wash my long hair. Eventually I stopped caring about the sweat, the smell, the dirt that could never be entirely washed away with the limited resources we had. We were all filthy. I loved it. No pretense of tidiness or perfection. It was entertaining to see how others in the group were feeling about the same circumstances. A few were reveling in the release from life's daily rituals while others were irritated and wanted nothing more than a real bed and a hot shower.

Sleeping in our tent brought me great delight. Twice our campsites sat precariously on narrow mountainside clearings. The clarity of the cold air, carrying a damp scent of earth and brush, was an inescapable reminder of our remote location. Only the sound of the wind wrapping around the mountains and rushing up from the valleys hinted at the vertical depths beyond the tent's opacity. Swaddled in my sleeping bag I deciphered the silly dreams created by the high altitude. In the mornings the sun would reach us late, having finally made its way above the erratic zigzag of the Andes' silhouette.

The Inca Trail passes successively larger and more important Incan sites as it leads to Machu Picchu, the final destination with the greatest historic significance. During the trek my mind made a parallel journey, digging progressively deeper into my system of values and interpretation of fortune with each day on the trail. What I was slowly discovering was that it didn't take much to be happy, not for the local people we met and not for most of us hiking along the trail. To be wandering the Inca Trail and sleeping in the Andes mountains was enough, and just enough to create an insatiable desire within myself to see more places around the world.

During our days in Cusco the locals greeted Michael and me with kind curiosity. This continued without fail along the entire Inca Trail, even as it sometimes led past the Peruvians' front doors and backyards.

At these points, most trekkers chose to tread the trail lightly. Others, however, trekked with disregard as if the trip they bought included a week's worth of entitlement to the land. These tourists would never have tolerated the world's travelers traipsing across their property on a quest to see ancient ruins. But the Inca Trail's significance and the community's economic need had created a situation in which the people living along the trail had little choice in the matter but to tolerate the traffic. Surprisingly, these residents were enduringly happy and welcoming especially if greeted with a smile.

Michael and I proved to be suitable traveling companions. He turned out to be neither a killer nor a snob, but an intelligent guy with character. We shared a tent because he had made his reservation so late which facilitated getting to know each other. At the end of each day's hike we would sit in the tent before dinner, talking about our lives or looking at the view from our vestibule. My experience in Peru was richer with Michael's companionship. Through a risky invitation I had been rewarded with the gift of a new friend.

After days of anticipatory hiking we reached Machu Picchu—an experience worthy of its own chapter. For two hours I sat at Intipunku, the literal doorway to the site, staring at the anomaly in front of me—the same view I had seen in that newspaper several months before. I didn't want the trail to end and I didn't want the final approach to begin. I tried futilely to take in hundreds of years of history in a single prolonged gaze. The site was immaculate and superfluousness non-existent. It was as if every stone of the mountain had been accounted for and positioned to fulfill its divine space and purpose. Every incline was cut with rectangular, terraced beds of soil hemmed by meticulous rock barriers. The huts, clustered in specific areas, were built with walls of a consistent infallible thickness. From irregularly shaped stones the Incas had crafted perfect corners and gables creating a picture of precise angularity. In the center was a long stretch of green grass—a flat respite from the cubism of the canvas.

Eventually I took the last steps down the trail into the site. When I stood in the center of Machu Picchu I could finally, personally comprehend its auspicious intensity. It seemed suspended in silence, its footprint perfectly matched to this apex whose slopes plunged sharply to the Urubamba River. It seemed sculpted from the mountain with a mythical chisel and hammer. It seemed thrust into the altitude like an offering to the Gods.

A man's mind, once stretched by a new idea, can never return to its original dimension.

Oliver Wendell Holmes

After a night in Aguas Calientes, a ramshackle train ride back to Cusco and two days exploring Lima, Michael and I returned to the U.S. We drove to his house where my car was parked and we said our goodbyes, promising more adventures together in the future. I pulled out of his driveway and drove through his neighborhood. I turned right at a stop sign on to the street leading back to my apartment.

And that's when my mind stretched. I remember the moment distinctly. It was as if the collective experience of Peru suddenly collided with the reality of my life, resulting in a mental thunder that snapped me to full attention. I turned off the car radio and drove in silence, tuning in to the louder epiphany.

My week in Peru had shown me universal human qualities of generosity, gratefulness, passion, selflessness and tolerance in the midst of a comparatively less fortunate world than my own. I had experienced the commonality between many Peruvians and myself despite our very different lives that outwardly seemed to have little in common. The traditions of tea and clothing gave me new value for the endurance of culture over time. And overall, the visible remnants of Incan civilization helped me to imagine the fear created by living in a place where peace was intermittent and home was a hunted frontier—a condition that exists in so many parts of today's world.

Through this realization, I was suddenly startled by the fortune of my life. Of all the places in the world...I had been born amidst peace in the United States of America, the world's wealthiest nation. I had grown up with a roof over my head, food on the table, clean water from the faucet and health care when I needed it—circumstances that existed without question. I had received a valuable education that enabled me to get a job. With this job I had supported myself and charted my course, following that American Dream. The lucky location of my birth had provided me with a select starting point in the world's economy and a palette of opportunities with which to create my future. It was a bit like winning the lottery without even playing.

I drove on and thought about all of this…thinking about my sheer luck, thinking about the fact that I even owned my own car, gaping at the sprawling homes I was passing. I was suddenly shocked that for some people this life of incredible abundance was still not enough. It was enough. It was more than enough, and I knew now that it was possible to be even happier with less.

I had never before perceived my life from this angle. I suppose I had spent twenty-eight years growing into the belief that people's lives around the world were not too dissimilar from my own. Any evidence to the contrary was brief—maybe a story on the nightly news that was a 60-second attempt at telling me otherwise. Until I literally stepped out of my life and into Peru I didn't begin to truly comprehend the myriad, often less fortunate lives of others. I realized in this moment, driving through Silicon Valley, that my trip to Peru had provided an acute beginning to my real world education. I had a new responsibility to continue learning.

This whole percussive epiphany meant the dream I'd been chasing in my skirt and high heels had just taken a turn off the trail into life's real wilderness. To keep chasing it I was going to need different shoes and different priorities because I was about to enter uncharted territory, at least for me.

My fortunate life was the very basis for my ability to travel to Peru in the first place. What I eventually promised myself was that I would use my ability to travel to gain a real-world education and awareness that no money could buy. I would try to see as many places and experience as many cultures around the world as possible. Traveling became the new dream in my life. Not the kind of traveling with posh hotel rooms and expensive meals—the kind of traveling where I board a 35-cent train to Pak Chong, Thailand to hike in the jungle wearing leech socks and track an elusive tribe of gibbons. The kind of traveling where I sleep on the floor of a bus and get dropped off at a remote Turkish village in the dark morning hours while Islamic prayers broadcast from the nearby mosque. The kind of traveling where I don't shower for three weeks and sleep in a tent in sub-zero temperatures just to witness the Sherpas' Mani Rimdu ceremony and have a look at Mount Everest. The kind of traveling that in some ways makes me uncomfortable but provides me with an indelible education about the world outside my own.

***

What I know now, and what I am continually reminded of as I travel, is that in the U.S. the evidence of fortune is rampant, and that fortune can be very easily mistaken as universal. In our grocery stores the produce is flawless and flown in from around the world. There are twenty-five kinds of soda, cereal and bread and you can buy the recommended daily allowance of any vitamin or mineral. You can even buy bottled water while over one billion people in the world do not have access to safe drinking water. The U.S. literacy rate is 99% compared to under 20% for Niger and Burkina Faso. People in the U.S. have cheap and easy access to the Internet, a source of information that only two percent of people in Nepal have access to or can afford to use. Americans are native English speakers with a distinct advantage in communicating with the rest of the world's people, who must often become bilingual for a chance at a better way of life. In the U.S. we have acceptable air quality and programs to keep the environment green, while in developing countries trash is burned in the streets and 90% of wastewater is released without treatment. How much money do we each spend daily? Three billion people in the world live on less than two U.S. dollars per day. American women have equal rights, voting rights and lawful protection from bodily harm while women in parts of Africa and the Indian subcontinent are brutally raped, burned as brides or their genitals are mutilated. There is tremendous disparity in the world that we must be aware of if we ever hope to affect or change it.

After Peru I half-jokingly began equating the costs of "things" with how far I could travel for the same amount of money. My roommate Devin had a ridiculous sixty-two inch rear-projection television delivered—more than enough and so expensive that to me it equaled a wasted trip to Africa. The TV would become obsolete but a couple weeks in Africa might have offered Devin some life-long memories and perhaps given him a broader perspective about life beyond his television. I'm not saying that Devin, or any of us, should eschew life's material pursuits but it sure can be rewarding to dream of other things made possible through the use of one's fortune or abilities. My husband and I are contributing to the education of two girls in Nepal who otherwise might not get the chance to achieve their full academic potential. No other use for our monetary gift could fill our hearts the way reaching out to them has. We dream of someday returning to Nepal to see where their education and dreams are leading them.

My hope is that people around the world share their time, their knowledge, their fortune—great or small, in whatever form it takes—to help others in the world enjoy the things that make life a better experience. It doesn't matter who you are, where you live or what you have. Smile at a stranger, teach a child to read, listen to someone's life story or just walk out your front door into the rest of your world and see, in the simple yet profound words of Marvin Gaye, what's going on. Participate, give, find your magnificence.

As I travel the world I think one of the things I value most is my belief in the importance of dreaming. Without a dream I would never have gone to Peru. Without Peru I might still be following a dream that wasn't teaching me compassion or awareness. A dream is a platform for prophecy, the place where possibility or change begins. And most importantly...a dream can be had by anyone, with no bounds of fortune, circumstance, place, time or body.

My experiences traveling in Peru and many other places in the world have brought significant perspective and purpose to my life, much like Isak Dinesen wrote of her enlightening experiences during the early days of flight in Africa:

Every time that I have gone up in an aeroplane and looking down have realized that I was free of the ground, I have had the consciousness of a great new discovery. "I see," I have thought. "This was the idea. And now I understand..."

CHAPTER SIX
A MOTHER OF A CHRISTMAS;
THE MOST WONDERFUL TIME OF THE YEAR???
Christine Anne Speranza

I am a fifty-two-year-old wife of almost thirty-three years, and the mother of a thirty-one-year-old son.

I am the eldest of five children (all born within eight years) and I grew up in the Air Force. When people ask me where I'm from, I say, "nowhere," but Denver has been my home continuously since 1972, the year my dad retired after twenty years in the service.

Both of my parents, Joe and Connie, are from New York City—my dad from the Bronx and my mom from Manhattan. They met at Fordham University, and could not have been more different in every way.

My mom was born in 1930, and grew up in what was then termed "a broken home." She had always known that she'd get married at New York's majestic St. Patrick's Cathedral, having gone through twelve years of school in that parish and graduating from (aptly named) Cathedral High School. She had elegance, grace and a sharp wit that could insult or correct you while still sounding polite. She taught me to never wear red, white or black to a wedding, never to call a boy except to break a date and never to call anyone before 10:00 am on Saturday or noon on Sunday. She also required that one "make an effort" in social situations, regardless of how boring or awkward the setting. Two things I will never forget her teaching us were, "Never be mean on purpose" and "Don't cry over anything that can't cry over you." I wasn't allowed to wear black until I was sixteen or to attend "R" rated movies because of the language she deemed "coarse." She was petite and slim and wore only lipstick and a little mascara. Pictures of her as a child would remind you of Elizabeth Taylor in *Black Beauty*.

My dad had little in the way of what my mom would call social graces. He could insult you when his aim was actually to pay you a compliment, not that that happened very often. He demanded love and respect from us. Everything was a reflection on him, and, as they say in the military, "If we'd wanted you to have an opinion, we would have issued you one." We had a weekly duty roster for all of our chores; you did as you were told. Period. To this day, I still clean the bathroom with a toothbrush. And you thought that part in *Private Benjamin* was fiction, didn't you?! The only acceptable responses to him were "Yes, sir," "No, sir" and "No excuse, sir." When I watched *The Great Santini* for the first time, I had to leave the room after less than twenty minutes.

My dad was twenty-two and had just graduated from college with a degree in chemistry when he joined the Air Force in 1952. My mother had completed two years of college and had gone to work at *Time Magazine* for something like thirty-five dollars a week to help save money to get married. So it happened that they got married at the base chapel at Sandia Air Force base in Albuquerque, New Mexico. My dad's commanding officer gave my dad a three-day pass and lent them his car, and they honeymooned in Santa Fe. Certainly not the wedding my mom expected! Someone sent them a congratulatory telegram with a typo that said, "Wishing you a long harried life together." They sure got that right!

Thus I was born in Albuquerque on April 15, 1954. It wasn't tax day back then; the deadline was March fifteenth, I am told. But at least now nobody forgets my birthday! I was twenty-nine years old and on a business trip when I saw my birthplace for the first time. I remember driving from the Albuquerque airport to a meeting in Santa Fe, looking at the Sangre de Cristo Mountains, thinking, "This is where I came from!" It was quite surreal. It felt both comfortable and foreign at the same time.

I was in seventeen schools in twelve years. My dad was in Viet Nam the entire year I was in the sixth grade. We kids were ages two, three, four, seven and ten that year. There were three times when I was in three different schools in the same year: second grade, fifth grade, and ninth grade. Christmas of my senior year in high school we moved from Honolulu to Omaha.

My mom was an only child, and my dad had only one brother who was eight years younger than he was. We were seldom able to visit my grandparents in New York, so we grew up without any extended family at all. I guess that's why my parents had so many kids—we were a crowd even without anyone else around.

I've read that "military brats" carry around a lot of grief over the many losses they experience as children. The uncertainty of never knowing how long you'll be living somewhere or where you'll go next are hard to deal with, and always under the surface, the unspoken fear with no name: will my dad get killed someday? And will we find out about it when we hear, "We interrupt this program..."?

All I've ever wanted in my life is a home that's mine forever.

I crave order, predictability and harmony. I guess it's no accident I have been married for so long and have only one child. I am very responsible (maybe overly so) and trustworthy, and I can be loyal to a fault. Having been a mom since I was eight years old when my last brother was born, I am good at anticipating other people's needs, and I tend to rescue people too early. I have been the administrative assistant to the top two execs of our local United Way for the last eight years; sometimes they call me "Radar O'Reilly." I have lost the same forty pounds more times than I care to remember. I am blonde and blue-eyed, but in my next life I want curly dark hair like Andie McDowell.

My husband's parents, John and Lorraine, knew my parents when we lived in Colorado while I was in junior high school. They and my parents and two other couples belonged to some of the same church couples groups. My husband, John, who was already away at college at that time, and I actually went to the same school as his sister, Janice, in the ninth grade when she graduated from our parish's Catholic school and transferred to the public junior high school where I was. I was acquainted with her, but didn't get to know her well.

John is nearly five years older than me, and he has two sisters: Janice is the same age as I am, and Donna, who is fourteen years younger than he is.

We were introduced at a surprise-party-for-these-people-that-we-used-to-know-when-we-lived-here-before. It was for John's parents' twenty-fifth wedding anniversary, and John and Janice were giving the party. It was on the first Sunday afternoon of 1973, and my parents dragged me to it. "Make an effort," my mother said.

John was nearly twenty-four years old, and I was eighteen. I was so impressed! He was intelligent, witty and handsome, and he was a grown up with an apartment! I still lived at home. Getting married or joining a convent were the only acceptable means of leaving home as far as my parents were concerned. Even then, my mother always called my wedding day, "The day you ran away from home." I think she was kidding, but sometimes I wonder.

Three months later, the week after my nineteenth birthday, John came over and said he had to "talk to me." Here it comes, I thought. He's a grownup; I still have to be home by 11:00, or the Colonel is out watering the front lawn at 11:01 watching for me. Both of our moms were excited that we were dating, and I didn't know what I was going to tell them when John said he never wanted to see me again.

After three or four hours of blah, blah, blah—I had no idea what he was talking about—I figured I'd make him come right out and say what he meant. I decided I wouldn't let him off the hook without telling me something concrete that I might be able to explain to our moms as the reason for the breakup. He was talking about what he wanted to do with his life, where he wanted to go, what his goals were, and on and on and on. At least I could tell his mom he was mean to me! So I said, "I'm not quite sure what you mean by all this." When he said, "I want you to marry me!" I said, "Oh, okay." I was shocked! I thought for sure he was trying to let me down easy. When I told my mom the next morning that we had decided to get married, she said, "You be nice to him. He loves you more than you love him."

Three and a half months later, we were married, and seventeen months after that, our son, John Joseph, was born on January 25, 1975. We called him J.J. when he was a little kid; now we just call him J. He was named after both of his grandfathers; John and I were glad that, because J.'s middle name was different from that of John and his dad, our child wouldn't be known as (as they would say in the Bronx) "John the turd."

So many people who are now rich, famous, thin, gorgeous, successful, etc, say, "I had a wonderful childhood, and I didn't know we were poor until I was grown up." Yeah, right. How can you not notice that? Maybe I'm overly sensitive, but I was pretty small when I realized that there wasn't enough to go around. Like we never got our own can of soda. Except holidays. On Sundays at dinner we were allowed to share a can with one other sibling. It became so cutthroat and ruthless that the rule finally became: "You split. I pick." So, if the other kid was going to try to short you, you got the one they thought they were going to get!

When my youngest brother was born and I was eight years old, I was crowned "third in command." That meant I now had many of the responsibilities of an adult, but none of the authority or privileges. I was precocious, and learned a lot more about sacrifice and caretaking than any eight-year-old should be expected to learn.

This was especially apparent at Christmas. My parents assumed that I would understand that preserving the littler kids' belief in Santa Claus was of paramount importance, and that often meant that I received less than what I deemed would have been my fair share of presents. I promised myself that, when I grew up, Christmas would be a magical experience for my future family, with no scrimping. I would never give my kids a pair of socks wrapped separately that counted as two presents!

Our family's tradition was to painstakingly open presents one at a time. That's important when there are about fifteen presents for seven people, I guess. And another major clue that your family is poor. It wasn't much comfort that we were serving "our country." All of us. I'm not sure how, but being in the Air Force was judged to be a family mission, even at a young age. We were suffering for the greater good, and keeping America free from the Communists.

So it was horrifying when I first got married that on Christmas day, my husband's family handed me a stack of presents, and we all opened our presents at the same time. Essentially, we all sat there with whatever boxes we had been given and opened them alone while everyone else opened theirs at the same time. Alone. I always wondered if you had to thank everyone for everything you got, or just for the ones that you didn't hate. It took all of five minutes, and you didn't get the chance to see the delight (you hoped) on the face of the person for whom you were sure you had found the perfect gift. I really hated it.

About my in-laws: John's mother, Lorraine, came from a Polish family of eight children with a mostly absent father, and was forced to leave school early to help her mom care for her siblings. John, Sr.'s parents were both born in Italy, and he had two younger sisters. His parents were divorced while he was in the Army during WWII. His dad was very displeased and offended that his daughter-in-law was Polish, so he would only speak Italian in front of her, and he never addressed her directly. So he would say to his son, "Ask your wife to pass me the salt," in Italian at the Sunday dinner table.

I don't know about you, but I would have thought that when my only son got married, I would never be mean or rude to her, right? But nooooooooooo! Not her!

When we were newlyweds in the fall of 1973, we stopped by John's parents' house on the way home. Lorraine proceeded to tell John (in front of me) that one of his old girlfriends who had not heard we had gotten married had called to see about getting in touch with him again. Lorraine, of course, had to wistfully mention how much she had always liked this girl. Had no one ever taught her to "never be mean on purpose"? I was devastated. I cried in the car all the way home, and once we got inside, John called his mother and told her that, if she was going to force him to make a choice between his mom and his wife, there was no question that she would lose. Okay, case closed, I thought.

When we went over to his parents' house a few months later in the spring of 1974 to tell them that we were going to have a baby, her only response was, "I didn't want to become a grandmother again this soon." Well, we were also pretty surprised that we were going to become parents so soon, and it frightened us to some degree, but we had no idea that preserving her illusion of her own youth was part of our responsibility. I have never since heard anyone who wasn't overjoyed at preparing for a grandchild, have you? I could have understood if her concern were for John and me being unprepared for parenthood, or for cutting short the time we had for the sweetness of being newlyweds, but it was all about her. Not to mention that, once I stopped working to be a mom, our income would be cut in half. We would be poor, after only a few short months of being able to indulge each other.

When our son was born in January of 1975, I called my mom from the hospital to ask her to buy me a couple of nursing bras, having figured out that one wasn't going to be enough. Lorraine showed up at the hospital at the same time as my mom did and made a snide comment about my mom bringing something for me but not for the baby. I was not only shocked by her meanness—again—but I was embarrassed that my mom was the target of her barb. My mother-in-law was being mean to my mom on purpose. In front of me. I have still never been able to think of a suitable retort.

Remember, the baby was born seventeen months after we got married, so multiply these nasty comments by sixteen years. That's how long we had been married when the infamous "Christmas Eve incident" happened in 1989.

The first year we were married, we bought a kit with wooden paint-by-number Christmas ornaments that we started painting on Halloween. We did that for quite a few years, and we have never bought anything shiny or store-bought for our tree. In fact, I love to see all those ornaments so much that I hate to put any of them on the back of the tree, so John usually has to tie the tree to the wall with twine so it won't fall over.

Christmas was a complicated matter between the two families. There were only a couple of Christmases when all we had to do was go to my parents' and John's parents' houses and spend exactly the same amount of time. We were never able to get through it without one side or the other or both mad at us—if we went to my family's house first, they were upset because they wanted us there for dinner; if we were at John's house for dinner, they were disappointed that we hadn't been there earlier in the day. John finally told his mother in early December one year that if she was going to be in a snit over which shift she got, the two of us would go away for the entire holiday season.

Then it got worse.

John's parents separated in the fall of 1976, and John, Sr., and Lorraine could not be in the same room in the same house after that.

John's youngest sister, Donna, was fourteen. John's other sister, Janice, was divorced with a little boy who was two and a half years old at that time. The only solution we were able to come up with was for John's dad to have a Christmas Eve event at his house for our little three-person family, Janice and her son, and Donna; then for John, J. and I to spend Christmas day with my family; and then for John, J. and I to go to Lorraine's the day after Christmas. Janice and her son and Donna saw their own mom on Christmas Day. You might wonder when the three of us could have our own Christmas celebration, and we did, too. Well, we just sucked it up and we had virtually no time in our own home with our only child for days on end. We hated it, but never could marshal the guts to tell our parents that.

The first Christmas after the divorce in 1976, J. was not quite two years old. We had adopted my family's tradition regarding the Christmas tree. We wanted to buy it during the day on Christmas Eve, and we told J. that Santa would decorate it when he brought the presents later that night while we were asleep. I don't know why we did it that way while I was growing up, unless it was too hard for my parents to keep five kids aged eight and under away from it during the exciting days leading up to Christmas. But we did, and traditions sometimes carry on in spite of their impracticality.

So after lunch on Christmas Eve, I sent John and J. out to buy a small tree with ten whole dollars I had saved from doing day care after school for a little girl in the neighborhood. I stayed behind because I was baking banana bread to give our families as their gift. (I have never been able to stand the smell of banana bread baking again!) I had also been making Christmas ornaments that were practically free by cutting up a large block of Styrofoam into small squares and rectangles and covering them with Christmas wrapping paper, using gold twine as hanging loops. I felt I was being quite resourceful!

John and J. came home fairly quickly. They had found a tree for ten dollars, but they needed seventy-five cents for the sales tax. We put J. down for his nap, and John took the soda bottles back to the grocery store to get our deposit back. By the time J. got up from his nap, it was late afternoon and starting to get dark. They went back to the Christmas tree lot and the owner gave the tree to them for free, probably because he was starting to pack up and close down for the year. Or maybe the young dad who looked like Sonny Bono with the cute toddler inspired some Christmas spirit in the guy.

Ten dollars that was now unspoken for! That was a lot of money to us at the time—John was selling life insurance and making nine hundred dollars per month before taxes. So we put the little tree on the end table in the living room and covered the tree stand and table with a white sheet and pretended it was snow. We told J. that, when Santa came to bring presents, he would decorate the tree with ornaments and place a beautiful angel on the top of the tree. And he said, "No. A Christmas tree always has a star on top!"

John and I looked at each other in horror. What the hell were we going to do? Even if there were a star that cost ten dollars (including tax, don't forget), every store was now closed until the day after Christmas. You can't tell a two-year-old that Santa doesn't have a star for the top of the tree. We were in a panic.

But wait. The Styrofoam.

John cut it into the shape of a star, covered it in aluminum foil and used a pencil to make a hole in the bottom. Voila! Hang a shining star atop the highest bough! Just like the song! We were very proud of ourselves. We mistakenly thought that we would be able to raise our child without ever disappointing him. Somebody needs to tell the Lamaze people to cover the eventuality of failing our children in (hopefully) small ways in their training!

Even years later after we were earning enough money to be more than comfortable, I couldn't bear to use anything other than that goofy star and the homemade ornaments on our tree. We've kept it all the same ever since, and when J. moved to California at the age of twenty-seven, I had John make him his own star that we could send to him.

1976 was the same year that J. got what he called "the circle house". It was an indoor apparatus with a three-step ladder up to a platform leading to a slide, and it had an enclosure underneath the platform with an opening to climb through shaped like a circle. J. was absolutely thrilled with it. It was really hard when we had to leave on Christmas day to go to my family's. He threw a huge fit. I finally covered it with a sheet and told him the circle house had to take a nap while we were gone and that he could wake it up when we got home. It seemed cruel, but we didn't know what else to do. There was no way we could tell our parents we wanted to stay home with our little guy and so that he could play with his presents.

Another consequence of having to be out on Christmas Eve was that I was responsible for decorating the tree and wrapping the (few) presents while John had his best friend come over at 11:00 p.m. to help him put the circle house together until heaven-knows-what-time. We were exhausted from being at Grandpa Speranza's so late before we got home and had to start on our own parental Christmas duties. Sitting here now in our fifties, it would be so easy for us to tell our three groups of parents that they were being selfish and unreasonable, but, at the time, it was the elephant in the room that no one could bring up for discussion. Our parents were still able to make us feel too guilty to object.

After Christmas day with my dysfunctional family, the next day we had to go to Lorraine's. She was newly divorced and in her new apartment, and had invited some of her friends over. It was all grownups except for John, J. and me.

At one point, I went into the kitchen and found J. sitting on the floor eating from can of pitted black olives. I have no idea who gave them to him. This is just great, I thought. Day three of eating god knows what, no naps, late nights, tons of excitement. How not to raise a two-year-old. I bet the Department of Social Services had us under surveillance. Maybe they are still looking for us.

I have never been so glad for Christmas to be over in my life.

What happened to my promise to myself that my future family and I would experience the magic of Christmas every year? If I had tried to design a messed-up Christmas, I could not have done a better job.

When my dad retired from the Air Force in 1972 at the age of forty-two, we decided as a family that the favorite place we had ever lived was Denver, so we moved here. In September of 1978, my parents must have decided that there truly is "no place like home," and moved back to New York. Just like that!

As far as Christmas was concerned, it made things a lot less complicated for us. My youngest sister, Joanne, was in her freshman year at Colorado State University in Fort Collins, and was welcome to go with us to John's family's celebrations. That meant we were tied up on Christmas Eve and Christmas Day, which was somewhat of an improvement. It continued this way until 1985.

That year, John's youngest sister, Donna, graduated from college, and by then both of John's parents had remarried. When her graduation party was organized, everyone was informed that there would only be one party, and anyone and everyone who wanted to come was welcome. We were officially finished organizing multiple events to make sure that the two couples would never be in the same room together again. So expanding upon that concept we came to the decision that there would be only one family Christmas event: Christmas Eve at our house. Everyone now gets to stay home on Christmas Day.

Because money was always scarce when I was growing up, Christmas was usually a disappointment for me. The only decoration we had was the Christmas tree, and broken ornaments were never replaced. The vocal displeasure of the Colonel when you accidentally put more than one strand of tinsel on the tree at a time was loud and humiliating. It felt like, even during the holidays, you didn't get a break if you made a mistake.

One year—I think I was in the eighth grade—my mom and I were at K-Mart minutes before it closed (remember, this was before anything was open past 9:00 p.m., much less open twenty-four hours a day). We were in line at the checkout counter—and I am praying: oh, please, don't let them tell us they are closing and we have to come back tomorrow because there's not enough time to check us out—with my mom checking her list of what she had gotten for whom, written on the back of the envelope she was using to hold her Christmas money. I'm pretty sure it contained not only the money that my dad had given her for presents, but also any money she had been able to squirrel away from her "household money." I remember making elaborate Christmas wish-lists long after I knew there was no Santa, but still hoping that maybe, just maybe, this year I'd get something on my list.

I'm pretty sure the next year—when I was in the ninth grade—was the year that I went through my parents' closet and found everything that I was getting for Christmas that year. I could not have been more disappointed. There was absolutely nothing on my list in any of the bags I found. I hated being technically a grownup while still actually being a kid. I just wanted to be only a kid.

Even worse than that year was the year that I was pregnant with J.—he was born exactly a month after Christmas. We were so poor—how poor were we? We were so poor that we couldn't even afford a Christmas tree. As people sent us Christmas cards, I threw them away because it was too, too upsetting. This is not what I had promised myself when I had a family of my own. It was miserable. I was eight months pregnant; we were barely able to make the rent. We could hardly take care of each other, and within a month we would also have a helpless baby to take care of.

My point with all of this (as if you need me to point it out) is that Christmas is a big, big deal to me.

After moving from Air Force base to Air Force base to Air Force base, we only spent one or two holidays with any extended family in New York. And we didn't know half of the people who were our relatives. As only a three-person family after J. was born, I was yearning to create some sort of Norman Rockwell or *Father Knows Best* home and hearth where everyone is loved and cherished. John and I were just trying to pay the rent and put food on the table; how were we ever going to be able to afford to take care of a baby? The care part I knew how to do. The afford part was another story.

As I said at the beginning, I had decided as a new bride that Christmas was going to be different at my house. It took a while, but, finally. Christmas of 1987. A big house. Enough money to make everything beautiful. I have to tell you…every horizontal surface was decorated. Some vertical ones, too. Living room, dining room, kitchen, rec room. All decorated.

Our kitchen was a long rectangle, with a counter that ran unobstructed for about ten feet. It worked well, on holidays, to line that counter with every possible electric appliance on the counter to keep everything warm: electric skillet, crock pot, rice maker, and even a glass topped hot tray that fits two pots on it that we got for a wedding present. I've often worried what I'll do when that hot tray finally gives out, because I don't think they make them anymore.

The subject of my particular epiphany happened, as I mentioned, on Christmas Eve of 1989. I had made a giant pan of lasagna and the meatballs and sausage ahead of time. On Christmas Eve morning, I made the accompanying items so all I would have to do once everyone arrived was toss a salad with dressing and ask someone to fill all the salad plates on the tables. I really hate having anyone "help" me cook. There are only two ways to do things in my kitchen: my way and the wrong way. Actually, even outside the kitchen that's my attitude: my way and the wrong way.

Around the crack of noon, I start setting the tables. Our stay-up-all-night-and-sleep-all-day teenager comes upstairs and complains that the dining room floor above his bed is "crunching" too much when I walk on it. Obviously, ceremony, ritual and family tradition are lost on a fourteen-year-old. I tell him to deal with it, but I try to continue with as few trips into the dining room as possible. The things a mother does for her child!

I had told everyone to arrive around 4:00, and we could eat at about 5:15 or 5:30. That would leave plenty of time to open presents, and give any parents of small children who still had gifts to assemble and wrap plenty of time to do so after they got home. Not like the year we had to put together J.'s circle house and decorate the tree after we got home at 11:00 pm! *But I'm not bitter!*

I put everything in the oven around 3:00 on low, and did what my dad would call "police the area." That means inspect everything and make sure nothing has been overlooked. Bathrooms have clean towels, toilet seats down, and generally making the house look like no one lives here!

I had purposely left the arrival time a little loose, because I remembered how tough it is to wake up a little one from a much-needed nap to go out. And if they've had their naps, we all know there's a lot less crabbiness! My sister, Joanne, brother-in-law and two nephews arrived first, and she helped me with a couple of last minute things. Then came Lorraine (John's mother) and her husband, Bill. (John's dad and his wife lived in Florida from October to May, so they weren't coming.) John's youngest sister, Donna, and her husband were next.

All the "men" immediately went downstairs to the rec room to watch football and shoot pool, so I was having a glass of wine in the living room with Joanne, Lorraine and Donna. By this time it was close to 5:00, but everything in the oven was covered and would stay warm in all the appliances on the counter anyway.

Soon it's 5:15, then 5:20, then 5:25. I finally said to Lorraine, "Do you know what time Janice and her family are coming?" Janice and her husband, Steve, have two kids: Ian, who would have been ten at the time, and Courtney, who was six.

"Pardon me?" Lorraine says, as she glances across the room to Donna.

I sort of looked at my sister as if, "What's so hard about that question?"

I repeated myself. "Do you know what time Janice and her family are coming?" Am I speaking English? I think so.

Lorraine says to me, "Oh, they're not coming."

"What do you mean, they're not coming?" I replied. Now it seemed like I was the one who couldn't understand English. How could they not be coming? It's Christmas Eve, for god's sake. And they'll still get home early enough to have their own tradition, get their kids' presents assembled and wrapped. Everyone has to eat, don't they? Especially Italians.

Lorraine repeats herself: "Oh, they're not coming."

I could not believe my ears. It WAS like she wasn't speaking English.

"Why aren't they coming?" I asked calmly (I think).

"Well, Ian is singing in the choir at church at 7:00, so they have to be there at 5:30."

"Are you serious? They're not coming at all?" Sometimes it does take a brick house to fall on me.

Lorraine is looking at Donna with an expression on her face like, "What's so hard for her to understand?"

Then, in one of those moments that go in slow motion, Lorraine says to me, "And Bill and I and Donna and Al have to eat right away so that we can get to church by 6:00."

Joanne looked at me, not believing what she was hearing. She also correctly assumed that the sister she had idolized for twenty-nine years was about to break the 'never be mean on purpose' rule.

I saw red. It had taken us years and years and years to come up with Christmas Eve as a compromise for everyone—grandma and grandpa can be in the same room if necessary, and you get to be home by 8:00 on Christmas Eve! How hard is that to handle? I'm not even asking for appreciation for all the blood, sweat and tears that went before to make this a reality. But I never, ever in my wildest dreams considered that not showing up was an option. Even back when it was a three-day, exhausting, gastronomical disaster. Black olives, remember...

In the brief time it took for all of that to go through my mind (and I'm sure you've noticed that I'm pretty quick), I went from incredulous to FURIOUS.

I looked Lorraine straight in the eye and said (probably using my outside voice), "Then you can all go right now."

Now it was Lorraine's turn to be in the slow group. "What?" was all she could come up with.

"I said, you can all go right now."

"No, no, that's all right. We just have to hurry."

I'll never know where I got the courage. From tremendous anger, I guess. "You don't understand what I'm saying," I said. "I want you OUT of my house."

"No, no, we can manage," she says.

How about managing to get out of my house?

So I said (in my definite outside voice), "I want you all OUT OF MY HOUSE. NOW."

My sister gets up and runs downstairs to get John. Donna helps Lorraine out of her chair. (I guess I forgot to mention she had a broken foot. Too many martinis one too many times, and she tripped over the newspaper on a Sunday afternoon a month earlier.)

John comes running up the stairs with my sister right behind him. She had obviously told him there was a huge problem but didn't have time to provide details. I felt compelled to fill him in.

"Your MOTHER tells me that, not only are Janice and her family not coming, everyone else has to get to church early to hear Ian sing at 7:00. There will be no Christmas Eve dinner."

"Christine." John says to me.

I turned around and looked at him. THAT look. That look that means I-gave-birth-to-your-child-and-never-once-said-a-bad-word-and-you-won't-live-long-enough-to-make-that-up-to-me.

He turns to his mother and says, "There's nothing I can do."

I'm starting to giggle writing this, but, believe me, I was getting madder by the minute. You have got to be kidding me.

So Donna gathered up the people of the male persuasion downstairs, and John helped his mother down the stairs on her backside, the way a two-year-old goes downstairs, because of her broken foot. God forgive me, because now I'm guilty of being mean on purpose, but I guess I was reacting to sixteen years of meanness and spite.

John comes back in from helping his mother to the car, and I start ranting.

"Your mother has given me nothing but shit for the sixteen years I've been part of this family. But I guess she's decided that I'm not part of the family, am I? That's obvious. I don't know what I ever did to deserve this, but I am sick of it. I don't know who she thinks she is, coming in here knowing full well that everything I've spent days doing will be ruined. And YOUR SISTER. This is absolutely unbelievable." I don't think I took a breath for twenty minutes. But you get the idea.

You have to give John credit. He never said a word, except, "You're right." "I know." "You're right." "I know." "You're right." "I know."

Luckily no one asked me when we were going to eat.

Joanne helped take the lasagna, meatballs and sausage out of the oven and put them in the fridge. I made her take home so many leftovers, she and her family will probably never willingly eat lasagna again. I hope John made J. a sandwich or gave him McDonald's money, because I finally just sat down and started crying. Sobbing, really. *But here's my epiphany: People don't stop shitting on you as long as they get away with it. You have to MAKE them stop. As long as they get the result or outcome they want, why WOULD they stop?*

Up until that point, all my life, I would leave the room, lock myself in the bathroom, turn on the water in the sink and the tub, and cry and cry and cry. And I would never say a word to the person who hurt me.

This time, I stood up for myself. I didn't have John handle it for me, and I didn't make him tell his mother what a witch she had been. Or call his sister and tell her that she was beyond rude. I did it myself!

This was only the second time in my life I let someone know that I was finished taking any shit from them. Finished. Forever. Game over. And that other story is even longer than this one!

Lorraine has been nice to me from that day forward, at least to my face. There was never another snide remark or criticism of anything I did. She did a complete one-eighty, and if you had met us the day after this event, you would never have thought there could have ever been any friction! She never actually apologized, but the nasty behavior stopped that very day.

Every Christmas after that has been well-attended and scene-free! If only I had known years and years ago that I had the right to speak up and set boundaries and minimum standards for acceptable behavior at my house!

I have met a few girls of the girls J. has dated. When my friends ask me if I like the girl, I tell them, "That's not the question. The question is whether or not she likes me!" As God is my witness, I will do my best to be the nicest mother-in-law that ever was!

I'm telling you. If you don't protest and there are no consequences, there is absolutely no reason for people to treat you respectfully if they get the outcomes they want by dumping on you.

***

Afterword

Sadly, Lorraine passed away suddenly and unexpectedly on July 2, 2006, only a couple of weeks after I wrote this chapter. At that time, we had known for three months that John's dad had stage four lung cancer, even though he was a nonsmoker. He fought bravely, but he lost that battle on October ninth. At the moment of his death, I was checking John into an emergency room across town with what we now know was complete and irreversible liver and kidney failure. On November 14, 2006, I lost my beloved husband, and my life as I knew it.

I dedicate this chapter to him.

He was my protector and my champion, and he gave me what I needed to go out into the world and ultimately become who I am, because I knew he'd always be there to catch me if I fell. In many ways, his family was nicer to me than my birth family, and, as you saw, if they weren't, they suffered his wrath as well as mine. His greatest pleasure was to provide for me and for J., and his greatest pride was in seeing us succeed. Our love for each other and our son was and is boundless. What we created together was much more than the sum of the two parts we started with in 1973.

He gave me the roots I never had, and his unfailing love, support and encouragement gave me the wings I will now have to use to write the next chapter of my life.

I love you, Sport!

Chris

March 28, 2007

CHAPTER SEVEN
THE GIFT OF GIVING
Laura Rietmeijer

I had entered a world so different; not my own.
Walking down streets I felt so alone.
Pain and hardship I saw all around,
I realized happiness was no where to be found.
Men with skin hanging off their bones still carried huge loads,
Women with children strapped to their backs sang in deep tones.
Was this what I came so far to see,
a world that lay in complete misery?
The next day I came to a place, not the same
as the streets I had walked the previous day.
In this place, there was laughter and song,
In this place, I found love pure and strong.
Children orphaned by aids lived there, from far and wide,
Left behind by parents who had not survived.
Now alone and in need of some love and some care
I finally knew in my heart just why I was there....
Until they too must say farewell.
Laura Rietmeijer

I am now a twenty-two year old woman, and I can honestly say it wasn't always an easy path. People never tell you that growing up is hard, but it is. You have to find out who you are and who you want to become, and that's just the beginning. You have to find out how to get there too, and although so many have walked the path before you, no two paths are exactly the same. You have to find yours all on your own. My path, just like any other, was unique and one on which I sometimes lost my footing. However, my path was the particular one that led me to becoming a woman and to living the life that I could only have dreamed would come true.

I was born in the heart of Amsterdam to a wonderful and loving family.

My father had a son from his previous marriage who on this day of my birth became my only, but most favorite older brother. I lived in Amsterdam for the first two years of my life and then moved with my mother and father to the states when my father was offered temporary placement as a doctor in preventive medicine at Denver Health in Colorado.

We lived in Colorado for about two years and during that time my mother became pregnant again. We stayed in Colorado long enough to fall in love with the state, and then our stay, as well as my mother's pregnancy came abruptly to an end. My mother lost the baby girl she was carrying just days before she was to deliver and at such a young age this event strongly impacted my life. My parents had grown fond of Colorado and had hopes of expanding our family and now we were on our way back to Holland the same way we had come two years before.

Thankfully after only a few years my father was asked to return permanently. Colorado then became our permanent residence and the place where I would grow up. I began attending school and brushing up on my English, and as I made friends, America and Colorado became my new home. It was several years and a lot of effort, as I understand it, on my parents' part, but when I was nearly seven years old I became a big sister. It was great! Now I had a real live baby to play with, and boy oh boy did I love dressing my baby brother up like a girl.

Life continued to go our way. My older brother was still living in Holland with his mother which made his visits all the more special. My younger brother and I grew up in a loving home where my mother was constantly around.

In the meantime, school was difficult for me. I liked my friends and playing outside but the academics didn't come as easily. It wasn't until third grade that I was diagnosed with dyslexia, but it was clear by then that it was the reason I had struggled with learning from the beginning. With tutoring and extra help, I was soon doing much better in academics. I continued to succeed in school even after life outside of academics got increasingly harder.

It seems like everyone has fond memories of high school except me. Although I might have had a few great times, the last years of high school were the most difficult few years of my life thus far. I have always loved people and been a social person and when I went to high school this was the case more than ever. I had so many friends and never failed to find someone to hang out with. Life was great; I was young and so naïve, yet having so much fun. Then at the beginning of my junior year everything changed. In the time span of eight months seven people I knew died. I needed my friends more than ever and not one of them was there for me.

To say that I was in denial is perhaps the biggest understatement, but I was. It was like every time I had stopped crying for someone I would have another person to cry for. I realized how fragile life is and I realized how few people really cared. I thought I had all the friends I could ever want but not one of them was a real friend. It's really easy to find someone to laugh with but finding someone to hold you, when all you can do is cry, is really difficult.

So I realized that no one was going to change my life for me and that if I didn't do it myself I would not survive. I had to leave everything behind and start over, and so I left all my so-called friends and my school and I entered a world in which I never in my wildest dreams thought I would belong. I remember that day as if it were yesterday. I met with four teachers from an Outward Bound School, and as I sat there in my preppy little outfit across the table from this group of rugged adults, I thought to myself, this can't be the place for me. But as I left the small building that day, I decided it would have to be.

In the next year I changed. I left the *old me* behind and started forming someone new; a person that I could be proud to say was me. I went backpacking through the Copper Canyon in Mexico for almost three weeks with my classmates. During that time I did not shower, did not eat good food, and did not sleep in a bed. I was more uncomfortable during that trip than I had ever been before, and I loved it. I finally learned what life was about. It wasn't about the clothes you wear, or the amount of money you have; it's about what is inside of you and what you have to give. No clothes can cover what's inside and no money will ever be enough. During this trip, I met Tarahumara people who had nothing, yet were happier than any person I had ever known back home. In helping them through digging in trash pits, by teaching English in the schools and with simple tasks around their homes, I learned that they could help me too.

After this amazing experience, I wanted more out of life. I didn't want to live the way I had lived for so long. I wanted meaning, and wanted to give. And so when I was given an opportunity to do so, I took it whole heartedly. At this new school we had to come up with a senior project. The guidelines were not strict; all we had to do was make a plan for a community service project and accomplish a goal and document it before graduation. I was beyond thrilled.

My uncle and aunt had recently moved to Malawi, Africa and I wanted to go there and give all that I could to people in need. My uncle was working as a pediatrician for children with malaria and so I thought I would try to do some work in the hospital. Lucky for me, my uncle found an alternative; one that would be far more uplifting than the grim realities of the patients in the hospital. He found an orphanage in the center of Blantyre, Malawi, called *Open Arms Infant Home* that housed forty babies from birth to age two who had lost their parents to AIDS. Having been born with a mothering quality, this could not have been a better fit for me. My mother, thankfully, would be joining me for the first two weeks of my trip to help me adjust and support me while I experienced the initial shock of third world realities.

Once my plans were in place, I contacted the parents at my school asking them to donate baby clothing so I would not arrive at *Open Arms* empty handed. Within only a few days I received a large bag full; enough to fill any wardrobe for a decent amount of time. But just when I thought my attempts had been effective, I got the biggest surprise ever. I received a call from one of the parents, Kim Downing, who was a board member of a non-profit organization called *Somewhere in the World*. She told me about the organization and how they raised money for orphanages world-wide to support children who might never be adopted. She explained that she had heard about my trip and was very excited about what I was embarking on at such a young age, and said that she would be thrilled if I would take a donation to *Open Arms* on their behalf. I was absolutely blown away! All I had asked for was a clothing donation and here was a woman who wanted me to bring a substantial amount of money. I was honored to be given such a gift; I would be making a difference just by being the one to deliver it. So, after having started my week by casually asking parents to donate clothing their kids had out-grown, here I was at the end, receiving $1500 in traveler's checks.

Finally after what seemed like an eternity, the day came; the day that I would be leaving all that I knew and going to a place I had yet to discover. My mother and I then began our long journey and after nearly forty hours of flying we finally arrived. We were both fried; I had barely slept or eaten anything appetizing in more than two days, but when I stepped off that flimsy plane into a small hole-in-the-wall airport, none of that mattered. It was all new and exciting. After boarding the plane in Colorado with snow on the ground, it seemed unreal to be getting off with lush trees and warm sticky air all around me.

The first few days were hard, though; I did not start my work at the orphanage until Monday and it was only Wednesday when we arrived, so I had some time to kill before I could begin making the difference I had set my heart on making. My aunt, bless her heart, wanted to show us everything there was to see; we went around town stopping at the local markets and visiting the fabric store and having tea. It was all so beautiful, but it was a difficult sight to see, too. People had ragged clothing and their feet were badly calloused from walking for miles without shoes. Many of the people looked like they hadn't eaten a good meal in months, and because they carried huge loads on their heads and backs their skin seemed to barely cling to their weak bones. The people smiled but you could see pain and sadness in their eyes. And the hardship and poverty all around me were so overwhelming that as the days went by I wondered if it was even possible to make a difference in a place with so much need. I began thinking that even if I spent my whole life there it would only be a small drop in a bucket. What could I possibly achieve in six weeks?

Thank God for my mother being there to hold me when I cried and thank God that Monday finally came. My aunt drove us early in the morning to *Open Arms Infant Home* and as we entered the barbed wire security gates we were greeted by Rosemary and Nevile, a British couple who had been running the orphanage for over three years. The small white building had a humble entrance that brought us into the modest office space, and beyond another door the smell of porridge and the sound of crying and giggling infants having breakfast greeted us. We were given a brief introduction and then set to work. One of the Malawian nannies handed a baby covered with breakfast to me immediately, and it was at that instant I realized the difference I had so longed to make had just begun.

From that moment on my job description was simple: I had to snuggle, play with and feed babies. Although the tasks were not all together complicated, when I looked into the eyes of those children I knew that I was making a difference to them even if it was only for that moment. Because they felt loved and important, that in itself was difference enough for me.

About forty percent of the babies at *Open Arms* were HIV positive. Although they looked healthy and happy, their life expectancy was not long. I can't say it was always easy. The work wasn't hard, but reality was. I bonded with forty babies all of whom I learned to know by name, and realizing that many of them would not live, hurt more than any pain I had ever known. It was not fair because I knew that if they had been born in a different country; their possibilities for life would have been so much greater. We don't always realize how lucky we are to have been born in a first world country and to have the opportunities we do have. How lucky we are to be able to live the way we do and strive for the life we want. How lucky we are as men and women who can read and choose the books we like. If you are born in a first world country you are miles ahead of others before you ever take your first breath.

In realizing this, I knew the truth, but had to accept that the future of these children was out of my hands. *All I had was that moment and for that moment I made sure they felt loved.* I had known death but not this kind. Some of these babies were not only brought into this world alone and without parents to care for them but were brought into the world with a disease that would take their lives before they ever had a chance to make something of it. I can't really explain what that is like, because I can't possibly know; what I do know is that it's not fair, and that I know for sure.

Although *Open Arms* can't change the realities of these children completely, they do the best they possibly can, by giving them all the love, nutrition and medication they can get their hands on for the first and most crucial year of their lives. *Open Arms* is a transition home for these infants and takes children from birth to the age of two, because this is the most crucial period for proper nutrition, as so much development occurs during this time. They do not, however, keep the children much past these first two years because they need to make room for other infants. When the babies reach age two, they are either placed back with extended family in the village or in orphanages for older children. This transition is always a big one for the babies, so *Open Arms* tries to make it as smooth as possible.

For the children that go back to the village, *Open Arms* has a traditional Malawian hut in the back of their facility where the baby and its family stay for a week before they leave for the village. This way, *Open Arms* can monitor the child's progress in getting used to its new family situation and living conditions. If this process is successful, the child goes home with its family. They receive a care package that includes a month's supply of corn flower, vegetable seeds and starter packs, mosquito netting as well as clothing for the child. Once the child is back in the village, *Open Arms* visits monthly to make sure it is healthy and is receiving proper care.

As for the children who have no extended family, they move on to other orphanages in Malawi. Although the transition time and care packages are not necessary in this situation, they still do the monthly visits to make sure they are doing well. This process of transition is not an easy one, but is one that is taken very seriously after having invested so much in ensuring the baby survives its first years of life.

With this transition period, *Open Arms* becomes very familiar with the communities around Malawi and continually finds things that need to be done. They often find it hard to fund these projects themselves, but never fail to find other people who will. They know what needs to be done and how. By finding donors they create a win-win situation for the communities as well as the people donating because the projects are carefully chosen and done effectively. With the funding from *Somewhere in the World* and the help of *Open Arms* I saw how far money can go if used correctly. For example, with only $100, I was able to buy supplies and hire a local builder to rebuild the house of twins that had left *Open Arms* and were now living with their grandparents and five cousins, all of whom had lost their parents to AIDS. Their one-room hut had been completely destroyed by the rain, however, within less than two weeks, and with $100 they had a new home that was built to withstand the rainy season. Now think for a moment how often you spend $100 on things you probably don't even need, and then think about how this $100 changed the lives of seven children and their grandparents, who had been left to care for them, after all of their own children had died of AIDS. It sure makes our everyday purchases seem frivolous.

After six and a half amazing weeks, I had experienced everything wonderful and everything terrible in this life. I saw children who were malnourished being nursed back to health. I saw babies smile and giggle as they received true and honest love. I saw children leaving to start a new beginning in their lives. But I also saw sickness-weakened babies who had done nothing wrong. I saw life being taken away without reason. I smiled bigger than I ever had, and cried harder and shed more tears than ever before.

I learned the significance of the saying:

Life is not measured in the number of breaths we take but the number of moments that take our breath away.

Author unknown

During my six and a half weeks in Malawi I had more breath taking moments than I had in eighteen years back home. When I left, I knew that I was going back to the easy life but somehow I did not want that anymore. When everything is easy you don't feel like you are really living, and you don't realize how precious every moment of life really is. So when I waved goodbye to Malawi, I realized I had done what I had set out to do. I made a change, and in doing so I had changed myself as well. The funny thing about giving is that it's a gift to yourself as well, and it feels so good that when you start you can't ever stop.

When I returned from my trip to Africa, I knew it would be easy to slip back into my old life. But when you have had such a life-changing experience you should not try to fit into your old mold because you've grown out of it. *I had.* I wasn't sure what I wanted to do with my *new me*, but as I was a senior and graduating from high school, I thought college would be a perfect opportunity to come into my own. At the end of that summer I moved out of my parents' house and into my own place in downtown Denver and started school at the University of Colorado. I was not too sure what it was I wanted to do but I was eyeing anthropology as an option, because my trip to Africa had sparked my interests in learning about different cultures. College, right from the beginning, was so much better than high school had been. I could finally take classes I was truly interested in, and do what I wanted, when I wanted. The freedom was exciting and new.

In the next few years things were going well for me. I was continuing to make and have healthy relationships, some old and some new, and was feeling blessed that I was able to share my life with such wonderful people who loved and cared for me as I did for them. After having decided to study elementary education, in hopes of changing the lives of children by giving them knowledge, I was feeling positive about the future as well. Africa however, and my experiences at *Open Arms* stayed with me. I returned to *Open Arms* for a month after my first year of college and was thrilled to see some familiar faces. *Open Arms* had stayed true to its nature and had recently opened a nursery school to house children who had no extended family in the village. My trip was just as wonderful as it had been the year before. I wasn't experiencing it in quite the same way, but seeing my cousin Anna, who I had brought along on this trip, experience everything for the first time as I had, was a very uplifting and very special experience.

My mother and I decided not long after my return home that there must be something more we could do. After all, most of our lives are spent at home, and Africa is far enough away that we can't go there all the time. We decided to start a business that would donate fifty percent of its profits back to projects for kids in need in the third world. We decided that what you do for a living, after all, is such a large part of your life, and to not enjoy what you do, and still allow it take up so much of your time, is to not be changing the world or making a difference.

That summer, my mother went with my father to the AIDS conference in Thailand, then traveled to Vietnam, and decided that beautiful, silk pillow cases were a perfect product for us to sell. They were easy to import and a lovely product that all people use in their homes. While my mother was in Vietnam she found a small non-profit store that sold products made by tribes in Vietnam. They marketed these products to allow tribal people to continue living in their traditional ways, yet still make a living wage. We had no intentions of selling sweat shop merchandise, so we were excited to find a place where we could buy both beautiful and well made products that were helping the tribal peoples.

My mother's trip to Vietnam also put us in contact with a recipient for our Asian product donation money. We had decided that for every continent we imported from, we would chose one project to donate to, and for Asia we choose *Koto*, which is a program for street children in Vietnam. They take these children, of which 60,000 are living on the streets of Vietnam, and train them for eighteen months in English and different aspects of the hospitality business. During this time, they form friendships and gain skills that will ensure that they stay off the streets permanently, and with one hundred percent placement in the growing hospitality industry, *Koto* ensures their success.

Upon my mother's return, we started **The Pillow Dreams Project**, and although we were far from experts, we were dedicated to doing the best job we could. We were not only selling the tribal products to help the women who made them, but also raising donation money for *Koto*. In the beginning we sold our products through home shows but soon started selling our products at fairs and online as well. We were thrilled to find that people were excited about our project, loved the pillows, and that we were doing what we had so wanted to do.

Now, after two years, my mother has traveled to South Africa and I to Thailand where we found similar non-profits as we had in Vietnam. By visiting the villages where the products were made and gaining relationships with the non-profits we are now importing from both places, and have made *Open Arms* the recipient of our African donations. From these wonderful countries we have sold thousands of pillows and allowed our customers as well as ourselves to make a small difference in the lives of children in need.

It is our hope that all the people touched by The Pillow Dreams Project will strive to improve their lives with the gift of giving, because with purpose comes happiness, and happiness makes even the hardest of paths worth taking. After my experiences in Africa and Thailand, and with The Pillow Dreams Project, I have become so excited about life. I think many people are bored or depressed about life because they feel they have no purpose.

My epiphany is simply that no gift is too small, and you can never give too many gifts; no matter what, there is always someone to give to. As soon as you define what it is that you want to give, you find meaning in your life. People don't realize that even the small things make a difference and so they are always discouraged. But even if you have nothing, you can always give something. The babies in Africa had nothing material to give me, but they still had enough to change my life. I want everyone to feel that they have the power to make changes and make a difference in this world, because they do, and as soon as you realize that, life suddenly gets so much brighter.

So, as I said, my path hasn't always been the easiest to follow, and I have definitely stumbled along the way. But I learned to find meaning with the gift of giving and with it I have come to be the woman that I am today. One that is not afraid to cry, but never fails to try to make a difference, even if it's of the smallest kind. Because it's when you learn to give that you receive the single biggest gift, and that is the gift of giving. My path, therefore, may be filled with a million flaws, but it was my path, and if given the chance I would not change a thing.

What a gift!

Be the change you wish to see in the world...

Gandhi

Anyone who would like to become involved can find us at www.pillowdreamsproject.com.

CHAPTER EIGHT
AN EPIPHA-MINI

ONE

Anyone who would doubt that we have become one world,
one humanity
and one global economy should doubt no more.

The entire planet is our backyard.
One day early last spring I had that personal epiphany
when I received four long distance phone calls,
all in the space of one afternoon;
from my son in the jungles of Gabon, Africa;
my daughter and her husband in Thailand;
my friend Chris calling from the bush
of Kruger Park in South Africa;
and my husband from Mexico.
I felt like headquarters.

Remember when they used to ask,
"It is ten o'clock—do you know where your children are?"
Our children could be just about anywhere on the planet.

We are all citizens of the world.
One world.

CHAPTER NINE
AGREEING TO LIVE
Leela Kaisa Sundquist

April 2006: The Sex and the City Years
I'd always heard people say that women peak at thirty. The only problem is that they failed to mention I'd hit bottom at twenty-nine. So it was with discernable surprise that I rang in my thirtieth birthday this year after all.

The night before my actual birthday, I hesitated to set my alarm as waking up to the screech of my cell phone, and barreling down the ladder from my loft to stop the incessant ringing wasn't my idea of an ideal start to my special day. I had to get up though to meet my friend Bentley in Sausalito for a brunch date, so that's exactly how it did start. I'd mandated that Bentley bring her dog Zoe along for no other reason than the fact that I love animals. I love them more than people, for the obvious reason that their love is unconditional.

This very fact was displayed as I sat shotgun in Bentley's car with Zoe as she went into the grocery store for eggs. As I waited, I mindlessly picked open the cuticle on my thumb. Hardly unusual for someone who'd been biting and picking her fingers since the sixth grade. My cuticle began to bleed and a chunk of skin hung there, begging to be removed. I knew doing so would only tear it down to the first knuckle, so I managed to engage in some level of self-restraint. Zoe came between the two front seats, put my thumb in her mouth, began licking it gently with her blue-black tongue, then put my thumb under the edge of her cushiony left lip, then slid it over to her right side. She then gave me my thumb back miraculously repaired. I asked myself, which of my human friends would do that?

After we ate, I hopped in my car and drove to Palo Alto to meet my friend Rachael where we had a full "mani-pedi-botox" afternoon. The term was coined by Samantha on Sex and the City, and for some reason I adopted the phrase to represent any kind of self-pampering. Mind you, what we shared should really have been called "ghetto spa day" as it hardly resembled any uptown Manhattan establishment. We used old plastic toolboxes, the kind with two troughs and a handle in the center, to soak our feet, and food storage containers for our hands. The classiness continued as I only had seven cuticles on ten fingers, and was forced to arbitrarily decide where to stop painting the oddball nails. I can't claim the red polish leaking into my cracked cuticles like tributaries was sexy, but attraction in this case was not my intention.

Fully refreshed, I headed back to San Francisco to my eating disorder support group. After the meeting I went out to eat with one of the other women from the group; bit of irony in that for sure. With my recovery underway, I actually welcomed rather than shunned the opportunity to go out to eat. In a nutshell, things were really looking up for this gay blonde-haired blue-eyed alcoholic purging anorexic cutter. The time that I used to spend opening and closing the door of the fridge, or laying in the fetal position on the floor of my apartment drunk and trying not to cut, I got back. It was a ground-breaking month for me on all fronts: I celebrated sixty days of sobriety, sixty days of abstinence from purging, seven months of abstinence from self-injury and was eating enough food for the first time in a year. Oh, and I turned thirty.

May 2005: A Housewarming of My Own

My five-month-long search for a therapist continued. It seemed that despite the proliferation of mental health professionals in San Francisco, they were all either not affiliated with my insurance, had full practices, or couldn't return phone calls to prospective patients, which let's face it, probably means I don't want them as my therapist anyway. I finally had a trial session with someone that I thought I could work with, only to have her call me the next day and tell me "she knows someone from my story." I talked about my family on the east coast and my ex in the city and her new boyfriend, so it looks like seven million people in San Francisco wasn't enough for anonymity. She did give me three references in the hope for me to find someone else to work with. I called them all, and none of them were on my insurance. One of the three, though, offered to take a look at my list of providers to see if she knew anyone. I told her, Aimee, I'd print out the list and drop it by her office, which was right down the street from my apartment in Noe Valley. At this point, if my search for a therapist were a racehorse, I'd have a two-year supply of dog food in the pantry.

That Saturday, I went to my friends' housewarming party in Palo Alto. It was a nice excuse to dress up and get out. My social life largely amounted to nodding at other cyclists, and hoping the chick making my latte behind the counter at the coffee shop would ask me how I was that morning. As I drove up 25th street home from the party, I crested the hill and saw smoke. I thought to myself "Hmph, something's on fire in Noe Valley." As I got closer I saw that the fire was one block above the school that takes up the whole block below my house. That's right; the fire was on my block, about two-thirds of the way up the street, which made it either my house, or my neighbor's house. I drove closer. It was my house. I thought to myself, "This can't be happening to me again."

Thirteen years earlier I was a sophomore in high school and got called to the principal's office to be told that my neighbor was coming to pick me up and that there was some sort of an emergency. She arrived, I got in the car, and she said that our barn, which was attached to my family's farmhouse, was on fire. The fire destroyed the barn, smoke-damaged everything in the house and killed all of our animals, including my beloved horse Pecoy. She was my sweetness, my escape and my sanity. When my father would go into one of his rages, I would slip out into the barn and lay on her back in the stall. I would ride her into the woods and find peace. I suffered the grief of her death, and I lost the only thing helping me cope with my dad.

The cause of the barn fire was determined to be the heat lamp we turned on for the dogs, Sheba and Crystal. They stayed outside in the barn, even during winter, and since it was going to be one of those strange New England days that became colder as a weather front moved in, I'd turned the heat lamp on that morning. The fire was my fault. I had accidentally killed the one thing that brought me happiness and calm.

My hands were shaking as I parallel parked my car one block away from my house. I ran past the police at the intersection, past the fire engines lining the street, and saw firemen climbing ladders onto the roof heading towards the back of the house. I told the firemen on the street that this was my house, and gave them my key to unlock the basement door.

I told them I didn't know if my landlord and her family were home, that I'd been away for hours at a party. I told them my cat was inside and they had to get my cat out. They told me that they had to find out if there were people inside before they were going to go in looking for a cat. I stood there watching my home on fire with smoke billowing out of the windows. I saw about fifteen firemen standing on the sidewalk. Surely one of them could go in after my cat? I started talking to one after another. Eventually, I got one fireman to go in after my cat, and after three attempts to locate my boy, he came out with Ripley. The white of his tuxedo fur was grey, but he was okay.

The four departments on scene put the fire out, and while it would be left to the investigator to determine the exact cause, I was told the fire appeared to have been started because of an unattended barbeque grill my landlord hadn't extinguished properly before leaving. This left me with a shred of peace amidst the total chaos: at least it wasn't my fault. I couldn't have lived with that guilt again.

The next day some friends came up to the city to help me try to sort things out. I showed them into what remained of my place, through what I referred to as "my new Dutch door." The firemen had kicked in the door to my studio apartment, which must have been on clearance at the Home Depot, because it broke all too cleanly in half. There was very little to salvage inside. What hadn't burned was grey with soot or wet from water. I realized that the insurance company would have to deal with it when they came. My friends offered to take me out to lunch and suggested we head down the street for some wood-fired pizza or BBQ. Funny, kind of. They set me up with keys to their photographic studio, where there was a futon and a bathroom—enough for someone newly homeless to crash in for a little while.

June 2005: 7 Days and 585 Miles: A Vacation from My Life

Within a week of finding my road bike covered in the melted skylight that once was above it, I was back riding my repaired preferred vehicle of choice. The repairs cost more than many bicycles, but I was hardly going to let go of the goal of the last six months of my training, AIDS Lifecycle 4, slip away. The fire happened two weeks before I was to leave for seven straight days of riding five hundred eighty five miles from San Francisco to Los Angeles benefiting the SF AIDS Foundation and the LA Gay & Lesbian Center. The ride was a vacation from my life. In the preceding fourteen days I'd helped the insurance company sort out what to try to salvage, gathered a bag of basic necessities and walked away from my apartment for the last time.

Two days after the fire I put a call in to Aimee, the therapist who offered to review my list of providers. I spoke directly with her and told her that I was no longer going to be able to print out that list of providers for her to look at, as my apartment had just burned down. She told me that while she wasn't with my insurance, and only had a short-term opening to offer, I was welcome to come in and meet with her considering the circumstances. I thought that was probably a good idea.

I saw Aimee for the first time right before the ride. I laughed as I climbed the stairs up to her office. Each therapist I'd tried so far had remarkably similar office scenarios: an extraordinarily steep set of stairs that challenged even the fittest of people to make the climb (perhaps this was supposed to be a metaphor for the work ahead?), codes on the doors which were a challenge to keep straight when trying out various therapists, and the bathrooms in the converted Victorian houses that all still contained showers, which were almost invariably filled with storage materials and covered with functionally-appropriate shower curtains. Personally, I wondered if this was to prevent any suicides from happening on the premises.

The reason for Aimee only having a short-term opening was due to the fact that she was due. She was very pregnant and about to go on maternity leave. The session was great. It felt good. This was the fit I was looking for. I wondered if this was a new twist on my consistent attachment to unavailable women. Leave it to me. She could offer a couple more sessions, with the option to work together again post-partum. In the meantime, she gave me four references. I laughed, as if somehow I hadn't had enough contact with the therapeutic community yet.

The thing was, I knew I needed to pursue it. I was shutting down quickly. My first choice coping mechanism was restriction, a method to madness I had developed five years prior in the midst of a bad relationship and recovered from with the help of my old therapist Mary in Massachusetts. Right after the fire I stopped eating normally. I skipped breakfast, made insurance phone calls at lunch, and with no kitchen in the apartment where I was staying, it was all too easy to skip dinner. As the days went by, I stopped getting undressed or unfolding the futon at the studio. I slept on the floor in my clothes on top of the sleeping bag that reeked of smoke that I was simply too tired to get in.

Freud still had no place in my life. I stopped remembering my dreams which I considered a huge gift. After the first fire, I had reoccurring nightmares for two years. I would float through the charred remains of the barn always ending up at my horse's stall door looking down at her burned and contorted body. With dreams like that, I never needed courses in analytical theory to deduce the meaning.

I started having to really fight the urge to cut or burn. It was something I did in high school and then managed to stop when I went off to college. I used to do it when my dad would have one of his outbursts, but it was never that bad, only small scrapes, cuts and burns, or punching the wall until my knuckles popped open. I didn't engage in the behavior for ten years, until I broke up with my girlfriend of seven years and had three incidents in a single month.

After the break-up I was sleeping on the couch while I tried to secure an apartment for myself. To say the least, my ex was not in favor of the break-up, and I found myself trapped in a house with an angry person again. I was drunk when the cuts happened this time. I savored the beautiful zone when I cut. When I saw the white nodes of fat under my skin, I'd stop. During the following year I had a couple more cuts, always emotional and always drunk. I knew I had to get into therapy again, hence the start of my search that was going oh so well. While I'd found Aimee, kind of, the momentum of my problems was getting the better of me. I was desperate for the instantaneous calm and relief cutting provided me. I wanted that pretty much every hour of every day.

July 2005: An Undeniable Rebirth

There's an emotion that represents how you feel when you know you are slipping down a familiar slope that will lead nowhere good. At the time, I was not sure what that emotion was, but I knew I was feeling it. Now I call that feeling "dread."

I left the building where I worked mid-morning. I'd gone to check my phone in my locker for messages and it rang—it was Aimee calling me back. I walked next door to an open-air mall and sat down in a secluded spot. I pulled the hood of my red sweatshirt over my head and told Aimee it was getting to be too much. That weekend I had gotten up on Saturday, gone online to balance my checkbook and found that "I" had been shopping at Home Depot in Los Angeles twice already that morning. My checking account had nearly been emptied as I found myself to be America's latest victim of identity theft. I called my bank and then went down to the police station and filed a report. Great, now I was heartbroken, homeless and broke.

I was shutting down. I told Aimee I hadn't eaten in a couple of days. I had tried a couple of new therapists but it wasn't working out. I agreed to try another person on her list of references. It was with some hesitation because I didn't think I wanted to see a man, but I figured if he was good enough for Aimee to recommend, then I should call him. Right before we got off the phone she stopped the conversation, "Oh, Leela?" "Yeah." I said. "Go eat some protein." she said. I didn't question Aimee's request; I just walked upstairs at the mall and got a bean burrito. Little did I know this concept would later revolutionize my recovery.

I called Aimee's reference, Greg. To my great shock he answered his phone. Every therapist's phone I'd ever called had gone directly to voicemail. I only had my usual message prepared and was caught off guard to say the least. There was something about him that put me at ease, though, and I gave him the general gist of what was going on. He asked me what I was looking for in a therapist, and I answered from my gut, "I need someone to call me on my shit." I then apologized for swearing, and he just chuckled. We set up an appointment for that weekend.

My nights at this point were horrid. I was constantly consumed with whether or not to eat, typically purging if I did get myself to eat, and simultaneously trying not to cut. I was desperate to not cut, because I knew if it started again, I was going to have a hard time stopping. I found comfort in strange things. They were old ways of avoiding the behavior. I'd tape up my forearms or hands with athletic or medical tape. The tightness felt good, created a barrier and when I wrapped my fingers I couldn't hold anything such as a razorblade or scissors. I would sleep bits and pieces this way, which was a much-needed relief. I would wake up in the morning, however, to the very visible indication of just how out of control my life was. I'd unwind the tape or cut it off, put on my uniform and go to work. Some mornings my hands were quite swollen due to constriction and I'd just hope no one at the office would notice the circus sideshow quality to my proportions.

Right before my place burned down I'd gone to my doctor because of neck pain. My training for the AIDS ride had pushed my body to its limits. I was prescribed the painkiller Diazepan. When I went to pick it up, the pharmacist told me my doctor had failed to fill out the appropriate controlled substance form. Wow. My first controlled substance. The oversight was worked out and I was given the meds. Days later, the first bottle was lost in the fire, and I went to the pharmacy to refill it. I didn't particularly have the pain anymore, but I wanted to have it around in case I needed it to knock myself out and sleep. One night I was beside myself with wanting to cut, so I started drinking wine and taking the Diazepan. The indications were to take half a pill for pain. I took a whole pill and waited to feel drowsy. The desired effect didn't come, so I took another. No relief. I took a third one with another glass of wine. Finally, I got tired. I had successfully drugged myself.

About a week later on Saturday evening, I went to my friend Jim's birthday party. It was a casual affair with loads of his friends. I spent about six hours there, drinking from the keg and chatting with random people. Jim was the only person I knew at the party, and while I found my way adeptly through conversations with strangers, when everyone decided to go salsa dancing, I left to go back to my friend's place where I was house-sitting. I was drunk. On the drive there, I started to cry and bite down on my forearms. I knew it was going to happen. Hell, I had picked up fresh razor blades on Friday afternoon. Perhaps it was non-specific premeditation: I had no exact plan to cut, but was acquiring what I needed all the same. That night I cut my left upper arm. I knew the cut had to hide under my work uniform, which was short-sleeved. I savored the pain with many cuts across the same line. Then I cleaned out the cut and taped it shut.

I showed up to my first session with Greg with a wound just hours old. He asked me about something I had told Aimee on the phone, about the night with pills and wine. He asked me straight up "Were you trying to kill yourself?" Ironic; I was actually of the opinion that I was trying to save myself, and I told him as much. He asked me if I knew what the interaction between that drug and alcohol was, and how many times the normal dose I'd taken. I was had. I'd thought all along it was the cutting that would look suicidal.

July ended with me finding an apartment. I was about to move to Mill Valley, in Marin County just north of the Golden Gate Bridge. It was an area in which I had spent much of the previous year training in, and certainly was a lot more serene than the city. I told Greg that I hoped for a fresh start in this new place. He looked right back at me and asked, "While that's a nice idea, do you really think that you can expect that?" At that point I had cut three times, each about a week apart. Each as the other began to heal. I was purging only when I ate, which is to say I was distinctly not maintaining my weight. Most of my calories were coming from two liquids: coffee and Newcastles. Greg spoke the truth that I insisted on lying to myself about.

August 2005: Momentum

I moved into my new apartment and everyone around me acted like now everything was okay. Of course, no one knew what was actually going on, so yeah, on the surface, a new place was the only problem I needed a solution for. When the company charged with delivering my salvaged items showed up, they reported that more than half of my order was lost. They thought they might have delivered it by accident to an elderly woman on long-term vacation in Reno. Great, Grandma's got my Diesel jeans. I was understanding, but gave them two weeks to locate the goods or compensate me. In the end, it was a check I received, not my things. I thought to myself, "God must really want me to have a clean slate here." When I tried to throw a pity party for myself in my next session with Greg he told me that's always how it worked in his life, things came in batches. While initially I took this as dismissive of my experience, I later recognized it as his acceptance of things out of our control.

Greg was increasingly someone I trusted. He asked me if I'd ever gone to a twelve-step group to which I responded quickly, "No." He asked me to do some "homework" which was to find a self-mutilation or eating disorders group around the city. When I returned the next week having failed to find anything his only response was, "What search engine did you use?" I responded "Yahoo." He then said with a smile, "Well, I used Google, and here's a list of the meetings I found." He handed me two pages.

Greg asked me to go to one of the meetings on the list by our next session. Sensing my reluctance, he asked me what I had to lose. He was met with silence, then added "I'll tell you what you have to lose, about an hour of your time." He told me he hoped that a group would allow me to meet other people like me and feel less alone. Walking into my first meeting that night I said for the very first time in my life "My name is Leela, and I'm anorexic." Greg was right, the people I met that night said things that I thought were only in my head. I heard so much that I related to in just my first meeting that I felt comfortable enough to share with these strangers what was going on with me. My list of people who knew the horrid truth tripled in a single night. I was in therapy now twice a week, and with the addition of the E.D.A. meeting, I was now being truly honest for three whole hours every seven days.

I spent time reflecting on the origin of my issues around eating and my body. I recalled a conversation I had with my old therapist Mary during which she remarked that my cutting in high school usually followed some outrageous behavior on the part of my father, either in a fit of anger, or after he unleashed his belittling and vial commentary. She remarked on the horrible things he would say about my weight or body. He was awful. After college he would still make comments about my weight every single time I visited home without fail. My telling him to stop only gave him momentum as he realized the power of his words. When I became anorexic the first time and was at my thinnest, my weight was still a topic for him, this time in the context of being "unattractively thin." He always evaluated my body in a way I think every girl wished her father wouldn't, and he always approached it as his right to do so.

I found myself unsurprised that I landed in San Francisco, just about as far away as possible from little North Sutton, New Hampshire, a girl escaping her cruel father can go inside the lower forty-eight. It was an undeniable fact that the pain he caused my brother, mother, and myself invigorated a lot of emotion. How could it not? After moving out of the house, my pain faded to simple outrage, and then to sadness and regret. I guess I wish I had been able to save my mom, brother and myself a hell of a lot sooner than any of us can claim to have been saved. I wondered when that time would have been, when it could've been different. That chance may have been when I was eleven. That was when we moved from outside of Syracuse, NY up to NH. Before the move, I don't remember much about my dad; mostly that he worked a lot. After that, all I remember are the fights night after night between him and my mom. Years later, I found my sixth grade diary in which I wrote about killing myself to get away from the fights. I don't remember what they were about, just the sound of the screaming.

My dad is a smart man with an amazing talent for identifying another human being's weaknesses and exploiting them. For my brother it meant that he had to endure time after time of being told in new or old ways just how stupid he was and how embarrassed my dad was that he was his son. For me, it meant time after time of having my confidence of mind, body and actions picked apart. I had always had decent success academically, and that was the one area for which my father showed pride. So yeah sure, he called me stupid too, but in a "you should've known better" way. I learned to avoid my dad when I could, and walk on eggshells when I couldn't.

Each time I experienced failure, disappointment, or tragedy, there was the haunting voice of my father telling me that I was somehow not good enough to foresee it, fix it, or recover from it. There was no room for pain in his expectations. There was only disappointment dealt out through articulate means. He trained us to react a certain way, and that fundamentally was to believe we were not good enough, and that we should've avoided the pain that we were so selfish to say we were in.

I internalized it all. I focused on trying to be perfect so that I could gain some glimmer of approval from him. If I was 98% successful, I focused myself entirely on the two percent I hadn't succeeded at. I would accomplish something only to immediately push forward and fail to recognize anything I'd done well. I tried to be my own worst critic so that no one else would have anything to say that I hadn't already said to myself. It was a sick form of protection. Literally.

All these coping mechanisms I'd developed were undeniably unhealthy, but had a silver lining as they were born from my need to come up with some way to survive the environment I was in. Eventually though, they developed a life of their own, and my sense of control started to slip away.

One night at the end of August, I got up off the floor and cut a four-inch line across my abdomen. The next morning something new happened. I decided the cut wasn't deep enough. I'm not sure how I judged that determination, but I know I picked the razor blade out of the trash, took the tape off the cut, and used the dirty blade to further dig into my stomach. I was sober that morning. No alcohol to shift the blame of my actions onto. The size and number of red flags was increasingly alarming.

September 2005: Trading Seats on the Titanic

I showed up at Greg's office with a pressure bandage on my right wrist. He didn't notice it because I covered it with an oversized Nike sweatband. I told him about what happened. I had been ironing at work and had nicked my forearm accidentally with the side of the iron. The taste of the pain became a fixation for me and I spent the rest of the day wanting more. I wouldn't risk being caught intentionally burning myself at work, so I waited until I got home.

I walked in my apartment and turned on the oven. I heated it up to 400 degrees. When it registered that it had reached the proper temperature, I took out the pizza stone that had been inside and placed it on the stovetop. I placed the inside of my right wrist against the side of the stone and leaned onto it. My head rang beautifully with pain, becoming pure as the endorphins kicked in. As my flesh cooled the stone, I would turn it and press the same spot on my arm on the stone again. When the skin bubbled, I stopped.

Greg told me that the way that I described it reminded him of the way addicts talk about being triggered when exposed to their drug of choice. Hmph. Maybe that was why I had fought the urge to injure myself so much—it was like an addiction to the homemade drugs my body made. How convenient, I didn't need a dealer when I had myself.

On any given day I would force myself to vomit three, four, five times. I felt frustrated over allowing myself to eat when I knew I would simply throw it up. It was a waste of time, energy and money. The increasing deprivation from food had created compulsion when I did eat. I'd open my throat and chug wine only to thrust out of my nostrils while vomiting later, and digging the tortilla chips out of the bottom of the trash can because twenty-four hours after disposing of them, I decided they weren't that taboo after all. Put a fucking frame on that, that's a pretty picture.

When I was hungry and rationalized needing to eat, and actually got the food inside me, I was filled with such disappointment in myself for failing my commitment to starvation that I would purge. Firmly back at square one, I was still hungry, just with less enamel. This cycle was hell, and a lot less enjoyable than cutting. I didn't feel any of the relief that I did when I cut, just boatloads of failure. I was neither successful at eating, nor not eating. It was a kind of exponential cycle of disappointment in myself. I'd proclaim a new set of rules, a new place that I'd set the bar for myself, then break the rules and lower the bar further. I'd feel worse about myself and down, down, down the spiral went.

I'd taken to drinking every night. I'd stop at Whole Foods on my way home from work and pick up a six-pack of Newcastle Brown Ale. I was drinking as many as needed to knock myself out, usually four or five. Not eating had turned me into one hell of a cheap date. For some reason I refused to go the more economical route and head to the liquor store for the case, even though I would have easily consumed that much in any given week. I lived in happy denial, yet I'd make sure I didn't use the same checker two nights in a row for fear of being "discovered."

I'd drink and my eating disorder would rage. I'd managed to stop cutting for a few weeks. I was reflecting in a session with Greg about the day Aimee told me to go eat some protein. I didn't question what she wanted me to do, and I thought that if he told me he didn't want me to cut or burn, that I wouldn't. He began saying it to me at the end of each session, and it worked. It made it so that I didn't consider it an option for myself. I still missed the calm that cutting gave me though, so I drank, starved and purged my way to it instead.

I was up for promotion at work against two other equally-qualified candidates and it felt like a lose-lose situation: either I was going to fail and not get the job, or I was going to be greeted back from my month-long business trip to Boston in October with a whole new set of pressures.

As the days went by, my fantasies of cutting blended with thoughts of suicide. I couldn't get it off my mind. I'd always known that bleeding would be my way to go. The potential of only blowing half my brains out with a gun had no appeal for me, nor the Golden Gate Bridge, as I'd surely ruin the day for at least two hundred tourists and I couldn't handle the prorated guilt. It'd been clear to me since I was young: I'd thin my blood with aspirin and slit my wrists and cut my brachial artery. I'd die in the most beautiful place I'd known, which changed from time to time depending on where I lived and traveled. My suicide plan did however have a safety-mechanism, if a suicide plan can have one. My place of choice was a twelve-hour drive away, to Bear Mountain in Sedona, AZ.

After the drive I still had a three-hour hike ahead of me before I'd lay upon the white sedimentary rocks that cap the burnt orange that makes up Sedona's quintessential landscape.

As the month went on, I started seeing Aimee again. I was getting tired. Tired physically. Tired emotionally. Tired of living. I was showering at best once a week. I was sleeping in my clothes. I was determined to allow everyone to think that I was fine. I failed to be able to discern what I was happy for in this life of mine. I was facing every behavior I had faced before, which encapsulated the bitter taste of relapse with the added insult of dealing with them all at once. It was completely undermining to my confidence knowing that what I'd thought I'd conquered before had gotten the better of me. It was like I'd fallen for the wolf in sheep's clothing once, then mistaken the wolf again only because he was in a different outfit. I had only one answer for how to escape my pain for good.

In late September I didn't return home from work one day. I drove instead to a park and lay down in the grass near where the dogs play. I thought today might be "the" day, and wanted to think about it before going home. I thought about what would be comfortable to wear in the car for the drive to Arizona. I wasn't sure what the weather was like there. I picked up the phone and called an old friend, the father of two children I had taught at a preschool before moving out to California. I wasn't particularly close with Scott as I'd left the state right after getting to know him, but we were kindred spirits. I talked to him for two hours that afternoon and for once, did something different: I told him everything that was going on. I spoke the truth. I answered his questions without omission. He knew I was supposed to go to Boston for business in ten days and gathered I wasn't sure I was going to make it. He made me promise to tell Aimee everything I'd told him. I already had told her it was bad. At this point it was just updates on how bad.

October 2005: My Epiphany

I called Aimee from my apartment and told her I was done with life but too tired to make the drive to Arizona. I told her Mt. Tam in Marin was going to have to do. She heard the finality in my voice and asked me to consider checking myself in to a little white hospital on a hill. That's what I heard anyway. I told her I'd think about it. I didn't like the idea of making myself vulnerable to a batch of men in white coats that I didn't trust. There were only really two or three people that I trusted at this point in time: Aimee, Greg and Scott. I began talking to Scott daily, and it gave me one thing to look forward to. I wasn't sleeping and would call him early in the morning and talk to him before he went to work on the east coast. He told me he'd meet me at Logan airport, that all I had to do was get on the plane.

I woke up the first Sunday in October and had it set in my head: I'd get on my bike, ride to the top of Mt. Tam, take the aspirin I'd purchased, slit my wrists and bleed out in the second most beautiful place I knew. I got a call that morning. I was already dressed in my best cycling jersey and shorts. My friend Wayne from the AIDS ride was about to go ride Mt. Tam and wanted to know if I wanted to come. Fuck. I couldn't say no and then go off myself with him potentially riding by my bloody mess. I'd wait a day.

Monday morning I called out of work. As if I couldn't carry the guilt of an improper call out for the few hours to my grave. While I lay there waiting for the sun to come up, I realized that my store manager had asked me about Mt. Tam two days earlier. He thought he was going to take our visiting Scandinavian designer there on Monday. Great. I had told him to go to O'Rourke's bench, exactly where I was going to go. I'd have to wait another day. I called Aimee instead. She asked me why I'd waited to call her. I told her it wasn't really waiting when I was only thinking about one thing all the time. She asked me what I wanted. I told her I simply wanted to feel safe.

I called Scott. He was getting his kids ready for school. I didn't have anything to say, I just thought hearing his voice would give me a momentary shred of comfort. He asked me how the packing for Boston was going. I told him I didn't have the energy to pack and still wasn't sure I was going to make it anyway. He said he had someone who wanted to say hi. Maddie, Scott's nine year-old daughter, got on the phone. I'd taught Maddie when she was four, and she was decidedly one of the sweetest kids I'd ever met. "Hi Leela," Maddie said excitedly. "Hi Maddie," I replied quietly. "Is it true you're going to be at our house on Saturday?" she asked. At this point I cursed Scott for putting her on the phone. I hated him. He didn't know it, but he was making me choose to live or to die. I couldn't lie to Maddie. I would not do that to her. "Yeah Maddie, I'll be there." I said. *In that moment I had agreed to live.* She gave the phone back to Scott. "You know I hate you for that Scott," I said. "Yeah well, desperate times call for desperate measures," Scott countered.

What was to follow would be rough, but I never second-guessed it. To my own benefit and detraction, I'm very black or white. I am completely in or completely out. Love or hate. Pass or fail. Good or evil. My bull-headed stubbornness that was the catalyst in my self-destruction became my strength as I fought to get through each hour and each day. I talked to Aimee on the phone a lot that week. I told her that I didn't know how to get myself out of it this time. I told her I saw the light at the end of the tunnel but didn't know if it was daylight or a train. She said something that in the midst of desperation changed things for me: She said she had hope for me, and that I had to trust that she could see it even though I couldn't. I trusted her. It was clear to me that I wasn't going to get through this on my own.

In the three days before I left for Boston I packed, prepaid my rent and bills, had a phone intake interview from the fourth floor of the parking garage at work with an Eating Disorders Clinic in Boston, arranged for cat care, and got a ride to the airport with Wayne. Aimee and I were to have our sessions by phone, and I figured if nothing else, Scott could drive me to the closest white building on a hill in Western Massachusetts and we could take the carpool lane on the way. When I arrived at Scott's I felt safe for the first time in a long time. His three kids nearly knocked me down with hugs when I came through the door, and the relief in his eyes said it all.

I technically spent the month working at the new store, getting it ready for its November opening; but I remember very little about work. I worked to get to the weekends, leaving at first opportunity on Friday, and arriving back Monday mornings, never Sunday nights.

It was in Boston that for the first time in my life I interacted with God. In my 12-step E.D.A. program, we talk about handing our lives over to our "higher power," and I struggled as an agnostic with how to conceptualize this. One night I stole off with the shared gold Kia Rio to go to an eating disorders group. I was driving through the darkness of night and heavy rain with quintessential Boston drivers on each of my bumpers. I approached a rotary and knew enough to not use my indicator signals as to local drivers this would be interpreted as a clear sign of weakness. I made it across the rotary overpass, but landed on the other side adjacent to a strip of restaurants—not where I expected to be. I thought to myself: this is my hell—fast-food fest. I begged God out loud for help and guidance. "God, I fucking need to get to this meeting!" I began to drive again and for some reason had the desire to turn right down a dark, dank one-way alley complete with stray cat. At the end of the alley I stopped, spotted the street sign and realized I was only one block from my meeting. I found parking directly across the street and couldn't deny there was something to this thing of asking God for help.

November 2005: Calamity Jane

My time with Scott and his family was emotionally uplifting. I did, however, suffer a number of nasty physical problems along the way. I got a cold that left me sounding like a thirteen year-old boy, was bitten in the thumb by a cat which resulted in an infection and required antibiotics to stop the streaking up my arm, burned my eyelids in a French press coffee maker explosion, came down with a roaring stomach flu which had me experiencing severe fecal urgency for days and ultimately landed me in the hospital getting IV fluids pushed in, and finally, I was run down on the basketball court by a guy on my team who looked like Weird Al and got bruised ribs and a sprained sternum. Who knew you could sprain your sternum?

This all got me thinking that I may have compromised my health. I returned to California and went to the doctor to have my ribs checked out and to fess up about what else was going on. I'd never broken a bone in my life, and I really wondered if I'd fast-forwarded my bone density to be that of my elderly next door neighbor with the crooked back who couldn't stand straight enough to make eye-contact. My doctor agreed that a number of basic blood tests were in order. At the lab, the guy in the white lab coat with the graying super-mullet, a balding comb-over pony-tail, drew no fewer than four vials of blood.

The test results would arrive in the mail less than a week later. They were divided into a green column that represented numbers within normal range, and a red column, numbers in the abnormal range. The only red results had the letters AST and ALT. These letters meant nothing to me. I called my childhood best friend who was in medical school and casually worked it into the conversation. He said they were associated with my liver. When I got to see my own doctor face to face he said the same thing, "Your liver enzymes are off. Have you been drinking a lot lately, or taking a lot of painkillers?" I played it off, "No, I haven't even been on a bender lately!" Mind you, everything's relative. One person's average is another person's bender. He said it could be a few other things, including Epstein Barr virus, fatty liver disease or just a botched lab result. I laughed at the fatty liver disease and told him I thought the idea that an anorexic might have unusually large deposits of fat on her liver was quite ironic! He said I should get retested after abstaining from drinking and taking painkillers for three consecutive days.

It took me five weeks to get those three days. Nothing drags you out of denial and illustrates dependence like the inability to do something. Your car breaks down, and you realize you don't even know where the bus stop is, much less how much it costs or that it requires exact change. I'd have two days, experience what seemed to be an even shittier day than the last shitty day, and I'd say, "Fuck it. I'm going home and drinking." Or I'd get three days, the blood-drawing facility would be closed for the weekend and I'd drink.

As I began working again with Aimee, there was a lot to cover, current and past. I had twenty-nine years of life under my belt, and few were free from trouble. I had a "Why me?" attitude and recounted the various things that had gone on in my life. Why did my best friend get killed in a freak accident after college? Why did my dad have to be an abusive asshole? Why did I have a dozen tumors in my uterus at the age of twenty-six? Why did my place burn down, twice? I saw no meaning to that which was out of my control. I wondered how there could be a God that would want this life for me?

December 2005: The Monkey on My Back
I came to the difficult decision in December that I needed to cut off contact with my dad. The tricky part: how do I tell someone I hardly have any relationship with that I don't want to have contact with him anymore? I'd been thinking about it for about a year and a half. The two-way street had only one-way traffic for years, and I finally realized that if my dad were a friend, I would have ditched him a long time ago. I'd hoped that things were going to change and that I'd wake up one day with a father who wanted to love me unconditionally. I'd always give him chance after chance to change. I became sickened by my own willingness to repeat the pattern and my emotional pain finally outweighed my fear of what might happen. To separate myself from my abusive father would

finally allow me to take the control away from him and put it in my hands again.

I did it sitting on the bench next to the Mill Valley fire department with Peet's coffee in my hand. Creature comforts. I'd spent a few weeks with Aimee talking about what I would say, how I thought he'd respond and what I'd say back. I had my exit strategy. I was ready. As we talked about it in my sessions, I actually felt anticipatory relief. The call went about as well as one could hope for something like that to go. He said he didn't understand. He proclaimed he was different. I stood my ground and defended my decision to put what I needed first.

My second set of blood test results came back. I was fine. I told my doctor that I would try not to interpret them as a permission slip to continue on with my eating disorder. I continued to struggle to control my drinking though and had several unbecoming incidents. One night I drove home using brail, a term a friend used for driving drunk and using the reflector bumps as a guide. I got home, walked into my deathly cold house, turned on the wall heater which was under my desk and curled up in front of it for warmth. I passed out. Hours later I awoke to find my entire mouth was dried and cracked and my face was very swollen from the heat. I stumbled out from under my desk to the bathroom, looked in the mirror and said, to myself, "This is not my life."

On Christmas Eve I went out with friends to dinner. I told myself I wasn't going to drink: an affirmation that lasted about two seconds. My friend put champagne in my hand and I took it and drank it in three "sips." The holidays had always been hard for me. There were many bad memories, and the feeling of not having the place to go that everyone else seems to be running off to with presents packing their cars to the gills. I drank that night to make the feeling of isolation go away. When I got home I received a phone call. I cannot remember who it was. I went out to check my mail while on the phone and fell down my stairs. I remember my friend asking what the noise was, and I replied simply "Oh, I fell down the stairs...what were you saying?" In the morning I got up, shuffled into the bathroom, saw the bruises and remembered the fall.

On the 27th of December I called my friend Horace. I knew he was a recovering alcoholic with many years of sobriety. I knew when I called that I would tell him everything that was going on. I knew what he would say. He asked me if my drinking made my other problems worse.

I said, "Yes. Absolutely." He asked me if I wanted those problems to stop. I said, "Yes. Absolutely." He said, "Well then, Leela, it seems you have a desire to stop drinking."

He asked me, "Do you have any alcohol in your house right now?" I replied, "Don't you mean, 'Do I have any alcohol in my hand right now?'" He told me I had to dump it out. It was a pathetic display. I tried to chug the beers I had purchased just hours earlier, as I knew that they were going to be my last. I poured one into the sink as I poured another into my mouth. With my supplies gone Horace told me he was online finding me an AA meeting to go to tomorrow. He told me I would call him every day and find a meeting to go to everyday. He said he didn't care if it was AA, OA or NA, just to get to a meeting. He said after thirty meetings in thirty days I would undoubtedly be feeling some recovery. He didn't push me to tell him I was an alcoholic. He said that what I told him about my eating and cutting was like what alcoholics said about alcohol, that I would be able to relate to them, and them me. He was right. But I also related to what they said about alcohol.

My actions were changing. When I was stuck, I was telling people what was going on and asking for their help. I was taking suggestions. I was making my recovery my priority. I was being honest with others about who I was, and the number of baggage carts I needed their help pushing. I started seeing Aimee twice a week. It was a huge financial commitment, but I realized that without my health, I had nothing.

January 2006: Hello, My Name is…

I can't describe the panic I experienced in the check out lane at the grocery store when I was unexpectedly asked for my ID. I couldn't believe I was getting carded. Had I subconsciously picked up alcohol? I looked at my items and saw the six-pack. It was Diet Root Beer. I looked at the checker and said with a smile, "Hold on, you're carding me for root beer?" I'd taken up drinking root beer much the way a smoker trying to quit starts sucking on lollipops. This was hardly something I learned in the program, just my own special version of substitution. I drank them the same way as I'd drunk real beer. I started when I got home, left the bottles everywhere, and woke up in the morning wondering how I'd had so much to drink.

I found out that going to Alcoholics Anonymous meetings really wasn't that different than going to Starbucks, and I'm not referring to the weak coffee. A newcomer, anyone in their first thirty days of sobriety, was asked to introduce themselves by their first name so that the fellowship could welcome them. It seemed my name was as hard to get right in AA as it was when I got my latte. Nela. Leah. Layla. Lila. The program really was anonymous, just not in the way I'd expected.

Towards the end of January, my first thirty days of sobriety, neared. I knew some meetings gave out metal chips to celebrate certain lengths of sobriety. I wasn't particularly jazzed up about getting my "chip" but figured why not? Oddly though, as the moment came, I truly felt overwhelming excitement. The eyes of the hundred plus people said it all: Yes, change is possible for each and every one of us, if we are willing.

In therapy, I had no lack of things to talk about. I joked with Aimee that I was going to construct a large vertical "Wheel of Misfortune" that would be a pie chart of my issues. We would spin it at the start of each session as a means of determining what topic to focus on for the day. The thing was, I really couldn't stay away from any one topic too long before it began to fester. I was unrelenting in dragging skeletons out of the closet. I couldn't afford not to, and I didn't want any sequels to what was a fresh memory of misery.

I'd received the promotion at work and was taking part in a high-caliber training. One of the class modules focused on home furnishing with light, which shed some light on a problem I was having at home. When I'd moved into my new place, I bought all energy-saving bulbs. I did care about the environment, if not myself. The class taught us about the different color spectrums produced by bulbs and it turned out that all my bulbs were about as far from natural light as possible. They were likened to the dull grey glow of prison lighting. I had to laugh and speculate that this could not have been helping me dig my way out of my pit of hopelessness.

February 2006: A Relapse of Sorts

My mother came for an eight-day visit and this forced me to reconsider the supposition that February is a short month. Mind you, I love my mother, but I've kept her in the dark. Perhaps keeping her "blindfolded in a closet in the basement" is a better analogy.

In anticipation of her visit, I worked over various scenarios with Aimee and tossed around the idea of telling her about my alcoholism. I was feeling unready to share this information, but thought it might be logistically easier to explain my whereabouts because I planned to be at meetings most evenings. I likened the experience to being closeted: the days when I had to hang up a poster of pretty horses galloping through deep snow over my poster of K.D. Lang were upon me again. I would have to sift through all the AA phone lists and clean up my computer desktop to exclude the therapy writing and remove the bookmarks for various behaviors off the toolbar.

I did end up telling my mom, in a bar of all places. We sat waiting for tapas and she was going on and on about her time in wine country drinking. Having never heard my mom talk so much about alcohol in my life, I considered it a sign from God that I would never get a better opportunity for a segue. With my usual class, I said cheerfully, "So Mom, speaking of alcohol, I need to tell you, your baby's got a drinking problem." She leaned in and asked, "Like AA?" I smiled, and said, "Yes Mom, exactly like AA." She told me she was proud. My sick mind filled in the blank "I'm proud of you (for being a drunk)." She asked if I had told my brother, and I swear, it just fell out of my mouth "No, I haven't had the chance to call him up and tell him that I took the nipple off the Tequila bottle yet." I did try to offer her support in earnest in dealing with the news…"Mom, things aren't all bad, you did just get a free lifetime membership to Al-Anon!"

I spent a lot of time trying to get my head wrapped around how to get a sponsor in AA. I found it a delicate combination of finding someone that I could talk with, while also having just enough fear of them that I would only tell them the truth. I knew lying through omission wasn't going to fit the bill. I found myself waiting for that split second in meetings when members of the group are asked to identify themselves as available for sponsorship by raising their hands. Their hands always flashed up and down so quickly that I could only identify one or two people's availability each meeting. Given that math, it was going to take me a year. I was also painfully shy. I was the kid who used to hide behind the couch when visitors came to our house when I was little. Eventually I emailed a woman who I then met for coffee, who then became my sponsor.

I relapsed the night I picked my mom up from the airport, only I didn't recognize it at the time. I didn't drink, but I had substituted little pink pills for alcohol in order for my anxiety to go away at night. I wasn't experiencing any symptoms of an allergic reaction (itching, swelling, hives) so the Benadryl I took seemed to be a response to my prominent inner dialogue of "Fuck. I want to check out." I was saturated in disappointment in myself over the slip. I began to cry openly on Valencia Street after a Saturday AA meeting. My new sponsor was talking to me and suggested we move off the main street and onto the side block. As we turned the corner, as if a prop from a movie, there was a homeless man passed out on the ground, paper-bagged bottle in hand. Thanks God for the unmistakable reminder of life's possibilities. Maybe one little pink pill wasn't so bad. Maybe recovery was never intended to be a straight line. Maybe it's not all black and white. Maybe it is all gray.

March 2006: Serenity

It was a month of firsts, seconds and fourteenths. I saw myself through my first thirty days abstaining from purging, collected my second first thirty days of sobriety, and reflected on the fourteenth anniversary of the first fire.

I was realizing happiness more with each day. I found myself seeing life for the little things. I watched as a man crossed Dolores Street one day. I stopped to let him cross when most drivers would have continued to drive. I saw that the man was wearing a suit with a winter scarf tied as a belt around his waist. I admired his fashion statement as well as his gall, and the corner of my lip curled upward in admiration. His eyes met mine and we passed happiness between us as we smiled at one another. I was living life in the moment for the first time in as long as I could remember.

I'd built up a program of recovery. I was in therapy twice a week, working the steps with my sponsor, sharing in meetings and calling people. In my eating disorder meetings, I began to gain the perspective that I was no longer where I was when I walked through those doors for the first time seven months earlier. Seeing new women at their first meeting, and listening to others speak about their struggles helped me to recognize my own progress. I related to what they said and spoke from my experience about what I'd done that had helped me. For the first time, I felt like I had something to offer other people like me, beyond just company in misery.

I continued to speak regularly with Horace. He possessed a talent for asking me questions to which I had no good answer. One day I told him I was doing better with not cutting, drinking, using, or purging but that the restriction of food was something I still struggled with daily. He asked me, "What do you want from your body in the long run?" I told him I wanted to be able to be free of physical ailments and get out and enjoy being active for as long as possible. He then asked me how starving myself was supporting this goal. I responded simply, "My actions do not support my goal."

Aimee and I continued our work together. I looked forward to every session. I felt absurdly thankful for the fact that five months earlier I'd been dead wrong when I'd truly believed that there was no hope for my pain to be relieved. How can I communicate how glad I am that when I was at my worst I'd been able to trust Aimee and adopt her hope for me when I no longer had hope for myself?

I welcomed the day when I found my mind empty of my obsessions. It was the first time since I was a little kid that I remembered such contentment and peace. Mind you, the key to happiness is not nothingness, but for me it had a lot to do with the removal of expectations. I'd come across the line in the Big Book of Alcoholics Anonymous that "expectations are in inverse proportion to serenity." I had spent much of my life judging my achievements acutely as either complete successes or complete failures. I'd looked to my father for approval and given him the power to determine my value. It was time to rewrite my programming. I was deleting my self-destructive formula, and creating a solution that not only worked in the moment, but was sustainable too. I was able to build trust with myself, be honest with myself, and live with myself. For someone who'd been perfecting the act of self-destruction, this was a revolutionary gift. It began by agreeing to live, and became something wonderful called life.

CHAPTER TEN
SIDE-TRACKED
Vicki Rossiter Hand

Time is the coin of your life. It is the only coin you have,
and only you can determine how it will be spent.
Be careful lest you let other people spend it for you.
Carl Sandburg

God only knows where it all began; if or when it will finally end.

The school year had culminated in a frenzy of insurmountable paperwork, teary goodbyes, and the filthy cleanup of a rodent-arachnid infested classroom. As my spirits soared toward summer, little did I know they would come crashing down by fall, as stunningly as the Twin Towers themselves.

A teacher's summer calendar fills up as easily as a senior's mind on graduation night. There are the normal appointments inter-mixed with long awaited trips to see friends and family, lunches in restaurants instead of school cafeterias, the morning paper with coffee, and your husband's fifty Rotary friends for the Changing of the Guard dinner party. Oh yes, and there are home improvement projects.

My husband and I had decided to replace half the carpeting in our home with Travertine tile. After years of kids and dogs it was time, and because *HE* thought we could do it ourselves, and because *I* wasn't paying attention, four tons of stone pried from the deepest bowels of Turkey were delivered to our garage.

As with most of our projects, and they have been endless, he was the brains and I was the brawn. I like to think it is because I am five years younger and therefore stronger and healthier. In reality, it's because I always screw up the math and nothing comes out even, so Tom is the architect who plans and places, and I'm the Sherpa who delivers to his waiting hands. Luckily our son, Adam, had boomeranged home from college in between roommates, and contributed his brute strength—which was desperately needed to help carry and stack the fourteen pound tiles from the crate in our garage to the piles forming around the perimeter of all but the bedrooms in our home. This began, of course, after removing two thousand square feet of carpeting and tack strips, a job which we grossly underestimated. ALL of this was *grossly* underestimated.

Adam's "boomerang" back home was another story all its own. He is an artist. He collects things. He keeps odd hours. Our bedroom door is next to the garage and I am a light sleeper. As much as we love our children, any mother could predict where this was going. For me, it was the beginning of sleep deprivation.

It was during this time that my father called from Florida to report that his wife's surgery had shown her cancer was inoperable, and the diagnosis was terminal. She had suffered both bladder and colon cancer. There was nothing more the doctors could do, and so Millie was sent home from the hospital to finish her life under the loving care of my eighty-five year old father. He was both overwhelmed and heart broken. There were no words of comfort I could offer except a promise to be there when they needed me.

Dad had married Millie forty years ago, but his marriage to my mother had lasted nineteen years prior to that. Being a baby boomer, I was another victim of the sandwich generation, caught between the needs of aging parents and our struggling offspring. Following a series of strokes, my mother had been moved to a nursing home in Colorado where my brother and sister had the proximity I envied. Mother and I continued our Saturday morning ritual phone calls despite her inability to articulate—a tremendous frustration for a former English teacher. I would figure out what sounded good for lunch—pizza or Chinese food— the only two options, and have them delivered to her room. This was my only way to contribute to the little enjoyment she had left—good food and, when I would visit from Arizona, a movie outing.

"Lou- mon- ruge," she answered. We were making our plans for my visit the following week—lunch and a movie with our oldest son Matt and his girlfriend Donna who would join us from Las Vegas.

"I don't understand, Mom," I said.

"LOU—ROM- LOSE!" She was clearly frustrated.

"Moulon Rouge?" I asked.

"Easy for YOU to say!" she laughed. Her sense of humor was my favorite quality and she hadn't lost it.

Around the second week in June Tom and I left our beloved floor project behind, and headed for Denver, Colorado. We had been making this trip at least once a year for thirty-five years. It was easy: leave Scottsdale going east, turn left at Albuquerque, stopping only for gas and fast food, and you can be there in fifteen hours. During the second ten years of our marriage we lived in Denver, and did the same trip in reverse to visit friends in Arizona.

The older I get the more I appreciate the vast sky over New Mexico and an occasional stopover in Santa Fe where we reconnect with a childhood artist friend and go gallery hopping. But this trip was going to be the *express* trip. After dinner with Mom in Castle Rock, and a sleepover at my sister's in Denver, we headed straight to Fort Collins, at least an hour north, for brunch with Tom's sister, brother, niece, and father—a rare reunion which brought them from Virginia, Montana, and Idaho, along with Matt and Donna who were joining us from Vegas. We were all there to see Darby, my father-in-law, who announced, before we had even ordered coffee that he was ready to move to Arizona and live closer to us in assisted living. We were genuinely thrilled that he had made such a decision, and if it hadn't been for our upcoming trip to Alaska, we would have brought him along then and there.

Half-baked plans for Grandpa's relocation program were made, and we continued to our next stop, the family cabin in Estes Park. Visualize a rustic cabin, perched overlooking the Big Thompson River—catch and release fishing just outside the door and great antiquing all along the canyon. We had been going there for years and had learned to use it as base camp for seeing friends and family from the Denver area. We loaded up on groceries in Loveland, bought our traditional cherry pie at the fruit stand in the canyon, and headed for lucky Tom's cabin.

The following week was one of those never-a-dull-moment-let's-do-everything-all-the- time kind of weeks. Friends and family were coming and going, highlighted by a mid-week trip back to Castle Rock where Matt, Donna, and I took my mother, Peg, to see the film, Moulon Rouge. It was the only time she and Donna would ever spend together, and mother winked at Matt with her solid seal of approval. We would squeeze in one more visit with Mom on our way home. It seemed as though everything we did was being "squeezed" in!

This would be Matt's last vacation with Donna for a while. Both graduates in hotel management and hospitality, they had met while working for the Paris Hotel in Las Vegas. After months of dating they were in love and beginning to navigate their futures. Obstacle number one was Donna's green card expiration and deportment back to Canada, her permanent residence. Obstacle number two was the city of Las Vegas: too much crime, too fast, not enough family. Sooo, Matt announced that as soon as Donna was on the paper trail back to Vancouver, he would like to move back home to look for a job in Phoenix where they hoped to eventually settle. What more could a mother ask for than to have both her sons and future families living in the same town? Where would I put everyone? My summer was gaining momentum and I was wondering how I would deal with all the complexities of it as I laid awake at night unable to sleep, my mind like a search engine trying to Google the plans.

At home again in Phoenix, it was time for my yearly check up. Complaints of back problems spurred the doctor to order x-rays that, to my complete surprise, showed several kidney stones. I was secretly hoping I had suffered Travertine Tile Disc Syndrome and would be put on disability. Instead, I was referred to a kidney specialist and a urologist for more appointments.

What I haven't mentioned yet is the surprise that awaited us upon our return home from Colorado: an invasion of baby lizards. Whether it was due to our cranking up the heat while away, or having left the door open as we carried in the tiles, remains a mystery. I have even thought that lizard eggs from Turkey embedded in the pock marks of the stone, traveled half way round the earth to then hatch and set up residence in our home. These lizards were different from the Arizona variety I had seen—small and mottled white—hard to see on what little new floor we had. Amidst the continuing chaos of construction we would find their little albino bodies flattened like pressed flowers from the pages of a book, floating across the floor with the slightest breeze—"sail lizards" that crunched underfoot like pork rinds.

We worked on and on. Back pain made sleep uncomfortable and our fingertips were raw from being pinched and scraped. The stacks of tile were beginning to look like the ancient ruins of Rome, slowly eroding with the passage of time, yet still not noticeably smaller. And there were tricks to laying the tile—tricks we had not completely mastered. Too much quickset or too little quickset and the floor would be uneven. Once the tile was in place, (especially in the *wrong* place), the quickset grabbed onto it like a tick on a hound. The pressure to make headway was on, with Grandpa and his walker plus Matt both arriving in August. The project was going far slower than we had anticipated and our second vacation was rapidly approaching. Why would we try to cram two vacations into one hectic, over-planned summer?

Some time back in April, April twenty-eighth, to be exact, we were invited to attend the Denim and Diamond's Ball with our good friends, Mike and Maureen. Mike was, at the time, chairman of the Herberger Theater in Phoenix and often called on us to "fill in" when there were extra seats for a fundraiser. It was a free evening of dining, dancing, live entertainment, great friends, and sure to be fun; we could be ready at the drop of a trowel. Out of respect for Mike and the Herberger we would offset the "free" by purchasing raffle tickets. But as enthusiastically as we approached the evening, we excused ourselves before it ended, tired from our home improvement demands and in need of rest for the next day's lifting, mixing, measuring, sticking, un-sticking, project from hell. After years of fighting it, insomnia was finally a stranger at our house.

Early Sunday morning the doorbell rang. Mike and Maureen glided in with a bottle of champagne announcing from wide smiles that we had left the party too early, that we had been the grand winners of the Alaskan cruise! How could we be so lucky! We screamed and jumped enough to rattle the lizards right out of the floor. Mike and Maureen were so excited you would have thought they had won the cruise themselves! The idea of seeing Alaska thrilled us both and we booked our trip by mid-May, including a stopover in Vancouver to meet Donna's parents, and a brief road trip to see more of the fabulous scenery and wildlife. I couldn't believe we were going.

So with the cruise coming up at the end of July, the search was now on to find a new home for Grandpa, and then furnish it in a way he would enjoy. Lucky again. Three minutes from our home was a beautiful assisted living facility called the Freedom Inn. It was almost new, tastefully decorated, what looked like delicious food, and...it had a vacancy! Darby would arrive with Uncle Pete (I was running out of bedrooms) the second week in August, and the two of them would stay with us while we moved in the belongings he brought from Colorado. Now I was *really* beginning to look forward to the cruise as the running around town and the floor project were wearing me out. "Running around town" is my way of saying that I had to see every piece of furniture, towel, pillow, bedspread, and coffee mug until I was satisfied that Grandpa's place would be worthy of Martha Stewart herself. And then there were always the annoying appointments for my "stones". I was exhausted with summer only one third over.

Tom and I headed for Vancouver on July 21. I remember being so anxious about meeting Mr. and Mrs. Wu, Donna's parents. Our son was clearly in love with their daughter, and it was easy to see why. For all of us, Donna was the perfect choice, but how did Mr. and Mrs. Wu feel about our son? It was important for us to make a good impression, and I was as nervous meeting them as I was when I first met my own in-laws-to-be. I remember hearing once that if you don't make a good first impression; you may not have the chance to make a second impression! Also, I knew Donna was the kind of daughter who highly valued her parent's opinion. If they didn't have good feelings toward this family of ours, she could break my son's heart. These are thoughts that make a mother toss and turn at night.

It's a beautiful thing how life works out. Who knew that two people from China, who met in Italy, would have so much in common with a guy from Wyoming and a girl from Ohio, who met in Arizona, got married, and had a son who would marry their daughter. We were all so very much alike. Watching the young brides and grooms pose for the Vancouver photographers in Queen Elizabeth Park, I turned to Santos and pointedly asked, "How would you feel if that were Matt and Donna?"

"If it is their destiny, it is their destiny," he answered. I could see by the look on his face that he was remembering a day long ago when he and Denise had pledged their love, and I knew then that Matt and Donna, too, would someday be together. Our weekend in Vancouver proved to be time well spent, and the Wu's entertained us with an energy and enthusiasm that would put a five year old to shame.

We embarked on our cruise Monday morning. The ship was enormous, but if you had been a mouse on board you would not have bothered to store the crumbs of your crumbs in our miniscule room. "Room" was an oxymoron—barely enough space for a bed and two people to stand up, a miniature bathroom stuffed in the corner. I am married to a very large man! With no windows and only one door, my claustrophobia became debilitating. During the day I wandered the decks and reclined on lounge chairs, wrapped in wool blankets, and watched otters float by on their backs in a Disneyesque panorama. At night I stayed up as late as I could, attending nature talks, vaudeville shows, midnight buffets, karaoke bars—anything to avoid going back into my cage. I needed to be one nano-second away from falling asleep or I would lie there in my designated space riddled with anxiety, enduring the torture night after night. We had tried to upgrade to a larger room, but because the trip was free and paid for, we could never cut through the red tape. Exhaustion layered upon more exhaustion.

When we finally disembarked in Anchorage I felt like a caged animal placed back into the wild. Thankfully we had planned to see more of Alaska from the ground. We hopped into our rental car and headed for the Kenaii Peninsula, a fabulous spot, we were told, for salmon fishing and spotting bear. We had a cozy little cabin, next to a mom and pop restaurant, near a great little fishing spot. Perfect. It was all so rustic and remote; there was not a piece of Travertine tile or a dried lizard in sight. The scenery in every direction was breath taking and the cool clean air was electrifying. The next day we fished along the fringes of the Russian River where salmon were begging to be caught. A young boy at the cabin filleted our catch and the restaurant prepared it for dinner—nothing had ever tasted as good. It was *soooo* cool. I was learning everything about the five kinds of salmon and how to remember each, fantasizing about staying there forever on the Kenai Peninsula the way every vacationer does when he has found Utopia.

Up at dawn the next day, we slipped on our waders and headed for the river again; but today the fish wouldn't bite. Check out time was 11:00 am and by 10:30 I had a plan that would allow Tom to keep fishing. "I'll get us checked out and pack up our bags while you keep fishing and keep our place here on the river!" I returned to our favorite fishing spot, car loaded, in less than an hour, trying desperately to experience the same thrills as the previous day, but by 3:30 we finally gave up and headed to our last destination, Denali.

The daylight lasts so long in Alaska that you can lose all track of time. Driving to Denali we were fascinated by the scenery: a miniature train table with a winding railroad track, perfectly shaped conical pine trees, and strategically, artfully placed lakes. We saw eagle, caribou, and moose. Alaska is so enormous, so magnificent, that to see it all is like an inch worm contemplating the Empire State Building. By the time we reached Denali it was almost midnight and we were now beyond exhaustion. Another two days and we would be home where I could catch up on some much needed sleep. Why worry now.

We arrived home at midnight August 2 completely dead tired. Early the next morning I started in on the laundry, surveyed the stacks of tile, sorted through mail, e-mail, voicemail (" beep…Dr. Yee's office calling to remind you of your appointment"), and made out the grocery list. Again, I would be meeting with the kidney guy to check results. Our fishing trip was now just a memory, with only my mosquito bites to prove it had really happened.

Phone calls from my Dad were getting more frequent, and Millie's condition had begun to deteriorate. Because of the pain, she was on morphine that he would administer (at age eighty-five) and keep a log of; home care nurses would visit each day to monitor her chart and keep things going smoothly. They had recommended Hospice but Dad wasn't ready to take her, and I could detect by the frailty in his voice that this was clearly wearing him down. I booked a flight for my October school break and hoped that would be soon enough.

Saturday was spent helping Adam move out—divine intervention had found him a roommate, and Sunday was spent cleaning and getting ready for Matt to move in. And on Monday—school started again. From then on it was meetings, files, forms, meetings, files, forms, bulletin boards, then open house to meet the new students and their parents. The classroom was ready and so was I, I said to myself. Of course school always begins ready or not, and although I was already running on empty from "vacation", and although the floor was only half finished, this would be a welcome change from the hard labor and gerbil wheel pace I'd been keeping all summer. Right…

There is a destiny that makes us brothers:
None goes his way alone:
All that we send into the lives of others
Comes back into our own.
Edwin Markham in *A Creed* 1900

Thursday afternoon Darby and Pete arrived. Thursday evening Matt arrived. Thursday night I remember complaining to Tom that my mosquito bites were driving me crazy. He had none. Mine were all on the back of my head, under my hair where no one could see them.

That weekend we moved Grandpa into his new place (which he gave the Good Housekeeping Seal of Approval), and as soon as Pete's car pulled out of the driveway Sunday morning, Tom and I were busy working on the floor again, thankfully with Matt's help. It had been three full months since we began the floor project; it was endless, and the lizards were now full grown.

Having Grandpa and Matt living in Scottsdale presented new opportunities for entertaining. On that first Monday night we had a Denver Bronco football dinner and our whole family watched the game together. If you're a Bronco fan you can live anywhere in the world and do this. Everything stops for the game. You can have a floor or no floor, you can be exhausted or exhilarated, and it can be a week night or a weak night. Because you are a Bronco fan forever—that much I have learned from living in a house full of men and seeing John Elway pass the pigskin.

It seemed I had just drifted off to sleep when early the next morning the phone rang. "Turn on the TV!" It was my sister, Jo, calling from Denver in a tone I had never heard. I don't have to tell anyone what I was feeling when I turned on the TV and witnessed the planes heading into the Twin Towers. Everyone today knows how he felt, where he was, what ensued. It is as vivid today as it was when it happened, just like the assassination of J.F.K. After the initial expressions of shock, horror, and confusion exchanged with my family, I headed for school. Students were arriving and teachers had no direction from administrators how to deal with this crisis. Would there be more attacks? Who had done it? Why did they do it? The ten year olds' questions were no different from my own. We watched the news in my classroom, and when it became too much for any of us to bear, we turned it off and began to write, silently and with tears. It was our therapy. For the next few weeks America was glued to the news around the clock and I would catch up on these reports at night, staying up well past my bedtime in disbelief and fear.

That Saturday I had my kidney stones pulverized by a procedure called lithotripsy. I had never heard of this procedure, but I had heard the oft reported horror stories of other people's kidney stone trauma, comparing it to pushing a basketball through fifty feet of garden hose. Pain is my enemy and this was a great option. The lithotripsy was a walk in the park and I prided myself in only needing one or two of the potent painkillers prescribed, saving the rest for some unknown future emergency.

It came sooner than I had expected. During the next ten days my head began to hurt. Really hurt. I have been a migraine sufferer but these were not migraines. Migraines always started with an aura, a visual blacking out followed by headache. I had medication for migraines and I now used it along with over the counter headache remedies, but no relief from this pain was in sight. This burning pain seemed to be centered around my left jaw, and so I determined that a tooth must be the cause. I would have paid to have all my teeth pulled if it would relieve the agony, but the dentist could not find a thing. I went home in tears and got out the heavy duty pain meds.

I soldiered on to school the next day. There were rockets to launch in science class and an important Colonial Day meeting after school with the parents, but by 2:00 in the afternoon I was in so much pain I called the front office crying for help. Mrs. Jewell, the assistant principal, came to my room and after one look at my face, contorted like the wreckage of a train, said "GO HOME."

Screaming in agony, I maneuvered home, the side of my head with a fire that was relentless. What was wrong with me?! I was terrified. Was it an aneurysm? Was it a brain tumor? Was it encephalitis? Had I contracted some rare disease carried by albino lizards? Roof rats? Spiders? Salmon? The cat? The cruise ship? By the time I reached home I ran for the bathroom and started projectile vomiting with a force that would power a mill wheel. I grabbed my secret stash of pain killers from the medicine cabinet and crawled between the covers of my bed.

The next day I cancelled my trip to Florida to help my father, and arranged for a substitute teacher. Not able to get an appointment with my doctor, I *was* able to get an appointment with the nurse practitioner, Sara. The appointment lasted a full hour. When did this start, what have you taken, what medications do you normally use, what have you been exposed to, where have you been, out of the country? What else hurts, what does it feel like, what have you eaten, what's *different*...We discussed my summer, where I'd been, what I'd done, what and where I'd eaten. She examined my body inside and out. Just when I thought we had exhausted every possible cause, I remembered the mosquito bites that by now were almost gone. Sara began to comb through the hair on the back of my head like an ape grooming his mate.

"Shingles...I think you might have shingles." Lab tests ruled out other possibilities and confirmed the diagnosis.

Shingles? I'd always thought shingles was something old people got...I took the prescription she held out to me and left, relieved to know my problem was solved. Or so I thought.

Shingles is the second invasion of the chicken pox virus. Anyone who suffered from chicken pox as a child is a candidate for shingles. It becomes active when the immune system is weakened and manifests itself as a rash, but with significantly more pain than itch. The outbreak can be treated with drugs, but the damage done to the nerve cells can last indefinitely. I was not told about this part. An immune system can be weakened by several things, but for me the cause had been lack of rest and stress. Damage had been done to the nerves as the virus traveled to the skin where it created the rash. This can happen to any part of one's body, but happens only on one side. Some people believe that if you ever get shingles on both sides of your body, you will die.

The pain continued for weeks, then months. I continued to take the medication not knowing the medication was only meant to cure the outbreak, yet the outbreak had been gone since my first prescription. Reading the paper one morning I noticed an ad that read, "Do you suffer from post herpetic neuralgia?" I went straight to the internet to find out more about this condition, the condition which can follow shingles for a lifetime of pain. It was easy to make the diagnosis myself, and terrifying to read about this debilitating condition brought about by a weakened immune system. Italians call it St. Anthony's Fire, and if manifested in the head as mine was, shingles can even lead to blindness.

Again in the doctor's office, my suspicions were confirmed—post herpetic neuralgia. I was referred to a neurologist to rule out any other possibilities. After an MRI, which showed my head to be normal (despite what my brother has always thought), the neurologist took me through a series of questions and motor skill tests. Everything checked out—I had post herpetic neuralgia. In about 80% of the cases the pain in the nerves will eventually "burn itself out" and for the other twenty percent there is NO recovery.

I was given a prescription for an anti-seizure medication which is a preventative for this pain as well as migraine pain. I still depend on this medication to the tune of twelve hundred mg a day. It has made a huge difference in controlling the burning, but the neuralgia still exists and has certain "triggers" just as migraines do. For me, migraines can bring about neuralgia and neuralgia can trigger migraines. Learning to discern between the neuralgia and the onset of a migraine has been complicated. Suffering from either of these conditions incapacitates me, affecting my work and my general disposition. For many sufferers, depression is an additional side effect.

I had always thought of myself as an extremely healthy person. Being a teacher supposedly builds the immune system—I rarely get a cold or flu. I've never had a broken bone or stitches. I always felt I took good care of myself, and prided myself on how much I could accomplish in a day. What I didn't recognize was that I had been *sidetracked* by commitments—to family members, to work, to my house, even to my so-called vacations. My immune system broke down because I had completely and utterly worn myself out. I had neglected my own well being, and I am still living with the consequences.

My story is not uncommon. Women today perform a high wire act—balancing between family and career. Many of us are afraid to say no. We volunteer in our children's classrooms, take meals to sick friends, host the husband's company party along with our own, care for aging parents and do anything it takes to get our grown children on their feet. We do this in addition to having marriages and careers that deserve a full time commitment as well. We want to be everything we can be for everybody but ourselves.

A good friend taught me to use these five words: **Let me think about it.** I had to practice using these words; I had to repeat them to myself before even answering the phone. I have done a better job of managing my time, not over-planning my days, scheduling more downtime, and allowing vacations to actually *be* relaxing. My home is more of a haven and I'm careful not to invite the world in and to save time and space for myself. My son gave me an old piano and I'm playing for the first time since I was ten because it soothes me. I'm no good, but I don't allow that to matter. I'm more reasonable about what I can do in a day and how much of it is really important in the big picture. If I'm not well, I'm of little use to the people I love; the people who want me to be a part of their lives. They won't care if I've crossed off every item on a long to-do list.

My epiphany is this: Don't overlook yourself. Don't underestimate the importance of a healthy immune system. Being in good health is a luxury often taken for granted, and a weakened immune system has the power to subject anyone to a host of illnesses, only one of which is shingles. Being good to ourselves enables us to be at our best for others.

Taking responsibility for our own health includes taking responsibility for our own time—how it is spent and how much of it gets set aside to rejuvenate our minds, our bodies and our spirits. That time should be sacred. Being good to ourselves is not always selfish, and being self<u>less</u> is not always good. Please. Never get so side-tracked that you are not able to be good to yourself. Take time to renew and replenish that which you so generously and frequently give to others—the gift of your time.

Slow me down, Lord!
Ease the pounding of my heart
By the quieting of my mind,
Steady my harried pace
With a vision of the eternal reach of time.
Give me,
Amidst the confusions of my day,
The calmness of the everlasting hills.
Break the tensions of my nerves
With the soothing music of the sighing streams
That live in my memory.
Help me to know
The magical restoring power of sleep.
Teach me the art
Of taking minute vacations, of slowing down to look at a flower:
To chat with an old friend or to make a new one,
To pat a stray dog:
To watch a spider build a web:
To smile at a child:
Or to read a few lines from a good book.
Remind me each day
That the race is not always to the swift:

That there is more to life than increasing its speed.
Let me look upward
Into the branches of the towering oak
And know that it grew slowly and well.
Author Unknown

[Signatures: Patti Heapy, Ruth Chesley]

CHAPTER ELEVEN
FUTURES EXPLORED
Ruth Evelyn Chesley's Story
Written by Patricia Heapy

If you treat an individual as he is he will stay as he is.
But if you treat him as if he were what he ought to be,
he will become what he ought to be and could be.
Goethe

This is a story of love, sheer determination and dedication, involving three extraordinary women—my mother, Ruth, and my developmentally disabled sister Judy, who was born at a time when the future of such children was considered limited and bleak. Then, Helen Young, Judy's inspirational teacher who was the Founder and Director of *Futures Explored, Inc.*, an enterprise for disabled young adults; the very foundation of our epiphany.

Future's Explored was established as a non-profit organization in Lafayette, California for the sole purpose of enabling disabled young adults to reach their individual potential as contributing citizens and help them become as independent as their abilities would allow.

My name is Patti. I am Ruth's middle child, two years older than Judy, and three years younger than my brother Dennis. I will be writing this story on my mother's behalf as she tells it to me. When I was invited to write a chapter about a life-changing epiphany I knew exactly what I wanted to write about.

I wanted to tell about my sister's lifelong struggle to be treated and accepted as a "normal" human being. I wanted to write about my mother's struggle to maintain her sanity while she fought her own debilitating illness. I thought it equally important to share the emotional roller coaster ride my parents experienced raising a handicapped child. This may be typical of the hurdles that millions of parents of disabled children face each day, but I think we were a lucky family. Judy's disability was considered mild within the huge range of severity that exists in brain-damaged children.

My hope is that by sharing this story with parents and relatives of developmentally disabled family members, they will be encouraged to seek the help of professionals, and demand answers to their questions. My mother was a very non-aggressive person. As a young mother faced with the dilemma of raising a disabled child, she was, in the beginning at least, easily intimidated by professional people. Therefore she suffered a great deal in silence, unsure about where or even how to seek help. I think that she thought she could just handle this problem herself, as was her normal modus-operandi. My father was the epitome of a loving parent in denial. He thought Judy could learn to do anything that any other child could learn to do; it would just take her a little longer. He was a willing and able teacher with the patience of JOB.

Let me begin this literary journey by introducing you to my ninety-five-year-old mother Ruth. I liken her to one of her favorite flowers, the Iris, because no matter what Mother Nature pummels her with, she remains tall and regal. My friends and I call her "The Energizer Bunny" because she just keeps going, and going, and going...When I asked her if she would help me write about her life raising a handicapped child, she agreed, as long as she didn't have to write it herself. She seemed a little worried when I started to interview her. She said to me, "Now we have to make sure that every thing we write is the way it really happened because we don't want to get into trouble like that fellow on the Oprah show. You know, the one who didn't tell the truth about some things?" I thought to myself, "THAT is my mother in a nutshell. As honest as the day is long." Her biggest concern was if she would be able to recall the details of the events that took place over sixty plus years ago when she was in her thirties—a very long time ago. You will see that she has an incredible memory! I welcome you to join us on this journey, fraught with obstacles that seemed impossible to surmount, but to also witness the joys that we reveled in along the way.

I'll let her tell you the rest of the story.

My name is Ruth Longanecker Chesley. I am ninety-five years old, deaf in one ear since I was about thirty and blind in one eye due to a stroke after five-bypass surgery sixteen years ago when I was seventy-nine. Those scars between my breasts from the open-heart surgery are still evident, and if I had known I was going to live this long, I would have asked the surgeon to "lift 'em up a bit" while he was in the neighborhood. I used to stand about five foot eight, but I seem to be holding at about five foot six nowadays. The bone density tests tell me I have the bones of a thirty-seven year old, albeit they do creak a bit and get a little stiff. I still walk without help most of the time but at my daughter's insistence I do take her hand now and then if we're treading on uneven ground. I use an old wood shovel handle for a walking stick when I climb the hill to my garden in the backyard.

My hair is snow-white, my eyes are green, and my skin resembles a topographical map, showing every rut in the road. I am of German, Dutch and English descent. I still have all my faculties, so they tell me. (Gosh darn, if I could just remember my name...smile.)

My great-grandchildren call me Omah. The teenagers call me Grumpy Old Lady (I yell at them when they cut through my garden) and friends and neighbors call me The Cat Lady, because I feed seven feral cats that live outdoors and I have one that sleeps at the foot of my bed that I have taken care of since he was a kitten.

I am the mother of three, grandmother of five and great-grand to two young adults. Most of my family and dear friends are gone except in my memory. My youngest sister, who is ninety years old, lives a few hours away in an assisted living residence. I am getting older by the second and sometimes I get tired, but I keep on going.

I have miles to go before I sleep.

Robert Frost

My husband Floyd taught me how to repair almost anything, I have my own set of tools and I guard them closely. I do my own hair, prepare my own meals for the most part, and clean my own apartment except for the heavy-duty stuff. And I take care of my garden, which is my true passion. I would much rather be outdoors than indoors and I get real restless during the winter months when it's too cold to be outside. Every year I swear that I'm not going to buy more flowers to plant but, come spring, Patti and I traipse off to the nursery and come home with a trunk full of plants and fertilizer. Let the spring gardening begin!

I have been widowed for thirty years and have lived with my daughter for the last twelve years. My apartment is on the ground floor of my daughter's home. I feel very lucky to have such a nice living arrangement with my own entrance as well as an inside staircase to my daughter's living area on the second floor. This neat arrangement gives us both our privacy and independence yet I know she is close by. Besides, she does my laundry!

I have a "lifeline" necklace to use for emergencies, when I remember to wear it. It is comforting to know that my daughter is within calling distance day or night, thanks to the intercom and her cell phone. My daughter Judy, the subject of our story, lives less than an hour away and comes to visit most weekends using the local bus service. My eldest child Dennis, (are they still considered children when they're almost seventy?) lives east over the Sierra Nevada Mountains in Nevada.

I love living near the mountains in Auburn, California. The high country has always felt like home to me, although I spent most of my youth and later my adult years living in the central valley of California. I came to California on a four-day train ride from Nappanee, Indiana where I was born, when I was three years old. My mother and I and three older siblings rode a buckboard wagon from the train station in Stockton, California to Mokelumne Hill, a small gold mining town named after the local Indian tribe. My father, who knew nothing about gold mining, had purchased a gold mine there. About five years later he lost the mine because the men who worked for my dad knew more about the mining business than he did and they snookered him right out of the mine. He was sweet and soft-spoken, but not much of a businessman. We were very poor, but we didn't know it. My father made heroic efforts to keep his wife and six children fed and clothed.

After the mining fiasco we moved to the small, rice growing community of Biggs, California, in the Central Valley. My father took a job building highways all over California. My mother used to drag us kids along with her in the summertime when she visited him at his work sight. He died in his late fifties from tuberculosis, a common disease at that time.

Biggs is where I spent the rest of my youth. My mother and all four of us girls worked in the local cannery peeling fruit to help make ends meet. My two brothers worked in the rice fields. We swam in the canals to cool off on those God-awful hot days of summer when you could hardly get your breath. We slept with wet towels spread over our bodies at night to get relief from the heat, humidity and mosquitoes.

I met my husband Floyd at Biggs Union High School. He was two grades ahead of me. During the school term I spent a lot of time gazing out the window, wishing I could be outside instead of inside a stuffy old classroom. Floyd was a very good student. I was an OK student. We often met at the local library in the evenings...and it wasn't always to study.

We eventually married, but not until we were in our late twenties, after Floyd had spent several years in the Marine Corps. He enlisted because we had one doozy of an argument. I can't even remember what it was about. While he was overseas in China and the Philippine Islands, I attended college. I still didn't like being stuck in classrooms.

When my husband and I married in 1936, our first home was high in the Sierra Mountains in a little railroad town called Portola. I loved that little town. Those years before World War II broke out were the happiest of my life. We first lived in back of the office of the company my husband worked for, then moved into in a tiny little miner's house. We stayed for five years.

Now the year is 1942; it's war-time and jobs are scarce. We feared that Floyd might be recalled into the Marines. He had a lot of experience as a mechanic. So we left our home in the mountains (with me bawling all the way) and moved in with my widowed mother in the valley. My husband went to work helping to build war ships in the shipyards of Richmond, California. That job would keep him safe from re-call. We eventually bought our first home in a small river town called Antioch. With the war nearing its peak, we were lucky to have a paycheck. We paid $4,500.00 for our brand new two-bedroom house in a nice new neighborhood. Floyd built an additional bedroom later.

Life was sweet then. The war ended and the economy grew stronger, Floyd had a good job working in town and we actually had a nickel in our savings account. We were thankful. We were happy. All was well with the young Chesley family.

Our lives changed forever on the seventh day of July, 1943.

That day I was in the Antioch hospital giving birth to our daughter, soon to be named Judith Anne. But, because the doctor wasn't able to be there right away, the nurses crossed my legs to delay the birth. Judy was already in the process of being born! By crossing my legs she was held in the birth canal, preventing her from getting oxygen. It was about twenty or twenty-five minutes before the doctor arrived to finish delivering her. By all appearances, they deemed her to be a healthy baby girl.

But Judy cried ALL the time. We finally realized she wasn't getting enough to eat. She appeared to have difficulty sucking. I made the holes in the nipples of her baby bottles bigger. Still she cried, almost constantly. Something was not right, but we tried everything we knew. Boy, was she unhappy. We found out later, Judy's difficulty in drinking and eating was because her tongue action was underdeveloped and it hampered her ability to move the food to the back of her throat and swallow. Judy seemed to have difficulty doing a lot of the things that came so easily for my other children. She wanted to feed herself because she was so darn hungry but she just didn't have the coordination. When I fed her, the food would just roll right back out. Later on she had difficulty drinking from a cup. She would get frustrated and throw it. She literally pushed the food into her mouth. Not all of it stayed, but apparently enough of it made it to her tummy because she began to flourish. That made for a more contented child and a relieved mom.

Over time Judy's disposition improved and her frustrations diminished somewhat. She was a beautiful baby and an even prettier toddler. She had blond curly hair that bounced like little springs when she moved. She had azure blue eyes and skin like peaches and cream. She became a happy, bubbly, adorable little toddler but at the age of three still was not walking or talking. It was obvious that her motor skills were not developing within the normal time frame. She pointed and grunted. She crawled instead of walked. She loved music. She used to wriggle and jiggle when she heard music. She rocked. Literally. She rocked and rocked. The older she grew, the harder she rocked, usually while sitting on the sofa or even in a straight chair banging her head against the back cushion. She continued to rock even past her teen years. (Today she rocks to her portable CD music!)

Finally, when she was about four she learned to walk. Then she ran. Everywhere. She escaped the yard and ran down the street. I would have to call the police to help find her. She would latch on to some one else's toys, especially doll buggies, and hold on for dear life. The policemen would bring them home with her thinking they were hers. We bought her a buggy of her own thinking it would keep her from running away.

She still bolted every chance she got. We finally resorted to keeping her in the backyard and wiring the gate shut. She had to be watched *constantly*.

I was tired all the time. I knew Judy wasn't developing like a normal child her age, but I was just too ill to pursue the problem. I didn't pursue much of anything. I was too sick. I was having dizzy spells that lasted for days on end. I started having terrible ringing in my ears. I needed help caring for the children. My sister took one of the children, my mother took Judy and I kept Dennis at home. It was a struggle for me just to get out of bed, and some days I wasn't even able to do that. I became even more tired.

My sister started taking her six-year-old son to a pediatrician that had been recommended to her in a major city close by. Since I was not real happy with the local doctors, she suggested I take my children to see the pediatrician she thought so much of, so I did. We went together to see Dr. Bennett, taking all four of the children. The female pediatrician put all the children but Judy on a regimen of vitamin pills. Two-ascorbic acid, one cod liver oil, and about ten Brewers yeast tablets a day. That turned out to be the smartest thing we ever did. The three older children took them for the next eight to ten years and rarely got sick with anything except the normal childhood illnesses that were common at the time. They never had colds, runny noses, sore throats, or earaches. She closely examined Judy and suggested that she be tested further at U.C. Hospital in San Francisco. The doctor suspected that she was retarded. The tests proved her correct. On my return to her office to learn the results of the tests and listen to her suggestions for a variety of therapies, I felt overwhelmed. I just broke down in tears and cried, "But what if I am just too tired to do all of that?"

"I will **help** you," she said. FOUR LITTLE WORDS. THOSE INCREDIBLY MAGICAL WORDS. I...WILL...HELP...YOU!

That was <u>my</u> epiphany.

I was dumbstruck! I had felt awful since I was a teenager and and didn't know why. The only doctors I ever saw where obstetricians, and they just brushed me off. After all, it was "all in my head." You mean someone was actually going to FIND OUT WHY I FELT SO DARN LOUSY? Do you know what else she said to me? She said, "If you had been under MY care during your pregnancy, this would never have happened." She was referring to Judy's brain damage. *I often wonder how many other children suffered brain damage just because their arrival wasn't conveniently timed.*

She sent me to a specialist. He determined that I was acutely anemic. Not enough iron in my blood. The Dr. wondered why I was even standing up! I was put on a regimen of Vitamin B1 shots for the next year. My life was pretty miserable. My children were scattered, living with relatives. I spent weeks in bed in a darkened room. Finally, after a year, the vitamin shots began to take effect, and I started to feel less tired but I still had that terrible ringing in my ears, along with some dizziness.

Off to another specialist I went. This time, tests at UC Berkeley. It was determined that I had tinnitus and Meniere's disease and the nerves in one ear were irreparably damaged. They thought the anemia might have caused this, but they didn't really know for sure. I just had to learn to live with the hearing loss, and I have ringing in my ears to this day. (It's no wonder I'm a little cranky now and then.)

Our lives began to improve after I was treated for the illnesses that could be treated. There was no cure for the tinnitus and Meniere's disease. Those were permanent. With the help of my husband, family and friends, I was better able to cope with the daily demands of raising three active children including one child that required ten times as much attention as the other two. All of my energy went into caring for Judy. Keeping her safe, protecting her from hurting herself. She did not understand boundaries. She fought to be free from everyone's grasp. She could not comprehend warnings like the other children. She was needier than the others, and so completely demanding of my time. But, other than that, she was just pure joy!

In retrospect I think my other two children probably suffered from the lack of my attention. I wasn't even aware of it because I was so involved with this 'special needs' child of ours. Oh, if we had just known then what we know now; *but we didn't know.* We just did the best we could. At a much later time in my life, Helen Young sent me the following poem one day when she sensed that I needed a lift. She always seemed to know when I needed reassuring. I felt so guilty sometimes about "what I *should* have done."

Before God's foot stool to confess, a poor soul knelt and bowed his head; "I failed," he cried. The master said, "You did your best. That is success."

Author unknown

Judy's first epiphany took place when she was about seven years old.

We were driving home one summer evening, Floyd and I in the front seat, all three children seated in the back seat with Judy in the middle. We were passing by a field of freshly mowed hay that was formed into huge mounds. Judy began to yell loudly, with great gusto, "Hay! Hay!" Floyd, who used every opportunity to encourage her to speak said, "Hey what, Judy?" in response to her shouts. Patti chimed in, shouting, "She's talking! She's talking! She's talking about the HAY STACKS." Finally, her first word at the age of seven, loud and clear! "HAY."

It was like the time Helen Keller finally associated the word "wa-wa" with the cold water being pumped and splashed into her hand. Judy began to associate words with objects. OH HAPPY DAY! Judy actually had the potential to communicate! From then on she tried saying words, mixing them with sounds, interspersed with giggles and shouts of glee as she discovered her new ability to express herself in her own garbled language. "What's that? What's this?" she would shout, as she pointed to objects and attempted to repeat our responses. She was eager to hear the sound that we would say when she pointed at something.

Judy showed other signs of brain damage, some so very subtle that I can't even remember now. I remember thinking that maybe if she were around other children her age it would be good for her. She loved people of all ages, friends or strangers. She feared nothing and no one. She was a happy, curious child. It was time to enroll her in school. So I thought!

Feeling full of confidence and anticipation, I went to the local public school to enroll her. To my dismay she was rejected. At seven years, *she was too old and too retarded.* The year was 1950. There was no one to teach the retarded children. The so-called slow learners and handicapped children were on their own. They were either kept at home away from the curious eyes of strangers or institutionalized. The school authorities offered to test Judy. As a result of the tests she was labeled "severely retarded." One of the school administrators felt sorry for us and suggested we place Judy in a 'facility' for the mentally handicapped.

My two sisters, who were both teachers, went with me to visit the recommended facility. It was utterly heartbreaking. We witnessed children of all ages as well as adults who were caged in cribs like animals, obviously for their own protection. Some were just vegetables. It was a horrendous experience. As we left that institution we all agreed that this was <u>not</u> a place for Judy. There was no way that I would ever agree to place my daughter in a facility like that. It was obvious that the patients being cared for there were so much more disabled than Judy. Physically, Judy appeared to be pretty normal and we knew she didn't belong in an institution. God willing, I would find a way to teach this child myself if I had to.

When God closes a door, he opens a window.
Author Unknown
And open a window he did.

One of my sisters had a friend who taught at the same school where I had tried to enroll Judy. She agreed to accept Judy in her classroom and help her as much as she could. Judy stayed in her kindergarten class for two years. She showed some small improvements. The best thing, however, was that she was amongst other children, and she was happy. A few years later the state of California passed a law that public schools would establish a special class for handicapped children of all ages and with varying degrees of disabilities up to the age of (I believe) eighteen.

The next several years are kind of a blur. My time was filled with the challenges Judy presented. She was like a "forever" child that never grew up. I worried constantly. My mind was always filled with thoughts of what was best for Judy. I was exhausted mentally, and physically. Judy, on the other hand, was just plain happy. No worries, no fears. Just happy. Judy continued her schooling in the "special" class for the slower children.

There were two skills that Floyd thought Judy needed to learn, "In order to get along in the world," he said. The skills were counting money and telling time. Boy, did this man have patience. He spent hours and hours trying to teach her to tell time. He made a clock out of cardboard with big numbers and hands on the clock that she could move. She would try but she just couldn't "get it." He never gave up on her.

She was about twenty years old before she could count and tell time. She learned to tell time when she was given a watch of her very own by a friend of the family. The day she got the watch is the day she finally pieced it all together! She actually saw the hands moving around the face and voila! She announced the exact time to all of us! An epiphany? You bet! All it took was ten years of repetition *and* a new watch. Floyd's plan was to give her a watch as a reward *after* she learned to tell time. It seems that he had an epiphany that day also. Suddenly he realized that he should have given her a watch to wear <u>years</u> before. He would have liked the phrase we commonly use today to apply to a situation like this: DUH!

Everything we learned about helping our retarded child was by "trial and error." There were no instruction books for us to read. No support groups, no medical advisors to call upon.

Floyd's Next Epiphany:

Judy loved animals. Especially horses. When we took her to the county fair she always wanted to pet them. She was not the least bit afraid. My husband was raised with horses and was an expert rider. He had a brilliant idea! We would buy her a horse! Not a pet hamster or a dog, mind you. A horse!

Judy was about twelve when the search for the gentle horse began. He had discovered that we could board a horse at the fairgrounds nearby for a small fee. One of the horses he tested shied away from a fence post and rolled over with Floyd sitting on it, breaking Floyd's collarbone. That didn't stop him one bit. He finally found a gentle giant Appaloosa and they named him Rusty. Judy loved that horse.

Her dad taught her every thing she needed to know about taking care of a horse. Then he taught her to ride. She walked to the stalls every day to be with Rusty. He was unbelievably patient with Judy, and she with him. They were best friends.

She couldn't read or write yet, but she took great care of her horse. She was a natural. She won several show ribbons with Rusty. Owning her own horse gave her such a sense of pride and accomplishment. She had Rusty for about five years. She reluctantly gave him up when she started attending the Lynn Center a year or so after high school because she just didn't have the time to devote to him. She never quite forgave us for selling Rusty. She still misses him. Judy's most meaningful treasures are several large paintings that Mrs.Young's husband, Lowney, painted in oil. Two of them feature Judy working at *Futures*, but her favorite one is the one of her riding Rusty. It reminds her of some of her happiest days, when she was, in her words, "a real cowgirl." The paintings hang in her home.

Judy struggled in high school. Fellow teenagers teased her and other students that were in the special class on a daily basis. She wanted so badly to fit in, to be like the other teens, going to dances and football games, etc. Her dad took her to many of the school functions. Having

Rusty helped to ease those painful teenage years. When Judy was a sophomore another significant change took place.

Enter Helen Young:

This woman was a fifty-piece orchestra in one body. She was blessed with an incredible insight, aptitude and an unwavering devotion to teaching the handicapped "young people" as she fondly named them. She opened doors, windows, and even raised rooftops to help them reach their full potential.

Helen was a petite, green-eyed redhead with a smile as big as her heart. She was the youngest of twelve children, born in Wiscasset, Maine. She followed her husband to California when his firm transferred him there. They lived in Lafayette, California where they raised two daughters. Mrs. Young became Judy's teacher, friend and mentor. She became one of my dearest friends and my confidant as well. Little did we know the amazing impact that Helen and her own giving family would have on our lives. They lifted our spirits, instilled us with hope, and took us into the fold of their warm and loving family.

People will forget what you did. People will forget what you said, but people will never forget how you made them feel.

Maya Angelou

Helen taught Judy's special class at the Antioch High School for the next three years. She loved Judy unconditionally, and Judy loved her back. Judy began to gain confidence in herself. She walked taller. She smiled more. She began to look at people when they spoke to her instead of lowering her eyes. Helen was so encouraging. She didn't talk down to Judy like other people did. Helen began to teach Judy the basic skills of reading and writing as well as some social skills. Judy blossomed under Helen's no-nonsense, straightforward, loving tutelage. Judy graduated with her class in 1961. She received a "special" diploma. She was so proud of herself, and we were all so proud of her.

Now what was she to do? Helen to the rescue again. She had decided to accept a teaching position at a center for handicapped youth in a nearby town. We enrolled Judy there at her suggestion. After about two years, Helen became somewhat disenchanted with the curriculum. I believe that she wanted the freedom to teach handicapped young people using her own carefully thought-out techniques. She believed that they should be treated and taught as the unique individuals that they were based on their own individual capacities. She gathered several parents, teachers and volunteers whose opinions she respected and told them of her vision to open a center in a different location and asked for their support. That was the beginning of *Futures Explored, Inc.* My husband and I were part of that support group.

The very first thing Helen did before establishing *Futures* was to pay a social call on all the local business owners and homeowners in the area where the center was going to be located. She had leased a small house that would soon become the main center called, "The Enterprise" in a residential area bordering the downtown business area in the small, rather elite, mid-sized town of Lafayette, California, twenty-five miles inland from San Francisco. She introduced herself and explained to them what her plans were for the center. She told them about the handicapped young adults that would be attending the center daily and asked for their understanding and support. She assured them that there was nothing to fear. In other words she educated them using her own special technique; by *pulling on her soft, kid gloves.* We would be witness to this special gift of hers hundreds of times in the next twenty years. Only after everyone was contacted personally did she open the door of *Futures* in 1964. Her support group consisted of dozens of adult volunteers, many of them parents, but also volunteer educators from the local community. Eventually there were fifty-one young people, and a staff of nearly twenty, of which just a few were paid a salary. Helen was a paid staff member—she was the Director.

Helen's explanation of *Futures* follows. She wrote this and it became the creed of *Futures Explored;* it was printed in the brochures that we passed out to our visitors when we held our annual open house.

"Futures Explored is a group of handicapped people seeking respectable and dignified ways to blend into the community scene; attempting to form behavior patterns and personal characteristics to lessen the fear of the "normal" person for the "different" person; providing services to the community to demonstrate the ability to be contributing and participating people; resisting the culture pattern of begging for money at local, state and national levels; hoping that respect will be gained because of our desire to do whatever we can to support ourselves."

Within a year or so *Futures* consisted of three separate buildings. "Our Enterprise" or "center," as it was commonly called, housed the workrooms where the young adults made handcrafted objects to sell in "Our Shop," a gift shop located a few blocks away. Across the street from the shop was "Our Place," a small "home away from home" close by that the young people could go to during the day for a break or where they could make a reservation to spend one night or a weekend, fully chaperoned. That way they could be on their own, away from their parent's home. It was like a vacation place and it gave their parents a "vacation" from them too. There was always an adult on the premises. I chaperoned there many, many times.

As word of *Futures Explored* permeated the neighboring areas, young people that were hidden away in closets, or kept inside their homes because their families didn't know what to do with them or how to deal with their disabilities, were coaxed out of hiding. The young people were brought into the light to discover that there *was* hope and that *there could be a future for them.*

The Young's daughter and son-in-law lived at "Our Place" for awhile when it was first established and later often volunteered on weekends. Both of the Young's daughters made huge volunteer contributions to the successes of *Futures.* They were so friendly, giving and warm. Everyone loved the entire Young family. They were always popping up to volunteer, much to the delight of the young people. The young people could even cook their own meals in "Our Place" if they chose to, with supervision of course. There were games, television and a record player with their favorite records to dance to. There were numerous parties, potluck dinners and holiday celebrations held at "Our Place." Extended families were always welcome. The young people always participated in the menu selection, choosing the theme and making the decorations for all of the parties. There were also many excursions away from the center as well.

Later, "Nifty Thrifty," the thrift shop, and "Bob's Books," a used bookstore, were opened. Each one of these businesses was staffed with young adults, under supervision and according to their ability and desire. The object was to expose the young people to the public, practice their social skills, and for those who were able, to eventually transition into the work force. By the way, every one of the young people that worked in the various stores was paid a small salary.

I was what you might call the maintenance lady; one of the worker bees. I built shelves, bookcases, tore out walls, replaced walls, painted, refinished furniture and was basically the local handy-woman. Some of the young people worked right along side me. I also helped establish the thrift store. We realized that because so many local folks wanted to donate wonderful objects for us to sell in "Our Shop" we needed to establish a second hand store. "Nifty Thrifty" was born. Donations poured in. We kind of wanted to keep "Our Shop" pure. In other words just for the handmade art and crafts the young people produced in the Enterprise. People came from miles away to shop in our shops. We had quality merchandise and the word spread. We didn't do any advertising at all. Only when we held our annual "open house" did we print out brochures stating our purpose, our goals and information about the various shops. We became highly regarded in the business community as well as the local up-scale neighborhood. It was an enormous undertaking, and required hours upon hours of help from dedicated people.

You may be wondering why I refer to the young adults as "young people." That is how Helen referred to them. Helen never called them students or children; they were known as "the young people." Kind of ironic don't you think? *Mrs. Young's "young people."* As they matured they were referred to as "our people." Or by their own name, of course.

While at the Enterprise the young people practiced dynamics every day. It was an open forum with Helen as the facilitator. She encouraged people to talk about anything that bothered them or anything that made them feel good. It was an opportunity for them to vent as well as share their hopes, dreams and ideas. The young people also participated in the governing of the center. Judy was an original member of the all-client advisory board. Every one was encouraged to voice their opinions about the environment they worked and lived in.

The walls of the Enterprise were covered with large posters featuring famous quotes, poetry, inspirational thoughts and artwork. Interspersed among the art and quotations were also reminders of how to behave that the young people wrote. There were also lists of their goals, daily reminders of what they hoped to achieve. There were remarkable poems that they composed themselves. It was so inspiring and beautifully presented. I found the center to be such a warm environment. It was a place that compelled you to linger. It was, in a way, almost *spiritual*. The doors were always open to visitors.

The amazing work ethic that was instilled by Helen was evident throughout the center. The dedication of the volunteer teachers, college students, and parents of the students helped keep the young people focused and happy in their work. Not to say that there weren't times when situations developed that required a special meeting of the minds. Just as in any learning environment with so many diverse personalities, there were bound to be ruffled feathers that required smoothing. Helen's words of encouragement, incredible patience, and firm, but consistently gentle voice usually thwarted any personality clashes. She was always "tuned in" to what was going on.

I would like to share a few of the lessons the young people said that they learned at *Futures*. These are excerpts that I saved from a local newspaper called The Contra Costa Times. The article was written in May, 1966.

Jerry Wade said, "You have to be a gentleman, more than anybody."

Someone else said, "You have to accept yourself," and "We put on no false fronts here."

"When you ride on a bus you have to act better than anybody," Jerry Wade said.

"You have to give things a try," said Judy Chesley.

Judy also said, "Don't quit, and do your best."

Someone else said that this was one of *Future's* mottos; "Whoever you are, if you behave like an idiot, you'll be treated like one."

In the same article Helen Young was quoted as saying the following: *"Brain damage that can prevent learning to read has nothing to do with usable intelligence. Right away, people start judging you on whether or not you can read. One of the first humps we get over is to demonstrate that mechanical and social skills can be developed quite independently of the ability to read. Also, any kind of learning is easier once the person himself recognizes the need for it. All the young people, for instance, have gained much more understanding of money from working in "Our Shop" than they would if coins were shown to them in a classroom."*

The final addition and clearly the ultimate goal that Helen had for the people of *Futures* was the purchase of a home appropriately named "Our Place." This was "the icing on the cake", the "cream in their coffee," and truly "the proverbial pie in the sky" dream come true. The possibility of enabling the first chosen few, the earliest pioneers of *Futures,* who had proven them selves capable of learning to live on their own, *to live independently* was going to become a reality at last. Hooray! (There had been another "Our Place" earlier in the life of *Futures* that I mentioned before, where the young people stayed overnight or weekends. That one was a rental. This one they owned! This house was to be the stepping stone that would enable the young people to learn the skills that they needed to be able to live independently.)

Judy and five others were the first residents to reside at "Our Place." It was a two-story house that *Futures Explored Inc.* was able to purchase with the income from the small businesses that were so successfully operated over the years. I think some of the funds were donated as well. Judy and her five roommates learned to make out a grocery list, purchase groceries, cook their own meals, clean house, do laundry, practice basic personal hygiene skills and even create a budget with help. They were taught basic security precautions, and had to show that they were very responsible citizens. Judy lived in "Our Place" about a year and a half.

When Judy and her roommate at "Our Place" had successfully learned all the skills necessary to allow them to move into their own apartment and live *independently*, they took the big leap! An apartment was located. Hooray again! The year was 1988. It only took forty-five years for Judy to achieve this goal; twenty-three of which were spent at *Futures Explored.* The complex that Judy and her roommate moved into was selected because the owners accepted subsidized rent. Not all rental units qualified for subsidized housing in Lafayette. The complex had well over one hundred units and was near the transit station, grocery stores, and a ten-minute walk from the *Futures* center.

For the next ten years Judy lived in the apartment in Lafayette. She had a terrific support system. She had an Independent Living Services instructor provided by the state who helped her with her finances, grocery shopping and in the beginning, her personal shopping. She was also placed under the umbrella of "Supported Employment," an agency that would be responsible for finding Judy a job.

She was assigned a job coordinator who arranged her first job. She worked in a restaurant washing dishes and busing tables in a town about ten miles away. She was assigned a job coach who was responsible for checking on her progress and her work environment, then reporting it to the coordinator. Judy was taught how to use the transit system, which she used not only to get back and forth to work, but she soon learned that she could get to San Francisco on it too. San Francisco was about twenty miles away and it beckoned to Judy often. The young people were not allowed to travel by themselves, only in small groups, so she would round up her friends from *Futures* and take them all to Fishermen's

Wharf for the day. She loved to be on the go and enjoyed being the tour guide for the group.

Eventually, Judy was able to find a job closer to home working in the kitchen of a nearby convalescent home. She held that job for a few years. Her next job was her favorite one; working for Penny's in the stock room. It involved using the transit system again. She felt so grown up. She was riding to work like all the other commuters, traveling to a real job working for Penny's Department store! She liked telling people where she worked. "I'm a J.C. Penny's employee," she would say proudly. Heck, she even had a charge card with her name on it. How lucky can you get? She often rode the bus "home" to visit us. Her hometown was only about thirty miles away.

Judy stayed in close contact with her friends at *Futures* at first. It gave her the opportunity to share her experiences out in "the work force" with her young friends and with Helen. After so many years being at *Futures*, it was hard to break away from "the mother ship." Eventually, however, the need to return to *Futures* dwindled for Judy. Mrs. Young, as Judy always called her, retired and *Futures* was no longer the same without her, in Judy's eyes. She saw the Youngs more on a social basis.

I'm sure that Helen, in her infinite wisdom, had this all figured out when she established Futures. *I am positive that Helen fully expected to watch many of her charges struggle with their new wings before they would fly. But she also knew that they could fly. And fly they did!*

Today, Judy is sixty-three years old and she says she's too young to be a senior citizen. She is tall, fair skinned, and youthful looking. There are strands of silver starting to glisten in her wavy light brown hair. She lives about twenty-five miles from us, and spends most of her weekends with us. Patti takes us for nice rides in the mountains. She warns us to bring along a toothbrush and a change of underwear because she never knows for sure where we'll end up. We all love to explore the back roads, often packing a lunch and searching for a place to picnic along the many rivers. Judy and Patti go hiking and collect river rock for the garden. We play word games and sing along to music while riding along. Judy loves these outings. Heck, she just loves riding in the car and being with her family! It takes so little to make her happy. She loves movies. *Shrek* is her favorite because her nephew is a Senior Animator at PDI/DreamWorks and he helps create the *Shrek* movies. She loves to listen to music, especially Country Western. She knows all the singers by name. She also searches the newspaper for events that she is interested in and wants to attend, like the Ice Follies, state fairs, horse shows etc. She lets Patti know when she finds something she wants to attend and they make a date. She doesn't read books, but she does enjoy simple puzzle books. She knits, and does cross-stitching, and can put a complicated puzzle together in a flash. Patti tries to take her on an annual vacation; it usually involves horseback riding if at all possible. It gives Judy the incentive to save some of her money for her vacation and gives her something to look forward to. She usually has her suitcase packed *months* in advance in anticipation!

Judy has accepted, for the most part, that most "normal" people don't befriend her. Physically, Judy appears to be perfectly normal. Strangers and new acquaintances are friendly to her at first, but sooner or later realize that she has a disability and then shy away from her. It is heartbreaking to witness. She admits that she prefers the company of people who *are not* disabled. Because she is outgoing, fun and adventurous, she wishes she could be included and accepted by the "normal" people. She has learned to just put on a happy face and do things on her own during the week.

The other senior residents in the community where she lives are nice to her, but no bonding has taken place in the seven years she has lived there. It's a nice, safe location, however, and there are stores, shopping centers, bus service, and especially job opportunities for her. The owners accept housing subsistence. She has support agencies similar to the ones that she had in Lafayette. She sees her Independent Living Instructor a few hours twice a week. She still has help grocery shopping and with her finances. Other than that she is fairly independent. She takes care of her own one bedroom apartment, and her cat. She does her own laundry and prepares her own meals. She is only allowed to work twenty hours a week because she gets state aid and housing assistance. She carries her cell phone and calls us to let us know where she is. "Just checking in," she says. I wish she had a friend to keep her company.

Judy says that people find it hard to believe that she has a handicap so they often expect more of her than she can manage. She says it's very frustrating when people give her too many instructions at the same time. Other than that, *"I'm just fine,"* she says.

She still often wonders why she can't have a car, yet she knows that one of her biggest disabilities is depth perception. I try to help her understand that *that* is a very important part of driving a car. She doesn't agree. Her father always told her she could learn to drive someday and she has never forgotten that. She wants to drive a <u>HumVee!</u>

Judy still faces many challenges on a daily basis, but she never quits learning, tries to stay up-beat and just wants to be accepted. Helping to smooth the way for her is a life long commitment of ours, and her happiness and well being are top priorities for everyone in our family.

The two special women in Judy's life, her mother Ruth, and Helen Young, had a vision and never wavered, and still are the two brightest stars in her life even though one of them is guiding her from above. Our dearest friend Helen Young passed away on December 13, 2003. She taught Judy that she could do anything she wanted to do…except drive a car. She requested that her memorial be held on her favorite day of the year—The *DAY OF EPIPHANY.* Hmmm…

***

Postscript from Ruth

Writing this chapter has certainly stirred up my memory bank! Thank goodness we have come a long way from the ignorance that prevailed when Judy was born. I hope that anyone who has a disabled child, knows someone who is disabled, or has a disability himself or herself will remember that we must never accept no for answer. And never, never give up. There is help and financial assistance waiting out there for each and every one of you. Start with a visit to your doctor. A <u>HIGHLY</u> RECOMMENDED DOCTOR!

P.S. I'm ninety-six now and I just planted a new crop of flowers. After all, it's Spring! Hooray, Judy has a new job working for Safeway. And best of all, she has found a new friend!

***

Dedication

This story is dedicated to the memory of Helen Young. She would not approve of our holding her up to be the magnificent bright star that she was, because her goal in life was simple. It was to treat every individual with respect and to help each one achieve his or her greatest potential.

Her daughter Nancy described her best. *"Her greatest gift to her family and friends was her strong and clear sense of herself. Therefore, she could be of great help and comfort to others."*

Without Helen's unassuming and humble entrance into our lives and the lives of scores of other individuals too numerous to mention, none of us, disabled or otherwise could have reached our full potential as contributing human beings. We will be eternally grateful to this beloved woman for the gift of *herself.*

CHAPTER TWELVE
AN EPIPHA-MINI

WILD-EYED INNOCENT

Never assume that you could not be mistaken for a terrorist
given the right circumstances.
In the chaos of preparing for a family wedding, fatigued and
scatterbrained as I was,
I kept randomly and unintentionally transposing syllables in words
I was saying—
changing words in several conversations to crazy, hybrid, mix and
match gobbledygook—
often hilarious and yet sometimes oddly more appropriate
than the correct words themselves.

Somehow the "kitchen gadgets" that were to be part of a shower
gift always came out as "chicken gadgets." My sister and I found
this so funny that we just decided to go with it, making it a
permanent "family slang term", and use it from then forward.
Later, traveling to Scottsdale to visit my sister, I had placed in my
carry-on bag some colorfully wrapped items I was going to give her
and her husband for their new vacation home. Included were some
"chicken gadgets" for her kitchen.

Airport Security stopped me, seeing weirdly shaped items in the
x-ray of my carry-on bag. The security guy (who was so obviously
in over his head with his position as airport bag checker, and also an
obvious stranger to the kitchen) asked me what they were.
Without missing a beat, I said they were chicken gadgets.
"What do you do with them?" he asked.
"They are gadgets for my sister's chicken—I mean *kitchen*," I
replied.
"Do you use them specifically on chickens?" he asked.
"Well, sometimes."
"To do what?"

"We use them to cook with!" I said, looking innocent and yet wild-
eyed and crazy.
"Haven't you ever seen spatulas and a hand beater
and a pair of tongs?" I said.
"A pair of tongs for a chicken?" he asked, with wonder in his voice.
"I think you are confusing the word "tong" with the word "thong,"
I said. "Chickens don't use that underwear thingy that girls wear...
but chickens can be served with tongs, actually."
He looked blank—apparently humorless and clueless.
Vacant as a box of rocks.
He asked to unpack all the contents.

He motions for the other security attendant who is a woman. He
tells her these things are called chicken gadgets
and I have a pair of chicken thongs. She looks at me...I look at her.
She does not want to make her fellow bag checker look like an idiot
(a tall order, under the circumstances) so she continues questioning
me about the items, purely for affect.
"These instruments are for your sister?"
"Yes."
She obviously thinks I am a chicken terrorist.
I try to explain the origin of the term...that chicken gadgets were
originally shower gifts and I could not pronounce it correctly
because I was...over-extended and fatigued...it was just too hard to
think of the right word so...my sister and I just call them...oddly
enough...and I know it is sort of nutty...chicken gadgets.
It is family slang talk..."
"It is *what* kind of talk?" Now she is concerned that I am using
another language that she is unfamiliar with
and I don't fit the profile for it.
She takes the utensils to show someone else...

"WAIT! HEY! Don't start grabbing stuff...these are gifts!...we just
use them to cook...we don't really use them just for chickens...that
would be *so weird*...but, so what if we did?...is that illegal?...these
are harmless...geez, I bought them at Crate and Bar...just give
them back to me please...these are just little GIFTS!"

Cooler airport security heads finally prevailed
and I got my gadgets back.

But, never assume...

CHAPTER THIRTEEN
FINE DINING
or
How I Survived Divorce on Cheap Wine, Potato Chips, and Onion Dip
Leilah Diekman Schou

Advice—What I Learned in Divorce School.

There's no way anyone can experience a traumatic episode or period in life without evolving into a different person. To stay the same would mean, in my mind, that he or she had not been fully engaged in the process (perhaps they just couldn't help it). I believe that, in the words of **Gary Zukav in *The Seat of the Soul*: *Authentic empowerment is not gained by making choices that do not stretch you.***

This divorce experience certainly stretched me. There were so many words of wisdom sent my way, along with bad advice, that I had to navigate through a sea of murky water before a logical, sane path finally made its appearance. I strongly urge you, if you are in the midst of such a journey, to the best of your ability, to reach out to others. In my desperation and pain, I practically begged others for The Answer. Of course, I was the only one with my answer, but people responded with compassion, suggestions (fortunately I didn't take them all literally), opinions, advice, and amazing openness. You'd be surprised how eager people are to share their own tales of woe if they sense a sympathetic ear or a similar situation.

The hardest thing ultimately, for me, was to let it go—to surrender it to the universe and to acknowledge that the harder I clung to what was turning into a fantasy, the less control I actually had. I needed to re-establish enough self-respect and faith in something bigger than myself to finally realize it was out of my hands anyway. **Gary Zukav also states: *Authentic needs are the needs that are always met by the universe.***

I fought this whole concept of surrendering for the longest time, but eventually came to believe it. Mick Jagger said it best when he told us that we can't always get what we want, but we do get what we need.

I say, embrace others who are going through the same thing. I shared this time with friends who were also in "divorce mode" and we truly kept each other afloat. I think it's vital to wallow in self-pity, baby yourself, treat yourself as the wounded soul you are—put one foot in front of the other; then bit by bit, see the little signs that appear daily for the true epiphanies they are. Realize that there is life, joy, laughter, and a Technicolor world waiting for you after divorce. Even though this new life isn't what you signed up for, it's actually your reward for having survived, for having taken the high road, and for being strong enough to transform yourself into a vital and more compassionate person, able to construct a world of new experiences, friendships, and empowerment.

You'll no doubt spend countless hours examining your marriage, what caused the whole thing to shatter and how to make it work, even when your gut tells you it's over. If you still have hope that there may be a reconciliation, hang on as long as you can, as tight as you can. One way or another, you will know when you've had enough. After awhile, even *you* will tire of your story—so imagine how boring it will become to those around you. There will be alternating accusations and guilt trips—you'll blame yourself, then your spouse, for the collapse of the marriage. But in my case I eventually stopped beating myself up and realized I was seeing myself as a scapegoat—and that unless I could become a different type of person, I had to now save myself. I was sick of the psychobabble justifications (this wasn't a "moral" issue, it was a "lifestyle" issue, for example, in his words) and demeaning situations. At that point, I hired a great attorney and stopped any contact with my ex. From then on, I started to regain my strength (physical and emotional), realizing he had been sapping me of my energy as well as my health.

So many years have now passed—to say that I am older and wiser would be an understatement. The person I fell in love with so long ago no longer exists—but neither does the couple we once were. Really, a death has occurred, but out of the ashes new growth and life can emerge. There are so many subtle signs that life will go on, if only you can be open to them. It may not be life as you imagined, but acknowledging this will open you to the epiphanies that are sure to follow.

And so, who am I today? WOW—what a question to contemplate at this stage of one's life. At any stage, for that matter. For sure, I'm a proverbial "work in progress"—and hope to be for the rest of my life. Vital statistics would describe me as sixty-four years old, divorced, living in the

Southwest in my renovated (by myself and some great professional help) old house with my rescued dog, Molly (and lots of company from time to time). I've experienced so much over the past few years and these experiences have created a monster, in the form of someone able to look life in the eye, speak my mind, embrace people with different views on life, and be thankful for all the good that is part of every day. I can also deal much more effectively with the unpleasant that is bound to be part of life.

More than anything, it has become important to be surrounded by people I cherish and who place value in the person I've become. My home is a gathering place for all sorts of wanderers and wayfarers and nothing warms my heart more that fixing a good meal for the multitudes and sitting around discussing the meaning of life (or how the latest game is going). I love the ritual of cooking while enjoying a glass of wine and listening to some great Cuban or Reggae music, knowing the evening will nurture a few souls as well as tummies. And, I believe good wine and food are vehicles for some great conversations (as well as heated discussions along the way) and fellowship.

Some of my favorite dishes are Mexican, Chinese and Indian; not to mention the many party dishes I used for years when we entertained. I must say I love the ritual of shopping for weird and exotic spices, unique ingredients, and different "accoutrements"; taking them home, roasting the spices, then grinding them, making a monumental mess in the kitchen, flinging pots and pans, stirring, pouring, and finally managing to pull it all together with not much time to spare. My goal is to have the whole chaos cleaned up, be cleaned up myself, and have a glass of wine in my hand about five minutes before my guests arrive. Whew.

Food was always a passion for me until my world kind of fell apart and then I learned I could live on cheap wine, potato chips and onion dip for extended periods of time. For someone who had been chided by my then loving husband for making too much fuss over food, a process I enjoyed as did our friends, this is one of many recent ironies. In addition to the menu items mentioned above I have also made a lot of comfort food—I guess we really do crave these things when life is hard and simple food is one of the few things that makes us feel better.

Here is my "Family's Favorite Casserole" recipe that tastes great and qualifies as comfort food:

1 12-oz pkg wide egg noodles

11/2 lb ground turkey
red wine
pinch of sugar
1 small chopped onion
1 chopped green pepper
1 12-oz can tomato sauce
1 small container sour cream
1 small container cottage cheese
1 8-oz pkg cream cheese
Cook noodles & drain, then place ½ in bottom of casserole, set other ½ aside.
Fry onion and green pepper in a little oil until tender, add turkey and fry until
cooked through. Pour in tomato sauce, large pinch of sugar, and about ¼ C red
wine. Simmer about 20 minutes. Spread cheese mixture over noodles in casserole,
top with remaining noodles, then pour tomato sauce mixture over all. Cover and
bake at 350 for 30 minutes Great made ahead and can be served at any family
function.

In addition to being a decent cook, I think of myself as a tolerant, contemplative person who is still dealing on a daily basis with the cards dealt me over the past few years. People say I have a great sense of humor—I actually crack myself up from time to time. In a relatively short time I faced a hysterectomy, divorce, two surgeries for breast cancer, and a "reversal of fortunes" which was caused by a decline in the value of my financial portfolio. As I try to reflect on the person I am today and think back on events that led me to this place in time, I am aware that these are *my* recollections. In the many stories of my life, there are also that many versions, variations, and conclusions, depending on the point of view of who is telling them. I am telling this story from *my uniquely personal perspective.* After all, I was there—I can only tell you, in fairness, how it was for me. However I found it challenging and gut-wrenching to accurately describe the powerful emotions I experienced during this divorce process, and so I offer you my accounting of the main events with little fluff. And, out of respect for our children, and for the extraordinary life we shared for many years, I will refrain from relaying the most gruesome details.

These were surely some very dark days of self-doubt, sadness, emotional extremes, and tears. Lots of them—would I ever stop crying? I really did live on wine, potato chips, and onion dip far too often.

Ultimately, though, there was a sense of wanting to survive and there emerged some sense of peace. In the immortal words of **Johnny Nash and Jimmy Cliff**, *"I Can See Clearly Now, The Rain Is Gone"*. Even now when I hear that song, I think back on all those times of such intensity and sorrow, and I feel like a real survivor.

In asking myself how fulfilling my life is now, I'd say some areas are blessed beyond belief, while some are missions unaccomplished. There is a world of friendships and relationships that are as substantial as any I've ever had. Trying to figure out the meaning of life certainly forges connections that bring us all closer together—whether or not we actually come up with The Answer. More than likely, we produce many answers and raise even more questions. I'm also blessed with a whole lot of boy friends (okay, so they're mostly my girlfriends' husbands, or relatives) who've been of invaluable help with practical, financial, or legal matters. The men in my life actually seem to care about what I have to say.

I'm proud to be an animal-rights nut and I support those organizations which protect and rescue the creatures that need it most. I'd love to adopt all the poor sad critters in the local shelters, but lack of space prevents that! Molly was a "pound puppy" and she's just the best!

Like so many people, I'm worried about the state of this country. I just don't remember a time in my life when things seemed so overwhelmingly hopeless or beyond repair. Perhaps it's a generational thing—younger people don't seem to have such a sense of gloom and doom. They have their work cut out for them—there just don't seem to be as many safety nets available any more to protect the average citizen.

I'm grateful to have my parents in my life—living independently and very much "connected" to the outside world and, I treasure memories of all my grandparents, and even a great-grandmother! Not to mention countless aunts, uncles, extended family members and even invisible friends from my childhood!

Whenever I contemplate the next phase of my life (what does that mean, anyway? It's not as though there are clear divisions between "phases"—they usually blend together. And the hell with being in the autumn of my life—each day has four seasons) I'm aware of the increasingly rapid passage of time, however, and don't want to waste it. How I want to be more "in the moment" and to be aware of the epiphanies that come our way daily. That being said, I don't have a burning desire to climb any more mountains again or to turn my life upside down in an effort to beat the clock. I earned the right to come home to my adorable house at the end of the day, feeling contentment and being at peace. Yet, I look forward to what each new day brings. Not bad.

I grew up in the suburbs of New York City. For kids living in the shadow of the Big Apple at that time (the 50's and 60's), it was a pretty idyllic environment—still a country atmosphere, but close to the pulse and vitality of the City, which was an hour's train ride away. But what a world away! I always loved New York and spent my junior year of college there—majoring in Spanish and commuting from home. It was one of the best and most exciting years of my life and I'll always be a New Yorker at heart. Nothing better for my fellow students and me than being in the prime of our lives, renting bikes in Columbus Circle and riding to Tavern On The Green in Central Park where we conversed with the waiters in Spanish, convincing them to give us sophisticated cocktails like rum and Cokes, and feeling as though we were on the top of the world. And we were. How could I forget attending world-class theater, hearing Harry Belafonte in concert, traipsing through stores where I couldn't afford a thing, visiting museums, and being aware that there was a whole new world out there?

The best childhood memories, though, were of summers spent at my family's cottage in the Thousand Islands area of the St. Lawrence River in upstate New York. These were innocent days spent swimming, fishing, (my old fiberglass fishing pole is still hanging from the rack with all the other gear at the cottage) searching for crabs under the rocks on the shore, catching lightening bugs to put in a jar (how many of these poor things sacrificed themselves this way?) and gathering "night crawlers" (big worms) for the next day's fishing trip. What a memorable and peaceful time it was—kind of an "Endless Summer" without the surfing. Our mode of water transportation was an old wooden rowboat that we painted red every year. It was a sad day, indeed, when we had to pack up at the end of every summer to head back to reality. That being school. The River is what my memories and heart most often connect to, especially when I feel the need to center myself. And it never lets me down.

Speaking of school, I was an average student (pretty good in language, literature, social studies and the like, but terrible in math and science) and was quite shy as a kid. I loved to read and had a couple of good friends, but sitting in a classroom when I'd rather be outside was a challenge. How things have changed! I now treasure my many friends, love to socialize, and nobody would describe me as shy. Once I got to high school and college, I discovered my love for the Spanish language and that became my major. During my many trips to Mexico over the years it served me well and now that I'm living in the Southwest, I use it often, though my fluency isn't what it once was.

While a junior in college, I met my husband who was attending school nearby. Our families had known each other for years, so it was inevitable that we meet. We were head-over-heels about each other and I fell in love with his strength and intelligence. It was a rich time and this connection that we established with each other, and the world we made together, lasted for thirty-five years. Unfortunately, the things that brought us together and kept us together may have been the things that ultimately brought "us" crashing down. This union took us from a motel complex in Columbus, Georgia, to a house on the beach in Hawaii (where our daughter was born) to historic quarters in Washington, DC (Where our son was born), to a trailer park in Texas, student life in Boston, then a "normal suburban lifestyle" in the picturesque farmland of Pennsylvania, to a flat in England, to Evergreen, Colorado, which I still believe to be one of the most beautiful places on earth. I'd never smelled air like that, never seen a sky so brilliantly blue, and never felt such a sense of awe at my surroundings as I did there. And then finally to the Southwest. I became a seasoned packer and un-packer, and could pretty well get the family settled in and feeling at home in short order.

The physical or environmental background is pretty easy to describe and portray—but the larger issue of the emotional/spiritual/character-building background truly defines who we are and who we eventually become, and how we face the real challenges in life. This can be a little more troublesome to explore. When people of my generation were growing up, there wasn't a lot of tolerance of or encouragement for expressing our emotions (particularly if they were regarded as "negative" or, heaven forbid, LOUD). So, over time, we learned to suppress our emotions and to assume that we didn't have a right to them. And, it was inappropriate to impose them on others. That certainly does little to instill a sense of owning these emotions let alone allowing you the idea of your own power or strength. It puts people at a real disadvantage when it comes to having fair arguments, standing up for oneself, and going toe-to-toe with your adversaries. The end result for so many of us has been to try to reclaim our own courage and to build on it as time goes by. And that takes work. There is something so rewarding in this process where strength builds on strength, and inner peace builds on inner peace. Bit by bit, you morph into someone who is gaining strength and being a more substantial (hopefully) human being with each passing day.

***

My Epiphany

So, what exactly is this concept of epiphany we're all contemplating these days? Is it a gut-wrenching, between-the-eyes blast that appears like a bolt of lightening then suddenly, quietly makes the muddled mess clear? Does it enable us to finally and instinctively see the light, or the forest for the trees? Or, is it a lengthy, sometimes excruciatingly slow process that takes us on a journey from that first inkling that something just isn't right, to the point where we can see that our odyssey was just what we needed to experience? Or, is it a hint of insight that finally, thankfully, shows each of us our individual truth, and allows us to accept our own reality? I believe it can be any of these things, some of them, or maybe different ones, depending on your journey.

My epiphany evolved over several years during the time my husband and I were going through the divorce. There were epiphanies galore during that awful time, but one stands out above the rest.

It was January 2, 1997. A typical post-holiday day. The Christmas tree was still up, remnants of a small New Year's Eve gathering still in evidence, and chaos still reigned with the usual piles of greeting cards, presents to be put away, and debris from our annual holiday party. I had just returned from attending my grandmother's one-hundredth birthday party, and as usual, I was looking forward to my husband's return home from work that evening.

As he walked in the door, I almost immediately sensed that there was something wrong. As it turned out, something was terribly wrong and our lives were about to change forever. There would be no turning back.

I was sitting at the kitchen table, dinner was probably ready, and we would be enjoying our customary drink while chatting about our day. I remember what we were each wearing, and he told me I looked pretty. My heart is racing now just re-living what was to come, and what was more than I could bear to hear. He said he wanted something different in his life (paraphrasing now) and I said that we'd been through so much together, that we'd try something different, and that we could surely get through this. By now he was sobbing uncontrollably and responded that he didn't know if I could handle this. I clutched his hands, not even beginning to imagine what was wrong. When he was able, he told me he was in love with another woman whom I knew as an employee of his, and who had become a friend of our daughter's. She was actually considerably *younger* than our children.

This person had lived with us and with our daughter; I had given her furniture and housewares to set up an apartment (conveniently near our house), and she accepted it evidently conscience-free. Didn't I see it coming? No. Weren't there red flags? Now that I look back, yes. But of all the things that could have faced me in my life and in our marriage, this was just too preposterous to wrap my mind around.

The rest of the night is largely a blur. I remember wanting to throw up; I thought my heart would explode; I was totally dazed and literally in shock, anger, desperation, grief, rage, and, yes, love. I don't think I slept that night or for hundreds of nights after. As time went on, we sobbed together, held each other tighter than ever, talked this thing to death, yet all the while in my heart, I just knew we were dying a slow, agonizing death. My heart was broken. I was broken. We were broken. I had lost my best friend, or so I had thought. *And, I was suddenly living with an adolescent again.*

And so, it was no joke. I felt sick to my stomach and could hardly breathe. I know what it is to be literally in shock, and it seemed to take forever to lose that awful sickening sensation. I went on the divorce diet that instant—couldn't eat, couldn't sleep, concentrate or think straight—I could barely function. I couldn't tell a soul for months and as people were wondering what was wrong with me, things deteriorated on the home front. Eventually our kids were told and that was that. I can't imagine how it must have been for them. The effect of all this has taken its toll on them; it shook their very foundation. All our friends and relatives were told, once I finally had enough of what seemed like torture, and I filed for divorce. It was almost a relief by then to be making some decisions rather than waiting for another day to pass in limbo.

The emotional roller coaster was exhausting. One minute I wanted to destroy him, but the next minute I was desperate to hold him and feel his strong arms. How could I live without his touch? Who would I dance this dance of life with? Very early the next morning, he left for the day, pleading with me not to do anything rash. I spent the day taking down the tree—this tradition was always one of mixed emotions anyway, but this time I was wailing my heart out, not knowing, truthfully, if I wanted to live or not. For the next year or so, I bounced between thinking (deluding myself) that we might make it, figuring we probably wouldn't, then wishing I'd made him leave right away and thus having spared the angst this drawn-out ordeal had produced. But I can look back now knowing there was nothing else I could have done to make us ONE again. Those were times of intense emotional and physical intimacy which I clung to, aware that once I let go of that, it would really be all over.

During the time I was re-inventing myself (or, trying to put Humpty Dumpty back together), there were many epiphanies which guided and encouraged me. It seemed that when things were their darkest, I'd get a phone call out of the blue, or receive a card or encouragement from a long-lost friend. There were even prayers sent forth to a "Higher Power". Not being a particularly religious person (in the conventional sense), I was humbled and appreciative of these gestures and do believe that their power carried forth into my soul and somehow gave me strength. The conclusion I made was that although I might interpret these as mere gestures, I chose to regard them as signs that I should not despair. *And one of these epiphanies was that I mattered to quite a lot of dear people. These mini-epiphs gave me moments of relief and something to smile about.*

Nothing in life could have prepared me for that mind-numbing divorce journey and those memories still lurk in the back of my mind— kind of like the breast cancer I developed shortly after the divorce was final. I don't believe the medical community has placed nearly enough emphasis on the concept that stress is toxic to our bodies as well as to our minds.

We struggled through therapy, copious amounts of wine (some cheap, some not so cheap), living apart, living together in some sort of weirdly constructed conjugal arrangement, reading self-help books (I called them psycho books), emailing insults and threats; but the lure of a different lifestyle was too strong for my husband, and I finally realized our marriage was over since the first moment this ordeal had started. So, after almost three years, I stood in a crowded courtroom in front of a judge who asked me if this marriage was irreparably broken. And I tearfully acknowledged that it was. A dark day for me, indeed, but it forced me on an incredible journey of such intense emotions and experiences which I wouldn't trade for anything.

I traveled a lot in the time right after the divorce and did things I'd never have done otherwise. I hiked with friends from a Divorce Recovery Group into the Dolomite Mountains of Northern Italy (think World-Cup skiing scenery—it took my breath away) on trails so steep and narrow you had to brace for every step. These were black-diamond ski runs in the winters, and some were so rocky it was like being on ball-bearings. At one point, we crawled over a narrow path of crumbling rocks with my right shoulder brushing a sheer cliff, and a VERY long drop about a foot off my left hiking boot. There was no other way down besides following the trail, and I had a HUGE epiphany that I didn't want to go crashing and bouncing down the Italian Alps—I went from not caring if I fell, to knowing that I wanted to live to tell the story! Our little group hugged each other after some of these daily forays into the unknown—relieved the day was over and that nobody had toppled down a ski run.

I also braved (the operative word, in retrospect) an eight-day white water raft trip down the Colorado River with eighteen new and not-so-new friends. I was struggling with the same feelings of despondency over the collapse of my marriage one minute, screaming at the top of my lungs the next, while being pummeled by the violent rapids (check out Lava Falls on the internet) and whipped by the roiling frigid waters. I knew I didn't want to go this way, either! I had to survive this trip of a lifetime. Thoughts of my wonderful kids were constantly at the back of my mind and always what kept me wanting to see their precious faces again. Planning these adventures and anticipating them was such a *positive* thing. These trips, and several others, seemed to come along at just the right time—timing being just about everything, again. *Epiphanies!*

I have observed that in so many marriages which don't make it to the finish line, couples go along taking each other for granted. We are passive in our contributions to the relationship, rather than being pro-active partners. That being said, we all bring our own baggage to the table, and when couples marry young (as we did), there's not always a lot of opportunity to figure out who you are and before you know it, roles have been established and life seems easier for someone like me to be the good wife and put other's needs first. I eventually lost the will to stand up and be counted. After the dust had settled and the divorce was over, friends commented with an observation I hadn't ever noticed. *Whereas I sometimes felt not seen or heard, he became all I saw and heard. I was becoming invisible to both of us.*

Still, I am thankful for the good times, the great friendships established because of our travels, and the family that was created. The circle of life, as they say. Mostly, in all my life, I am exceedingly grateful for my two children who were rays of light through this dark time. They helped keep me (relatively) sane with their unconditional love, maturity, and understanding.

So, the big question I ask myself is, what is the most important epiphany gleaned from all the thoughts, angst, soul-searching, and lessons of this time in my life? How do you know when an epiphany has appeared before you, and do you recognize it as such, or are you tempted to shrug it aside as so much voodoo or desperation to have AN answer—any answer?

I believe that for me it is the realization that I can take my rightful place on this earth as the person I am truly meant to be— knowing that it took many tears, much laughter, and a whole lot of introspection to get to the top of the hill and survey this new life. It is a gift to finally be able to accept one's worth and value (still knowing we all have our flaws) and to build on that newly achieved self-confidence. I still have a small sense of sadness at what could have been, but I am finally at peace with who I am and I am comfortable in my skin. I like that quality in a person. Life has a way of interfering with your best-laid plans, or with no plans at all. I guess we all try to handle the cards dealt us the best way we know how given our circumstances and ability to cope. Change sometimes comes crashing into our lives whether or not we're prepared. I don't necessarily believe the adage that, "Change is Good", but it probably is inevitable. Small changes are acceptable. We rise to the occasion to the best of our ability. But being able to accept a monumental change, forced upon us, then, learn to adjust to it, and actually move on and begin creating a new life is a very different matter.

Now, that is an epiphany!

There is often in people to whom "the worst" has happened, an almost transcendent freedom, for they have faced "the worst" and survived it.

Carol Pearson

CHAPTER FOURTEEN
BLOOM
Brenda Louise Mossa

If we don't change, we don't grow.
If we don't grow, we are not really living.
Growth demands a temporary surrender of security.
Gail Sheehy

There is a plaque in our kitchen that says "Bloom Where You Are Planted" and those have been words to live by for me. Over the years we have been dug up and replanted many times. Just like a real plant, we've had setbacks in the transplanting, needed time to establish ourselves and set out a root system before the new growth happens. It is an amazing feat of nature and human nature as well that with time, nurturing and sunshine, plants and people come back better and stronger than before. The plant food of transition is *attitude*, which adds strength and resiliency to the mix.

We've owned nine houses in five states plus temporary homes and apartments. We've raised three sons, each was born in a different state and each graduated from a different high school. Amazing; each lives in a different state now. Most people think we were military and our youngest son used to swear it was the 'witness relocation program', but it was the corporate ladder that kept us on the move. We've been through some serious illnesses with the kids and I have experienced some of my own. I went to three colleges before I finally graduated at age forty-six! Frank and I have been married thirty-eight years and as the saying goes "It's never dull in Laredo"…it's never been dull at our house. Change has been a constant companion.

What's life like today? I've always "worn a lot of hats" and that's one thing that hasn't changed over the years. Staying engaged with life and challenged keeps me energized. I don't "work" anymore; officially I am retired, but honestly life is busier than ever. One of the rewards of retirement is the ability to take time for yourself, but for the most part my life is hectic and full with little down time. It is a different kind of 'busy' than working; the focus is now on my family and friends. I take things seriously and at times my jobs have taken over my life; I became my job and put it ahead of myself, quite willingly, but at a cost. Now the focus has shifted to home.

My sister Cathy lives with my husband Frank and I. She is a brave woman facing health challenges and the loss of her husband. Cathy also lived with us when our children were young and we were the ones needing help. What goes around does come around and we are glad we can help her now. Our boys are grown but Cathy's cat Mr. Pudders keeps our parenting skills sharp. He is truly a cat with personality, adding humor and trials and joy to our lives.

Sometimes I think our home is Grand Central Station. We have lots of out of town visitors and often also have friends in for coffee or brunch, a casual dinner or my husband Frank's homemade pizza. The welcome mat is always out. We love to entertain and touch base with old and new friends. We've lived a lot of beautiful and interesting places and our 'retirement home' is in the Suisun Valley, halfway between San Francisco and Sacramento and very near the Napa Valley. It's a great community; cows grazing on beautiful rolling hills, green in the winter thanks to "rainy season" and "golden" in the summer. I am humbled to be living in such a lovely area…it is a far cry from the cramped apartment in Queens, New York where I grew up.

Our home is typically "California"; stucco with a red tile roof. There is a big dried flower wreath on the front door. I noticed this morning the birds have been confiscating little pieces to build their nests. The back door is off the kitchen and we have a large deck Frank and his brother built. Our home is casual and comfortable, nothing fussy or ornate. Over the years I've dispensed with anything that needs polishing or ironing. Life is too short and I can think of better things to do with my time. We have a super-sized kitchen / great room and that area is the heart of our home and the perfect style for entertaining. My taste is eclectic and I love things that have been made by hand…anything that has had a human touch it…artwork, pottery, sculpture and unique items that make your house your own. We've also weaved in many mementos and photos to remind us of family and friends. Nothing in our home is high end or worth very much except to us, but it is warm and inviting.

A fitness club opened in our neighborhood a few years ago and that has been icing on the cake; a perfect place to exercise and also linger awhile for coffee and meet the faces you pass on the road. The people here are friendly and open. We've bought and sold a lot of houses, and I always wished there was a section in the multi-list to rate neighborhoods for being neighborly. Some people would be interested in "don't bother me areas," but I like to know the neighbors and find friends. I've learned over the years that good neighbors and friends enrich your life. This neighborhood would get a good grade.

I belong to two book clubs; both include interesting women in a wide age range with broad and fascinating backgrounds. I enjoy the discussions and exchange of ideas. Book clubs are great, giving you an opportunity to read things you ordinarily wouldn't pick up and to hear different perspectives. I've always loved to read. Books were a great escape growing up and then entertaining and educational as I got older. I learned a lot about myself from books and poured over parent education, home improvement, self-improvement, business books…whatever it was I needed at the time, there were always books to validate or teach, put things in perspective, get a project going or to just get lost in the story. I like movies, but I love to read. Frank and I enjoy live performances of any kind, especially theater. I am definitely a people person. I truly need my friends and enjoy having people around, but I also value being alone, enjoying my quiet time reading or browsing the shops or sitting at the computer.

I have learned some significant lessons in recent years. One is that age is just a number. As one of the first Baby Boomers, I'm living a different retirement than my parents had. I've learned that retirement is not an ending, but instead a new beginning and a chance to reinvent ourselves again. It's pretty cool to be retired! Frank and I have enjoyed expanding our horizons and learning about our world and different cultures through travel and also reconnecting with our huge family, now that we have the time and resources to do so. We've tried our hand at real estate and other business ventures, not willing to totally give up the excitement of the business world. I tell people we are not participating in old age or old ideas, and I mean it. Our philosophy is to enjoy life and continue to be constructive, productive and fulfilled. A few months back we attended a workshop where we "ate" fire and broke boards. This definitely was out of my comfort zone, but sometimes you just need to stir things up.

I've learned to make time for myself. My day starts with my walking buddies, out the door at 7:20AM three days a week. There are seven 'regulars'; we leave our houses about the same time and meet along the way. We do four miles, walking and talking, laughing and venting and sharing our joys and our problems...believe me it is better than therapy and lovely to start the day with hugs and smiling faces. The other two weekdays I go to a strength training class. I also practice yoga and during summertime I take a water aerobics class. Being healthy is a priority for me and I can honestly say I am healthier at sixty than I have been in many years. Frank and I have vowed to stay healthy for each other and knowing how things can change in a moment has kept us on track.

If I had to describe myself, I would say I am a good wife and mother and friend, task oriented and a hard worker. Flexible and spontaneous... spur of the moment things are fine with me...I can be out the door with a moment's notice and we are happiest on trips without an itinerary! If I get a bee in my bonnet, just get out of the way because I am going to do it now...my husband just rolls his eyes when he sees me with a hammer in my hand or heading for a piece of furniture he said he would help me move tomorrow. I am high energy, but sometimes I just plum give out. I like to think, find solutions and look at a problem or situation in different ways. This has come in very handy with all our moves where we've had to go from plan A to B to C...all the way to plan twenty-seven (that means you've run out of letters!). Another lesson I've learned: you can't get too attached to any one plan or outcome. It just causes grief and disappointment. Let things roll and if one thing isn't working, try something else. Usually the universe will take care of the details.

I am told I am kind and considerate. People tell me I am upbeat and a good listener. I don't have too many down days and attribute that to my wide support group of friends and family and a positive attitude. I have learned not to get bogged down with every little thing. Let it go. I am reliable; if I say I am going to do something I do it, even if I stay up all night getting it done. Can't help it...just one of those things that defines who I am.

I am empathetic and sympathetic especially to people in new situations. I know how much it meant to me to be greeted by name or invited for a cup of coffee or to participate in a group activity when I was feeling alone in a new place. I smile a lot and really like people. I am shy by nature, but I have learned that if I don't let people know me, then I will never get to know them and that is a lonely existence. When I am in a new situation I like to take the lead and introduce myself and get a conversation going. Over the years I have gone from introvert to extrovert, but sometimes revert to the quieter me. It sounds silly, but I love little benign, arcane sayings…things like "Whistle a Happy Tune," "Just Do It!" "Reach Out and Touch Someone" and my all time favorite "On the Road Again"…little ditties that pop into my mind; profoundly simple but encouraging and useful.

I am a wife to Frank, mother to Frankie, David and Brian, mother-in-law to Michele and Carolyn, a new grandmother and another grandchild on the way. Nothing has brought me more joy than our children; loving them and being loved by them is priceless. Raising our boys was the most challenging job I ever had and also the most rewarding. They have taught me as much as I have taught them and it is incredible to know them as adults. Frank and I are very proud of our wonderful sons and daughters-in-law and I get teary just thinking of our infant grandson and soon to arrive, granddaughter.

I am a sister and caregiver to Cathy and sister to Lynn who lives three thousand miles away. We have a wonderful extended family on both my parent's sides and are blessed to have Frank's mother, three sisters and brother and their families in our lives. It would be great to say we are all one big family living in one town or at least one state, but we are spread out over thousands of miles and have immediate family in Hawaii, California, Nebraska, Illinois, Ohio, Maryland, New York and nieces, nephews, aunts, uncles, cousins from Vancouver, Canada to Ft. Myers, Florida, back up to Montreal…and all in between. Thank goodness for email to keep in touch!

I am proud of our big extended family. My Dad was first generation Italian, one of nine children, brought up in New York City. Mom was one of five sisters, born and raised in South Carolina; a real southern lady who still said "Ya'll" and "Yes, Sir" and "Yes, ma'am" after forty years in the Big Apple. My husband Frank came to the USA when he was twelve from a small town in the boot of Italy called Sannicandro, near Bari. No one in his family spoke English and his parents were close to forty years old when they immigrated, leaving everything behind for a chance at a better life for their five children ages six to eighteen. My father-in-law worked nights in a factory to support his family and Frank seized that same opportunity for a better life. He recently retired from upper management of a billion dollar company and has his own story of change.

We've lived away from our immediate and extended families almost our whole married life. **The French poet Deschamps said, *"Friends are relatives you make for yourself"*** and I thank God for our many friends and neighbors who have filled the gap of family over the years. Our friends are precious to us in so many ways and I wouldn't trade any one of them for the world. They are my mainstay and my history and I know who I am because of what we've shared in our lives. They encouraged and cajoled. They got me through hard times and shared the good times. They included us in their lives when we moved to a new area and stayed in touch when we moved away...you know how it is with people who are loved and hold a special place in your life.

Growing up in New York City, I was protected and isolated by our big Italian family and strict parents. Well, I should qualify that and say my father was very strict. Mom was sweet and kind; too soft to stand up to Dad. I was shy at school and it was hard for me as the bookish, quiet type to speak up, but I earned decent grades and enjoyed a few close friends.

My father was a difficult man with a very strong personality; set in his ways and unbending. You did not express your opinion. He loved us underneath but often it was hard to see or feel. If he said he wasn't going to do something, he wasn't going to do it. I can be stubborn and know that comes from Dad. The first time Dad told me he loved me he was eighty years old and suffering dementia. I always knew, but still it was important to hear it before he died.

For all his troubles, he really loved Mom and he loved his three daughters. Dad might have been difficult, but he wanted good things for us and felt that being strict was only being protective. My parents were married forty-seven years when my mother passed away of pancreatic cancer. They were inseparable; sometimes we wondered why she put up with him, but they were a pair. Her softness complimented his roughness and it worked. He took good care of her in her final months and I respected him in his quest to get her well. We knew it wasn't going to be, but Dad called many doctors looking for answers and kept a bell by the bed so she could call him. Often he would fall asleep in a chair in her room. He was good man but not an easy father.

I had a huge support group in our New York and South Carolina families. My grandmother and seven of Dad's eight siblings lived near us in New York, half of them walking distance from our apartment. Our Grandma was the best person in the world, sweet and kind and accepting. Her house was a place of refuge especially when I was a teenager and needed to get away for a while. She was little and feisty, had a heavy Italian accent and many sets of rosary beads under the cushion of her chair that she used to pray for her huge family. She loved us unconditionally.

There was always a houseful at Grandma's house on Sunday afternoon. Everyone brought food and aunts, uncles and cousins were all over the house and the front porch balancing plates on their laps. It was always a noisy fun time. I bet you can picture "Sunday sauce," homemade bread and meatballs and spaghetti...but most often our feasts were garnered from the local Italian, German and Jewish delis and bakeries. Even back then, families were busy and there were just so many of us to feed! At Christmas and Thanksgiving, tables and chairs were rented so we could have twenty-five or more around the same table. I think the reason I love to entertain is a throwback to those happy family gatherings.

Most summers we would spend our two weeks vacation with Mom's family in South Carolina. We would pack up the car and drive seven hundred miles from New York City. That was before the interstate system so just getting there was an adventure in itself. We always looked forward to seeing our South Carolina family. Oh, the fresh air and the fun! No electronic games back then; we would chase each other around the perimeter of the house until we fell exhausted in the grass, and then beg for a turn at churning fresh peach ice cream.

Somewhere along the way it occurred to me that when I grew up I could have a different family life and could live anywhere I wanted. Of course it wasn't any big insight back then, just a child's wishful thinking, but doesn't it all begin with a thought? As I got a little older I visualized that "my" family, my future husband and my own children, would be different from my birth family. I was too young to get married and certainly no husband was on the horizon, but it was definitely going to be different when I grew up; no yelling and kids had rights too...yep, that's the ticket!

That was a child's reflection, and I didn't understand then where the road of life would take me or how my life experiences would mold me. I did understand, even as a child, that it was up to me. The first class I signed up for in college was Psychology. I wanted to learn what was going on in my family and how to remedy it for my future. That long ago thought of change was being implemented, changes were percolating and new ways of thinking and acting were coming.

Being from a large family I had seen a lot of major life changes, but one day I had a flash of insight! Big and small things happen every day; there is a lot in life we just can't do much about, and even little happenings can have a major impact on us.

But what we can control is our attitude, and being positive or negative determines how situations affect our lives. It was profound.

It was an epiphany.

"If it is to be, it is up to me," another of those little sayings I like. Long ago I realized I could beat myself up because I wasn't happy with how life was going...or I could go out and create challenge and self-esteem. I could be lonely or I could find friends and activities...Life throws curves and stepping up to the plate or in some cases stumbling to 'home' has shown me who I really am inside. For me it wasn't a big plan...life unfolds in unexpected ways and the choice is very simple: to resist it or grow with it.

I have learned that it really is up to us and that attitude, perseverance and resiliency is everything. I believe it all starts with a thought: I can do it or no, I can't. I will stick with it or I will give up. I am strong or I am weak. I can embrace life or life is too tough. What does your self-talk say? For me...well, I think it is better to make lemonade. "Just do it."

I have learned when something is amiss in my life to ask myself simple questions:

What can I do to improve this situation?

When I am sick...how do I get well?

When I am bored...how can I be challenged?

When I'm overworked or overbooked...how do I find time for myself?

I have learned what you give out to the universe comes back to you. You know, what goes around comes around. I have found this to be true over and over. For example I really enjoy people, I genuinely like to hear what is going on with them, help out if I can. I like to smile. I send out love and positive energy and am rewarded with an abundance of happiness, a loving family and warm friendships. It is an amazing phenomenon!

Someone visiting our home once said, "Your sign must be Cancer; they love their homes and they like to nest!" I don't know much about astrology but I remembered that because...well, that is me. Over the years I've created many nests for my family where I wanted them to feel protected and loved, but secure enough in themselves to test their wings and then fly. It is always difficult to leave those nests that became homes and the friends who became family to us. There were always teary times as we packed up to "new adventures." Before the movers came I would go room-to-room, tucking away memories, saying goodbye and thanking God for that part of our lives. Being part of a larger community of friends, work, volunteerism...giving our kids a secure and happy home gave meaning to my life and 'creating nests' over and over revealed strength and resilience I didn't know I had.

Most men find meaning in providing for their family and Frank has always thrived in his new assignments. He worked for the same company for thirty-seven years and going in as the boss with an immediate sense of security and belonging is a far cry from starting over from scratch with three disgruntled kids and a house full of boxes to unpack. We always did our best to convey a sense of excitement and adventure to the boys. Looking at the positive side, a new house means a new area to explore, new friends we haven't met and new challenges as we settle and adapt to our new surroundings. The truth of the matter is new beginnings are stressful, some less so than others...but we gave it our all, things always fell into place, we became comfortable in our new neighborhood and soon it became 'home'. Sometimes people ask, "Where did you enjoy living the most?" That is hard to answer because it is difficult to leave each place; we've made friends, planted ourselves in the community and leave behind many happy memories. Each has a special place in our hearts.

My husband Frank is terrific...he is kind and supportive, with an amazing energy, quick smile and distinctive laugh. He is my rock. He listens and doesn't make judgments and he has always shown me he feels I am worthy and capable and strong. Frank is my best friend and I love him dearly. That doesn't mean we have always agreed on everything or that I have always been happy. Sometimes I was furious because his expectations and my feelings didn't jive. I needed him to be there live and in person when he was thousands of miles away at a new job or on a business trip.

No one waited for Dad to get home when they needed a trip to the emergency room. Blizzards didn't wait or broken pipes or a blue jay who managed to get in the house and was dive-bombing the windows. No one jumped up and down and yelled, "YEA! We are moving again." Sometimes I just needed a little help...three kids going in three directions and only one of me. There were times I wanted to throw my hands up, but I got through a lot of very tough situations, from medical and household emergencies and the daily demands on my time and energy, to the logistical nightmares and emotional drain of moving our family state to state. It's always something, Gracie...but I learned I am strong and capable and I can do it.

Frank has been the source of many changes in my life. They say be careful what you wish for it might come true! I wanted to live away from the big city. I wanted a husband who would promise me that, and also a husband who would treat me with respect as an equal partner in our marriage. Well he did and he does, but I didn't know it was going to be a winding twisted road from one coast to another and back and forth again. I had something a bit more stable in mind!

Frank and I were raised in the 1950's and early 60's. We came from intact families and there was no divorce on either side. That didn't mean everything was hunky-dory, but it did model good old-fashioned stick-to-it values. There have been rough times in our marriage and several instances where I mulled over a divorce request in my head...thankfully we kept communication open and the pain passed. There were times I felt our family life and family stability were being sacrificed for Frank's career moves, but we've always loved each other and we've always considered ourselves a team. When you are on a team it is all for one and one for all, even when you are down a few points! Our marriage is strong; we have been through a lot together.

I have learned that the keys to a happy and successful marriage are mutual respect, understanding and good communication skills. It allows you to bring out the best in each other. But honestly sometimes you just have to scream..."What were you thinking???"

We married fairly young; I was twenty-two and Frank twenty-five. His first promotion came a year later; we moved from New York to Connecticut, not far in the scope of things, only two hours from home. I was pregnant with our first child, so off Frank went to his new assignment and I stayed in New York waiting for our baby and hoping the blessed event would be on a weekend so Frank could drive me to the hospital. Our beautiful son Frankie arrived on a Sunday afternoon! He weighed in at ten pounds seven ounces and it was my first (and only) shot at celebrity as nurses and visitors stopped by to see the little lady with the really big baby.

We moved two weeks later; not much time to adjust to motherhood or recover from the C-section. I had not seen the apartment and literally had no idea where it was in relation to the town or to Frank's office. Let me tell you I had a very sinking feeling that first morning Frank left for work and I realized how isolated I was from everything I'd always known. There wasn't a bus on every corner like New York City and I didn't drive. I was lonely and somehow the instruction manual for new babies got lost in the move. I had no experience with babies and no one to help. It was the middle of winter. I cherished the thought of being a new mom and was really excited over the move. It *was* what I wanted. But instead, those first months dragged as the realities of motherhood and isolation of the move set in. I felt lonely, emotionally drained, unsure of my mothering skills, isolated from my support group and pretty pudgy too.

This first huge change for me was a very difficult time; a double-whammy of motherhood and move, and more than I bargained for. I left the safety of family, friends and work for what seemed like the abyss. The isolation was debilitating. How was I going to make this place OK for me?? It was already OK for Frank. He was very content with his challenging new position and happy to have his wife and son with him.

I must admit I was a little, well maybe a lot, snively those first months as I considered how to deal with our new reality. We live _here_ now. That wasn't going to change, so I needed to dig deep and figure out what I needed to do to be comfortable, happy and make it _home_. I had a husband I loved, a beautiful new baby, and a spacious apartment in a beautiful area. So far so good! It's all about attitude, self-talk and how you view life. Success has everything to do with the actions you take. No excuses!

What did I need?

I needed friends and projects to sink my teeth into.

I needed to learn to drive.

Most of all I needed to stop feeling sorry for myself.

I threw myself into domesticity...being a good mother, trying new recipes, decorating the apartment…by spring I was driving, had joined the Newcomer's Club and took my first of many volunteer positions doing publicity for that group. I have learned volunteering is a great way to meet people and get to know an area and what is going on locally. Over the next few years we became homeowners, home improvement experts, parents to our second son, David, and enmeshed in the community. In my mind we were set; close enough to our family so we could visit on weekends, enjoying a happy life with lots of friends and a cute little house with a yard and playhouse for the kids. I was active in the community and enjoying an idyllic life.

We must be willing to get rid of the life we've planned so as to have the life that is waiting for us.

Joseph Campbell

Wrong. We sold that cute little house, had a big party to say goodbye to our new community, and five months pregnant with our third son we moved again, this time to New Jersey and spent six weeks in motels before we could actually move into our house. Now that was a lesson in patience and fortitude! Brian was born with pneumonia and over the next two years he was hospitalized numerous times for various respiratory problems. He was critical twice. My sister Cathy came to live with us to help with the older kids so I could be at the hospital. Frankie and David had a lot of illness too, at one point all three kids had pneumonia and two were hospitalized. I was trying to keep a positive attitude but it was more like "Whistle A Happy Tune." I didn't want any one to know how afraid I really was.

The two years in New Jersey were a nightmare. Besides the kid's illness, Frank had a long commute and was finishing his degree at night. Did I mention it was also a "one hundred year" winter? So much snow fell, the town stopped plowing our little cul-de-sac. The baby wasn't thriving and Frank requested a move to a dry climate. A lateral position opened up in Denver and that was the perfect spot. The only caveat was Frank had to report right away. Cathy and I packed up the house and got it ready to put on the market. The older kids were sick, the baby was in and out of the hospital and we weren't doing that well either. It was stress city. The coup de grâce was chicken pox Frankie brought home from kindergarten a few weeks before the movers were scheduled. Two weeks later David had them and two weeks later Brian, with pneumonia as a secondary infection. I hand carried all their health records and Brian was still healing but we headed to the airport and were out of there.

I knew when we left New Jersey I could handle anything and the adversity of the past two years had given me a new perspective on life and on myself. *I learned that nice little families like ours were not exempt from life threatening problems and that I would have sold my soul to the devil to make my child well.* Instead I bargained with God and my prayers were answered. When I didn't think I could handle one more thing, one more thing came roaring in. Sometimes more than one thing and we got through it. "I can do it." I've seen it in myself and in many other people. The colloquial would be "When the going gets tough, the tough get going" but believe me there is an amazing well of courage and resiliency within…I believe we all have it if we are willing to release our fears and trust the outcome. This too shall pass.

We all hit our stride in the beautiful Colorado mountains. The schools were top notch and the kids had loads of great friends and activities. The health problems were on a back burner. I was very active in the schools, with cub scouts and kid's sports and enjoying many volunteer and club activities. It was a busy active life with an incredible group of friends; we were all so close I felt the support group of our big childhood families again. Of course there were bumps in the road and we were further from our family than we had ever been, but we depended on our community of friends and they depended on us, forming deep and lasting friendships. Many of those friendships continue today. We all loved Colorado and felt grounded there. Frank had a nice promotion and was feeling challenged and appreciated. Even Frank could have stayed, but the recession of the late eighties hit Colorado very hard and Frank was transferred to the Bay Area of California.

We went from the mountains to a small beach town south of San Francisco. It was a tough move for the kids because they were older and didn't want to leave their schools and friends. After ten years we felt like native Coloradoans and considered it home. Frankie was a senior in high school and he moved with us, but at semester break decided he wanted to graduate with his friends. He headed back to Colorado and David and Brian wished they could go back too. The schools in California were the pits and the kids missed their friends and activities and they missed the mountains. When Frankie left, they missed him. Ditto for me.

A lot of the kids at school had known each other their whole lives, so it was rough being the new kid in town. I picked Brian up at school one afternoon and he looked pretty down. When I asked him how his day went, a tear rolled down his cheek and he said "Oh, Mom, if only *one person* would say, 'Hi, Brian'." Then it was my turn for tears. I did a lot of listening, validating their feelings, inviting new friends over and finding new activities. They wanted a little black kitten a woman was giving away in front of Safeway, so Webber came into our lives. He was not much bigger than my fist but he was a good listener and believe me they gave him an earful. We had Webber for sixteen years, so he saw a lot of changes too! Things improved when the kids made some friends and we were able to move out of the apartment and into our house, but I always wondered, given the choice, if they would have traded us in for parents who stayed put.

I had my first paying job since the kids were born when we moved to California. Feeling very insecure about my experience, my resume was pretty sparse. The astute woman doing the interview got me talking about the volunteer positions I'd held and requested I re-do my resume to reflect what I had "really" been doing. I had a viable background and was not just a displaced homemaker! I learned that change is also an opportunity to grow and discover new abilities. She hired me and mentored me for the next three years seeing potential in me I didn't give myself credit for. I will always be indebted to her for raising the bar and making me stretch. I went from wondering who the heck would hire me after so many years out of the workplace to knowing I was smart and 'promotable' and an asset. I learned to place a value on my life experience.

I was side-tracked with back problems in my thirties. The change from health to non-health is a blow on many levels. Surgery was not on my agenda...my kids were six, nine and twelve years of age and I was too busy carpooling them in all directions, being the den mother and team mother, PTA, helping out at their school, community volunteering, working with my sister at her store...but, when you stop functioning, there is no choice. Our loving neighbors and friends took care of my family and me, bringing food and driving my kids to sports and activities, stopping by to say hello and leaving their favorite books for me to read. I learned to just say thank you and not try to do everything myself.

Finding out so many people cared was a humbling experience. I've always been the one taking care of others and it was very difficult for me to accept so much help. Frank and my sister Cathy did a lot, but Frank worked an hour from home and Cathy ran her own business. It's ironic because I never hesitate to give help to others, but was so resistant to be on the taking end. I learned some things can't be paid back in kind and, in time, to offer my hand of friendship to others in need. Over the years I have been able to repay the kindness shown to me many times over and it always comes back ten fold. I'm still pretty independent, but now willing to ask for and accept help when I need it and not see it as a sign of weakness. **Don't you love this line from a Beatles song...*"I get by with a little help from my friends"*?** It is so true. I was always able to give but I have learned to accept the love.

I finished college at age forty-six. It was a life goal and an important accomplishment for me. When we got married I had ninety three credits but between the wedding and overtime at work I skipped a semester and didn't go back. When the kids were older and we were living outside Denver I enrolled at Metro State taking a Parent Education minor and Psychology major. My first class was an entry level Parent Education class. I had taken many local workshops and read many parent education books and articles and somehow I believed, after the trials and tribulations of being a mother it would be a piece of cake!

It was not as I expected. The class had some undergraduates but also students with advanced degrees who were employed in the field and working on certification in Parent Education, a new program at that time. I felt I was in over my head, stupid and inadequate. The others seemed so polished and professional and here I was, just a mom, in my jeans. I knew I was smart enough, but my old shyness and insecurities returned in the classroom. My thought pattern went something like...you have nothing to offer this class...what made you think this was something you can do? Yada, Yada, Yada. The first test was a killer and I was sick as a dog. I guess my subconscious felt if I was sick at least I had an excuse to not do well. I surprised myself! Sneezing, coughing and unable to breathe...I got an A. I kept at it. A couple of semesters later I took psychological statistics and aced that one too; in fact I got an A in almost all my classes. I attended classes until we moved out of state and it was put again on hold.

I finished up several years later after my resume was rejected because I didn't have a college degree. I was well qualified for that job and the snub made me mad. Forget the job, back to school I went. Graduated Summa Cum Laude and proud as a peacock! I'm not sure I was a whole lot smarter after I got that piece of paper, but I was a whole lot more confident in my abilities. I learned that the change to college graduate, so long on the back burner, made a big difference in how I felt about myself.

1993 was a year where change brought me to my knees. Just as I was finishing my degree Frank was on the move again. He was offered his dream job three thousand miles away in New York. He had started with his company in the warehouse as a nineteen year old kid and was going back at age fifty in charge of the whole district, occupying the corner office overlooking the 59th Street Bridge. I knew he couldn't and wouldn't pass it up, but I also didn't think it was the right thing for the rest of the family. I argued to stay in California. We would be taking home base away from Frankie and David who were living nearby, Frankie in college and Dave a couple of years out of high school and on his own. We had moved twice in less than six years. I was angry and disappointed that Frank would even consider moving again and especially so far away. Brian, our youngest had already been to two high schools and found his niche in a magnet program for performing arts. He certainly didn't want to move. I was finishing up my college classes, feeling very confident and with contacts in the area felt I could get a challenging job. Seemed to me it was my turn to shine.

I was wondering how we got on such different wavelengths. I tried to rationalize moving again and put a positive spin on it, but it was hard to do. Yes, men are from Mars and women from Venus! My dear husband was telling us he loved us by providing for us. I felt he was being insensitive to how we felt emotionally and our family was being jerked around. Parents don't move away from the kids. That is backwards... when the kids are ready, they move away from the parents. We were both right. My mother had just passed away...Dad was recovering from brain surgery...moving three thousand miles from Frankie and Dave and uprooting Brian...was too much change for me. Honey, I love you and I don't want a divorce...but I'm not going.

There came a time when the risk to remain tight in the bud was more painful than the risk it took to blossom.
Anais Nin

Well, we did go. Brian and I. Frank moved to New York in February and we had a lot of time to think things over until school was out. We made lists of why we should move and why we should stay. New York had a spring blizzard and we put "snow" on the stay list. Actually weather was way down on that list and being with Dad was always at the top of the "go" list. When push came to shove, "go" outweighed "stay."

Change is like that though...deep down we probably knew all along we were going. I have learned that there are cycles you go through just like grief and it was the right thing to do. Frankie and David encouraged us to go and did fine (well, most of the time, and it offered them their own opportunities for challenge and change) and Brian and I did very well too. Brian tested out of high school and went directly to a junior college with a performing arts program and continued on to graduate from Tisch School for the Arts at New York University; a feather in his cap. I started part time in a financial planning office, and ended up with the most challenging job of my career. We made great new friends and reconnected with family and old friends. Our lives were totally bonkers, working stressful jobs, traveling, and yet it was exactly where we were supposed to be; closer to my father in his final years and challenging ourselves as we approached retirement.

We purchased our retirement home on a whim. We saw a house we liked while visiting California. Time with our older sons was less and less, due to distance and all our work schedules and we wanted to be closer to them. We were "thinking" about retirement, but no decisions had been made as to where or indeed when. The day we were browsing for houses was a perfect spring day, sunny and warm, flowers everywhere, beautiful hills and abounding birds and butterflies. New York was experiencing a wintry mix of sleet and snow. Somehow we short-circuited and decided...Let's go for it! An hour later we made a bid and an hour after that it was ours.

What were we thinking? Women spend more time than that at the hairdresser! Flying back to New York we made our to-do list...quit jobs, sell house, line up movers...MOVE to California! It was exciting, but it wasn't that easy!

Three months later I moved to California. Frank's plan to stay in New York and work until the end of the year seemed fine at the time, but when he left and flew back to New York I crashed. I was alone without a couch to sit on or shades on the windows and a couple of hundred boxes piled everywhere, knowing no one, and my car was still in transit. Looking back I had a meltdown: everything that had been my identity was stripped away. I hadn't touched base with "me" for quite some time and needed to figure out who I was at this mid-life retirement stage of my life.

In our six years in New York both my parents had died and all the kids had become independent. Frank and I both had demanding jobs. I was working long stressful hours and also traveling and entertaining for business with Frank. Every moment was filled and I mean that literally... the candle was burning at both ends. I immersed myself in my job, and looking back I see there were a lot of stressful events I just didn't want to deal with; it was easier to stay busy to the point of exhaustion.

My identity was tied up in the sum of my husband, my kids, my job, my house, my friends and family. But now those anchors were absent, as were my doctor and dentist and the all the familiar faces in the community. It was just "me" starting over and I felt naked without all my familiar surroundings. I wasn't sure who I was with all my roles removed. Everything seemed disconcerting and overwhelming to someone who knew she was confident, in charge and could do it all. I learned that even the positive changes of retirement and moving to a place *of my choice* was stressful.

Besides the emotional drain of the move, I faced the sheer physical challenge of opening and placing the contents of several hundred boxes in a nine-room house, then breaking down the boxes and getting them to the garage. At fifty-three years old and out of shape, my arms and my back ached under the weight of the cardboard and abundant packing materials. Slowly the house began to shape up and I did too.

Frank didn't join me for a year! It was a demanding year, but also a year of great opportunity for introspection and getting to know myself again. I knew intuitively it would all work out. I'd been through it many times before and though it was unsettling at first, the results were predictable. Positive action and taking control got me going. I met neighbors and joined a walking group and book club. I reveled in having Frankie and Dave just a couple of hours away and seeing them once a month instead of twice a year. Girlfriends took advantage of my "bachelorette" status and visited during the year and we shopped and laughed and did girl stuff. I bought furniture, hung pictures, had the yard landscaped and made new friends. I traveled and Frank and Brian came "home" when they could. I found I enjoyed this time of new freedom and adventure. I learned I was OK spending time with myself and I am still who I was...strong, resilient, and challenging and reinventing myself one more time.

Promise me you'll always remember: You're braver than you believe, and stronger than you seem, and smarter than you think.

Christopher Robin to Pooh (AA Milne)

Folks, life happens and change is a fact of life. Some change is invited and some is imposed, but either way, change keeps our lives colorful and interesting and keeps us active and engaged and on our toes. I have learned the trick is to go with change, not resist it. Yogi Berra said it best: "When you see a fork in the road, take it!"

The road might be bumpy, but give yourself credit for being brave and strong and smart! Remind yourself of all the challenges you have handled so well in the past and all the opportunities that keep life so intriguing! Go with the flow and persevere. Keep a positive attitude because it is our attitude and how we deal with life's ups and downs that allow us to grow and mature and really experience life's blessings

My favorite t-shirt says, "Life is Good." I believe every day is a gift offering new opportunities and adventures. Notice the shirt does not say, "Life is Easy"…but even when things aren't going well, life is still good. Go ahead. Enjoy the ride. Change and challenge are good. Attitude is key. That's my story and I'm sticking to it!

***

Dedication

One year later…life has changed again. There are two new branches on our family tree…tiny but strong, growing like weeds and spreading sunshine to all. As a grandma I enjoy"instant wisdom" and can pull baby photos out in a flash…I am brushing up on nursery rhymes, shopping in stores I barely noticed before and breaking into a smile whenever I think of them. What a blessing and a joy to have these beautiful children in our lives. This chapter is dedicated to Leo and Carlie. May your lives abound in love, laughter and opportunity and may you always…"Bloom where you are planted."

CHAPTER FIFTEEN
SHE'S MY SISTER
Jerusha Anne Blackmer

I wake up and feel the water running between my legs. I look at the clock. It's five-thirty in the morning. I know what's going on, but I don't want to believe it. I run to the bathroom and realize that my water broke. It's time, I guess, but it's two weeks early—or so I think, at the time—I will come to learn, in the next twenty-four hours, that it's actually a month early. I tell my husband to start calling work because he's going to have to drive me to the hospital. I call my doctor. Her answering service never calls me back. I take a shower to clean up and calm down and then call again, an hour and a half later. They say that I had the wrong number and I should already be at the hospital. I'm a little concerned because I haven't had any contractions yet. So, we start the hour long journey from our small house in the woods and get stopped in morning, rush-hour traffic—still, no contractions. We get to the hospital and find the last bed in the delivery ward, that day. They hook me up to the monitors and drips and still no contractions. I rest for a while and still no contractions. They start the Pitocin drip and finally there are contractions, but they are not what nature intended and they hurt! Still, I'm not dilating or effacing well and they up the dosage. The contractions get worse and worse. They take me off of the Pitocin from time to time to see if my body will take over and start making its own contractions. It doesn't—ever. They keep checking my blood pressure (I'm totally pre-eclampsic and have been for weeks). They are constantly threatening to put me on blood pressure medication unless I can calm down. Yet, they up the Pitocin dose every hour because nothing is happening. We're on the clock. They have told us that if this baby isn't born within twenty-four hours they will have to cut me open. After the tenth hour I become crazy. Not just "ha, ha, look at how messed up I am" crazy—no, I mean really crazy from the pain, frustration and fear. I start sobbing uncontrollably. I finally ask for pain medication somewhere around hour twelve. My blood pressure is sky high. I'm exhausted because of the high blood pressure. They can't find a vein and have punctured both of my pudgy arms about twenty times to start another drip. It's another while before the medication can be fed into the tube that they shoved into my spinal cord. Then, finally, it takes effect.

I feel almost nothing and I rest, in the dark, while my husband sleeps beside me. I rest so I can be ready for when they cut me open in a few hours. Then, just as I'm nodding off, the lights in the hospital start flashing and the sirens start to wail. I see people running in the corridor, outside. I shake my husband awake and ask him to find out what's going on. He comes back with the news that the hospital is on fire. They have told him not to worry, however, because our section isn't burning—*lovely*. I feel something when he comes back to sleep again. It's a feeling of pressure on my pelvis. It feels as though someone is trying to push a sack of potatoes into my pelvic bone. I wait for a while—hoping...then, after an hour, I press my call button. It's awhile before a nurse answers; probably because the fire alarm is still going off. She's a little gal who snaps on white gloves and feels around inside me like everyone else that day. Yep. It's true. The baby's head is in my pelvis. I'm all of a sudden fully effaced and dilated. She's coming down. Now, the little gal goes running out to call the doctor. She snaps on the light and starts busying herself with getting the room ready. It's time. She calls in the other nurse. She teaches me how to push. I do exactly what she tells me to for about ten minutes. Yep, there's another gloved hand groping around inside me, as usual today (Isn't it amazing what you get used to in a twenty-four hour period?). The nurse tells me to stop. Well, I'm sorry lady—I can't. It's time. She calls the doctor again. I hear her on the phone saying that she better get here in another five minutes because I'm having a baby. I'm still not sure how she got there in time. Really, she didn't. I was already starting to tear—*lovely*. I could feel my skin ripping apart as the head came out. Then, all of a sudden, Anne was there.

She was there, in the room with my husband and I. She never cried. She just stared and stared at us. I got to hold her on my chest for awhile. I remember saying, "Oh good! It's so nice to finally meet you!" I remember looking into her eyes while she looked up at me. That was such a powerful feeling—to gaze into the brand new eyes of your first born child that you had waited seven years for. But then, they had to take her away. I was bleeding—not just that usual bleeding afterward. I wouldn't stop bleeding. They started anticoagulation drip after drip. They gave me suppositories, they gave me pills—I think. I hadn't slept in over a day and a half. I was exhausted and crazy. I could hear what sounded like buckets of my own blood gushing out of me as they pressed on my abdomen. The nurses and the doctor would not let me eat. I begged for ice chips and they said no. I couldn't eat because I couldn't stop bleeding and they were going to have to wheel me in and cut me open to stop the bleeding. I finally opened my eyes and gave my husband that meaningful look. His face was ashen. His eyes were huge. He locked in on my gaze and he understood. He had watched it all.

I was starting to hallucinate. I could see waves of water floating everywhere. It reminded me of the hallucinations I had before seizures. I knew I wasn't doing well. All I was trying to do now was stay awake—because if I was awake, I knew I had to be alive. I asked Matt, my husband, to wheel Anne over to me so I could look at her because the nurses and doctors were not letting me hold her. I asked him to take a picture of the two of us because I wanted her to at least have one picture of her mommy. So she could see that I was with her for a little while. I pulled the oxygen mask off of my face and leaned in. I was sad that I wasn't going to get to see my little daughter grow up. I made Matt promise to guard her and take good care of her in case I didn't make it. Then, they wheeled her out of the room to go and get her first bath. One of the young, little nurses leaned in and whispered that I needed to rest now. I felt as though Anne was safe. I finally closed my eyes and passed out. I don't remember if I dreamed. I do remember thinking about my mother. I missed her so much. I wondered if she felt what I felt during childbirth. I wished I could talk to her again—even to see her once more. I wished she could meet Anne. I wished Anne could meet her grandma. I missed my mommy. Those were my thoughts as I drifted into unconsciousness.

Nineteen months later, I look at my little daughter toddling around the house and I cannot wrap my mind around how far I've already come in this lifetime. Some days I think I'm just a nobody, without a story to tell, but today, I remember—I remember it all. It has come flooding back into my brain. The main story of my life comes flowing in and with it come the little, incidental memories like a wash of water brings leaves to a storm drain.

Choosing to stay at home and raise my daughter, in my thirties, has changed my life. It has changed everything about me. It has also afforded me the chance to stop and smell many roses and reflect on what has happened to me. That's when I realized that I *am* somebody, with a story to tell.

When Anne was born, I wasn't sure I was going to survive. However, I *was* sure I wasn't going to get pregnant again. Being pregnant and giving birth was far too difficult for my old, war-torn body. I'm pretty sure it's not going to be able to go through all that again. Some of my friends talked about how they sneezed and out popped their child, but I'm obviously not one of those women. Yet, when I see Anne cry and cry when her little friends have to go home after a day of play, I feel like we are all missing a part of our little family. Anne needs a sibling and I know how important siblings are. I had many when I was growing up and I miss them. I haven't seen many of them for years and I have no idea where they are. I want my daughter to know the love of a brother or sister, just as I did. My brothers and sisters changed my life, my heart and my mind. I wish I could see them again. Maybe someday I will get to see most of them. Yet, I know I will never get to see Erika again.

I remember waiting for what seemed to be an excruciatingly long time for a little girl. It had only been a few hours since my parents left. Yet, it seemed like an eternity. I sat there on the couch, with the babysitter, waiting for my little sister to arrive. I already knew her name—it was Erika. My parents showed me a videotape of her, in the hospital, and tried to explain it all to me. Now, tonight was the night that she got to come home. I couldn't wait to meet her. I got all of my dolls and toys out so that we could play when she got there. My mom warned me that she would probably be too tired to play with me when she showed up, but I wanted to have all my toys ready for her, just in case. I finally could wait no longer and fell asleep. When I heard the garage door go up I raced down the stairs to meet my new little sister.

As she rounded the corner from the garage I could see her crutches first. Then, I saw her face. She smiled a big smile at me. I think she was very happy to be out of the hospital. Then, I saw her leg—or where her leg used to be. It was hard not to stare at it or rather, the absence of it. It's just human nature to want to learn about something that we don't understand. We learn through our senses and sight is a perfect way to do that. So, I couldn't help myself. I stared. I stared long and hard at where Ericka's leg used to be. I stared, that is, until she started to talk to me.

She learned a little English when she was in the hospital, in Connecticut. I remember her saying "Hi!" in this big, perky voice of hers, filled with a thick, Honduran accent. Looking back on it now, she only had stuffed animals to play with at the hospital and I bet she was so excited to see another little girl! I remember being so excited to see her, as well, because I didn't have a little sister. I only had little brothers, thus far. I couldn't wait to start playing with Erika. I wanted to take her upstairs to see the playroom. So, not knowing a lot of Spanish, I beckoned her to come up the stairs with me. She set her crutches down and proceeded to pull herself up the stairs with her arms and push off of every step with her one leg. It took a while but she made it to the playroom, crawling across the floor once she got to the top of the stairs. Once there I put the toys on the floor so she could play with them. I always sat on the floor anyway. To my surprise, she knew exactly what to do with Barbie dolls. She wanted to see everything I had and I got it all out. It was so fun! I realized that Erika was just a little younger than me. This was going to work out well! We played and communicated in broken English until my mom told us it was time to go to bed. I couldn't wait to get up the next morning.

That night, as I fell asleep, I thought of what my mom and dad had been preparing me for. As any young girl, I hadn't been completely paying attention to what they were telling me about Erika, before she came. Yet, now that I saw her, I remembered a lot of her story. They told me about what happened:

Erika's mother worked at a bank in Honduras. She took Erika with her to work, one day, and Erika wanted to cross the street to get a cookie (What kid wouldn't?). She crossed the street as she had done so many times, in the past. However, this time it was different. A large semi-tractor trailer came barreling along and hit her. Her leg was ripped from her body and thrown across the street. The rest of her landed in a ditch. The truck never stopped. Many witnesses never stopped. One cab driver finally pulled over and placed most of Erika in the back of his cab. He radioed for an ambulance and waited with her for help to arrive. Help never arrived. So, hours later, afraid that Erika would die in the back of his cab, he drove her to the nearest hospital. Erika's mother found out what happened to her. She came to visit her. She brought with her pamphlets from the local mortuary. She asked Erika which coffin she would like to be buried in. "She wasn't being mean, she was just being honest," my mom told me. Everyone thought that Erika would die. They gave her blood transfusions, but that was all they could do for her. Then, a doctor from the United States heard about Erika and tried to find a way to help her. He chartered a helicopter and brought her to the United States for surgery. He wanted to save her life. Surgery after surgery later, Erika became part of *Healing the Children*. It was a grass-roots organization that worked to find foster families, doctors, hospitals and airlines to donate their time and efforts to children that lived in "third-world" countries, who needed surgery and medical attention that only the United States could give them. So, after a few surgeries, Erika was healthy enough to take a break and come to stay with us. As a child, I never understood the trauma Erika went through before I met her, that day. As an adult, I still cannot understand fully what it must have been like for her. Yet, I realize that because of my lack of understanding, I treated her like any other little girl. Maybe it was the innocence of childhood or maybe it was something greater. Either way, I was just glad to have a sister for as long as I was allowed to keep her. My mother kept reminding me that she wasn't going to be able to stay with us forever. I knew that. I just didn't want to think about the day we would have to let her go.

I'll never forget the day we had to let my foster brother go. His name was Maykool. I fell in love with him the minute I laid eyes on him. He was just a few months old when *Healing the Children* found enough money to fly him and another baby girl from Guatemala to the United States. Both babies were born with a cleft palette and a hair lip. This is a common birth defect in countries where the drinking water is not as sanitized as our water is. A cleft palette was a very serious aliment for Maykool. It meant that there was a hole in the roof of his mouth. So, every time he tried to drink breast milk from his mom he spit it back out his nose. Thus, he became very emaciated, very quickly. He couldn't eat, so without treatment, he was slowly starving to death. Maykool's mom and dad knew what was going to happen to their baby. They did what they could to save him. They had great faith and gave their starving, little baby to complete strangers who flew him to another country. I could never imagine how horrible they must have felt when they let go of him. At least I did not understand it until we had to give him back.

My father still has a picture of my mother, feeding Maykool, the night he came to us. He was completely emaciated and had a large, distended belly from lack of nourishment. My mom saw his condition and she kept shaking him awake, all night and feeding him a bottle with a special nipple that looked like a long piece of spaghetti. She would shove this little bottle down his throat, past his cleft palette and force him to drink. He would start to pass out again, after a bit of feeding, and she would shake him and herself awake and start again. She stayed awake with him all night. When we woke the next morning, Nick and I went in to peek at our new baby brother. My mother had finally allowed him to sleep and we watched him dream.

A few days later we found out that the little baby girl who was with him, on the plane, died that night. Yet, Maykool found the strength to survive. He grew and grew and finally the day came to take him to the hospital for a surgery to correct his cleft palette and pull his lip back over to the other side of his mouth. My mom stayed with him at the hospital. When Nick and I finally got to visit him after the surgery, he was crying and trying to rip out the stitches on his face. So, the nurses had to tape tongue depressors around his elbows so he couldn't bend his arms. He just cried and cried. I felt so bad for him. We took him home and tried to make him as comfortable as we could. Nick and I played and played with him day in and day out. Just about the time he started pulling himself up, we got the news that it was time to send him home. There was nothing more we could do for him until his teeth grew in. So, we needed to send him home, well and healthy. It was time for him to see his parents again.

I'll never forget the day we went to the airport with him. I was crying and crying. Nick was crying. Dad was crying. Mom was trying to hold it together but she wasn't doing a very good job of it. Finally, we were at the gate and it was time for us to give our sweet, little brother to the young gal that volunteered to travel with him to Guatemala. As the young woman took him from my mother's arms she collapsed on the floor and my dad had to hold her arm. She was sobbing. Years later, all I remember her saying, over and over again was, "He's *my* baby. They're taking *my* baby. He's *my* baby..." In the car she choked back enough tears and turned to my father, to say, "No more babies. I can't do this again."

After that, we only took in older children. There was Choo Nu, Mejung, Autuwelpa and Carolina. Yet, there were no more babies. That's how I got my sister, Erika.

After a few days of getting to know one another and playing, as all children do, it was time to start Erika's continuing treatment. She would never be completely well and there was always much to do. My mom would give Erika a water and medicinal enema every day to wash out what was left of her intestines. Then she would help Erika change out her colostomy bag (what Erika had to defecate into because she lacked a large portion of her colon). She would cleanse the wounds around her backside and where the doctors needed to take grafts of skin from her thighs to close up the wounds where her leg used to be. My mom told me honestly, one day, after they needed my help in the bathroom, that Erika was never going to be able to have children because those parts of her body had been ripped away, as well. I didn't understand the complexity of things, being so young, so I asked why the doctors couldn't help her with that. I'm not sure if I ever got a straight answer from my mom but she did tell me that maybe some day, when she was older, they could perform another surgery on Erika so that she could enjoy having a husband. I think I figured out the rest, on my own. It made me sad to think that Erika would never be able to have children. I think she was sad about it, too. Yet, when you are a little girl, you get over that stuff fairly quickly. What else could she do?

Soon enough it was time to go back to the hospital for a checkup. My mom pulled me aside, the night before, where Erika couldn't hear us. She whispered that it was going to be rough at the checkup, the next day, and that Nick (my little brother) and I might hear Erika crying because they were going to have to do something to her that would hurt her. As we made our way to the hospital, I braced myself, yet again. Even with my mom's words ringing in my ears, I didn't know how bad it was going to be. It was very upsetting. Nick and I couldn't get away from her screams of pain. My mom told me that they gave Erika some pain medication but I guess it wasn't enough. Erika had the bottom part of her pelvic bone sticking out of her skin on the side where her leg was missing. For whatever reason, they couldn't get enough skin grafts off of her thighs to cover the entire bone. Until they sent that poor, little girl back into surgery, she had to keep a little, sticky patch of foam on the protruding part of the bone, so that she wouldn't get infected.

Well, that little, sticky patch of foam had to be removed and replaced because it was getting old and dirty. Just imagine how it would feel if someone gave you a little pain medication and then proceeded to peel a thick sticker off of your innards and pelvis. Imagine how you would scream as it was happening. I will never forget Erika's screams that day. I will never forget them for as long as I live. I looked over at Nick as we stood, alone, in that hallway and I had to look away because he was crying and I was trying so hard not to cry, myself. Mom made us promise to not leave the hallway so we just had to stand there and listen to her scream.

Finally, after what seemed like hours, Erika and my mom emerged from that room, both of them with tear-stained faces. Erika was still crying and hyperventilating. All I wanted to do was hug her, but she pushed me away. I understood. We drove home in silence that day. It was a long drive home. Some days, I would forget how much Erika had gone through already, but that day, I did not.

Life went on, as usual in the coming weeks. Erika and I ran errands, played, fought and made-up, like sisters. Yet, sometimes, it's those mundane days that can truly shape a person. It's the simple tasks and conversations that can have the biggest impact on one's thoughts. So, there we were, waiting for our friends to get out of the public school, down the street. For some reason, my brother, Erika and I did not have school that day, due to the fact that we went to a private school, but our friends did and we were there to pick them up. As I waited for them, I remembered how one of these friends stared at Erika the first time she met her. Just like every other kid we encountered at the grocery store or the library. She, just like everyone else, stared at Erika or should I say that she stared at the lack of her leg. Lots of times I just wanted to yell at kids and say, "Yes! She's missing a leg. It's no big deal! Get over it!" But, mostly I just ignored everyone who was staring. So did Erika. What else could we do? We were the folks who had to "get used to it"—so we did.

The school bell rang and a flood of screaming kids started running to the busses. Then, two disheveled young boys stopped. I saw them start to point at Erika and I braced myself. I knew what was coming (at least I thought I did). They started to talk louder, very purposefully. I could hear what they were saying now.

"Look at that girl. Ewww! Gross! She doesn't have a leg. That's disgusting! Yuck! Eww! Don't go near her!"

They wouldn't stop. I just stood there—frozen. I couldn't believe that children could be so mean. I was blown away. When I finally shook myself and looked around, I caught sight of Erika, behind me. She was working so hard not to cry. She was so brave. She was trying to look around like she didn't hear those boys and it made me so angry. I looked at her and I began to cry, too. I believe I lost a little faith in our humanity that day. Couldn't those boys see how much she must have gone through already? Couldn't they see that it was no big deal and it wasn't gross that she was missing her leg? Couldn't they see that she was my foster sister and I loved her? I turned back around to yell at them, but they ran off to catch their bus.

A woman (possibly a teacher or mother) who was standing next to us turned to me and asked who Erika was. "She's my sister," I said. The woman laughed. "No, really—who is she? She doesn't look like you or your brother." I told her about *Healing the Children* and how Erika came to stay with us. "Oh!" she said, "So she's your *foster* sister."

It was at that moment that I remember having the first epiphany of my life. All of the emotions I'd had in the past few months came flooding back. I remembered Maykool leaving us at the airport and Erika and I playing all day. I remembered what those boys said and how much it hurt me and I turned to this woman, with great defiance blazing in my eyes, and my back arched as much as it would and I said, "*No*, she's my sister!" I have not uttered many prouder words in my lifetime. She *was* my sister and I loved her very much and I wanted everyone to know.

Well, this woman (whoever she was) kept trying to convince me that I was wrong and kept trying to explain to me what a foster sister was— like I was stupid or something. Finally, my friends arrived and my mom motioned for us to get in the car. I was relieved to get away from this woman, yet elated at how I finally realized that I was tired of explaining my life to others and was ready, with my new answer, whenever anyone asked me about my siblings. "Erika is my *sister*." I kept repeating it over and over in my head. I realized that I didn't care how long I got to keep her with me. She will always be my sister.

I didn't get to spend as much time with Erika as I wanted to. She lived with us for only a short time. During that time my father lost his job and we had to move to Colorado. It was best for Erika to stay in Connecticut and keep receiving treatment from the doctors and nurses who knew her and knew of her conditions. It was a difficult decision for all of us but we had to leave and she had to stay. We found another, loving couple who did not have children of their own, yet. They were willing to take care of Erika while she stayed in Connecticut and received more treatment. I remember the day we said goodbye. I was very upset and crying. I remember how Erika looked so stoic. How she just stood there and looked at the ground. She had already moved on, I thought. I realize now, as an adult, how hard it must have been for her to make so many new relationships with people only to have to leave them abruptly, every few months. She had to leave her mother and her home town, the doctors and nurses at the hospitals and now, our family, as well. I kept begging my parents to let her stay, but there was no way that she could. All I could do was hug her. I gave her our pet goldfish and told her to take care of them for us. We left that day and my mother told us we would probably see Erika again and not to worry. She would grow up and we could always write to her and keep in contact, somehow.

It started out that way. Just as children move, they move on, as well. I wrote letters to Erika and Mom spoke to her new foster family on the phone, from time to time. We tried to keep in touch. After a while, the letters and phone calls grew sparse. Then, one day, we got a call from them. They told us Erika had been diagnosed with a rare, blood disorder. They called it H.I.V...I didn't know much about it at the time. Mom had to explain it to me. She said that there was nothing that anyone could do for Erika anymore. They were sending her home, to Honduras, to die. To this day, I will never understand those decisions that were made. As a child I could not understand why the doctors could fix Erika when she was bleeding to death, without a leg, but they couldn't cure this disease. I remember saying, "How can they just let her go?!" I had heard about what happened to children with amputations and physical deformities in the poorer parts of Honduras. That's why *Healing the Children* tried to keep Erika in the United States as long as they could. That's why they tried to get the best prosthetic leg made for her. I didn't want to think about what would happen to Erika when she went home. I was so afraid for her.

I sent letters to Erika at the only address I had for her in Honduras. They were never answered. I may never know what happened to her once she was home. Years later, my grandma, who donated money to *Healing the Children*, every year, sent me a calendar she received from them. There was a note attached, "I think you should look at this." I flipped through the calendar and looked at all of the faces of the children who were being helped. Then, at the end of the calendar, I saw a face I recognized. It was on the page titled, "In Memorandum." There was Erika. "There's my sister," I thought. She was smiling back at me. I knew now, what had happened to her. She was finally at peace. There would be no more pain, no more screaming, no more suffering and no more sadness. My sister was gone.

Yet, life goes on and so it did. In Colorado, my mom began a new chapter of *Healing the Children* where there was none. She enlisted the help of everyone who would listen and she spearheaded the entire Colorado chapter, herself. She went door to door at the hospitals and airlines in town to gather free medical attention, surgeries and flights for many new children. We cared for many other children in the years to come and then my mom was able to do the unthinkable.

Over the years, Mom kept in touch with Maykool's family. She'd written them feverishly and called them every now and again with the aid of our friend Carmen, who could speak fluent Spanish and English. I chose the country of Guatemala for my fourth-grade social studies project and Maykool's father graciously mailed me recipes, pictures, songs and information about their country to help me with my homework. Our families became good friends and we sent one another pictures every year. We saw our baby brother grow to be a toddler, right before our eyes. Somehow, some way, my mom got her little baby back. She fought to get his teeth fixed!

Children who are born with a cleft palette and a hair lip usually have problems with their teeth when they start to come in. Maykool was no exception. His teeth were very crooked when he was just a little boy and my mom could see that in the pictures and letters from his family. He needed dental surgery and he needed help. If he got this help he would be better able to have a normal life, later on. My mom loved Maykool so much. We all did. We did not want him to be ostracized or teased for the rest of his life, due to his appearance. So, Mom was able to find doctors, nurses, hospitals and airfare to get Maykool the help he needed. Then, she was able to get him an extra plane ride to our house in Colorado. We had our little brother back again!

Maykool stayed with us for a few months. It had been a long, three years since we'd seen him. He wasn't a little baby anymore. He was a toddling, little boy who ran around and in his broken English yelled, "Oh! My Shoe!" every time something fell or broke. He would smile and blow us kisses and dance and play. He was the sweetest little boy. I remember at Halloween, I felt that I was too old to go Trick-or-Treating so I stayed home. As a toddler, he did not understand why I didn't get to go, so he kept trying to give me his entire bag of candy. It just made me cry. We were all glad to have him back for a few months. We had all missed him terribly. Yet, once again, we had to say goodbye. Maykool flew back to Guatemala. We never got to see him again. That was tough.

Maykool was our first foster brother and he was one of our last. Not long after he left us again, my mom went back to work as a school teacher, full time and she didn't have as much time to devote to other children. She didn't think it was fair to bring kids here if she didn't have the time to take care of them. She always left the door open to having more, though. She never wanted to say that she was finished.

As I write all of these memories down on paper I look back at who made them possible—my mother. I will never be able to understand where she came up with the strength to do everything that she did. She was not only a wife and mother of her own two children, but she was a foster mother of countless sons and daughters. She was also the head of the Colorado chapter for *Healing the Children* and was known, by many, throughout the world. She did all of this and more on a daily basis. Yet, I knew her as my mom. To me, she was just my mom. She sang to me. She did the chores around the house. She taught us every summer that we were out of school. She did all of those little things and she did a lot of big things, as well. Yet, sometimes it's the amount of little things that add up, over a lifetime to create one, big, powerful life.

I look at that picture of her holding the limp, little, almost lifeless body of Maykool in her arms. His little appendages are just hanging there. She's not looking at the camera. She's looking down at the little baby in her lap. She had just met him at the airport, only a few hours earlier, yet she knew that he was her job. Even though you can't see her face, I know what look is on it. I'd seen it many times before. Her jaw would set and her eyes would squint with that far away look. She was determined to keep this baby alive. If one person could fill another with determination, it was my mother. She was determined to see him live and he did.

Standing only about five foot, one inch tall, my mom packed a mighty punch into a tiny package. She was so strict with us kids. It always made me jealous of the other children I went to school with. I never did see another kid at school who had to follow as many rules as we did. She governed our days including what we ate for breakfast, what we said, what we listened to and what we read. To this day, I never pass through the cereal isle at the grocery store and don't think of her and how many fights we had over Lucky Charms. Yet, as a new mother I have seen the light. I am already stricter with my little toddler than many of my friends. I know now that I owe all of my character (whatever I may have) to my mother. I wonder how I would have turned out if I had eaten Lucky Charms every morning. I will never know. Just recently, my little girl stopped eating her granola for breakfast. I bought her a box of Fruit Loops. She loves them...hmmm.

I guess that it is impossible for me to believe that some girls never grow close to their mothers. I have a hard time believing that because I became so close to mine. Sure, we fought (and fought quite heavily during my tween years). But, we also made up and we did so much together. We enjoyed the same things. We even looked alike. Every dirty old man we came in contact with would always talk about how we looked like sisters. That would make Mom beam from ear to ear. Especially after all that she had been through.

When she went back to work, she became very sick. They didn't know what was wrong. I remember Nick and I having to carry her into the bathroom because she didn't have the strength to get out of bed. After living in her bed for a week, she finally threw up and couldn't muster the strength to even tell my father what happened. It was at that point that my father took her to the hospital. She stayed there for what seemed like an eternity. I couldn't bear to talk to her when she was there. She looked so frail and pale. I had never seen my mother like that before and it scared me. I didn't know what to think. The doctors said that they didn't have any idea what was wrong with her. They put her on the floor with the A.I.D.'s patients. We would hear everyone moaning and dying as we walked to her room. She was shaking and weak. They kept drilling core samples of her skin. My dad made a brief and failed attempt to broach the subject of my mother's possible death with my brother and me. He worried that her end may be near. Finally, the doctors chalked her problems up to an overactive immune system and put her on Prednisone. Then, within days, they sent her home. Aside from the weight gain due to the steroids, she looked as if nothing happened. After a while she said she felt fine. She was a strong woman, mentally and physically. I don't know if everyone could come through such an ordeal. Could I?

I think that after all of that, my mother and I became closer. I realized when I almost lost her, just exactly how important she was to me. She was my mommy and I loved her very much. I think I started to mature, as well. I went from fighting with her over a box of Lucky Charms to finding a constant friendship with her. We began, almost like clockwork, to discuss things in a civilized manner and have adult conversations about so many things. There was finally a peace in our house that had been missing for so many tumultuous years. I truly enjoyed every minute of those few years I got to spend peacefully with her. She promised to slow her life down and concentrate on a few things rather than everything. The doctors didn't know what sparked her overactive immune system but she would come to tell me, years later, that she truly believed it was because of all the stress in her life. So, she focused on us and her new career: teaching. She found so many other children to help when she taught. I think she really loved being out of the house again and back in the workforce. She became good friends with many of the teachers in her school and she began socializing so much more. I hadn't seen her smile like that in a long time. It was so good to see.

Then, *I* got sick. I don't know where I picked it up. It may have been on a doorknob, payphone or drinking fountain, at school. Wherever I picked it up; it tried to kill me. It was an ear infection. I went to our ear, nose and throat specialist, who was a friend of my mother's. She was from South America and my mother got her to help with translation for *Healing the Children*, after striking up a conversation with her, when Nick needed an appointment. The doctor let me know that it was a serious bug. So, I went home with giant horse pills for medication and lay in bed. I got worse—a lot worse, in the next few days. My ear swelled so much that I couldn't eat. It pushed on my jaw so that I couldn't close it. Soon, my jaw became unhinged. My eardrum already popped about two times from what I could tell. (It is horribly painful.) I tried to suck on popsicles for nourishment. I started to throw up the giant, horse pill antibiotics. Things were not going well. I remember not knowing what time of day it was and all of the hours started running together. I hadn't eaten much in days and I couldn't keep the antibiotics down. My face was so swollen and throbbing. I wasn't paying attention to much.

This whole time, my mother stayed home with me. She moved me into her bed and made my dad sleep with my brother. She had a substitute for her students during an entire week. She washed my face, cleaned up my vomit and tried to get me to eat anything at all. Nothing was working. It was Sunday afternoon. I hurt so much. I couldn't keep from hurting. All I could do was ask my mother for a favor. I could barely get the words out because my jaw wouldn't move. So, I asked her, in a whispered voice, if she would hold me in her arms and rock me like she did when I was little. She would always sing to me and hold me in her arms, as she rocked me to sleep. She sang soulful songs—deep songs filled with meaning. As a child, I didn't know what songs they were; I only knew how they made me feel—awash in the deep love of my mother, without a care in the world. All I wanted was to feel that once again. So, she pulled me up and cradled me in her arms. She held me tight and rocked us both back and forth. She sang a song I heard many times in my youth. I would come to know later, that it was a Negro spiritual. A song so filled with power that you could not help but sing it with a powerful voice. My mother was such a wonderful singer. Here she was, not singing in front of an audience, but singing on a bed, holding the tired and pain racked body of her teenage daughter a mere foot from where she lay dying a few years earlier. Her voice cracked at the end of the song. She apologized. I was still in great pain, but I now had a new found peace about me. She left to go downstairs and I drifted deep into thoughts of nothing.

After a while Nick came into the room. I asked him where Mom was. He told me she was downstairs, crying on the phone, to Dad. She was telling him that she was afraid I was going to die and that she couldn't take care of me any more. She came back upstairs a few minutes later and announced to me that I was going to the hospital the next day. Dad would take me there and care for me for the next week. I remember coming out of my stupor long enough to yell, "Don't leave me with him!" I didn't want her to go. I didn't want anyone but my mommy to take care of me. I didn't want to share her with anyone, but her decision was final. I couldn't talk her out of it so I went back to staring at the wall and trying not to think about the pain in my head.

The next morning, as were all of the days that week, was a blur. I remember waking up in the darkness to see my mom curling her hair in the bathroom mirror. Then, as if in a dream, there she was sitting next to me at the edge of the bed. She was dressed in her clothes for school. She was very peaceful and quiet. She told me something comforting and kissed me on the cheek. Then, she was gone. I fell back asleep or maybe I just passed out, I don't know which one it was. When I awoke again, my father was there. He helped me get dressed and he carried me to the car. We headed down the hill to the hospital.

When we got there, it took my father a long time to fill out the paperwork necessary to turn your child over to a hospital. I waited in a wheelchair for it to be over. They then wheeled me up to a room, got me in a bed and started an I.V. drip. They said there was a man to see us. He needed to talk to my father and me right away. He came in with a manila folder in his hand and introduced himself. He was from the coroner's office. My father asked him if something was wrong and he said that my mother had been killed. Someone drove a car into her while she was on her way to the children, at school. I remember someone screaming. Only later did I realize that the sound was coming from my own mouth. With not even enough strength to get into the car that morning, my father had to pin me to the bed. I couldn't stop thrashing back and forth. I couldn't wrap my brain around the fact that I would never get to see my mommy again—that I would never get to hold her hand or smell her hair or see her smile at me. Just like that—she was gone.

Everything that she did for this world, and its children, went with her. For many years after, I would visit her grave only to find little, wooden apples with her name on them, left by her little students that she was driving to on that day. When Maykool's father heard of her death, through the legal system, he hopped on a bus to come and visit us. It just reminded me of all the courage, strength and love that was gone from this world, now that she was gone. Where had all that energy gone? Where could it go? Something—no someone—was terribly missing from all of our lives. And more than all of that—I missed her. Nick has a hard time remembering her. My baby will never get to see how wonderful her grandma was. Just like that—she was gone.

When Anne was born I saw that she looked like her father. Everyone said she looked like her father. She still does. Yet, the day after, in the recovery room, when everyone came to visit us, I got to see my mother again. Someone was holding my little girl, next to me and those beautiful, thick, orange rays of sunshine where highlighting the profile of her little face—and there she was. There was my mother. After all of these years, I finally got to see her again.

It was then that I had the second epiphany of my life: Now, *I'm* the mommy. Waiting all those months and years for her to appear and she finally did. "She's *my* baby," I thought. And just like that—there she was. I turned to my husband, with a puzzled look on my face and said, "It's like we've known her forever, isn't it?" and he agreed. I was one day into motherhood and I couldn't remember life without her. I realized that not only is there a cycle of life, but there is a cycle of love, too. The giant hole in my heart that was carved out by the death of my mother became filled that day, with love for my daughter.

The next few months of new motherhood, with a sickly baby, overwhelmed me greatly. Recovering from childbirth and taking care of a newborn baby, who had to be on oxygen, was almost too difficult for me. I mustered through. I still don't know where I got the strength to do so. Every two and a half hours I would feed her—every day and every night. Many times I would have to feed her twice because she had acid reflux and would throw up her entire feeding. Thus, getting only an hour's sleep in between feedings left me groggy and forgetful. That's why I didn't know what day it was when Nick called me.

He sounded sad. I knew that tone of voice. He never called me so I thought it was unusual. I asked him what was wrong. He reminded me that it was the anniversary of our mother's death. I couldn't believe it. I stopped what I was doing. How could I forget one of the most important and sad days of my life? How could I forget the day my life changed forever? How could I forget?

I looked down at the little face snuggled in my arms. There was a reason I forgot. It was a wonderful reason. Nick asked, "Oh wow, did you forget what day it was?"

"Yes," I told him, "but Nick it's so wonderful! *I'm* the mommy, now!"

I *am* the mommy, now. I do see my little girl sad that she can't play with her friends forever. I see how she needs siblings, but I don't know if I can give them to her. I remember Erika and wonder, every day, what my other brothers and sisters are doing. I wonder where they are. I remember my mom and how full my life was because of her. I want all of that for my daughter, too. Someday—*someday* I will find the strength my mother possessed. I will be ready to help other children, too.

At my mother's funeral the priest spoke a few words about a woman he barely knew. Yet, all of her friends came to tell him about her. So, on that very sad day, he relayed a story I hadn't heard before, but one I will remember forever:

One day a man was walking down the beach. He saw that it was strewn for miles with dying starfish. He then saw a woman who was throwing the starfish back into the water, one by one. He came up to the woman and said, "You know that you can't save them all." To which the woman replied, "Yes, I know. But, that starfish I just threw back is happy that I stopped to help."

What have I learned in this short life of mine?

What have my epiphanies taught me?

I have learned that family is not a last name.

Family is not who you look like.

Family is familiarity.

Family is love.

Family is everything!

It is what you make of it, every day.

May there be peace and love in your family, no matter who they are.

Cherish them always and fill your life with your family;

it could be tomorrow that they are gone.

CHAPTER SIXTEEN
AN EPIPHA-MINI

GRANDMA R.

My husband, ultimate techno-computer geek and practical thinker, had an insight about death that I had never before heard from him. I was comforted by his brilliant flash of truth, coming from such a black and white, no nonsense kind of mind.

My daughter was to be married in July at a lovely national park in the west, in the meadow behind the lodge, with the waterfall in the background. My elderly mother would be the only one in the family who could not attend, having become a nursing home resident and unable to travel. She was crushed to have to miss the wedding of her oldest granddaughter, but she died just three and a half months before the ceremony.

Outside the funeral home I stood with my daughter and my husband as we waited for the others to join us. I said to my daughter, "Well, your grandma's death has actually solved the agonizing problem of not being able to get her to your wedding."

My husband spoke, "You don't understand…this is your grandma's way of *ATTENDING* her granddaughter's wedding."

We all smiled, knowing that realization was absolutely true.

CHAPTER SEVENTEEN
HE SOMETIMES EATS SOUP WITH A FORK
Barbara B. Knowles

WHAT IT IS

It's not the car I drive, the clothes I own,
the watch I wear, the beach house
I share, the daily workout routine, the full time, part time
employment as adjunct college instructor, forty years of teaching in
public, private and international classrooms, the reunion diet, the
hovering blood pressure,
the shaky cholesterol, the a.m., p.m. medications, the mention
of Botox, the life-lined, laugh-lined face...
It's that I'm suddenly 60.
The joints jest; the knees kink;
the hips haunt; the crowns need crowns;
the memory muddles; the ears elude; the eyes edit; the teeth
tarnish;
the weight whines and wanes...Why?
It's that I'm suddenly 60.
It is the 40-year marriage to the Wiesbaden High School prom
date, post college; the 20 years as an Air Force fighter pilot wife;
the 17 major moves, US east to west
and South America, final settlement in Virginia...
It is having two middle-aged married daughters, one in Virginia,
one in Texas; it is giant hugs from 3 tow-headed granddaughters
and one Italian vintage Dallas grandson with
a sister on the way; it is receiving no proof
senior discounts automatically; it is free lunches for portfolio advice,
living wills, tax management, insurance counseling; and everyone
looks older, except the presenter who is boyish; it is the security of
relationships, the freedom to travel...
It is that I am suddenly 60.
It is looking best in black pants with white non-sleeveless shirts,

never wearing a skirt, rarely exposing arthritic knees, removing
earrings only for slumber. . .
It is the laughter of adults and the giggles of "little people," the
echoes of celebrations; it is closing my eyes and bowing my head
and being grateful, ever so grateful. . ..
that I am suddenly 60.

HE SOMETIMES EATS SOUP WITH A FORK

His death is much on my mind these days. Biological father,
daughter touching each other's lives after years of separation
caused by wartime romance, marriage, and divorce, making a
past impossible and the present a frustrating, fabulous reality. All
penetrating my life at suddenly sixty.

William Paul Brown, rising 87 year old bachelor,
former Smith-Barney broker,
current resident of Williamsburg Landing, Woodhaven Hall,
assisted living 1999-2002, Memory Enhanced Unit 2002-2005,
Skilled Long Term Care Unit, 2005-present,
married 4 years, 1942-1946,
one offspring, 2 granddaughters,
Great-grandfather of 5

My father came from Detroit to Virginia in December, 1999,
never left and won't. He had a slight stroke at the Williamsburg
Community Hospital, followed by a diagnosis of Alzheimers.
My family owns those words; he never heard them. Stories
from Detroit pals about missed engagements, lost in familiar
neighborhoods, cancelled checks, unpaid bills, penalty payments,
periods of daydreaming, unbalanced market orders, sketchy phone
conversations were warnings of dementia. He retired at 78, but
continued to arrive at the Smith-Barney downtown Detroit office
by lunchtime each day. The phone would ring in my classroom in
Virginia.
Barb, he's here.
Is he dressed, clean, shaved, coherent?
Yes.
What do you want me to do?

Weeks into this routine I attended a conference in Detroit and
spent a Thanksgiving week with Dad.
You're retired. Why do you keep going to the office, Dad?
I'm afraid not to.

I didn't put that answer and beginning dementia together. I
realize now that in that answer was real sadness and fear. In clear,
cognitive moments, fleeting reality hit him. I began to realize
slowly that our lives were changing. I began to call frequently
and he would relate a former routine of Country Club golf with
pals, dinner with friends at the Athletic Club, board meetings,
grocery shopping and Sunday mass. He was unable to give specific
information about these familiar routines, except 12:00 noon mass
at St. Mary's, located two blocks from his apartment. Truthfully, I
longed for someone else to handle this parent agenda.

Older daughter Katherine and I planned a surprise 80th birthday
party, October 23, 1999, in a favorite Grosse Pointe restaurant
with 30-50 guests. As I reflect on this event, I realize our success
of surprising, planning, inviting, celebrating was overwhelming to
him. He was a guest of honor among familiar names and faces, but
his demeanor was that of a stranger. This vagueness was confirmed
on December 25, 1999 in Williamsburg, when my family presented
him with a photo album; he could not recall the circumstances, the
event or put names to the guests. Five days later the stroke and the
diagnosis, all placing him in the state of Virginia.

At first we were in the denial, defensive phase of this disease.
This comes in the following forms: *I've been here all day and the
phone doesn't ring busy; the electricity was off this afternoon and
the remote control hasn't worked for days, so the phone doesn't
ring....I have never been late....you just show up.....I would
have brushed my teeth, but no one told me I was going to the
dentist; let's stop at a mint store....I shower and shave every day;
you never give me time...I don't tip the barber in Williamsburg,
but I tip nicely in Detroit....Don't buy a box of cigars; I'll have
to pack them...*
Bering Imperials, remember?....Never grow old and cranky...
Where are we going and can you help me find my car?

We began to live in Polaroid moments. His former life recast. He
was like the pressed prom corsage falling from my childhood diary,

a childhood he never witnessed and a teen-ager he didn't raise, making flashback impossible. He became a character in a novel whose plot isn't his and I, the editor, with so few notes.

In the beginning our outings were frequent. We would run errands, visit the library, stroll around the college, eat on our deck, lunch in town, make cigar runs; he witnessed yard mulching, car washing, tree pruning, deck sealing, all chores he had missed in his privileged upbringing and adult life style. He was an eager, pleasant companion. Someone from my family visited every day. He was quite comfortable and settled in an elegant, upscale assisted living facility, 10 minutes from my home.

He fancied himself on spring vacation in Florida, a thirty-five year routine. He would look for his rental car in the Landing parking lot and ask staff for directions to the ocean. He would mention daily his returning to "1300 Lafayette East," his downtown Detroit apartment, 1200 square feet frozen by his departure.

In June, 2000, my husband and I rented a van, drove to The Motor City, home of the Tigers and cleaned out apartment 2012 in the southwest corner, windowed on renewing downtown Detroit, the Detroit River and Renaissance Center. He witnessed his car being stolen on two occasions from this 20-story view. It was a household exodus from family strangers, his voice hovering, "when I return to 1300" and my rushing regret, locked guilt, unsettled sadness; his sanctuary, empty now, secretly sold. In the attic of my mind I have memories of musty cigar smoke, bags of cookies, frozen Stouffer's meals, petrified greenery, TV's echoing sports commentary, a rotary dial phone with a one foot cord, burned out light bulbs in tall, dated lamps above angled checked sofas and a fatigued Henredon chair with thread-bare ottoman. We removed clothing, two paintings, his golf clubs, silver trophies, bookshelves and the retirement gift clock. We integrated these items in his two room assisted living apartment and he wanted to know what he owed us, not realizing these had belonged to him for 36 years. His independent life over.

I try not to make his days identical. I am reminded of Toni Morrison: *All water has perfect memory and is forever trying to get back to where it was. Writers are like that: remembering where we were, what valley we ran through, what the banks were like, the light that was there and the route back to our original place. It is emotional memory—what the nerves and the skin remember as well as how it appeared. And the rush of imagination is our "flooding."* I am thinking not if the dam bursts and the fiords flood and the rushing pollutes memory and the mind stream is barren of thought.

"If he can't give words to thinking, is it thought?" I asked the neurologist. On the examining table he drew a map of the brain and described the cell death and the ailing neurons with disconnecting Schema. "Prognosis is poor," he repeated, "with fleeting moments of lucidity." He ordered another brain scan; his nurse asked, "For who?" My father corrected, "For whom?" As a professional, educator daughter I swell with pride and treasure a fleeting moment of lucidity.

My father informs me that he is not ready for "a major life change." The adjunct, college instructor only daughter reminds him that these changes often "come unannounced."

"I'll just come home with you." A tangled knot in my innards. *"Live together...you're 80, I'm 60; we've rarely spent seven consecutive days in the same house. You want to start now???"*

There is no attic to his mind; the silverfish have chewed his winter memories. I consulted with the neurologist, "What did you expect?" he wanted to know. I struggled for an answer; tears of hope floating. "I want to make him whole again."

New Year's Eve, 2001, three women nearly had a fist fight over where he should sit in the festive dining room, as Mrs. K. and Mrs. S. were grabbing at his red sports coat, insisting that he dine with each. The maitre'd had to pull them apart before they created a scene worthy of the "Jerry Springer Show." The whole affair was the talk of the staff meeting on Monday morning. When I described the events humorously to my father, he commented, "I wish someone had told ME about that." Brownie had established a routine at the Landing; breakfast, lunch, dinner, followed by walking with a Bering Imperial. He had several lady friends, some of whom would join us for outings and Sunday dinner on our deck. *"If the cigar smoke bothers you, don't mention it."*

My father had smoked three stogies a day for 30 years; his dessert. He had mastered the lighting, puff, puff, light, never inhale, puff, puff, light, no dropped ashes; he could light a mere inch with the dexterity and precision of a hole in one. I've had a box, 25 cigars, of Bering Imperials in my refrigerator for the past four years; he smoked his last stogie on my deck while watching golfers play through. I watched him puff, light, puff, light his thumb. He remembered the routine, but not the process. I took away the book of Detroit Country Club matches and the cigar. "Dad, you gave up smoking for Lent." *"No, Barb, I gave up sky diving and deep sea fishing."*

Several ladies had eyes on cute, buff, bachelor Mr. Bill. Mrs. S. pulled me aside one morning to discuss with pantomime and choppy phrases that a double bed would be helpful because this single bed…..I got the gist. I queried Father Brown about the purchase of a larger bed; his reply, "Not at this juncture." Sometimes I would find Mrs. C. napping in the single bed and I would question Pops, "Who is that in your bed, Dad?" He would saunter around the corner, still keeping an eye on Market reports, "Barb, I can't answer that question."

The morning of 9/11 I was with Father Brown, picking him up for a haircut. *"Why not get them all cut?"* Passing the Woodhaven parlor I heard the announcement of the first plane hitting the Trade Towers as I gazed at the large screen TV in stunned silence. My father wandered in as the second plane hit. There was no possible explanation for the few residents who were staring. When life knocks you to your knees, that's the best position in which to pray. Staff and residents began holding hands, about 7 of us; we formed a prayer circle and through tears mumbled, "Our Father who art in heaven….." It gave comfort to each of us. "Dad, do you have your rosary?" *"In my pocket, in my pocket."* The reality of this event was never stored in his memory.

In April 2002, following several "fate of our father" meetings where the staff presents and I defend, we were required to move him to the Memory Enhanced, 15 resident unit within Woodhaven. He had advanced beyond the 7 levels of assisted living. He could no longer negotiate a toilet or shower independently. The move was

made with dignity and ease; he did not recognize the change. He
acknowledged the room, but not the belongings as his.

I was the person struggling. I walked into the ME Unit and saw
stick people, scarecrows and I could not place my father among
them. I began to move through the halls at gazelle speed, while
his flank speed was that of a sloth. A female resident, babbling
letters and sounds, often followed us; my father reassuring her,
"Mildred, we'll get back to you on that." Ever the kind gentleman
my grandmother Adele raised with his social skills intact. I marvel
at this. Every Friday at 3 p.m. he chaired the memory impaired
support group in the parlor of Woodhaven. He called the meetings
to order and dismissed the residents at 4. For him, one hour of
reality; again the cufflink man, senior vice president at Smith-
Barney. This was supposed to comfort me. It didn't. Silly, sad,
hollow, I know, but words don't count when words don't matter.

Meals were silent; tables of various levels of dementia victims
speaking in syllables, random verbs, disconnected phrases, a few in
paragraphs with no transitions. I could not place him among them.

As this disease progressed we lived in peaks and slumps; the
slumps were frequent and lengthy. His life became a hopeless
confinement within a mind in the process of decay. Visits were
measured in stares and silence.

We lived in non-events: visits from golfing buddies and family
from Detroit, the baptisms of grandchildren, the marriage of our
older daughter, the birth of her son, deaths of his former girlfriends
and pals from Detroit, golf tournaments, Saturday mass, many trips
to the emergency room following slight stokes, 8 stitches around
his mouth, gums and eye after a tumble on our aggregate driveway,
physical therapy sessions, emergency surgery for a bleeding ulcer
with a 10% chance of recovery.... all events he could not process.
His comment was usually the same, "Well, that's a good report."

Early in this life-change for both of us, I began a one-page
correspondence with 40 of his pals, some of whom I knew. I would
keep the letters upbeat, informative and truthful. Just this month I
completed the 33rd update. I included pictures of him alone or with

great grandchildren or new friends from the Landing. These letters
became my private emotional flooding. Once he became confined to
a wheelchair and was unable to feed himself, we moved him to the
long-term, skilled care unit in 2005. The pictures of him stopped.
He looked unbearably empty. I wondered if he had cleared all
traces of his former life and self. I struggle.

The epiphany comes in the form of our first grandchild, youngest
daughter of our younger daughter Sara. Katherine Kenyon began
visiting her Bapa at 5 months; she is now a rising second grader.
She knows when she is seven, he will be 87; when she is 10, he
will be 90. She unknowingly became his lifeline; her still, small
voice anchoring Detroit's child in the state of Virginia, providing
a childhood for him to witness, but not record. Has he lived a full
life, not yet. He had a pal and so did she. The Landing recorded her
walking, talking. Kenyon was absorbing seven words a day while her
Bapa was tracking toward a verbal shutdown, as words to thought
escaped him. She understood that he had a fever in his brain that
burns memory; he will never forget her, but he will forget her name.
When she was five, she suggested to our neurologist that he give her
Bapa a shot and then "he could remember her name." Alzheimers is a
lonely, boring, hopeless disease.

Our Kenyon would attend the 30-minute Sunday Vespers service
with me. "B, I want to go to the vegetable service with you," left
on my answering machine. This four-year-old had not learned the
word Vespers. We adults enjoyed the humor of "vegetable." Words
don't count when words don't matter.

Sunday afternoon in the parlor of Woodhaven, I am surrounded by
an apparition of stoic faces, men and women braced by walkers or
wheelchairs, aging hands gripping canes, Parkinson heads bobbing,
tethered oxygen pumps seeping, a rhythmic snoring and whispers
of "Our Father who art in Heaven..." hesitant chorus "This is my
Story; This is my Song." There is the smell of permanent stuffiness,
the staleness of life escaping slowly. My father is slumped in his
wheelchair; there's cadence to his breath worth breathing, the
rising, the falling, measuring a life in limbo. The circuit of his
brain faltered five years ago, first in flanneled memories, then in

cotton thoughts and now numbed thinking, a complete brain funk, a mind unplugged. I learned not to ask him questions he could not answer. There is safety in silence with deep sadness beneath unspoken words. The present disappears in the present.

Six year old Kenyon leans into me, "B, he's asleep, isn't he?" I fully understand this concern because I drove her to pre-school on the "10% chance" day, so that her parents could visit with Bapa. I watched her in my rear view mirror processing my answers to her questions from her toddler car seat. "I know he's sick B; he's been in his P-jamas all day." "How old do you have to be to die?" "How will he get to Heaven?" "Does God know he needs his wheelchair and sometimes eats soup with a fork?" "When I am 10 on Earth, will he be 90 in Heaven?" I deliver her with tears floating a surge of childish hope. WPB recovered.

Kenyon is testimony to the belief that as long as he creates fog on the mirror, he has purpose. I am a teacher; I work in terms of "fix-it" strategies. Where is his zone? What keeps him here? I am a spouter of information and he is a careful listener, never a responder. Every day for him is a workshop as he deals with disconnected retention, fractured recall, unraveled reasoning, stranded Schema. There is no evidence of repair. Kenyon reminds me that Bapa is like Dorrie in *Finding Nemo;* she can't remember either.

In her still, small voice, Kenyon modeled forgiveness in place of anger, patience in place of numbness as she demonstrated remarkable wisdom.

"B, he smiled and that's why we're here." He has bonded with those blue, baseball eyes; he knows her, but not her name. "Beautiful child, Mr. Brown." *"Good Morning."* The warmth of his smiles and gestures remains. Detroit's child is a Virginia gentleman.

My father and I bonded 60 years too late. There were no walks around the block, packing U-Hauls for college, congrats for high grades, advice after missed opportunities, wiping of tears caused by broken relationships; we had no resume and I caused no hassle in his life. I am in a personal struggle of expectation and reality.

He did teach me to catch a fired baseball in a seasoned glove and reminded me always to shake hands with strength and conviction.

His pockets emptied and mine filled. Where is his rosary; it is in MY pocket, MY pocket.

My epiphany comes in writing about him; it isn't biographical; it's about me. I am writing to discover him and have access to myself. Blood is thick. I am often asked, "Does he know you?" Yes. "Well, you're lucky!" The perception of "luck" escapes me. I cannot anticipate the final exit though his death is much on my mind these days. I fear that grief may be a welcome feeling.

My day breaks and shadows flee away; my life-rope reaching my hand and in her voice a tapestry of emotions.

"B, I think he is a pretend father."

My epiphany.

CHAPTER EIGHTEEN
LIVING THE ABSTRACT LIFE
Jo Ann Brown-Scott

Inside you there's an artist you don't know about...
Say yes quickly, if you know—
if you've known it from before the beginning of the universe.
Rumi, 13th century poet from ancient Persia

I was born an artist. I inherited the DNA component from my talented Dad and chose to not just acknowledge it but also accept it, and carry the torch for a lifetime. I am an artist by profession, not hobby, although I have also held productive and satisfying positions that paid far better, in sales, marketing and teaching through the years. Doubting, at just one of the numerous insecure junctures in my life, the strength and potential of what was becoming my official art direction, I took another of those tests that reveal in harsh black and white scores where one's talents might best be put to use. They don't hand you a paintbrush, or a musical instrument for these aptitude tests...you are supposed to be good at something else besides the "arts." Nobody ever says, "Well, let's see if this one over here has artistic potential because we are looking for another Picasso." The test determined I would make a good journalist or TV news anchor; perhaps a "color commentator" for public events and sports. I would be the person who describes the context surrounding the event. Well, maybe so. I "take in" everything that is around me—I am a visual person to such an extent that I am constantly parched for pictorial stimulation—new views, new color combinations, new faces and places, new foods, new books and new movies. But then I just use it all to paint. I am creative because I *must* create. I call it a sickness and people laugh, but it is truly an ongoing malaise.

Sometimes it hurts. It can be emotionally painful—the actual process of squeezing out the image onto a canvas as well as the process of then showing it to perfect strangers, looking for reactions. Intense scrutiny of your work is your way of life. Anyone can and will pass judgment—they certainly do not have to be art critics from the newspapers or museum curators. People who know nothing about color theory, composition, or contemporary abstract art can wander into a gallery, or your home, and spout off about your latest and greatest work as if it were completely disconnected from you. Don't they realize it is like an umbilical cord to your soul? As an artist, you are always setting yourself up for rejection. It is one of the things you do best.

Most everything in the art world is trial and error, off and on, brilliant or horrific, in fashion or suddenly out. It is a chaotic industry. People find original paintings hidden in the attics of their homes that are worth millions—other people who spend millions find that they have bought a forgery. Galleries close overnight when the discovery is made that fraudulent Dali prints are being sold just as the crew from "60 Minutes" walks in the door with cameras; even the knowledgeable gallery owner oblivious to his ignorance. Celebrities who can sing or act brilliantly can often also paint fairly well and are likely to command more attention than the art of a budding Andrew Wyeth type of genius. Paintings are sold done by monkeys or elephants flapping around big wide paint brushes on paper as they beg for peanuts. Peanuts is what most artists are paid, however, so that is not so unusual...If you are an art groupie—a gallery walker—a fan—a follower—then you know that it is a fast and loose scene. Hilarious. Scary at times. But endlessly fascinating. It sucks you in.

The only people for me are the mad ones, the ones who are mad to live, mad to talk, mad to be saved, desirous of everything at the same time, the ones who never yawn or say a commonplace thing, but burn, burn, burn, like fabulous yellow roman candles exploding like spiders across the stars...
Jack Kerouac

I once attended a special gallery show for a well known artist who was a full blooded Crow Indian. He and I hung in some of the same galleries and I knew him casually. He was gifted—a genius—very prominent in Colorado, with paintings selling well into the thirty-five thousand dollar range and above. He is dead now, but his images are still sought after and of course even more expensive to collect since his death. His life was the stuff that art legends are made of—but he was authentic. His girlfriends were all strippers from a local watering hole; he had a problem with substance abuse. It was said that when he was thrown in jail for DUI's he asked for his paints and did murals on the hard masonry walls. My God could he paint. He arrived at this particular show at the last minute, rushed, carrying in several enormous canvases, one by one, barely finished, paint still wet, in the nick of time as the people began arriving; I noticed immediately that all the Indians' horses were missing their tails. I tactfully and quietly pointed that out to him, and he replied, "Oh my God, am I doin' that again?" He got out his paints and took care of it right on the spot, as everyone watched, endearing his fans with that human touch.

Putting your soul on the gallery wall and inviting remarks is not so much fun. It might look fun, with the lovely assortment of hors d'oeuvres and the wine flowing freely and the gaggle of funky, fashionably dressed, art-hopping people who disembark the "art bus" shuttle that arrives to the gallery district from the four corners of the city and drops them at the door. But that is illusion. A gallery show is merely a cleverly disguised disaster area where they should be handing out coffee and donuts outside the yellow taped area. Behind the scenes it is mayhem. It is anxiety personified. Rarely does the evening leave happy memories. Rarely do many people actually study the art and ask intelligent questions. Rarely does your best painting sell. Often nothing sells. But I am not complaining. I always go back for more.

It takes a thick skin to be an artist, and yet a sensitive nature to paint. You must learn to sell yourself without being an egomaniac. You must demonstrate confidence but remain humble. Your most fervent wish is that your work will be appreciated for the message you intended, but people often misinterpret, leaving you wondering why you paint. They tell you what they think you must be saying in your images. They speculate. You want to scream "Wrong! Wrong! And wrong again!" but instead you look intent and fascinated with their obtuse interpretations of your message. You do not want to sound like a victim of your art, and yet you are at the mercy of it. A friend with a great sense of humor gave me a rubber stamp that says "ART CAN'T HURT YOU," and I stamp it on the back of my finished canvases; but I think it can.

The greater the artist, the greater the doubt; perfect confidence is granted to the less talented as a consolation prize.
Robert Hughes

The only advantages, as I see them, to being an artist are: 1. People you rub shoulders with are often a fascinating crowd—always lively, show-bizzy and eccentric; and 2. Your work gets better the older you grow, providing you stay sane. That is the trick. When you die and your canvases are scattered on the walls of some little hole-in-the-wall gallery for your retrospective showing, you don't want the onlookers to be pointing to that certain canvas in your "art journal" where you so obviously lost your noodles. Madness is hardly ever a good thing. Except with Van Gogh. Or Dali. They made it work.

There is one other advantage to being a painter. It allows you to make a contribution to the ages. It gives you a voice that speaks long after you are gone—the chance to leave something of yourself behind that you worked very hard to achieve. Something you spilled blood for at times, something you breathed toxic varnish fumes for, something you cried and laughed and agonized over. Pieces of yourself that, if carefully studied, reveal the messages you wanted to leave to the universe. When people ask me, "How long did it take you to paint that?" I reply, "All my life."

My particular art career, modest as it is compared to the "greats" of my chosen field, has resulted in far more humorous, odd-ball situations and bizarre circumstances than the success stories I have enjoyed. Such as the pilot who wanted a painting in the shape of a large trapezoid, to fill the special niche above his mantel where the wall met the sloped cathedral ceiling, or the deranged person who asked me to paint a maudlin image of an invalid slumped in a wheelchair in an impressionistic style using happy Easter egg colors, or the frivolous requests from numerous Parade of Homes type designers who wanted the art to match the colors of the drapes and identical paintings above twin beds. The fascinating, hilarious and weirdly textured stories like these are the ones that stay in my mind, in spite of the pride I feel for the stories of my triumphs.

Timing has been everything for me, and the big breaks fell into place effortlessly it seemed, as if pre-ordained. I got my first big break while living in Evergreen, Colorado when I was asked, out of the blue, by the Evergreen Chamber of Commerce, to create a winter snow scene from which five hundred signed and numbered, limited edition, Christmas posters and thousands of Christmas cards would be printed and sold. It was the very first experimental year of that idea, in what was to become a long tradition of yearly contests for local artists competing for that special honor. After that year, 1982, my career took off to a higher level.

This powerful art gene has surfaced in my family in many incarnations. We have a professional wallpaper designer turned serious weaver; we have a skilled rock climber who sketches the routes of his technical climbs and has had them published in climbing magazines along with his accompanying article; we have a talented graphic artist whose career has taken her to prominent positions with a major film company and a global outdoor equipment organization; we have a brilliant young artist who paints like he has been here for centuries and we have an elderly artist—my ninety-two-ish Father—who was still sculpting as recently as a couple years ago. There is no beginning and no end. It flows like a deep blue river of dreams. It carries me with its current and I am powerless to resist the lure of it.

I also inherited my Father's and my Grandfather's salesmanship skills and their minds for business. I can think logically and mathematically on the other side of my brain, oddly enough. I once had an H & R Block guy tell me that I should be a tax accountant because I had a technical *and* creative mind for figures. I stared at him as if he was nuts. WHO, ME? The same foggy headed slob who gets out of bed and wanders into her studio space in her jammies, to paint, before she has even brushed her teeth?

It is my dirty little secret that beneath all of my mad abstraction there resides a meticulous person. Like Georgia O'Keefe, I must have my underwear drawers tidy and my kitchen clean to be able to free my mind to paint. I have to maintain an undertone of order in my life because the art images in my head are so disorderly. I need a solid foundation. I am one of those especially neurotic artists who does not thrive on chaos. The world is so brutally random; I am so quietly structured, as I paint with wildly focused, yet abstracted abandon. I am a walking talking contradiction.

***

I had a sobering realization not so long ago. I was at a gathering in Boulder, Colorado in the home of our dear friend Sally Kingdom, for a special type of college reunion—just the six of us who had remained life-long friends; college students of the sixties, now in our sixties. Sally placed ten of her sterling silver forks out on the dining room table, lined up side by side like armless people standing in a row. She told us that these ten forks represented the ten decades of our lives, assuming we lived to be a hundred—a very big assumption to start with. She immediately removed five forks on the left end. Those were the five decades that had already passed. Then she removed two forks from the right end, because from the ages of eighty to one-hundred you had pretty much passed the time when you could have the types of quality adventures you used to have. That left three forks. We had three good forks left, and we were well into the first of those three. Time is short.

As this day dawns, I am a youngish sixty-four-year-old woman, and holding firm. I do not want to be any older than this; of course I do not want to die, so there you have the problem. I find myself restless and ambitious, with acute awareness of the passage of time and the fact that I don't have enough of it to do all that I want to do. I feel as though the saloon of life is nearing closing time and I still have quarters for the juke box and people to meet. Sort of like the Little Bear Saloon in Evergreen, Colorado at 1:30 am. I don't want to go home yet.

I am considered an optimist by friends, fun to be around, an animated story teller, an attentive listener and an active person in mind and body. I have a lot of energy. My mind will not turn off; and I have an intense curiosity about people and relationships, places, animals, science and everything the universe has to offer. I am a "news junky." Earth is a three ring circus of a place. I want to be in the loop of life; if not in the center ring then at least able to see it from here...

I am an extrovert one day and an introvert the next. I need my private time to paint and read and incubate; until I no longer need that, and then I really, really need my friends. My mind seems to be half creative thinker, half practical thinker; half conservative, half liberal; half romantic, half cynic; half meat eater, half vegetarian, until I get a craving for a cheeseburger; half eccentric and half traditional. I am a "child at heart" kind of adult. Still, I am a deep thinker—I feel forty-something in my skin, but with wisdom from having lived into my sixties. I figure that if you are not a deep thinker by this time in your life, you have just flat missed the deep thinking boat of life. I have known some—been in love with a few—who are indeed still waiting on shore for the boat they missed.

I am capable of yelling, but usually I am quietly rebellious. I continue to fight the type of conformity that was expected of me and continually thrust upon me as a child. In my household, children dared not speak up, and were to be seen and not heard. That was typical of my parent's style of parenting, and many others of that generation. I hated it. I felt stifled and without a voice for much of my early years. I swore I would never banish my children from the room when adults were engaged in interesting conversation, and they are wiser for it.

Although people tell me that I am one of the sanest people they know, as an artist I do not relish that remark. I would like to be weirder. Any deliciously eccentric tendencies I revealed as a child were squelched for the sake of good behavior, like sweet syrupy juice quickly extracted from an orange. My favorite color in high school was actually flame orange—a color that was a shocker to my Mom, who thought it an eccentric choice; probably indicative of some wild streak or deviant tendency. She encouraged me to make more conservative choices in clothes. I went off to college trying to stifle the orange like a good daughter (kidding us both—art school. duh) and so for a period of time in my final two years my favorite color actually began to change to Prussian blue. Mom was satisfied that I had matured, but my years away at college were the most crazy-fun times, and the most reckless years of my life. I barely got out of Boulder, Colorado alive; it was a hair-raising four years. After graduation, orange changed back to being my favorite color, in all shades from bittersweet to pumpkin to tangerine to coral, and has remained so ever since. I use it tastefully in my home and wardrobe.

I am a voracious reader of everything from serious books to National Geographic to People magazine, with a heavy emphasis on interior design publications and art books. I once taught an interior design class at college level, when my children were grown. This is odd, because I was told, while a fine art student at the University of Colorado in Boulder, that I must get my teaching degree (which I resisted) because my chances of ever selling a painting, much less earning a living at it, were slim—to none. I had the talent, but few artists were fortunate enough to actually *sell* their work, especially women, in those days. Additionally, I was a student of abstract art, in the time leading into the Viet Nam era—people were not exactly taking a number and standing in line to buy art unless it was the hallucinogenic flower child variety. During times of war or economic uncertainty, art's popularity usually takes a dive. Everyone's mind is on other things. Art follows trends, as a general rule, and a liberal political movement brings about a looser style of artistic interpretation; a conservative political movement brings about a resurgence of realism in art. During the Ronald Reagan years most of the galleries swung their inventory over to realistic western art, because Ronnie liked it and displayed it in the oval office, sending abstract art into a long period of relative unpopularity in galleries.

One of my favorite professors at C.U. during that period of the sixties, when being an art student seemed divinely in sync with the hippie movement, was a wonderfully eccentric man who was one of several professors instrumental in bending me to the abstract style. After a semester in his tutelage, he literally threw down a tall, weathered and beaten wooden ladder, flat on the floor, and told us to give him our best interpretation, as our final exam. Are you kidding? Everyone knew he was not looking for realism. He wanted some funk. He wanted some grit. I got an A. My most comfortable artistic niche, I discovered in four years of fine art classes, was not to be realism.

He had a wife who was reportedly also quite talented. No one heard much about her. Just this morning, I opened the Sunday Denver Post to find an immensely complimentary article about her long struggle for success and her great achievements as a woman artist, against all the odds for someone of that generation. ("Met Exhibit Glazes Artist's Uphill Career" by Kyle MacMillan, Denver Post Fine Art Critic, June 11, 2006) Her career is now peaking at the age of seventy-six, with a current retrospective show at the Metropolitan Museum of Art in New York. The article states that she is one of the five most accomplished artists to ever emerge from Colorado. She states that her prominence as an artist came after a long uphill climb, overcoming many hurdles—the most primary hurdle simply being a female. She has unquestionably reached the pinnacle of achievement for any artist, but especially so for a woman. Her name is Betty Woodman.

In spite of the discouraging odds for artistic recognition, I hated the thought of a lifetime career in teaching—finger painting at grade school level was what I envisioned at that point in time. So I remained a fine art major with minor studies in psychology and English literature, fully expecting to starve as punishment for my arrogance and impracticality. Just who did I think I was, thinking I could be a real artist? Van Gogh did not sell a painting in his entire life.

I sold my first piece of art (in the form of a mosaic) at the age of eighteen, then my first serious painting to a serious collector in my late twenties, and have by now sold hundreds of others, in spite of my gender. My art has certainly not provided me with a comfortable living—I have always found it necessary to have "real" jobs too. So I did indeed teach interior design for a six- year period of time, at a community college where my life experiences alone qualified me as a professor. What a hoot. See what happens? Never say you will never do something because you could have to eat your own silly words someday. (Once I said I would never choose to live in Kansas, and the next thing I knew, my husband was transferred there. We thought we were going to be transferred to Santa Monica—what a shock to find we were going the other direction, to be landlocked in a very small town in the southwestern part of the state in tornado alley. We spent a lot of time in the basement. I was shocked to find a level of prejudice and small-mindedness there that was intolerable to me. I wrote a letter to the local paper and expressed my concern and I was instantly thrust into a love-hate relationship with some of the town's population. But the experience is a piece of the puzzle of my life.)

I am married for the second time, having recently celebrated that occasion on the beach at Half Moon Bay, California with a couple handfuls of dear people and joyfully colored accoutrements, after fourteen years of stalling, while living in sin, with the second man in my life whom I have ever loved with all my heart. Before, I was married a full twenty-five years to the father of my son and daughter; children I treasure to the full extent that it is humanly possible for us mere mortals to treasure our children. In spite of the termination of that long marriage, I would not change the course of my life even if by some time-travel, "back to the future" miracle it became possible for me to do so, because I needed to have the exact two children that I had with the exact husband I had them with. (I was brilliant in my choice of my first husband in many ways.) I also believe that I chose my children and they chose me, in the larger scheme of things. *I believe that our souls manage to find the company they like to keep.* My children are my best friends. They are often my teachers. They are my loudest laughs. Their safety is the subject of my most fervent requests of the universe.

Yes I do talk to the universe, but I cannot say I am religious; I am spiritual. I believe in a higher power. Call it what you will. I believe that if you are in tune with the universe it will mother you well. I believe we all have a portion of this higher power within us, in our souls, and we can listen to it speak to us. It has a voice. I concoct my own recipe of beliefs by adding and subtracting pieces from many ideologies, stirring them together and tasting frequently for flavor. If I really had to choose, I'd probably be a Buddhist. I can barely snuff out the life of a bug—I always attempt its relocation. But if an animal is suffering I feel it should be put out of its misery. I believe in reincarnation—I have the ultimate respect for life. It is because of this respect for life that I want life to begin and end properly. I want a birth to be joyfully anticipated and cherished and I want a death to come after a long and productive life well-lived.

But it is not a perfect world, and I am not a predictably liberal artistic type. I am an advocate of the death penalty for criminals who commit heinous, barbaric crimes, and in my opinion have chosen to live like vicious animals. In my opinion, they deserve to die. I am pro-choice. I am concerned about our open borders and I take a tough stance on immigration. I am alarmed about global warming. I find it inexcusable that we still have people starving in this country, or any other for that matter, in the prosperous times of the 21st century. I am a mixed bag of beliefs.

Believing that tough stuff, and yet being so thoroughly the artist, I am probably *still* too sensitive for my own good. Way too sensitive to have been allowed to witness the slaughter of the neighbor's pigs one bright and sunny Saturday morning when I was just about seven. Much too sensitive to have my looks frequently criticized as I was growing up. Far too fragile to have expressed any youthful opinions that could be laughed at and ridiculed. It took me years to develop bravery. Eventually I became intolerant of rudeness, repulsed by arrogance, totally impatient with stupidity and bureaucracy, and finally, after I had really gelled as a human being, too frank for my own good…and then still, at other times, shocked back to speechless silence at the insensitivity of people. Full circle character development. Not perfect by any means, but a start.

I am somewhat the perfectionist and always restless and wiggly. I can't hold a grudge very well, although I have been guilty of skillfully hiding brief messages of rebuke in the compositions of certain paintings—yet generally I will not spend my valuable energy in resentment. I will just remember it if you have wronged me and take it under consideration for everything that comes after.

I love the quote from Maya Angelou, *"When people show you who they are, believe them."*

I pay attention to what people show me of themselves. I am observant. I watch body language. Passive-aggressive people greatly irritate me and I am triggered by their manipulations, because I value honesty and directness in thought and action. I try not to be a fool, but I have indeed been foolish in my life, mostly from trusting the wrong people at the wrong time. I try not to make the same mistake twice, because the first time you are a victim—and the second time you are a volunteer.

I believe that a louder voice and a greater force in advocating peaceful solutions for the world must find its expression in women. Our husbands and sons and daughters are the ones who are asked to give their lives in wars almost always declared by men. Women need a deciding voice in determining under what circumstances peace is no longer an option. I see women as the more compassionate voice for social reform and feeding the hungry of the world. Women get things done. Women multi-task. I doubt you would see truckloads of food, sitting idle along the road somewhere for lack of instruction, while people starve less than fifty miles away if women were in charge of such things. The centuries-old subordination of the women of the world has taught us that our path to greater independence and representation lies in skills and education, followed by a voice that is heard and respected. Progress is not happening fast enough for me. I believe strongly that the empowerment of women can and will change the world. I believe that our collective "mother bear instincts" in wanting a better life for our children could well be the salvation of people everywhere, when those instincts are finally able to kick in at full strength.

***

I was successfully born in Dayton, Ohio, after my Mother had experienced at least three agonizing miscarriages. I was the first of three children, with a younger brother and then the youngest sister. I lived the bulk of my childhood in an elegant, gargantuan, enfolding mother of a house on Munger Road hill, surrounded by eight acres of beautiful, green southern Ohio countryside. It was a glorious, old country house—I found it comforting and yet mysterious. I still walk the rooms in my mind when I can't sleep. I remember every inch of the eight acres and all the trees I expertly climbed to alarming heights, the hayloft in the barn where I was first kissed, the caretaker's home where I often visited that wonderful family when they had weekend fish fries out back, the swing from the biggest tree down by the school bus stop where Stephen R. wrapped a dead snake around my neck and sent me nearly to the moon with repulsion, the babbling creek and collecting eggs from under screeching chickens in their coup. I was a serious tomboy. I once had a fist fight with the kid who bullied my little brother, pinned him to the ground and spit in his face for the grand finale.

Snowy winters were great fun since we were in the hills and the sledding was wild, with scary, steep, icy routes through trees and around rocks; we made igloo-type snow forts by packing snow into cardboard boxes to make cubes for stacking. We often took peanut butter and jelly sandwiches for lunch so we wouldn't have to go back to the house, and we found places to relieve ourselves in the bushes. We were outside all day; rain, snow, hail or summer heat; spending our summers barefoot, playing until the sun finally set and even then collecting lightening bugs in jars. We stopped briefly for a noon-day rest, believed to be a buffer against contracting the dreaded disease of polio. Horse flies and house flies, duck and chicken droppings, horse manure and such were thought to be carriers of the virus, but they were everywhere and unavoidable. The well always ran dry by August and so we had precious water trucked in—bathing in the tub was three-kids-at-once and infrequent, and in between full immersions we just went to bed with dirty feet, sticky with pine sap from climbing trees, and sweaty hair.

I was fortunate enough to see it all again in 1991, just days before they tore down the main house, once featured in Better Homes and Gardens magazine. Timing is everything—this experience was arranged in the nick of time, by the man I now love, with prior research and permission for us to explore. Someone was in the process of salvaging the best parts of my old home to build a *new* house, undoubtedly lacking in the same rare character as my old house. Chunks of my childhood were ripped out and scattered on the front yard—hand forged hardware from the doors, chandeliers, porcelain bathtubs—and inside I saw wallpaper and carpeting I remembered. The house seemed in pain. The windows had obviously been open to birds and bats and whatever else in the final weeks of its dying. We wandered around for several hours until I couldn't stand it anymore, but what a gift to give me. You see, in my family, residences and furnishings were the hub of our existence.

My Grandpa Rossiter, who I dearly loved, founded a fine furniture store on Main Street in town and therefore our home was beautifully furnished. It was just pure luck, plus the hard work of my Dad and my Grandpa, to be able to live like that. My Dad and my uncle were sales people and interior designers. I found out a few years ago that my great, great grandfather had sold fine linens and lace in England—my sister and I both said, in unison, "Well! That explains a lot!" The genes don't lie.

When I was seven or eight years young my favorite Saturdays were spent going to the Dayton Art Institute for my watercolor class and then on to the furniture store. I first ran up the stairs to Grandpa's office in the loft area overlooking the store, sat on his lap, showed him my latest creations from art class and got some hugs. Then I wandered the showrooms, loving the art, the furniture and the accessories. I said hello to Mr. Barlow, the "colored" (as we said then) gentleman who was the janitor; one of my favorite people. I spent time in the basement watching the seamstresses in the work room turning bolts of fabric into bedspreads and curtains and upholstered furniture pieces. If I was lucky there would be some fabric scraps for doll clothes and some old wallpaper sample books and art catalogues to take home. I absorbed all this creative activity and spit it out later in life, transformed. It was in the genes.

My Mother was a blue-eyed blonde beauty with brains who graduated with honors from Miami University in Ohio where her father, Arthur Evans, was a botany professor. She was born in Boulder, Colorado however, one summer when her parents were living there temporarily—her father was a visiting professor for that period of time in 1915. Mom and Dad were a movie star gorgeous kind of couple. Dad looked like Dean Martin, and loved to sing and paint and sculpt. They had eloped; her parents strongly objecting to the relationship. My Mother and Father had a stormy relationship, fueled by drinking, and my relationship with my Dad was difficult at times. I was lonely and even fearful for much of my childhood but it made me creative, and the big house *usually* gave me plenty of room to escape the violent arguing. My parents were divorced when I was finishing seventh grade, and I was both sad and relieved about that change in my life. Yet I felt guilty to be so relieved, and as many children do, also afraid that some of it had been my fault. I know now that it was not. The big old nurturing house, along with the acres I loved so much, was sold. Our horses, including my own pitch black pony named Thunder, cats and various other adored animals were gone, over night; a different life began.

I became listless and melancholy. My brother, sister and I moved with Mother to a city house. I was sure that I was unattractive and would never fit in my new school or my new neighborhood. After having just changed schools for seventh grade, in the fall I was to attend the next new school for eighth grade, and then I was promised that I would attend the high school where my cousins would also be going, and that was of some comfort and support to me. But just before high school started, we discovered that the boundary that divided the two rival high school districts was the street alongside our house, and I was living on the wrong side. I had to face another drastic change of schools, leaving behind my brand new friends (including my first boyfriend) from eighth grade and continuing on without my cousins, to attend the *rival* high school. That discovery made for a very dark day in my life and a rocky freshman year.

During those years the furniture store suffered a three alarm fire that nearly took its three floors to the ground. We raced downtown when we got the call that the store was on fire. We could feel the water spray from the fire hoses three blocks away as we ran to Main Street. Then we stood across the street and watched it burn, drenched by the water and sobbing. Not long after, Grandpa died quite unexpectedly of complications following what had been referred to as routine gall bladder surgery. They said he never recovered from the shock of the fire and his health suffered because of that. In the years that followed, what was left of the furniture business that Grandpa had built from zero (he started out as an elevator attendant in the building down the street) into a multi-million dollar, family owned company, was sold to our competitors; a transaction that I found deeply embarrassing. My parent's divorce, the death of my Grandpa, the fire and sale of the business were reported in all the local papers. Tongues were wagging. Mother became depressed. We saw Dad, on what became unpleasant weekends with his new wife and her undisciplined kids, when I would rather have spent time making new friends. My world changed so drastically that I hardly knew who I was for quite a while. But I turned my struggle inward and realized later it had helped make an authentic painter of me. In what seemed like a lifetime later, when I was in my early fifties, I was able to locate my half-brother (born to my Father with this second new wife during their brief marriage) whom I had not seen since he was less than two years old—and establish a very loving relationship with him.

Gradually my life brightened and I went off to Boulder, Colorado to attend college in 1961 and never turned back, falling instantly in love with the west. My decision to go west, against the strong family suggestion that I attend Miami U. in Ohio, was my official rebellious escape from home in the direction of independence, combined with the strong pull of the fine art department that the U. of Colorado had to offer. And remember, my Mother had been born there—she had no memories of it, but she was fascinated with Colorado. I felt that I had finally arrived where I needed to be. I loved Boulder, and still do. I fit in beautifully and made life-long friendships there. It is one of the most wonderful places on *my earth*; it was a four year period of happiness.

In the summer after my sophomore year, at my suggestion, my Mother (newly single and in need of a fresh start) visited me during spring break at the university; then interviewed for and accepted a teaching position in Denver. Finding her groove again, in a gutsy little move, she sold the house in Ohio and moved west with my brother and sister. Reminiscent of my escape to Boulder for college two years earlier, she never looked back. She loved Denver until the day she died at the age of eighty-six.

At this writing, my Dad is alive and living in Sarasota, Florida, still very much the eccentric artist that I always knew him to be. He is an elegant man; grown old gracefully, wildly funny and still able to tell a great story. I get a kick out of him. And of course I got much more from him.

I married in 1966, a year after college graduation. A boyfriend from Dayton, Ohio, caught and released during one period of high school time and then warmly re-accepted after four maturing years spent in college and in his case, college and Air Force Officer's Training, was the person with whom I intended to live the rest of my life. I became pregnant on our honeymoon, joyfully had the son I had always hoped for, and almost immediately got the news that my husband was off to Viet Nam. I had experienced a major paradigm shift. (Funky art student straight from predominantly anti-war university campus marries straight-arrow Air Force Officer—tries to blend into highly regimented life as dutiful officer's wife—complete culture shock ensues—they have a baby barely ten months later—husband leaves for Viet Nam.)

Thus began a long history of Air Force and then civilian positions that took my husband away from home on a regular basis. We were blessed with a beautiful daughter in 1970, completing our family. But in the years approaching our twenty-fourth year of marriage I had begun to feel the same type of deep loneliness and neglect I had felt as a child; my husband and I had grown apart; I initiated a divorce which was finalized in 1992. In the years since, we have remained good friends, able to talk and laugh again. We made our children the focus and kept things comfortable for all concerned. We are the poster children for amicable divorce.

During the time of my former husband's heaviest traveling, I wrote a three-page accounting, on yellow chief tablet paper, of how it was *for me* to be the wife of a husband who was constantly away from home. I sent it off to the Phil Donahue Show producers, when the show was located in Chicago. It was written as therapy, on a day when I really had just one nerve left with the entire lifestyle—I expressed my frustrations in a semi-humorous way; instantly forgetting about it as I put it in the mailbox. I told them that I was tired of being, for all practical purposes, a single parent, running a sort of bed and breakfast with my husband as the weekend guest, and that when he walked in the door on Friday night he was always horny, hungry and tired...and I didn't know which one to satisfy first as the "good little wife". I was amazed, months later, to be called by the producer of the show and asked to appear as the "expert" on stage for the hour-long discussion they had planned around my letter about husbands who travel. I flew to Chicago and this show was broadcast on national TV and overseas as well, and even went into re-runs...I can't say that I burned up the airways however. I provided valuable insights, but was constantly aware that my Mom, my mother-in-law, my grandmother and my *children* would be watching it. I softened my punches a bit, but I made my points.

With that experience I again realized, in spite of my soft voice and my smile, that I had a streak in me for frank expression that could arouse controversy. That was quite an epiphany, after being labeled a shy child. I was not ever shy—I just had never been given the freedom to be heard. No one had cared what I said, so I murmured things; observations; opinions; comments—sort of like a whispering commentary; microphone turned too low for anyone to hear. Maybe I should have been a TV journalist after all...

The larger epiphany I would like to tell you about came to me in my sixth decade. I have had others along the way but this one hit me clearly one afternoon. Quite simply, it required perspective for me to finally notice it. I needed to see backwards, peeling off layers over a long period of time. Epiphanies are always about some intuitive realization—some truth, manifested in some instant thought, surrounded by a context of certain activities or circumstances that push it to the surface of our consciousness where we suddenly see "IT" (the truth) as if a magic switch was turned on in a dark room of our mind. This one was all encompassing. I needed to uncover the hidden pattern in my tapestry of life. I needed to understand the recurring theme, the common but dominate thread; not running randomly but quite consistently.

***

My epiphany is that I have unconsciously but quite apparently, chosen to live my life exactly the way that I paint—my life is my ultimate painting, you might say. I have been perfectly consistent in the types of free form choices I have made for myself, in art and in life. I have lived structured underneath the more visible, unstructured layer. I have lived out of bounds at times, with confident enthusiasm and wild creativity, because the floor of my life—the foundation—is solid. I know myself well. My life is not like a painting of barns, sunsets and birds in flight, appreciated by everyone with an eighth grade education. It has not always been neat and tidy, practical, predictable or appreciated by those with less imagination, and that is precisely why I value the strength and the courage of my living breathing abstract composition.

I have chosen to live an abstract composition because of the valuable *variables* it affords me: great freedom for interpretation, constant opportunities to express myself 'out of the box', the joyfulness of spontaneity, rich and vibrant technicolor action, the excitement of living in the moment, and even the difficult struggle for achievements in the tough world of art. New choices for deepening the meaning of my life-art come to me in flashes of inspiration, 'on the fly'. Changing my mind is not a problem, because I live with great faith born from trusting my instincts. Finding a better path is a lovely surprise and accepted without hesitation. I remain flexible to change. I work every day to not make "fear-based" decisions. I know from the chills on my arm when something great is in the works. I can detect red flags as they are barely beginning to wave their warnings. I have a sense of timing. I feel in tune with the universe.

What does this mean, you might say, to those of us who do not understand or appreciate the nature of abstract art?

Let me explain. Painting in an abstract style is grown into—no artist starts out one hundred percent that way. Every artist first learns to use the tools available, adding certain techniques and the tricks of the trade and the rules of fine composition to paint *realistically*. That is the structured foundation for what evolves. You gradually grow into abstract painting, if that is your choice, after mastering the basic principles of painting and then wanting more intellectual depth and more room for individual interpretation in your work. You proceed to grow, to progress, and you allow yourself to explore—you take risks with your talent. You edit your work and you fine tune it, you condense it, you loosen your painting gestures and you blur the hard outlines a bit. You are on your way to being an abstract artist.

Abstract art is not a mumbo jumbo of color and shape thrown against a canvas. Effective abstract art has a strong composition, a path of lightness or darkness that draws your eye into the focal point of the painting, some exciting action areas and some areas for your eye to rest, and it carries a message. A good painting also reveals the signature style of the artist—a recognizably unique approach to painting that expresses the artist's personality. Even when a young Jackson Pollack "randomly" slung paint onto a canvas placed flat on the floor, in meandering dribbles and drabs of color, he was using an innovative, quick gesture, a free spirit and a particular color palette that were unheard of and unique in the world of art for that time. He made a breakthrough for the rest of us, not to copy him, but to modify his distinct freedom of motion and use that to whatever extent we chose in our own compositions, thereby giving us other artists the gift of exciting change.

About twenty years ago I read an article in an art publication about the evolution of a particular female artist from realism to abstraction. Although I have since lost the article, I will attempt to loosely impart that information in my own words, in spite of all the time that has passed. It explained the process so well:

An artist may begin painting by adoring waterfalls, aspiring to capture their splash and color and liquidity by setting up shop in the woods next to the very waterfall and painting her heart out for months, days, years even. She finally manages to paint the waterfall in all its realistic glory with the strict mechanics of her perfect skill. Every water droplet and splash shines with realism. It might be so technically accurate that it could be mistaken for a photograph. What a fine accomplishment.

After a time she gets bored and she needs a new challenge. She has developed a new distaste for predictability. She feels confident enough to loosen up. She becomes more impressionistic. She spreads the paint around a bit and lets the image become less distinct but more free spirited. (Remember Monet's water lilies?) This very freedom seems to represent the flow and power of the water in the waterfall more than the exact representation ever could.

After more painting, over a period of time, the artist discovers that in order to fully capture the essence of the waterfall she does not need to be outside at all, and against all the rules, her "plein aire" painting can now be done inside her studio, because she can *remember* the feeling of the falls and the colors and the downward splash of the water. She has come to know the waterfall *that intimately*. She begins to splash the paint around in her studio as if it were *the water itself*. She loves the wild abandon of the process. She likes taking the risk of doing something in a brand new way.

One day she has an epiphany. She has a huge canvas, the size of large window, which she props up against the wall. She mixes her paints to the colors that she wants *her* waterfall to be—not necessarily the blues and greens of actual water. She mixes some hot colors to give the waterfall some power and life, surprising even herself in the stirring of the paint. She places a ladder next to the canvas, climbs it and pours the paint colors down the front of the canvas, one by one; a pale teal green washes over apricot, raspberry runs in rivulets next to cerulean and then over-laps the Prussian blue, all then blending and running into each other in a lovely, improvisational, spontaneous action that is both strong and delicate and also breathtakingly beautiful. Then she puts the canvas on the floor and uses the paint brush as if it were a giant toothbrush—spraying and flicking splatters of periwinkle, lime and ultramarine blue in her final touches that mimic the wild and crazy water spray action of her waterfall. Now at last, after hours of using the paint in a poetic dance of living color, controlled and yet free, she has captured it—the very essence, the very soul of the waterfall in all of its abstracted magnificence. She has become an abstract expressionist. She had faith in herself. She remained flexible. She lived completely in the moment of her experience. She released her fear of failure. She used her finely tuned instincts and she did the best painting of her life.

As far back as kindergarten, when my teacher told me that I certainly could not paint a tree my choice of aubergine purple, I have been an abstract painter in my soul. That very first, innocent leap of imagination was coldly rejected when she embarrassed me in front of my class and attempted to eradicate my uninhibited flight of fancy. As young as I was, I knew it was wrong to dictate color to me as I was using my imagination to paint a tree. So the fire did not go out; it just got hotter through the years. By the time I graduated with a BFA, seventeen years later, I wanted to be like the artist on the ladder, pouring liquid waterfall color and splashing paint onto the floor, not only in my art but in the crafting of my life's journey. I began to live my life out of the box, and it has worked for me ever since. I have cherished the unique and special viewpoint that comes with the territory of living life as an artist; using that viewpoint as a foundation for approaching every life circumstance and struggle with a bedrock of imagination and creativity. I am grateful for the genes that have allowed me to be the kind of person who has been accepting of the sometimes difficult changes I have experienced and allowed me to view them as serendipitous opportunities. I can almost always think outside the box.

They say that life keeps teaching us its big lessons, with increasing force, until we finally learn them and apply them consistently to all appropriate situations. During a crisis of faith that came with my divorce, I needed to learn for the umpteenth time that by releasing fear, remaining flexible and living in the moment, I could open my mind to possibilities that would offer me wonderful, life-changing gifts of happiness. When that kind of a gift was offered to me at that particular moment in time, I very nearly refused it. I was asleep at the wheel of life. I was an emotional wreck at the time. My usual pluckiness having taken leave of its senses, I wallowed in the sad thought process of anticipating dismantling our home and seeing our little family scatter in four different directions. With my decision to divorce, I was racked with guilt that my need for happiness had broken apart our home. In that mind set, and with the fear and apprehension I felt in preparing to take my big leap out of the marriage, I lost my belief. I didn't know how to hang on to my faith; the faith that goodness could or even would present itself to me ever again, much less *immediately*, in the very eye of the storm—in my darkest hour.

I needed to trust more in the perfect timing of my life. When I finally decided to accept the gift without hesitation, the second half of my life opened up. This is a story of that gift I nearly refused.

When my marriage was over I let it continue in the shell of its former self for far too long, treading water and seeing marital counselors, who all kept assuring me I was normal and that my expectations for how a happy marital relationship should work were not unrealistic. I was also telling myself that by delaying the inevitable I was giving my children the time they needed to become independent and out of the nest. But I actually had a huge second reason for staying—I was terrified to leave. I had no idea what I would do, where I would go or how I would "land" when I jumped off the cliff. I was miserable and seeping self esteem with each beat of my heart, like blood from an open wound. Years had gone by and finally the process of accumulating courage solidified into a palpable thrust of action near the beginning of the twenty-fourth year of our marriage and I began to see some lawyers. I began to put actions to my miserable complaints because I had the epiphany that I was more worried about what I would become if I stayed in the marriage than if I got out of it. Not wanting to age into a sour old woman spilling buckets of regrets for what might have been, I decided to sprout my wings on the way down as I made my decision to leap off the cliff. I was focused, finally, on the task of getting unmarried. I took it logically. I had the talk with my husband, announcing my unhappiness (which he did not take seriously) and detailing the various reasons why I wanted to end the marriage; reasons which he continued to rationalize away as if he actually thought he might be successful in erasing them from my reality. I worked around him and continued with my plans. I had seen three lawyers and was still searching for the "good fit" lawyer I wanted when an odd thing happened.

I received a mysterious phone call from an elderly woman. She left a message on the recorder asking me to call her back, as if I would know who she was, but I hadn't a clue. A day went by. I finally called. She was the mother of an old boyfriend. She had always been like a second mother to me. I loved Esther...and her son had not been merely a boyfriend. He was an extraordinary guy I had loved deeply and long but dumped in my sophomore year of college in large part because of my Mother's strong disapproval of him but also because I was not at all ready to leave college, accept his proposal and settle down. I was having too much fun. I was young and stupid. I thought there would be others like him in my future. I did not know enough to recognize the rare gem among the other cleverly packaged but less precious chips of stone. It had been a cruel breakup, taking him by stinging surprise. He literally drove off into the sunset, tears welling up in his eyes and tires screaming as he made an instantaneous directional correction toward Montana. As badly as I had handled it at the time, I knew that the timing was wrong for our relationship to work

Esther was calling to offer me back my old high school ring which had hung around her son's neck and had been rattling around in a junk drawer for twenty-seven years. We had a lovely talk—I asked about her son; she told me he was in Texas, instantly providing his phone number with the *strong suggestion* that I call him because he "never got over you." Quite a shocking remark from Esther, since he and I were both married. I got chills on my arms.

Having not revealed to her that I was screening lawyers about a divorce, she could not know (or could she?), how unwise it seemed to me to call him. Why open that old door at a time when I was an emotional mess? That very day I had been agonizing over the loss of love in my long marriage and imagining my bleak future, fully aware of the ridiculous odds against my ever being happy with a man again. One idiotic "marital expert" on TV said that if you were a woman over the age of forty-five and divorcing, your chances of ever finding happiness with a man again in your lifetime were extremely slim—the same kind of odds as being sucked up by a tornado, in fact. Based upon ridiculous "research data" like that, I put up huge mind barriers against this man's re-entry into my life.

I struggled with myself all afternoon. Then, hating my weakness of character, I called. It was Sunday, April 14, 1991. This phone call could not be a good thing, I said to myself, as I dialed his number. I saw it as a silly rebound mistake. I saw it as a fluke, a diversionary tactic, a way of kidding myself; almost like a test to see if I was foolish enough to complicate things even further, over-lapping one messy situation with another.

He was astonished but happy to hear from me. Too happy…we chatted on the phone. We talked again. We began to talk nearly every day. This gift of this man came to me, through Esther's link, at what I thought was the worst time of my life. I resisted him. I fought with my instincts. I fought with him on the phone. But we got to know each other again, sight unseen. Was he a jerk? Obese? Handsome? Smart about life, or low on the emotional IQ scale? Kind? I was on guard against being foolish but I asked none of these kinds of questions of him, nor did he ask them of me. It was more abstract than that. *We found our way back to eachother through intuitive realization based upon long conversation.* Months went by. He finally revealed to me that his twenty-five year marriage had not ever been a happy one. I told him I was seeing lawyers, after having seen marital counselors. Finally I re-met this man in person. We fell madly, deliriously in love, and I still did not trust that it was real. I gave it time—and during that time I began to see that I was being offered a surprising and new, yet familiar, gift for the second time around, and the timing that had seemed awful to me at first glance was in fact perfect.

Lovers don't finally meet someone;
they are in each other all along...
Rumi

After I finally sprouted wings and leaped into his open arms without reservation, everything else fell into place and remained properly aligned. Great changes were made in my life, and the lives of my family and friends, because divorce causes a tsunami that sends tidal waves far and wide in all directions, even to the beloved family dog, Tenspeed, who died during the transition. It was not an easy time for any of us, but it was one of those times in life when you absolutely know what you must do and you do it because it is going to restore your entire being to the authentic "you" that had been lost for so long. I gradually began to remember the way I had laughed, the way I had loved, the creativity I had enjoyed, the energy I felt and the faith I relied on before—before the butterfly left my soul. Self esteem returned and joy flowed back in like light through an opening door. Solutions appeared, difficult details smoothed, decision upon decision was made, and although the transitional period was quite painful at times, the agony gradually diminished with the process of healing. I knew I had found a true partner in life.

When he joined me in Denver, the time came to re-introduce this lovely man to my Mother, who had never liked him much before. Imagine her surprise to learn that the young man she remembered from nearly three decades before—the same boy she had questioned so aggressively (auditioned, actually) about world events such as men on the moon and Communist Russia and monkeys in space—and then cheerfully dismissed and forgotten—had grown up and come back around after twenty-seven years to pursue her daughter once again. She could not figure out how this had happened! Then daughter invites Mother to lunch, to sit down with this guy, thus requiring polite conversation for at least a couple of miserable hours. In reality it all took months to unfold but to my Mother it seemed instantaneous. It was an embarrassment to her.

After her initial shock at seeing him all gown up and handsome, she took up right where she had left off, questioning him about world events, picking his brain to see if he was a thinker, and finding out quickly that he was. She expressed disappointment that she did not have cable TV and could not watch CNN where she was certain the best news reporting could be found. She scrutinized him. She observed his obvious love for her daughter. She actually found herself warming up to him—even joking and flirting a bit with the "boomerang man," now transformed and mature.

The next Monday morning a cable TV guy showed up at her apartment door telling her he was there to install cable TV—she explained that she could not afford it. He said that it was a gift. She said that she did not want cable TV for just a month of free-trial time. The cable guy said it was not for a trial time but for a lifetime—a gift of cable TV for the rest of her life, from a man who had lunch with her the week before. She was flabbergasted. She was stunned. She was won over. The gift giver was left wondering why he had never figured out before that it could all be that simple...

The moral of this story, and the epiphany I experienced, is the realization that if you are able to keep your mind open, remain receptive, release your fear and live in the current moment without letting the previous storm of dark moments cloud your perceptions, then you will realize there is a peaceful place on the other side waiting for you. That process is called "having faith". Faith has a voice. In order to hear it you must rule out the un-enlightened advice you are hearing from all outside sources and go within. You must listen to your soul. Give it a chance to speak and you will hear it.

Do not fool yourself into thinking that you are just a victim, and that you are powerless—embrace the experience of being humbled, brought to your knees, by the struggles of life. When these moments happen, accept them as proof that no one leads a charmed life and you are being given a chance to rediscover the core of strength within your soul. These hard times are the defining moments of your life. Get up off you knees and walk again, head held high.

Fearless improvisation, based upon solid intuition, often yields brilliant results that would not have come to the less confident. The rewards are sweet for keeping the faith. Living the abstract life is my adrenaline. It's in my genes. The exotic world that has opened to me as a result of my acceptance of the uncertainty of the artistic life has been my reward for taking the risk to paint. The artistic struggle has been delightfully difficult and rich with meaning, teaching me lessons that cross over to all other facets of my life. I believe that my life is my masterpiece, perfect in its crazy imperfection. My only plan for the fall and winter of my years is to stay at the top of the proverbial ladder, gleefully pouring colorful paint, for as long as I can still climb the steps. Then when my knees give out I will put the canvas flat on the floor and hobble around it with my cane, as I slowly, very slowly, sling the paint.

The resilient nature of my soul is rooted in my creativity. I am grateful for this gift.

The essence of all beautiful art, all great art, is gratitude.
Friedrich Nietzsche

CHAPTER NINETEEN
CALLING GOD—ARE YOU THERE?
Ann Thomas Hamilton

The newspaper referred to "an elderly woman in her nearby home." ELDERLY WOMAN, MY ROYAL ASS!!! Call me an old bitch, a "tough old bird" (I was actually called this by a physician when undergoing a gynecological procedure without benefit of anesthesia!), an aging hippie, an opinionated blue-hair, but PLEASE do not call me an elderly woman. This description of me involving an incident later described as my "greatest epiphany" literally added insult to injury. Reading it conjured up visions of an old woman, dull and benign, trudging through life tending her garden in her comfortable middle-class neighborhood. The phrase was likely taken from the police report by the young responding officer who took one look at my battered face and disheveled grey hair and noted "elderly woman." Throughout my sixty-three years on the planet I have confronted many challenges, undertaken a variety of opportunities and had blessings beyond my wildest dreams. But never will I accept the label "elderly woman."

My life has been a dichotomy—exhilarating and exhausting, astonishing and intriguing, frightening and passionate—not unlike many women my age who have confronted pain and despair and learned volumes. Curiosity and a sense of humor have been my good friends throughout—senses I often count on to pull me through the darkness of confusion and self-doubt. As I enter the autumn of my life, I know the best is yet to come. Fall has always been my favorite season.

As a woman, I am southern to the core—carrying within the eccentricities of a culture many find puzzling—sweet-pea on the outside, steel-belted on the inside. My female ancestors possessed these traits as well as a deep abiding reverence for the land and its bounty. Some of my fondest early memories are sitting on the screened-in porch shelling fresh-picked, purple hull peas with Grandmomma McNeill and her five daughters, listening to their stories and laughter. While preparing Sunday dinner for the large extended family, they discussed child-rearing, their youths in rural North Carolina, building and buying homes, and sharing future dreams of travel to far-away places with their husbands.

Conflicting personalities abound in many southern women of my generation. We were brought up to be compliant, to provide comfort, to conform, to follow our husbands and to act within the confines of a strict social code. These characteristics remain prevalent in southern women of today. Perhaps it's a deep-seated yearning for a more peaceful, family-oriented, church-based society free from the technologically-driven, fast-paced and often fear-mongering one we find ourselves in today. Many of us adapted to the conformity expected by the "old" society, but found within ourselves the strength, given to us by our mothers and grandmothers, to pursue lifestyles and professions far beyond what these noble women could ever imagine, having served society as school teachers, social workers and nurses before marriage. After the nuptials, however, they did what was expected and became primary caregivers to their children and husbands.

Deep down, I always thought Momma wanted and needed more in her life. But it was never discussed. She accepted her "lot in life" with trust and resolve and never complained. She willingly accepted what Daddy wanted—from employment opportunities to vacation destinations. She died at the age of sixty-seven from melanoma. Sometimes I think she died of heartache from being stuck in a place she abhorred—a place and a culture far away from her beloved sisters and soul-mates. I weep for her to this day. She did what was expected of her. She followed her husband.

Momma gave birth to me on March 9, 1943 in Kingsport, Tennessee where my Daddy worked as a civil/mechanical engineer at Tennessee Eastman Kodak Company. Seemingly, theirs was a happy, satisfying marriage. I never saw them argue in front of me or my sister. If they disagreed, they did it in the bedroom. Momma knew how to run a household having graduated and taught Home Economics before meeting and marrying Daddy. My father was a complex man, the only child of an older physician father and a younger nurse mother. When he was eighteen years of age, he discovered that *his* father had previously been married and had two other male children. Those first Thomas boys ended up in Mexia, Texas where they became doctors. Years later, while on a visit to Mexia, I found the historic cemetery and came upon the graves of the Thomas brothers and their families. What an eerie feeling

I had standing over those grave stones and wondering how different my Daddy's life might have been, had his secret family been revealed to him as a young boy. Southerners are good with secrets—some call it denial.

Daddy was gregarious, funny, smart and friendly to everyone. Momma went along with him, laughing at his antics, traveling to strange places in his recreational vehicle and just "being there" for him. They were both very happy when he retired at sixty-five, and had planned several trips to places they had always wanted to visit. Upon returning from one such trip, they found their home burglarized and all of Momma's silver, china and other very nice old family pieces destroyed. She was devastated. These were her only material links to the family she so adored, and she was not a materialistic woman. She never really recovered from this loss.

Daddy loved all things mechanic and collected antique cars. I benefited from this in that my sister and I had our pick of exotic automobiles to drive from a ten-passenger 1944 Cadillac limousine formerly owned by the governor of Louisiana to a 1927 Rolls Royce Roadster complete with a rumble seat. I suspect that Daddy's hobbies of cars and mechanics replaced the loneliness he felt by being an only child, not knowing who his family really was. He was a secretive man and seemed to relish being so. After his death in 1998, while going through some of his papers, I discovered both his birth certificate and my own. His indicated that his place of birth was Trenton, Kentucky, while mine indicated that he had been born in Bristol, Tennessee. Even in death, the secret remains.

My childhood in Tennessee and Texas was for the most part idyllic and happy. We really lived the Ozzie and Harriet Nelson lifestyle. We created our own entertainment without benefit of television or formal recreational/cultural training save the occasional piano lessons and Friday night football. In Tennessee, there was the excitement of my firemen friends and their dog (yes, a spotted one) at the firehouse across the street. I contracted scarlet fever when I was four and was quarantined in an attic room for about three months completely isolated from my Daddy and sister. Momma came with my meals on a tray three times every day wearing a mask. I don't recall being especially sad or lonely, but I do remember watching and waving to Daddy as he left and returned from work every day from the window high above the driveway. I vaguely remember my sister's reading to me outside the closed door. My imagination ran wild during this time. When I was finally let out of the "cell," I went right to the firehouse to see my firemen friends. At Christmas, I got a red tricycle and rode it endlessly up and down the sidewalks of our street. One day, a new family moved into the neighborhood with a little boy my age. We became friends. I found out he did not have a tricycle, so I gave him mine. After walking home, Momma asked what I had done with it and I told her I gave it to Billy because he didn't have one. Being Scottish and thrifty to the bone, she went marching down the street and retrieved it, but I was not permitted to ride it for several days. This may have been the beginning of my life-long quest to give to those less fortunate than I, which is what I now do professionally.

Shortly after this we moved to Texas where Daddy was transferred to oversee the construction of a petroleum/chemical plant on the banks of the Sabine River in deep east Texas for Eastman Kodak. Our trip in the dead of winter across the south was very scary and perilous due to a severe ice storm that hit the region that winter. From our old woody station wagon, we hauled a Model T Ford—Daddy's pride and joy—complete with its live contents, Howard Duff, the family cat. Once we got to Longview, we lived in the Dun-Roamin' Motel for about a month, until we could find a suitable home at 307 Morris Drive, a place where I remember attempting to dig to China and instead creating a great mud-bath, and building a playhouse that looked like an outhouse, much to the disgust of our neighbors. I remember converting a big fallen tree into a pirate's ship complete with hidden stolen cargo. Best of all, I remember being best friends with Jane Evangelist. She and I remained life-long friends until her untimely death from multiple sclerosis in 1999. Life in Longview was good, even though polio was a big scare for parents. Momma made us take two-hour naps after lunch throughout the summer. I would escape out the bedroom window to run and play in my own fantasy world while my obedient, erudite, older sister read. Guess which one of us was the better student?

During this time, Momma coped, but never really adapted to the nouveau riche ways of the oil boom in the late fifties and early sixties in east Texas. Longview was a fairly small town, but the Eastman folks were considered "transplants" and therefore not wholly accepted into society, even though the plant brought great economic stability to the region. For the most part, all the "transplants" were well-educated and bright, so they created their own community apart from the wild-cat mentality of that era. Many of my female friends in junior high school sported diamond rings their parents provided them as a reward for graduating from the eighth grade. After Momma died in 1981, Daddy married one of the women of that wild-cat era. He believed she would take care of him and bring him comfort. Not so. She wanted his money to feed the obsessive spending habits of her two grown children and herself. He was miserable for the next fifteen years of his life in Longview and silently mourned for his "dear Frances" until the day he died.

Momma introduced and inspired my love of the natural world. She had the proverbial "green thumb" and transformed the red clay dirt of east Texas into lush gardens of bold flowering, climbing plants, all from snips, sprigs, and root starters she found or "borrowed" from neighboring yards. Without formal training, she had an inherent understanding of the balance of nature and the cycle of life. Because of this and her deeply held religious beliefs, she possessed an inner peace and serenity when in her garden enjoying plants and wildlife, especially her beloved songbirds.

Momma did not suffer fools lightly and had a keen sense of humor and a biting tongue when describing some of the "buffoons" with whom she reluctantly came in contact. After meeting "Miss Longview" at a wedding shower, Momma came home and declared the young woman beautiful but possessing the "personality of a tree stump." My growing-up years in Longview burst with adventure and excitement for a small-town girl, but they were also darkened by narrow-minded people whose strict religious beliefs remain there to this day. I am glad to be from there and not still there. Its natural beauty is breathtaking, especially in the spring when the dogwoods and redbuds are in full bloom. The darkness of the piney woods has also made many of its human inhabitants rather sinister, judgmental and unforgiving to those who do not share their beliefs.

Most of my high school friends attended colleges in Texas. I wanted out—way out—and was ecstatic when the letter of acceptance came from Daddy's alma mater, the University of Colorado at Boulder. This was my chance to escape the wild-cat culture of Texas and experience the wild-west culture of Boulder in the sixties. And what a ride it was! Some of that time in my life is reflected in an introduction I made in 1990 of my former boss, Colorado Governor Richard D. Lamm, before he addressed a group of Earth Day participants at the Houston Museum of Natural Science:

Once upon a time in the land of "purple mountain majesty above the fruited plains", there lived a young housewife and mother. Just before Earth Day 1970, like a modern-day "uncorseted" Betsy Ross, she climbed the mesa behind her suburban home in Boulder, Colorado. There, in the shadows of the flatirons that her father had climbed more than 40 years before, she sewed 50 white stars onto a field of green cloth to finish a green flag of ecology. She flew it every day for the next decade, as a symbol of her commitment to protect the Earth.

We were part of a loosely-knit, well-informed group of young Coloradoans who migrated to the Rockies in the early 60s, seeking education and opportunity. We found much more. We watched eagles soar; drank water from clear, crystal, yet unspoiled mountain streams; refreshed our bodies in the cold blue lakes above timberline. We camped, we sang, we laughed together under starry skies. In attempting to find ourselves, we discovered and came to revere a great power— Mother Nature.

At the same time, we watched in horror as our heroes were assassinated. We felt great pain as family members and friends were maimed and killed in the jungles of Southeast Asia. We sat in silence as Neil Armstrong stepped onto the moon. We saw, through his eyes, the fragile blue sphere suspended in the darkness of the universe and we knew we were a very small part of a living whole. We tried to live peacefully, but we knew deep down that our planet was in peril. We participated with great passion and resolved to do our small part on that first Earth Day 20 years ago.

A leader in the Colorado Earth Day movement was a man with the gentle name of Lamm. As a member of the state legislature, he pledged his support "to think globally and act locally." His victory in the governor's race in 1974 was a victory for those of us who were genuinely concerned for the future of our state. I was fortunate to join the Lamm administration as director of the Colorado Office of Volunteerism that allowed me to travel statewide, building a network of voluntary action councils to address serious social and environmental issues facing the state. Working for Governor Lamm was not only exciting but a great learning experience. I learned plenty about politics and how to maneuver between three very diverse sectors—the public, the private and the voluntary.

How I miss those majestic mountains and golden fields of grain. Hopefully, that old green flag has flown again and again to signal a renewed effort to save the planet. I often wonder if we still have the resolve to accomplish that mission.

By reading this, you get an idea of the next twenty years of my life. My time in Colorado was one of pure enlightenment—an age of self-discovery and growth with pockets of intense pain and disappointment in myself and in those I dearly loved. Marriage right out of college resulted in the birth of my two children and with them came the awesome responsibilities, amazing joy and hard work that go with it. Adding to this challenge was the fact that I was living in an extremely dysfunctional atmosphere. As a family, we moved nine times in eleven years, and divorce finally came after thirteen years of marriage. I wrote the following shortly after the divorce about our union and its offspring:

BROOKE—child born of passion!

Strong, independent, stubborn, honest, straight-forward, sporadic, active, nervous, beautiful...

WELLS—child born of love!

Sensitive, introspective, kind, questioning, gentle, confused, supportive, frustrated, sweet...

At this time, violently opposed to each other and insecure.

Will they be friends again? YES!

Both have learned from examples set by their parents whose passion and love were diminished by immaturity and selfishness.

We will grow separately, but friendship and love will be the end reward!

I am happy to report, after three attempts at reconciliation and separation, my spousal relationship ended permanently with a move back to Texas in 1985. However, my prediction of eventual friendship and love has come to pass. Both children were badly damaged and carry the scars of their parents' highly emotionally-charged relationship to this day. To my surprise and delight, both have made the necessary "corrections" to their lives and seem to have comfortable, stable, solid relationships with their partners to the degree possible given the complexities of today's society. I have had multiple intimate, loving relationships with others, but remain friendly with my former spouse when we are together for family gatherings and celebrations like my daughter's fortieth birthday celebration in Saint Louis on Valentine's Day—a most joyous occasion.

Our marriage was one of enormous extremes. Being pregnant, I entered it with shame and reluctance. He joined it with pride and assurance that it was the right thing to do. In retrospect, we were just not ready to assume the tasks of building a family with the firm foundation of mutual respect and trust that such relationships require. We were simply too young, too inexperienced and completely unprepared for parenthood. Stability was not a part of the scene. While I have many sorrows and regrets over our inability to provide a secure, safe environment for the family, I am grateful for having my children. Because of this union we gave society two socially-responsible, productive, intelligent adult children who are friends today even though they live in different states. We have the incredible good fortune of having three of the world's most beautiful, talented, intelligent granddaughters. Additionally, I am pleased to know that my children have both selected mature, thoughtful, industrious partners whom I respect and admire. My children fully acknowledge the pain and hardship of being our off-spring, but both often say that, despite all the confusion and anger, they knew they were loved. I thank God for that.

On July 4, 1985—Independence Day—I packed the car purchased the week before with an income tax refund. My dog, Howard Earl Morgan, and I headed to Houston where I began a new life of making exciting new friends, finding employment and facing new challenges with the rock solid support of my dear sister and brother-in-law. My son had already relocated to Houston and a stable environment thanks primarily to his uncle by marriage—a true life-saver and role-model for an angry young man. My daughter stayed in Boulder with friends throughout the summer, but followed us in the Fall.

After three jobs during my first six years in Houston with the incredible help of a new and loving support group, I was offered an opportunity to work in philanthropy—a profession to which I had long aspired. My former positions in government, non-profit organizational development, establishing public/private partnerships, and fundraising gave me the skills needed to begin a professional career as a grant officer for a large private foundation. Since 1991, I have had the good fortune and honor to assist in giving away "someone else's money" to deserving causes.

The gentleman who established Houston Endowment in 1937 was Jesse H. Jones, a progressive thinker for his times, who was also known as "Mr. Houston," for his development of a major portion of downtown— both businesses and institutions—in the early decades of the 20th century. Mr. Jones, and his wife Mary, so loved Houston that they left their considerable fortune to the private foundation they established for the betterment of the city and state. As U.S. Secretary of Commerce and Chairman of the Reconstruction Finance Corporation he made the following statement in a CBS Radio Broadcast on January 2, 1937:

An enlightened world will find a way to live in peace. There will always be struggles for supremacy in governments, between governments, and among people, but these struggles should be confined to betterment of economic conditions and living standards. We would all do well to keep constantly in mind the thought that the people of one country cannot long be prosperous and happy if those in other countries are miserable and unhappy. This applies as well to people within a country, and especially our own country. There should not be too wide a difference between living conditions in the various strata of society.

I keep this quote posted in my office and refer to it often as I do the work that I believe Mr. Jones would expect of me. Being a grant officer in a major foundation is certainly not without challenges, but it is one of the most rewarding careers anyone could ever want. Not only does it feed my need to "do good," it provides me opportunities to meet a wide variety of committed people whom I greatly admire and respect. I am humbled in their presence. The persistence, dogged determination, and abundant energy of "my heroes" in the non-profit arena make the world a better place and provide me with positive reinforcement at a time when doubt, negativity and fear seem to be flourishing throughout the world. Indeed, we would all be well-served by adhering to the words Mr. Jones uttered over seventy years ago at a time when our world was facing daunting challenges as it is today.

Even though I think I have the best job in Texas, my life has not been free of stress, anxiety and pain. After I turned fifty-nine, I had three major health crises in three years. In 2000, I underwent major invasive surgery. In 2001, (eight days after 9/11) I was given the news that all women dread. I had breast cancer. And in 2002, I broke my first limb. All this for a woman who had never spent one night in the hospital except for the births of her children. I made it through these experiences with the help of family, friends and professionals and declared to myself that, after three life-limiting health issues in three years, I was "home free" for at least the next decade, or so I thought.

In 2004, a sinister force crept into my life and all the strength, perseverance, resilience, and courage I had accumulated over sixty years was put to the test. After experiencing a wealth of minor epiphanies, including seeing beautiful Boulder, Colorado nestled at the foot of the Rockies for the first time at the age of thirteen, and watching a flock of Blackneck Cranes land in the Phobjikha Valley of Bhutan amidst a colorful, cultural celebration at the age of fifty-seven, my greatest epiphany unfolded in the early morning hours of May 17, 2004 right in my own bedroom at the ripe old age of sixty-one. The account that follows is my best recollection of this pivotal event that brought the true substance and meaning of my life into sharp, permanent focus. I wrote it several months afterward, as a way to work myself through the trauma and to make a case for reinstating the neighborhood patrol to the residents of my subdivision who had let it lapse for lack of funding. I entitled it "The Victim's Tale."

My rational self tells me: Get over it, Ann! Being a victim is such a bore. Why the obsession? Be thankful. You are alive and still in one piece. It could have been much worse. Your friends tell you that you acted with strength and courage. Just get on with your life and focus on the positive!

*Then my irrational self kicks in. The slightest incident—a sudden sound in the night, a man shouting obscenities from a bicycle, the back of **his neck** in the courtroom—triggers the frightening experience. Tears streak down my face and the shaking starts until I convince myself back into that rational self...the comfort of my home...the love of my family...the wisdom of counselors and clergy...the kindness of neighbors...the efforts to reinstate the constable program in the Garden Oaks neighborhood of Houston where I live.*

Here is my story.

About 2:30 on the morning of May 17, 2004, I am sleeping when I feel a strange presence come into my room and wake up to see a massive hand turning on the light beside my bed. I shout, "What are you doing?" The hand comes down hard into my nose and I feel the pain of cracking cartilage. I hear, "Shut up, you motherfu...!" The body to that massive hand jumps on top of me in the bed. The face is partially covered with a blue and white bandanna, but I see the wild eyes. I fight back screaming to the top of my lungs...another blow..."Shut up, you motherfu...bitch". I grab for his "privates" imploring my dog, "Bite him, J. K., bite him!"...another punch to the jaw...the hand appears again with handcuffs...dark thoughts enter my mind of being cuffed to the bedpost...rape?... murder?...a slow death?...the hand pressing them around my left wrist...I am struggling hard to pull them off...falling sideways off my high bed...thump... onto the floor...another jump from behind...cuffs on both wrists...the lock tightening...leaving me helpless...hopeless...bleeding...shaking...crying...the hands enveloping me in my own bedspread, which is absorbing the profusion of blood..."Shut up, bitch...just be quiet...I want money! I know you have it. Where's the money?"

I begin to pray and to think as I hear the hands rummaging through my dresser pulling out drawers..."Shit! Where's the money?" A move to the other room...desk drawers being pulled out and thrown...My rational self says: "Okay,

Ann, you have nothing to lose. Treat him with respect—like a human being." He stomps back into the bedroom. I say, "Sir. I am a Christian woman." He responds angrily, "Don't give me that God shit!!!"...grabbing the purse...finding my wallet. "Sir, I have very little money. You are welcome to anything I have—my television, my video, anything, but please don't hurt me anymore, please, sir!" I silently pray, "God, guide me."

"Credit cards...that's it...we're going to the bank!" He unwraps me...pulls a suit jacket out of my closet...un-cuffs me..."Put this on! We're going to the bank!" I respond, "Can I put on my shoes and shorts?" He mutters, "Make it quick!"...the keys drop...the cards drop...I help him find them...high state of agitation...I try and calm him, "Don't worry...we'll find the keys." They fall from the bloody bedspread...he picks them up..." Sir, only one of these cards will work at the bank"...he grabs me by the arm...we walk to the front door. "Don't do anything stupid or you'll get this!" I look over to see a long knife cupped into that massive hand. I shiver with fear as he tightens his grip on me.

We leave...I lock the door...a puppy greets us...jumping...tail wagging...I ask: "Is that your dog?" He answers: "Yeh." I say: "Don't you want to take him with us? We probably won't be coming back here." He replies: "Nah, he knows his way home. Come on get in the car and don't do anything stupid." I do as instructed as he puts the passenger seat in a reclining position as he sits down in it. We're off to the bank on 19th Street. I remember the cameras there. As I drive down 32nd, he turns the radio to another station. A black woman is singing a melody. I say, "She has a beautiful voice." He grunts. We discuss the amount of money he wants...$400. I explain that I probably could only get $200. He says he had a card two weeks ago and it gave him $400 and to try that and if it won't work then he'll take $200. He asks me to drive faster. I tell him that I don't want us to get picked up. (What a strange thing for me to say.) I tell him that I am a woman with a forgiving heart and that I know he must be having hard times. I explain that I have had my share of tough times also. He says, "I've got kids. I'm doing this for them. I've got to get money for them." I tell him that I have three granddaughters but they don't live in Houston. He says, "That's good." He seems calmer.

We get to the bank and he tells me again to try for $400 first and then $200. I do as he says and $400 pops out. I hand it to him never looking straight at him. He quickly takes it and seems relieved. He tells me to take him back to 34th and Yale "up near the railroad tracks." I do as told and pull over to the curb to let him out. He instructs me to pull into the parking lot. My heart sinks as I think, "Now he's going to kill me." I pull into the parking area waiting for the knife to enter my heart. I stop. He opens the door, looks down at me and says,

"I'm sorry lady, I just had to do what I had to do. Now you go do what you have to do."

I pull out of the parking lot, look in the rear view mirror, watch him walk north counting the money. I immediately go to my neighbor's house; I pound on the door. The neighbor finally comes. I fall apart screaming, crying, shaking, begging him to call 911, that I have been assaulted. He comes to my rescue and before long the police are there, an ambulance arrives and soon thereafter, my sister and brother-in-law. At last, I know I'm going to be safe even as the chills and shakes persist. Dark memories of a long ago past envelop me.

My assailant was apprehended the next morning after committing the same horrible crime at the house of a young neighbor. This time the police caught him. He is in jail awaiting the trial he has requested. I have been to every hearing and will go to the trial as well. This man cannot do this to others ever again. As it turns out, he was seen in the neighborhood at least three weeks before my assault wearing that blue and white bandanna. I cannot help but wonder if this would have been a much different story had the constable patrol program been in place in May of 2004—a time that will always bring back those dark memories.

I have watched both of my parents die—one fairly quickly without pain, the other, painfully slow, but I never ever thought I would witness my own death. While the actual incident lasted less than forty-five minutes, it is true when they say your life rushes before you when sudden death comes calling at the hands of another. In retrospect, I was prepared. Throughout my life, when in danger or in harm's way, that inner voice has always spoken to me. But until the life-threatening event of 5/17/04, I never acknowledged that the inner voice was God's voice within me. I fought, I screamed, I cried and then I calmed myself down by listening to my heart—the inner voice of God—speaking to me clearly, asking me to see and understand my attacker as another human being—frail, scared, and most unfortunate. As I reflect back, that inner voice has said, "There but for the grace of God, go I." During this particular epiphany, I literally left my body and placed myself into the body of my assailant. In doing so, I began to understand that we were both an accumulation of our pasts—me, one of fortune and opportunity and he, one of poverty and hate. Despite our differences, we were connected in our humanity. There but for the grace of God go all of us as we move through "this veil of tears" (as Daddy called it). The lesson in it all is that we have but a short time on this earth. Live life full and well. Strive for goodness. "Do unto others as you would have others do unto you."

After six visits to district court, accompanied each time either by my loving family or friends, I saw my assailant sentenced to sixty years in prison for the crimes of aggravated assault with a deadly weapon and aggravated kidnapping. My recount of the event and a letter written by my son who had flown in to be with me in the aftermath, were not included in the file presented to the court by the district attorney's office as a part of the pre-sentencing report. Thankfully, the parents of the other victim knew some of the court officers, and we were able to get them introduced into evidence at the sentencing hearing. We watched as the judge read them from the bench. My son's letter was particularly powerful in its indictment of the perpetrator:

Judge Keel:

On the morning of May 17, 2004, my uncle wrote an e-mail to me at work. He stated that my Mother, Ann Hamilton, had been attacked in her home by an intruder during the night and that she had been beaten and robbed. She had been treated for her wounds and was recovering at his house. I immediately booked a flight and flew to Houston to be at my Mom's side.

Upon my arrival I noted that she had sustained bruises to her face, where the man had punched her and lacerations and bruising to her wrists where he had bound her with handcuffs as he rifled through her belongings she had in her bedroom. After that he kidnapped her, making her drive to a bank and withdraw the maximum amount of $400 from her checking account. After giving this man her money, she had the personal strength to talk him down and, thankfully, he left her there.

I remember we watched a news telecast shortly after my arrival, which depicted the scene of an arrest just blocks away from my Mom's house. The camera captured an image of the bandanna the man had been wearing as well as one of his face. It was then that my Mom said, "That's him". She had identified the defendant in this case, S_____ S_____, as her attacker. Evidently, this man had been stalking her neighborhood at night, and had broken into and attacked two other women during this same period.

Given the nature of his predatory behavior and the premeditation used in these attacks, I feel as though Mr. S_____ is a highly dangerous person who should be sentenced to the full extent the law will allow and incarcerated for the remainder of his natural life. It is my opinion that if S_____ S_____ is granted freedom again, he will murder his next victim, if given the opportunity. It is in your hands.

Thank you for you consideration in this crucial matter.

Thomas Wells Hamilton

In a case like this, one must trust that justice has been done. But let me tell you, federal district court in downtown Houston, Texas does not remotely resemble an episode of *Law and Order*. The courthouse is a place of intense sadness, filled with people who made very bad decisions in their lives. It is a place where families of both the victims and the criminals suffer in silence as they sit and wait for the wheels of justice to move ever so slowly in bringing incidents such as mine to conclusion. All of us suffer knowing that we will never ever quite see life in the same way again. My assailant will be eligible for parole in thirty years, whereupon I will be ninety-three years of age or dead. He will have reached the age of fifty-three or he too will be dead. After thirty years behind bars, if he is still alive, he will likely be but a shadow of a man, well beyond the hate and anger so prevalent on that fateful morning when our paths crossed. Perhaps he will hear that inner voice of God and find the reverence for life that he was never able to fully enjoy on the outside. Hope springs eternal, even in the Texas prison system.

My greatest epiphany came as I was wrapped up in my blood-soaked bedspread. Death can come at anytime. While I am not ready to leave this good Earth, I am fully prepared for my departure, thanks to a young man who has likely never known love—desperate and ignorant—a man who allowed me to hear the inner voice of God.

Robert Nozick describes the end of life on Earth in his book, *The Examined Life*. His description seems a fitting close to this chapter, *Calling God: Are You There?* My answer is an astounding YES!!!!

I understand the urge to cling to life until the very end, yet I find another course more appealing. After an ample life, a person who still possesses energy, acuity and decisiveness might choose to seriously risk his life or lay it down for another person or for some noble and decent cause. Not that this should be done lightly or too soon, but some time before the natural end—current health levels might suggest an age between seventy and seventy-five—a person might direct his mind and energy toward helping others in a more dramatic and risky fashion than younger, more prudent folk would venture. These activities might involve great health risks in order to serve the sick, risks of physical harm in interposing oneself between oppressors and their victims—I have in mind the kinds of peaceful activities and nonviolent resistance that Gandhi and Martin Luther King engaged in, not a vigilante pursuit of wrongdoers—or in aiding people within violence-ridden areas. Utilizing the freedom of action that is gained by the willingness to run serious risks, people's ingenuity will devise new modes and patterns of effective action which others can emulate, individually or jointly. Such a path will not be for everyone, but some might seriously weigh spending their penultimate years in a brave and noble endeavor to benefit others, an adventure to advance the cause of truth, goodness, beauty, or holiness—not going gently into that good night or raging against the dying of the light but, near the end, shining their light most brightly.

***

Postscript

Hardly a day goes by that I don't think about the young man who assaulted me three years ago. I wonder how and where he is imprisoned. I especially think about his family, including his three young children, and whether or not they see him or if they have given up and stopped visiting or supporting him. His family was at all the hearings when he was being tried and eventually sentenced. Their faces, especially his children, continue to haunt me.

I am a realist as well as an avid news junkie on issues related to the environment, crime and social justice. I have learned that the only way to survive the Texas prison system is to align yourself with a gang. Therefore I suspect that he has joined a prison gang and has become even more angry and hardened. However, my hope is that he has sought and accepted help in prison and is making progress in becoming a more responsible person, and an example of positive change for his children. *That* would be his epiphany.

CHAPTER TWENTY
AN EPIPHA-MINI

KEYS

No wonder kids are afraid in the darkness of their rooms at night.

As my three year old and I stood outside
the front door of our house,
car waiting in the driveway,
ready to leave for an afternoon of errands,
I put my house key in the door and locked it.

She looked at me quizzically and said,
"Mommy, why do you always lock the door?
Everyone in the whole world has keys!"

CHAPTER TWENTY-ONE
THANKFULNESS
Jean Marie Westland's Story
Written by Jo Ann Brown-Scott

This being human is a guest house.
Every morning is a new arrival.
A joy, a depression, a meanness,
some momentary awareness comes as an unexpected visitor.

Welcome and entertain them all!
Even if they're a crowd of sorrows,
who violently sweep your house empty of its furniture,
still, treat each guest honorably.
He may be clearing you out for some new delight.

The dark thought, the shame, the malice;
meet them at the door laughing, and invite them in.
Be grateful for whoever comes,
because each has been sent as a guide from beyond.
Rumi, 13th century poet from ancient Persia

Jean is a like a character out of the 1940's. At age seventy-nine, soon to be eighty, she has beautiful Betty Davis eyes, Lauren Bacall cheekbones and silver gray hair cut in a straight across, no nonsense bob with bangs. She greets us in her characteristic husky voice, Pall Mall in hand. You can almost hear big band music in the background—String of Pearls, Begin the Beguine. You can picture her all dolled up in the clothes of that era, but today her willowy figure is clothed in brown corduroy jeans and a gorgeous hand knit sweater of colorful design.

We meet again after many years, having known each other before in a casual friendship when we both lived in Evergreen, Colorado. Evergreen was simpler then, and she was part of an antique shop cooperative on Main Street that became a hub of activity for the little mountain village outside Denver. Some big names in the music industry, including one red bandanna-ed and pigtailed country music star who lived just up the canyon, wandered frequently into the shop, as did other folks that you would recognize as nationally known movers and shakers of that era. Politicians. Artists. Owners of prominent companies. The occasional film star. Many of these people made casual conversation, sharing local news and stories as they chose unique accent pieces for their mountain get-away homes. You didn't go into town without stopping there. Everyone loved Jean. She was a local treasure.

Jean and her husband Ken enjoyed a busy social life and knew a lot of people. Jean has dozens of stories stored up and she tells them very well. She also has well defined opinions on just about every subject—she says her life is an open book. Her dry sarcasm is legendary; she can knock you out with her irreverent remarks. She can slay you with a look. She will tell you flat out if you need to stop doing something that she finds a silly habit or a destructive train of thought. And you try to stop it then and there. She is the kind of person who stays your friend forever and keeps in constant touch with everyone she likes, going back decades in time. She is amused by keeping abreast of all the news that is "fit to print." She admires strong people—she especially admires Barbara Bush and Pope John Paul. Who you choose to admire says volumes about your character.

Jean now lives in Buena Vista, Colorado, a two hour drive from Denver to the south and west. My friend Lorelei and I visit in early April when winter is finally losing its white-knuckle grip, on the brink of surrendering to spring. The morning half of the trip offers breathtaking views of wide open grassland basins, turning a terrycloth towel texture of lush green, surrounded by snow covered mountains. We see large expanses of ranch land, some dotted with red barns, and elegantly weathered farms, along with a most abundant display of wildlife at every bend in the road. There are Rocky Mountain goats grazing by the roadside, delicate skinny-legged antelope and literally hundreds of elk in many separate herds, lazing and letting the pregnant females gorge themselves on new grass before birthing time. We could imagine Indians on horseback in the distance of another time and a different world.

Buena Vista is the most basic of little towns—flat, perhaps a couple square miles, friendly and natural, with not a hint of rush in the morning's unfolding. Nothing to rush toward. There is a new library, a poor excuse for a grocery in the opinion of city folk, a diner that doubles as an internet café, and a few other business establishments. It seemed the perfect place for Jean and Ken to settle in for the final chapter of their lives. It welcomes retirees, offering a moderate banana-belt climate, a dash of small town charm, plenty of peace and quiet and a community of likeable people including other retirees with whom they could socialize.

Jean's lovely ranch style house is located in a country neighborhood with winding dirt roads on the outskirts of the tiny town. As our car stirs up dry dust clouds we notice the houses are widely spaced and surrounded thickly with pinion pine. Outside her back deck, displayed as if in a movie set, is the Collegiate Range, this particular day dusted with just enough snow to clearly define every crevasse and craggy outcropping as if in a black and white etching. Feathery breaths of snow swirl in the wind around the top of the peaks and the view could not have been more stunning with the intense blue sky as a backdrop. There are six of Colorado's "fourteeners" in the Buena Vista area and four of them look as if you could reach out and touch them from Jean's backyard. Just that morning a spring snowstorm had blustered through—nearly a white-out, leaving measurable snow on the ground—but then melted off and cleared up by noon when we arrive.

Her home is filled with a tasteful collection of antiques that are most definitely not the grandmotherly curly-cue type. She was in the business and she has a good eye. The rooms are brimming with character and fascinating objects. The dogs bound around with wagging tails and smiles of curiosity for who we are. We begin talking in the kitchen, standing around a large rectangular piece of furniture used as an island, then proceed to the living room as we start the day with her. Jean keeps the conversation going and I am frantically writing and checking my tape recorder. Jean says again that her life is an open book...I am a sponge. Lorelei goes into town for some antiquing while we talk. Later we all drive to near-by Salida for lunch in a classic home-cooked food diner and the conversation never stops. This is a place still light years away from the big city hassles of living in Denver, and after a short time there I find myself shifting down to a slower gear. Why hurry.

Jean and her husband had made a good life in Buena Vista. He served her breakfast in bed every morning; she says just to prevent her from talking his arm off as he sipped his coffee and read the morning paper. Neighbors were close enough for comfort and companionship, but far enough away for privacy. The last five years had been their happiest. Until Kenny died last August.

Before marriage Jean had been a wedding consultant with Marshall Fields; then a recreation worker with the American Red Cross stationed in Northern Africa in the mid-fifties. After a year and a half there she was sent to France where she met Ken.

Jean's husband was a hunk of a guy—a good-looking, "right stuff" kind of fighter pilot during the Korean War, then a commercial pilot, then a corporate pilot until he retired. He and Jean were married forty-eight years, and it was one of those long and happy unions that are now just about extinct. A legendary marriage. Every other word that comes out of Jean's mouth is Kenny...they were pure opposites but madly in love. He was a true gentleman. Humble and self-effacing, but extremely accomplished. He handled things. He was a man's man, but also a great husband. He was not a church go-er; she is Catholic.

He was an outdoorsman, loving the rustic life. Jean hated camping unless, she says, it would be in the lobby of the Waldorf. He was a neat-nic; she a self-proclaimed scatter-brained slob. His glass was half full; hers half empty—he was an optimist. Jean *claims* to be a pessimist, but she seems more of a realist to me, accepting life's challenges and forging her way through them with sheer determination and grit. She has good instincts and uses them. She has known death. She lost her brother when she was sixteen, and she and Ken lost two of their four children. Now Jean is mourning Kenny, but in her typical no-nonsense kind of way. She says she feels his presence. She says that he probably wishes she was doing better than she is, in coping with the loss of him. He would want her to lighten up and be happier sooner. Easier said than done.

She says that she believes he may have had a premonition that he was going to die, based on some clippings, lists and such that she found in his desk. "How To Prepare Loved Ones For Your Death" was one title. He was organized and had his act together, as was his style.

He once asked her if she was afraid to die. She said no, not really, except that she was afraid that she might not have a chance to say a few things she wants to say at the very end. Ken told her that if she had the chance to say all of those things it would indeed have to be a lingering death...she laughs.

Her frame of mind as we begin to talk is one of over-whelming loneliness. She looks the part. I want to hug her, and later I do. I ask her how he died.

He walked the dogs every morning and every evening. This particular morning she watched him walk from the front doorway down the long driveway, out of sight; then a bit farther up the road and a few minutes later he collapsed under a tree. A neighbor found him, about a quarter mile from home with the dogs standing guard. Jean says he was probably dead before he hit the ground—it was that sudden. She knew, if he had a choice, he would have chosen to go out that way, but she has been struggling to accept it ever since. In fact, she said of his death, "Good for him...bad for me."

Let children walk with Nature, let them see the beautiful blendings and communions of death and life, their joyous inseparable unity, as taught in woods and meadows, plains and mountains and streams of our blessed star, and they will learn that death is stingless indeed, and as beautiful as life.

John Muir

We talk about the book *The Year of Magical Thinking* by Joan Didion. We had both read it recently. Ms. Didion lost her husband of many years quite suddenly at the dinner table one night. His head fell forward and hit the table, breaking a tooth. She saw it happen. She knew he was dead. But she lived for a year in denial. She resisted discarding his shoes, among her other bizarre behaviors, because he might magically come back some day and need them, all the while knowing in the rational side of her brain that he was forever gone. Jean could identify with that.

Life changes fast.
Life changes in the instant.
You sit down to dinner and life as you know it ends.

Joan Didion

The time since August has been spent resisting the impulse to make any major changes at a time when she is still so emotionally raw. Why sell the house? It is all one level and feels comfortable, and then there are those magnificent views...but why stay. Jean reads and knits and watches TV. Friends drop in and she makes a lot of phone calls. She stays current with the events of the world.

If Jean could change the world in a singular way *right now* in one quick and decisive act, it would be to somehow save the people in Africa from starvation. She believes that we all are just not that different from one another. It is one world, one people. She wants to hold a Somalian baby in her arms. She wants to feed the world's children. She does not understand why that is so difficult to do, if we all put our hearts and our minds behind that purpose.

Jean's epiphany came suddenly one day. She says it is a consistent thread that runs through her entire seven—nearly eight—decades of life. After Ken died, the first day Jean had to take the garbage out to the end of the driveway she realized what a long and tiresome trek that was, and she immediately appreciated that Ken had done that chore almost daily without complaint, and she had never thought to say "Thank You" to him for doing it. Oh, of course he must have known that she appreciated it, but she regretted never having said the actual words. Out loud.

The first time she had to call a plumber or pay a bill, Jean regretted not having said thank you to Ken for always handling things. Not for the major things so much, because she always said it for the big favors, but the daily tasks and the not-so-fun routine jobs went un-acknowledged as even being worthy of a simple thank you. She believes now, however, that they were quite worthy of a "Thank You" and she is remorseful that she neglected to say such an almost effortlessly simple two word phrase. And not just to her husband, but also to all the loving and caring people in her life; she feels deep regret that she has not said it enough. She has lived a big full life, rich with wonderful, fascinating people, a fair amount of tragedy, and a good amount of happiness, and on it goes. There is still time to say it, many times over. Her epiphany came to her in time to self-correct.

Now Jean is *not* a Pollyanna. She takes life seriously. She appreciates kindnesses and she notices everything. To have the realization that she had been remiss in the category of thanks comes as a disappointment to her. But I am sure she expressed her gratitude somehow. She is not a person who neglects such things. I believe she has lived a life brimming over with gratitude; perhaps, in her own opinion, just lacking a bit in the traditional way of expressing it.

The simplicity of the words reinforces their power. The statement is declarative and profound. It says volumes. It can be said with many different inflections. It can be whispered, shouted, drawn out and flowery or just briefly uttered. It can carry with it an implication of affection, respect, enormous gratitude, confidence, pleasure and even sarcasm as well as being just simple punctuation and closure for the act of kindness that preceded it. Jean thinks it is just important that it be said, any old way at all. In the 21st century chaos of our lives, it remains, after centuries, a thoughtful phrase for a thoughtful act. A phrase often neglected, often implied; yet often not said, especially to the ones we are closest to. The people we see every day. The loved ones we talk to long distance. The ones who are always, dependably, there for us.

Ken knew he was thanked. He really did. He knew Jean through and through and he was aware how she treasured and adored him. Everyone is sure of that. But Jean needed to say thank you for her own peace of mind. It is bothering her...it is sort of gnawing at her. She was so unprepared for his death, she says, but would being prepared have made it any easier? She doubts that it would have, after all.

I was once told by a professional person who attended many deaths that people die as they *prefer* to die, in most cases. Peacefully or dramatically, slowly or suddenly—privately or with loved ones all gathered around the bed—people do unconsciously, but almost always appropriately, choose the type of death they prefer, that fits their personality. Ken died as he lived, with a pilot's need for speed. He died with dignity. He was in control. The procedure was considerate of Jean. It was Kenny's perfect way to die. He took the burden for his death onto himself and handled it professionally, just down the road from the home and wife he loved so much, barely but yet safely out of her sight. He spared Jean the agony of witnessing it, and he spared her the agony of any lingering circumstances. For that too she now thanks him...and he hears her.

The idea is to die young as late as possible.
Ashley Montagu
Thank you Jean, for giving us the gift of your story.

CHAPTER TWENTY-TWO
LOVE'S LABELS LOST
Andrea Stoops Villarrubia

He who is in love is wise and is becoming wiser, sees newly every time he looks at the object beloved, drawing from it with his eyes and his mind those virtues which it possesses.
Ralph Waldo Emerson

Love isn't a decision. It's a feeling. If we could decide who we loved, it would be much simpler, but much less magical.
Trey Parker and Matt Stone, *South Park, Chef Aid, 1998*

It is Sunday morning, and I am waking up in Mexico, in love. Last night I could barely sleep, the thunder cracked so loud in the sky, the lightning alternating between flashes that turned night to day and razors that slit apart the blackness, the rain hitting the roof like buckets of gravel on tile. Like the saturated technicolor green of the jungle after the rains, life here is vivid, over-bright, intense. Days stretch forward like gifts, challenges, tests you can't wait to take. I roll over and nestle into the crook of my husband, who is sleeping soundly in the dark of our shuttered room, and drift back into sleep, thankful for the freedom we have created together in our life, with our love. We work when we want, sleep when we want, spend stretches of days tucked away in our house in the jungle, and with few exceptions here and there, pass all of our time together. It is a luxury we have worked so hard for; this freedom, this time.

After years of schedules, routines, sixty-hour work-weeks, commutes—fighting for stolen moments together in the chaos of the city, our high-paying jobs, our social calendar—I hope I never lose appreciation for the simple act of choosing when I start, pause, and end my days, and what I fill them with when I'm not nested here in my favorite place, the bed I share with my man and the occasional cat. This is what I have longed for, to live in a land that I fell in love with the second I stepped off the plane four years ago and into the open air hovering above the tarmac, thick with July's heat and humidity, laden with the promise of the unknown, of newness.

We are not wealthy, we are not retired; we are star-crossed lovers, renegade freedom-fighters looking for a better way to live, to love, to grow our family. Four years after our first trip to Mexico, two years after our wedding here, and one year ahead of our five-year-plan, we left our jobs as managers in the video game industry—a field in which the many rewards are easily matched and often exceeded by the strains placed on the lives of its workforce—to move to Mexico. We sold half of our things; hugged our friends and family; packed our van full of clothing, books, a laptop, surfboards; and drove into our future.

In the five months we have been here, aside from exploring our new world and new freedoms—of time, of responsibility, of rapidly-diminishing anonymity in our little village—we have started a business, purchased land, adopted a puppy, and stopped taking birth control. My husband tends bar two nights a week, learning a craft to support a lifelong dream of owning our own watering hole in the sand some day. I sit here writing a story about my life and the lessons I have learned through love. I am thirty-two, and until we have babies, my most important responsibility is to be the best, most loving and supportive partner and wife to my greatest friend in the whole world: my husband, the man that I love more than life itself, who showed me a love so true and pure, that I found my own lost self in its depths. This is my life. I have never been happier or freer.

My twenty-year-old-self would have bitch-slapped me across the face after reading those last three sentences, telling me to snap out of it and get a life. "Babies and a husband??" she might have yelled…"Is that what your life has come to? Your most important job is being the wife of some man?" She might write me off as just another wannabe-housewife-straight-girl, forsaking my life and career to lay beholden to the male of the species. That's okay. I can let her think that, because I know her—better than she knows herself actually—and I know that she has no clue about true love, or the truly revolutionary act of loving this one person who, whatever else he is, is undeniably, unequivocally, unconditionally perfect for me. So for now she can think whatever she wants—I know someday she'll see it my way.

Some people have always known what lives lay ahead of them—their childhoods like scrapbooks full of funny anecdotes that hint at futures as doctors, musicians, doting mothers, young wives...I am not one of these people. Looking back at my youth in search of clues that foreshadow who I am today, and how I got here, I find myself embellishing moments to force meaning upon them—shoving little memories into bigger shoes to increase their relevance. But this is not my life. My path has been more twisted, a series of long lines interrupted at abrupt 90° angles, which ease into more long, straight lines only to be interrupted again. Rinse...Repeat...Each turn a welcome awakening, a new perspective, all the sweeter for not having seen it coming around the bend. By now I've learned to live with—to love—the unknown paths that lead to new experiences and move life forward. If my future life choices had been limited to only that which I was able to see myself doing...I shudder to think where I would have ended up—I surely can't imagine I would have made it to where I am.

I was not a cool kid. As much as I would like to point to the hip clothes I wore and the underground music I was into, my adolescence was spent pretty much trying to fit in with the rest of the preppy kids in my Louisville, Kentucky hometown. By the time I was old enough to care about fashion and music, I was neck deep in Coca-Cola rugby shirts, Aqua Net Extra-Super-Hold, and Duran Duran. I went through a brief period of obsession with Heavy Metal, a poor attempt to co-opt some coolness from my sixteen year old step-sister who I'd spent the summer with in Kansas. But I missed the curve on that one too—*Girls, Girls, Girls* was far from Mötley Crüe's best album. Suffice it to say that the childhood years of my identity construction were all foundation-building, no style. It wasn't until I was seventeen that I finally started laying down trim and decorating, and by then I was ready to make up for lost time.

My parents divorced when I was ten, and I spent the next six years living with my active single mom in her early thirties—a high-school math teacher, swim coach, volleyball coach, and weekend softball leaguer. School was our life. I was as good a student as I was a kid, and this paid off academically. Among more traditional activities like band, cheerleading, and softball, I peppered my educational resume with such popularity winning exploits as math camp, debate team, computer programming competitions, and humanities camp. I had my head down, my nose in a book, and my track set for that Ivy-League scholarship, with my 4.0 GPA and my National Honors Society merit badge in tow. And then suddenly it was in front of me: the first of many decisions that would change my life.

For Spring break of my sophomore year in high school, I went to visit my dad. He and my step-mom had just moved from Wichita, Kansas—where I'd spent most of my summers since the divorce—to a suburb of Seattle. They were renting a two-story house with a picturesque view of the Cascades and the Puget Sound, a block off the water in a small community called Redondo. For my Kentuckiana-born-and-bred, Florida-vacationing sixteen-year-old self, Seattle was the epitome of West Coast cool. As the week was coming to an end, my dad sat me down and asked me if I wanted to come live with them after I finished the school year. Here was an opportunity to finish high school in an infinitely cooler world than my own, and to live with my dad who I'd always been close with. My mom and I were fighting a lot at the time, her bearing the lop-sided burden of being the custodial parent while my dad could do no wrong in my eyes. I was lost in layers of life plans that were far too rigid for my young self, and far too based on the expectations of others. Above all, I was not happy where I was.

I knew my mom would be none too thrilled to hear that I wanted to split town to live with my dad and his wife. After sixteen years, I was going to up and leave, just when all those years of parenting—many as a single mother—were about to pay off as I entered into adulthood from under her wing. In one of the more thoughtless and cowardly moves of my life, I opted not to inform her of my decision until my dad came to get me that summer. I finished out the school year business-as-usual, telling no one of my plans not to return the following year, nurturing my little secret and relishing the thought of everyone's shock at my sudden departure (even then I had a penchant for the dramatic). I can only imagine the heartbreak I unleashed on my mother, letting my dad tell her that I wouldn't be returning from Seattle that summer, just days before I left with him and two months before she was to marry my step-dad and start our new life as a family. I never regretted my decision to leave—I wouldn't have lived the same life if I'd stayed—but I recognize now that by failing to communicate or face my feelings head-on, I turned a difficult situation into utter agony for someone I loved. It took over a decade to heal those wounds with my mom. In the interim, I would manage to repeat this pattern—wallowing silently in unhappiness until I dramatically and abruptly changed the course of my life—once again destroying the heart of someone I loved in the process. I'm getting ahead of myself, though. Back then, I packed my sixteen-year-old bags and didn't look back.

Moving to Seattle gave me a sudden and unexpected opportunity to re-invent myself, in a world that was completely different and exponentially bigger than what I'd known my whole life. My dad and step-mom shared my honeymooner's infatuation with this new land of rainy days, coffee shops, and million dollar views at every turn. Together, we explored our world and made it our own. I took it all in, and, thanks in no small part to my free-spirited pop, began to cultivate an appreciation of difference and individuality that had escaped me for much of my young life. I stopped trying to look like everyone else, and started finding a new "cool" where before I would have seen "weird." I started listening to The Beatles, and shopping at thrift stores. I dropped acid and saw the world through new eyes. I became fascinated with hippy-chic and fell in love with the sixties, wearing flowered dresses, peasant skirts, and combat boots. I pierced my nose, joined the Seattle Atheists, and stopped saying "under God" during the morning recital of the Pledge of Allegiance. My grades didn't miss a beat, and I graduated at the top of my class as planned. But by then I wasn't interested in the Ivy Leagues anymore. I'd tasted freedom and I liked it. I applied to the one school I wanted to attend, and received a tuition scholarship for my first year at The Evergreen State College in Olympia, Washington, "Home of Environmental Terrorists and Homos[1]."

I first heard about Evergreen on a local Seattle-area sketch comedy show called *Almost Live*. Founded in the 1970's as a small state college with an experimental, integrated approach to learning, and a focus on environmental studies, it was a widely acclaimed institution with a student body of thirty-two hundred, offering the advantages of a small private school for the price of state tuition. It was also the butt of repeated jokes about degrees in cannabis cultivation and free love, its "tree-hugging," progressive student-body viewed with derision by much of the state's rural population of lumberjacks and farmers. With my new appreciation for all things left of center, it was perfect for me, holding the promise of enlightenment and education on so many fronts. I couldn't wait to move in.

Somewhere in the midst of transitioning from high school to college, I started thinking about girls, in, as my grandma would later say, a "funny" way. For me it wasn't some deeply-buried longing coming to surface, so much as a natural progression of thought. I'd had boyfriends here and there, though I did manage to stay a virgin by the time I finished high school, in spite of a few near-lapses in my better judgment. Somewhere between the repeated midnight screenings of Rocky Horror Picture Show, the library book of Lesbian Love Stories, and the Gulf War Protest—where my step-mom and I ended up marching smack in the middle of the Queer Nation Seattle contingent, screaming "We're Dykes, We're Fags, We Don't Want No Body Bags!"—liking chicks suddenly didn't seem that weird to me. In fact, limiting my options to just guys kind of did.

Though I had a few crushes on girls during my senior year, and managed to make out with my hot German-exchange-student friend during a particularly hallucinogenic sleepover, this did not exactly buy me my ticket to Queerville, and I had no idea how to break into the club. One summer day before college, while shopping at the newly opened Urban Outfitters on Seattle's Capital Hill, I came across a necklace I had to have. The set of six happily rainbow-hued rings dangling off a long ball-chain necklace appealed immediately to my (thankfully short-lived) raver sensibility, and I snapped them right up. I couldn't believe my good-fortune when the girl at the counter looked me up and down and asked if I knew that I was buying Gay Freedom Rings. "Of Course," I lied, handing her my ten bucks and throwing the rings over my neck. Within a few more weeks, I had talked one of my coffee-shop customers into giving me the VISIBLY QUEER sticker he had found at a concert, and I was ready for action—sort of.

Going to college was the break I'd been waiting for. If moving from Kentucky to Seattle had given me a chance to explore new sides of myself, going to Evergreen was like being re-born. I didn't know anyone there, and I wouldn't have had it any other way. No parents, no high school friends, no teachers—no expectations about who I was. I could be whatever and whoever I wanted, and no one would think a thing about it. I slipped my newly acquired sticker into the plastic sleeve of my Benson & Hedges Lights 100's, grabbed my freedom rings, and started making friends. The irony that this way of life and identity was something I dressed myself in like a new outfit, when the very notion of freedom for queers was so hard-won by so many before me, is not lost on me now. Then again, I've spent much of my life as a chameleon of sorts, surveying the landscape around me, and molding myself to fit into whatever it was I wanted to be: aspiring lawyer, hippy chick, alt-rocker, lesbian. It's not that I was pretending, or disingenuous, I just had a tendency to approach things with an intellectual curiosity: observe, research, assimilate. Some things stick, some don't—the experience therein being no less valid for having actively sought it out.

Adopting a major change in your identity is much easier in a world where no one knows you. Like water to a sea monkey, just calling myself queer was enough to make it so. Once I had that out of the way, actually being queer in the politically-charged world of Evergreen was absolutely liberating. I was surrounded by Riot Grrrls, Feminists, and Fags, and I had something legitimate to be passionate and pissed off about. I moved quickly from "Bisexual" to "Physically Bi, but Emotionally and Politically Lesbian," to straight up "Dyke." I had become a part of a world that made perfect sense to me now, which a year ago had barely crossed my mind. By the end of my freshman year of college, my education as a young lesbian was well underway, and my identity in my new world was a given. My only problem was that I had yet to sleep with a girl.

With no experience dating women, I had no idea what kind of girl I was really attracted to. This, coupled with my increasing desperation to get some experience under my belt, resulted in me having very few dyke *friends*, because I saw every queer girl I met as a potential date. This started to wear on me—here I was a good eight months into my new lesbian life, and I hadn't even kissed another girl (high school LSD adventures notwithstanding). What kind of credibility could I have as a lesbian when I couldn't land a date with a chick? Just as I was really starting to worry, I met Charlotte[2] at a Queer Nation Visibility Action at the Olympia Roller Rink. She was two years older than me and infinitely worldlier. We were both very girly—though I still hadn't accepted that in my baby-dyke self—and entirely too similar to last. After a week or so of making out, taking showers together, and snuggling, I was absolutely smitten, and dying to go all the way. She met a butch girl with a motorcycle and decided that we should just be friends. I cried to my Tori Amos record for days, and ended up sleeping with a straight girl who showed me how to love inside the box, so to speak.

In addition to providing my first lesbian heartbreak, Charlotte also introduced me to the world of Butch/Fem, a lesbian subculture and identity that had shaped queer history and would shape my life for the next several years. I read everything I could get my hands on about this subversive and sexually charged way of life, and I started down the path to finding my Fem self, another link in the chain of my self-constructed identity.

My second year in college, I decided to live at home with my folks—halfway between Olympia and Seattle—to save money on rent. This also gave me a chance to spend my weekends in Seattle, where my fake ID (another gift from Charlotte) gained me entrance to the lesbian haunts of Capital Hill. I became actively involved in Queer Nation Seattle and was a founding member of the Seattle Lesbian Avengers. I would spend hours at my local suburban Kinko's making Queer Nation stickers, which I would immediately plaster all over my clothes and bags before walking around the mall. Where I had once coveted a single sticker for its ability to gain me access to a new world, I now held the keys to the kingdom, and was running off page after page. It was right there in everyone's faces and I loved it. MUFF DIVING DYKE. WE RECRUIT. FUCK THE SYSTEM AND GIRLS TOO. I wore them like merit badges on my Queer Scouts sash. I came out to my dad when he asked me about the button I was wearing that said "I Like Women." On a trip back to Kentucky, I went to the grocery store with my grandmother wearing my seventies leather jacket, a neon orange sticker in the middle of the back blaring "WHY JUST DRESS LIKE A DYKE WHEN YOU CAN BE ONE?" I thought I was so fucking cool, and I dared anyone to question me. Bravery is so wasted on the young.

My dad and step-mom were nothing but supportive of my new identity, but they could not for the life of them understand why I would want to run around broadcasting the details of my life on every spare inch of clothing for everyone to see. From where I sit now, I have similar reactions to the thought of literally wearing my life on my sleeve—privacy becomes a coveted virtue in small worlds. Yet part of the magic of youth is that you do things that make little to no sense once you're older. In particular, finding and marking our place in the world by proclaiming otherness is a rite of passage that many of us continue in one way or another until we die.

So my nineteenth year consisted of school, activism, clubbing, and dating a string of women. Having decided from my thorough reading and research—more so than any strong instinctual attraction—that what I wanted was a very butch girlfriend, I set out to find one. Between my personal ad in *The Stranger* ("Foxy Fem Dyke seeks Tough Butch Top...") and my activist exploits, I managed to keep up a steady stream of dating for the year, but nothing really took. I found myself projecting more butch-ness onto my dates than they were usually comfortable with, which was a quick way of killing it for both of us. I was so hung up on finding someone who matched the picture in my head that I missed out on what my dates actually had to offer. There is a lesson here that I am still learning each day—to experience each thing for what it is, without measuring it against what I thought it would be.

Expectations of extreme butch-ness aside, I was actually starting to get the hang of the whole dating game, having finally developed my sense of self enough to actually attract members of the same sex. Up to this point, my attractiveness relative to whatever scene I was in had always been quirky at best. Now here I was, entrenched in a world of overt sexuality, finding my look and my hotness, and each new admirer was like money in the bank of self-confidence. I decided I didn't want a girlfriend after all—why be tied down?

That's when I met Mick[3]. She was supposed to be the first true one-night-stand in my new "swinging" lifestyle, with no girlfriend potential since she lived in San Francisco and I was only there for Gay Pride Weekend. We met at Club Q—a women's dance club in a huge warehouse on Townsend Street. She was cocky, good-looking, and extremely butch, though completely different from the cookie-cutter "dykes-on-bikes" image I had in my head. I remember a copy of my then-favorite book, *The Persistent Desire: A Femme-Butch Reader,* on her bedroom floor—no small point in her favor. We had a great weekend together, and made plans to see each other the following weekend in New York, where we were both headed for the 25th Anniversary Celebration of the Stonewall Riots[4].

By the end of the summer, we were living together in Olympia. We both threw ourselves headfirst into the relationship. There were plenty of reasons to be cautious: the nine year age difference, the fact that I was only twenty, the reality that we barely knew each other. But luckily love doesn't always listen to logic. If it did, most of us would be living vastly different lives than we are now. Besides, if you've heard that old joke about the Lesbian, the 2nd Date, and the U-Haul—well, there's a reason for some old jokes.[5]

We rented a cute little house in West Olympia next to the food co-op (how very lesbian, I know) and settled into the routine of our subversive suburban lives. By the time Mick moved in, we had probably logged a grand total of seven days together—late night phone calls notwithstanding. Getting to know someone while living with them is an interesting challenge to say the least, but it worked out alright for us. Between school, work, and nesting into our little home, routine came easy.

The snapshots I see when I look back at that part of my life all share the same tonal quality, the color of youth. I defined myself through my sexuality and my otherness. I read lesbian books, went to girl bars, wrote research papers about gay issues, worked on queer film festivals, and made films about being a dyke. I wore everything loudly, and I was constantly making a point—a habit I wouldn't outgrow until years later.

As planned, Mick & I moved to San Francisco in the summer of 1996, after graduation. From there, life continued to march forward. We were getting by, she as a Carpentry Apprentice, me slinging coffee at Starbucks. I eventually worked my way into semi-film-related jobs, but the main focus of our lives continued to be our home life and our social scene, which was almost entirely made up of dykes. All of our friends were queer women, and the only guys at our parties were Female-to-Male Transsexuals.

I got my first "career" job in my chosen field—as a Production Assistant for a retail advertising network—in 1999. It wasn't the most creative work, but it was production, and it beat working graveyard at the film processing lab. It was also the first crack towards widening my social circle beyond my small queer world, and the first step in defining my adult identity as an individual, outside of my relationship. To be sure, I was still very much identified by my sexuality and my coupled status, and I took great pleasure in plastering my cubicle walls with photos of me and my girlfriend. Yet as the lines of my social scene started to blur, for the first time in my adult life, I was making new friends—friends that lived their own lives outside the confines of the world that I knew.

Having spent the previous three years since graduation *constantly* searching for a better job and fearing that I'd end up answering phones or making coffee forever, I finally felt like I had a respectable gig—one that

I could keep for awhile and grow into to before I started looking again. That's when I got the call. I still remember that day—I had called in sick to work, and when the phone rang I expected it to be my boss (which ironically ended up being the case a month later). I had applied for a Production Coordinator position with a 3D animation company about eight months before. I got the standard postcard reply—"We'll keep your resume on file for future opportunities"—which I loosely interpreted as "Get Lost, Loser." It turns out they actually did keep those resumes on file, and they had a new position open which matched my skill-set. After a brief phone screening (I was so happy I hadn't gone to work that day), I was asked to come in for an interview the following week.

The interview was intense. Up to that point, I had never interviewed with more than one person. This place sent me a schedule for the day, which entailed meeting with six different people—potential bosses, bosses of bosses, peers, partners, heads of HR, etc. I showed up for my interview sporting my new black suit purchased on credit from Nordstrom Point of View (so very professional), my hair pinned back in a smart twist, the tattoo on my arm safely hidden beneath the sleeve of my jacket, my one-time uniform of Queer Nation stickers long since abandoned. I knew it wasn't a conservative company, but I always have believed in dressing up for interviews.

As I imagined myself getting this job—this job that I had been waiting for, my "big break" so to speak—working on an actual feature film for a real animation company, I knew that it would change my life...but to what extent, I hadn't a clue. The roller coaster year ahead of me took off that very day of the interview, when I met a guy named Gabbi. He stood out to me among all of my interviewers. Maybe it was the tattoos blazing across his arms & chest, maybe it was the nail polish coating his long fingernails, or perhaps it was the cool, casual comfort he carried himself with, along with his clear enthusiasm and passion for his job, which played its part in selling me on how great the company was. In any case, this guy clearly put some effort into cultivating a look, and it worked for him. He was strikingly handsome, with mannerisms and a fashion-consciousness that bordered on the feminine, but remained unmistakably male. My brain sized him up, saw a kindred spirit, and concluded—based on my neatly ordered, incredibly limited world view—that he must be gay. In my world, he was too cool to be a straight guy, and my young eyes were too used to seeing in black and white—the idea of existing somewhere in the middle of that spectrum of absolutes was way ahead of its time for my brain.

After landing the job, I was pleasantly surprised to learn that my kindred spirit from the interview would be my on-the-job mentor, doing the same job as me for a different department. Watching Gabbi's every move, I quickly learned the inner workings of the production hierarchy. He had mastered the dance, and did his stressful job with a grace and charm that I admired and sought to emulate. As I got to know him, I saw that he was unlike anyone I'd ever met. When I realized he in fact was not gay, it was like learning that I'd been mispronouncing a word that everyone else knew how to say. It was a chip in my perfectly ordered world—where I had everything and everyone figured out. Everything I learned about him made me want to know more.

Gabbi and I worked closely together each day, putting in the same long hours for little pay, and commuting the same two hour daily round-trip from San Francisco to Palo Alto. Unlike him, I was new to commuting, and I hated the hours driving to and from work alone. One day I experimented with taking the CalTrain to work, which would have been great were it not for the three city buses I had to take just to get to the train station in the morning. Unable to bear the thought of repeating the ordeal that evening when I knew he was driving into the city, I asked my new co-worker and friend if I could catch a ride home with him. I remember that night in his station wagon, smoking cigarettes, listening to music, and talking about our lives. I remember not wanting that ride to end, not wanting our conversation to end. While he enjoyed the company too, his want for privacy made him a reluctant carpooler, but my persistence won out in the end, and we started sharing rides two or three times a week.

Talking to Gabbi was different, challenging, and dynamic. He wasn't from my world—which had become so increasingly predictable in its stereotypical inhabitants—and he didn't take for granted the things that I had come to accept as gospel in life. Approaching topics with my trademark arrogance, assuming he would share my point of view like the rest of my friends, I would find myself instead faced with questions about my thought process, where I had expected only agreement and validation. Speaking about life, relationships, sex, music, whatever—he asked me things I wasn't used to hearing, questions which in turn made me think about myself and my choices in ways that I hadn't considered. Here was this guy that I respected and liked, who didn't automatically agree with me or share my particular view of the world. He said the weirdest shit that I never expected to hear, but that always made me laugh in spite of myself and my ideals about what was "acceptable" (read: politically correct) humor. He listened to the best music—bands that I had never heard of, and albums I loved that all of my friends thought were weird. He was utterly charming, extremely witty, completely cool, and absolutely gorgeous. He would look at me with his big green eyes and dark lashes, and I felt him looking into my soul. He was intense—no one had ever looked at me quite like that; it scared me and turned me on at the same time. Before I even realized what was happening, I found myself falling for him.

At first I didn't think much of it. He was a friend from work who I happened to like hanging out with a lot. After all—I was a lesbian, and I had a girlfriend of six years who I planned on spending the rest of my life with. When this new guy in my life—the first guy in my life in quite some time, friend or otherwise—started creeping into my thoughts and fantasies more and more, I had to face the reality that there was something else going on. As my attraction for him developed, so did his for me, and our friendship began to spark with the electricity of flirtation. The sexual tension was palpable, but at the same time completely diffused. As much as we both felt this attraction to each other, the realities of our lives and our individual circumstances allowed our friendship to flourish outside of romantic pressures.

It didn't take long for Mick to see that my interest in this "Gabbi" fellow went beyond the average work friendship, but having worked so hard to convince myself that it was mere curiosity, it wasn't much of a stretch to convince her of the same. Plus, in our sixth year together, she and I were both used to me developing crushes on other people. I'd had a string of them since early on in our relationship, albeit they had always been women up to that point. They were harmless enough, and we chalked them up to fodder for a healthy fantasy-life. Deep down, I always knew they were connected to some self-conscious need for external validation, but I thought they were just part of life—not a warning signal that something was missing. It's easy to accept a thing as normal when it's all that you know. It wasn't until I stopped getting crushes, and stopped seeking that validation outside of my relationship, that I saw it for the warning sign it had been. But I'm getting ahead of myself again...

Between long days at work, carpooling, and the occasional night out with other mutual work friends, my friendship (and infatuation) with Gabbi continued to grow over the next few months. As I found myself thinking of him more and more, I started to worry that this wasn't just another passing crush. I started looking for excuses to see him or call him—under the guise of friendship, but knowing that my motives went deeper than that, whether I was acting on them or not. I couldn't wait to go to work again on Mondays because it meant seeing him again.

Aside from this apparent crush on Gabbi, Mick and I were growing apart in other ways. For the first time in our relationship, I had a circle of friends from my new job that weren't part of our usual crowd and world. My new pals and I spent a big part of our weeks together at work and had a lot in common in terms of our goals, interests, and ambitions in life. Mick wasn't a part of that world. Maybe I didn't work hard enough to include her, maybe she just wasn't interested in going out with my new friends from work—most likely it was a little of both. In any case, it was one of many fissures in our relationship that would eventually lead to its demise.

With all of these factors swelling and colliding in my head, I began to drown in a wake of confusion, doubt, and unhappiness. As my attraction to Gabbi grew deeper, I came face to face with questions I did not want to answer. Was I seriously considering leaving the woman I loved, who I had built a life and planned a future with? For what—some obsessive crush on a co-worker? I couldn't even be sure how he felt about me. Even if there was a slight chance that things would work out with him, what if they didn't and we had to work together? Plus I had never lived on my own—what would my life be like and how would I support myself in a city like San Francisco on my entry-level salary? Add to all of that the fact that even being attracted to a man went against everything I stood for and thought I was. What would this mean for me as a lesbian, a queer filmmaker, a fem dyke? Would my friends still want anything to do with me? Leaving a woman for a man is tantamount to heresy or treason in the lesbian world. Could I deal with becoming what I had judged so harshly? I didn't want to be just another straight girl, and I certainly didn't want to be a "hasbian."[6]

These conflicting thoughts sent my head spinning. I was afraid to talk to anyone about what was going on. I knew once I verbalized what I was feeling, I would have to really acknowledge it and take some sort of action—which was incredibly scary. I began to take stock of where I was in life, and where I had been. Looking long and hard at the path that lay ahead of me and the commitment I had made to Mick, I had to face the reality that at twenty-six, I didn't want the same things that I had wanted and committed to at twenty. Mick was about to turn thirty-five and wanted to have children soon, which I was in no way ready for. I barely knew who I was myself—I couldn't fathom being someone's mother.

Still, Mick was a good woman, and all of our friends saw us as a model couple. We had been together longer than most people we knew, and it was hard to imagine life without her. I kept telling myself to just put this other thing out of my mind—that I was throwing away my life for a crush (on some boy of all things)—but in the end I knew it was more than that, and that the turmoil in my heart and head went beyond my attraction to Gabbi. Whatever happened or didn't happen with him, I had to come to terms with the fact that if I was looking so hard for something outside of my relationship with Mick, it wasn't fair to either of us for me to keep pretending I wasn't.

Mick and I grasped at last resorts—deciding non-monogamy might be a way for me to get this external need out of my system. Rules were established and guidelines laid down, but feelings don't follow rules. She saw me slipping away and tried to hold on by opening a door that leads down a dark and slippery path. Even the idea of an open relationship sounds utterly foreign to me now, but poly-amory and non-monogamy are common in the queer world, so it wasn't that far-out at the time. Of course the one thing that she asked of me—that I stay away from Gabbi—was the one thing I couldn't promise. I knew that I had no interest in just sleeping around for the sake of sowing my oats. At the same time, I knew that I couldn't leave her for him. That wouldn't have been fair to anyone involved, and I couldn't put a failure state onto any future chance I had with Gabbi. I had to leave knowing that I would be on my own. I had to face my fears about being alone, about being ostracized by my lesbian friends, about becoming just another girl who finally "found the right man" after some "experimental lesbian phase."

As I surveyed the paths that lay ahead, each forking sharply away from the other towards opposite outcomes, I looked back on my life up to that point—on the choices that led me to where I was now standing. I had made some pretty big decisions along the way, and as tough or as uncertain as those decisions had been, I had always been true to myself, and had always made the right choice for me. The idea of being alone wasn't so bad really—I thought it might do me some good, give me a chance to rediscover myself, get back in touch with things that I liked to do, things that had taken a back seat or simply fallen away in six years of molding my life to another's. The idea that I might fall in love with a man was trickier. How many times had I chastised others for this unthinkable act? How many times had I thought, "never—not me"? What satisfaction would I be giving to those in my family that had accepted my lesbianism through forced smiles and gritted teeth—assuming it was just another rebellious act to garner attention? Still, what did any of that matter in the big picture of my life as long as I was doing the right thing for *me*? I had never made any important decisions in my life based on what others would or would not think of me, and I wasn't about to start now. That twenty-year-old who walked around her suburban town plastered with Queer Nation stickers didn't live by the rules of those around her, and at twenty-six, I couldn't live by the rules of the Lesbian Nation if it meant denying something I felt in my heart.

That's when I knew I had to leave. Mick and I decided to separate for a bit—neither of us was ready to let go completely, though I suspected in my heart that I wouldn't be back. I see now that I bought into the idea of a separation as some sort of safety net, a way to give myself something to come back to if I got out in the world and realized I'd gone mad. Like all those years before when I left my mom, my failure to be completely honest about my intentions only amplified the pain I was to inflict upon someone I loved.

I spent two weeks crashing with friends before finding a month-long sublet in a house with two dykes. Thankfully they were more open-minded about my situation than I probably would have been before all of this. Within a week of moving out, Gabbi & I had our first date. Our mutual friends surely thought we were crazy, just as we both knew that logically we shouldn't be rushing into anything. Here I was, having just left my partner of six years, telling her that I needed to find myself, to be alone and live on my own for a while, to get my life together outside of a relationship, and within a week I was starting something else, with the guy that I had sworn over and over (to her and to myself) that I was NOT leaving her for. I tried to tell myself that I should wait, that I was going against everything I had told myself, my lover, my parents, and my friends about why I was leaving. Gabbi had plenty of his own reasons to stay away—what if he really was just a crush to me, or I was merely fulfilling some fantasy of being with a guy before I returned to Mick or to women in general? I was a lesbian after all—what did that mean for him?

Amidst all of this swirling chaos of logic, emotion, and consequence, something more powerful took hold, and led us to each other against all better judgment. There are some truths that you can only know in your heart, that are invisible to the rest of you, and to everyone else. In those first few weeks, I saw a chance—a chance at a love truer than I had ever imagined or understood, a love born out of friendship, mutual respect and admiration, of discovery—and I knew that taking that chance was worth any risk. As Machiavellian as it may be, there are times in life when only the bumpiest, most dangerous roads lead you to where you are supposed to be. Gabbi & I steeled ourselves for the ride ahead.

The night I told Mick that I wasn't coming back was horrible. We met at a bar a few blocks from our flat where I no longer lived, but had yet to move my things out of. While I had been discovering a new life and had already moved on, she had been living in our unchanged apartment, waiting for me to realize the mistake I was making and come back to her. The night ended with screaming on the street, her grasping at last moments with me, me wanting even more to break away when faced with the ugly reality of her heartbreak at my hands. While I can never undo that hurt, I am deeply sorry for it, and I think often on the life lesson it has taught me—that my inability to be honest with myself and my partner about what I wanted caused undue pain and suffering. I will not make this mistake again in my life—the stakes are too high.

Living out on my own, I started to discover the world again, outside of the box I had lived in for so many years. For the first time in my life, love was leading me, instead of me leading it, and the world was limitless. Once I wasn't looking for something so particular, I began to find everything I needed to be happy. I was experiencing life for what it was, and learning as I went. The simple act of letting myself fall naturally, where before I had always hand-picked my path like so many pages from a catalog, was a whole new freedom.

It no longer mattered whether I loved a woman or a man, whether I called myself a dyke or a wife; all that mattered was that I was falling in love with the most extraordinary person and friend. This amazing human, who was unlike any I'd ever met, who was every bit a man while relating to the world in a subversively feminine way, who opened my eyes to a love more vivid than I'd imagined and a world full of possibilities—this person loved me back, so intensely. Gabbi bared his soul to me, looked past the layers of chaos that would have sent most away screaming, and put his heart in my hands—he trusted me to see every bit of him, and to love him for all that he was.

In those months I realized that my identity belongs only to me, and I don't play by anyone else's rules. Loving a man doesn't suddenly make me "straight" after a formative youth as a queer woman. It doesn't make me bisexual, because I no longer define myself by what or who I am seeking. Put simply, I love Gabbi. He is my enigma: my best girlfriend and my strong husband, a self-proclaimed half-a-fag who has walked more lines than most would care to count. Who better to love him than a freak of a young girl who spent her early twenties as a radical lesbian feminist? Coming from a heavily coded world of Butch/Fem lesbianism, I am struck by the comfort and balance with which Gabbi embraces his feminine as well as masculine selves. I connect with him on a feminine level that I never did with my butch girlfriend, who built houses and watched football. Together, Gabbi and I find our *own* queerness in our *own* world, and celebrate it in each other, as no one else ever could. That alone is more revolutionary than any sticker I ever wore.

Together we grow, change, and learn to relish privacy—to keep things sacred and safe between us. We protect our love from the outside world, while simultaneously screaming its truths to anyone who will listen. We cherish each other by respecting the sanctity of our love in this world.

Gabbi and I are starting our seventh year together, and we have been married for two. We talk often of our life and our love, of the complicated path that led us to where we are. We constantly remind ourselves of the lessons that our past loves have left us with, the mistakes we cannot afford to make again. And we work—we work constantly at loving each other, at communicating, at being the best that we can be for the other, as we have both known the lesser side of love and have vowed not to go back.

We continue to celebrate our difference—as individuals with painted skin, as a couple who has traded our six-figure incomes to live a simpler life in a world where we can spend all of our time with each other and our growing family, as queers in whatever way suits us—but for me it is finally an unconditional celebration of who I am and who I love. I no longer define myself by how I fit into a supposed sub-culture. I cherish my unique history, and the path that led me to my husband and partner, that developed in me the mindset to accept him for everything he is, and to allow all of myself to be loved by him fully and unconditionally. The world is so much bigger than it was all those years ago...

I used to think I had it all figured out, but love has taught me that it's better to learn along the way. Gabbi always tells me I saved his life. I say I was merely returning the favor. I've a feeling that we will never stop saving each other as we continue to grow into our lives together, wherever they may lead us—I can't wait to see where.

CHAPTER TWENTY-THREE
THE GUY IN THE SKY
Dae Helena Leckie

We don't see things as they are; we see them as we are.
Anais Nin

Who am I, you ask? The first image that came into my mind was that of a diamond. In my late teens that diamond was roughly cut and not yet polished. The challenges of life and the many epiphanies of my sixty-seven years have slowly chiseled the rough stone to a finely cut prism. With each challenge, as with the slow but sure grinding of a stone, the gem has become brighter, more reflective and more polished. The evolution has, and still is, producing more and more facets.

As iron sharpens iron so one man sharpens another.
Proverbs 27:17

You know the song *The Way We Were?* Learning to know the guy in the sky and understanding His purpose for my life has made a critical difference in developing the multifaceted person I am today as compared to the undefined person I was before. The loved ones that God has brought into my life have also helped smooth my dull edges and have each contributed to the transformation from the person I used to be. Although the gem I have become is sparkling, clear and bright, as with any gem there are flaws that God will continue to polish and refine. The person I was is still within, and at times I recognize she has reappeared, but she no longer dominates my life. Throughout my life, finding God's purpose for me has been of major importance and the latest epiphany of what he wants has brought me much joy and peace.

I am a very different person from the nineteen-year-old that married forty-seven years ago. Learning to live with this man I still love, most of the time, has provided me with many chances to grow from the dependent, self-doubting, overprotected and frightened child I was into the joyful, competent, interdependent woman I am now. My two wonderful children, each adopted at three months, who are now forty-three and forty, have helped to polish away some of my jagged edges and have taught me the difference between owning my children and claiming them. They have taught me that just as I can love many children, they can love more than one mom. My daughter, who has offered me more challenges than I ever wished for, has taught me the way that God must love us. No matter how much we mess up, no matter how many mistakes we make, He is there, walking at our side and forgiving us. She has also greatly increased my prayer life.

Four and a half years ago we moved to Maui, Hawaii from California; I guess many people's paradise. I grieved the loss of friends and my wonderful career as a therapist working with adoptees, adoptive parents and birthparents. I missed a life I had loved. When I was sharing my grief with a friend, she said "Often in life we aren't where we want to be, but we are where God wants us." What a pearl of wisdom that turned out to be.

I learned during my first year in Hawaii that a life of rest, relaxation, fun and games was not what made me happy. I guess I'm a little like Angelina Jolie—a crusader for kids. But I combine that passion with a Reese Witherspoon, no-nonsense attitude of optimism and idealism. I need purpose in my life. God brought me together with another woman of vision who I found had been praying for someone with my background for five years (a social worker with adoption experience). My husband says when someone is praying for you it spells trouble. Together this wonderful woman and I were able to get a faith based adoption agency licensed in the state of Hawaii. Our passion for kids got the attention of the state and in January 2006 we were given a state grant to find families who would adopt older kids who have been in the system for many years. I told my husband, you can take a person out of adoption, but you can't take adoption out of the person. I know that by being instrumental in this great accomplishment I have discovered my main purpose in life, but it took a long and winding road to get there.

I am best described by words such as passionate, determined, stubborn and probably a little nuts. These days, life is like a candy store and I want to taste as many of the flavors as possible. My husband would say I make his life interesting and keep it from ever getting dull. He also recently said, "You are my joy," which truly touched my heart. Life was not always this joyful for me.

I do everything with passion and energy. I guess sometimes maybe a little too much, like "The Terminator." I learned with my new little granddaughter (my first red-headed one that I wanted so much), our son's first child, that sometimes I had to enter quietly. Now after two years she can handle my exuberance and loves to laugh with me, chase me and have me chase her. My five grandchildren are the joys of my life. Since moving to Hawaii my new name is "TuTu," the Hawaiian name for grandmas. I do wish the four in Indiana were closer, but they have gotten to visit us many summers.

I have many wonderful memories of those times in California. I'll never forget when my now thirteen-year-old, Alicia, came to visit at six years old. As we were driving off for my hairdresser appointment she shared, "My mom told me it was OK to cut my hair."

I was a little surprised, as my daughter loved Alicia's long hair. I said, "Are you sure?"

The reply came back, "Yes, grandma, honest."

So we got her the cutest, short little bob. When we got back to the house and walked in, her brothers, nine and eleven, said, "Mom is going to kill you."

Alicia turned to me, smiling, and said, "I was just kidding."

When we moved to Maui we bought a thirty-eight hundred square foot home with a four hundred square foot lanai and a five hundred square foot attic. It was the largest house we have owned and nicely holds all of my treasures. I told my husband I know some people who rent two or three storage sheds, so I'm not really that bad!!! I think it just caused him to panic that my next step would be to rent one. I have reassured him that will not happen, but I'm not sure he believes me.

I love shoes. When we moved I was embarrassed, but just for a minute, to tell my husband that I had packed over fifty pairs of shoes. My husband refuses to share a closet with me anymore. Can you imagine that? We do save money on hangers because my clothes just hold each other up. I have to admit many of them haven't been worn in quite a while, but each one has a special memory attached to it. I guess that says I'm very sentimental because as I go through my house each thing I look at has memories connected to it of people and experiences. I think my husband is afraid if I live to be a hundred my memories may outgrow our house. He also calls me incorrigible and says that I have an uncanny way of turning my worst liabilities into virtues.

I love to plan trips and we have made some wonderful ones by trading our timeshares. I have a passion for jewelry and am training my granddaughters by playing jewelry store whenever I get the chance. I also love scrapbooking. My problem is I like to make scrapbooks for those I love; therefore my own pictures are stored in shoeboxes waiting for their albums. Thank goodness I love shoes because I have an unlimited supply of shoeboxes.

I forgot to mention the collector plates I had been collecting for over twenty years just in case I wanted to start a mail order business. Ron started the mail order business when he retired as we were running out of room in our garage. He did sell off a lot before we moved to Maui, but I wouldn't part with the rest, so now I sell them on E-bay when I am not doing other things.

About two years ago the cartilage in my knee had gone and I was very crippled and had to walk with a cane. Since I am not one to sit around doing nothing I took up knitting again which my mom had begun teaching me when I was six years old. I decided to start a little business making hand knit scarves. Craft fairs are big in Hawaii so I go to craft fairs and sell them. During my recovery from my knee replacement I knitted over one hundred scarves. My husband is very glad that we have a five hundred square foot attic to house my scarves and the yarns I buy. The only problem is the attic was already pretty full of my Barbie doll collection and my Beanie Baby collection (boy was the hunt for those a blast). I also took up needlepoint, and to my hubby's horror, I have a box of unfinished needlepoint in the attic (I should say un-started). So you can imagine what his worries are about me doing this writing...every minute I spend means one more thing not listed on E-bay.

I adore Mexican food—could eat it every night. My son calls the music I like elevator music, but I have to confess I am an avid American Idol fan and I voted for Clay Aiken and bought his CD. My favorite color changes weekly and greatly depends on my mood. Red when I am feeling passionate and determined—pink when I feel quiet and shy—black when I feel sophisticated—turquoise and purple together in my elegant times—yellow during my bright sunshiny days—blue when I want my eyes to be the center of attention. I love orange, too, during my fiery moods. I do like to decorate myself for the holidays so needless to say you can usually see me coming.

You will soon understand that the carefree person I am today is light years from who I used to be.

My journey of sixty-six years started in Oakland California on July 3, 1939. My mother always referred to me as her Miss Firecracker. I was named Dae after her mother. My mother was twenty-five and was a stay at home mom. She had been a secretary before she married my dad. My dad was twenty-seven and had been raised in central California and at the time of my birth he was a butcher and owned two butcher shops.

My mother's childhood affected how she mothered my brother and me, as is true of all mothers. After her mother died of tuberculosis, she was molested before the age of six. She was also a child of divorce. Her step-father and his new wife sent her to an orphanage until her grandmother took her in, but the harsh childrearing methods of her grandmother were not much better than the orphanage had been.

My dad was raised by his mother and an alcoholic father who did not support the family and went off with other women on many occasions. I remember his mother as being cold, critical and not very loving. She called him the smart kid and my uncle was the loved child. Some of the discipline my dad received would definitely be called abusive today. When he wet the bed he was made to drink his urine. In order to ward off depression my dad had to listen to positive thinking tapes everyday of his life. Norman Vincent Peale's and Earl Nightingale's books were his Bible. When I would talk to him or ask him a question he would always quote his books. One of his favorite quotes was, "If you think you are green you'll continue to ripen, if you think you are ripe you'll begin to get rotten." Consequently, for years I had to point out my flaws, couldn't accept compliments and could not enjoy my successes.

My mother could not wait to have children. I was the first and my brother came two and one-half years later. We children were the most important people in her life, as was appropriate, but she loved us, me in particular, with an over-whelming, smothering love. She was going to give her children everything she did not have in the way of love. My mother was highly overprotective (given her own background that was understandable). She was very affectionate and was my major playmate until I was five. With my mother as my playmate I did not experience normal peer relationships. We moved to a neighborhood where there were lots of kids, but I was often hurt and crying because of the other children's teasing. I was shy and overly sensitive. It was hard for my mother to help me learn to cope and develop skills; she just wanted to love me and make it all better. I started school near an Oakland neighborhood and continued to have difficulty with peer relationships.

My desire to be the perfect child was impacted by my strict Catholic upbringing. Although my dad never really practiced his faith, my mom had converted when they married and had agreed to raise their children Catholic. She took that agreement quite seriously, and at five, I started catechism and began to learn about God. I felt I had to always be good to be loved by God and the early teaching I received in catechism cemented that belief. After taking first communion I went weekly to confession and communion. I remember feeling so good after confession and picturing my soul as the color white, after being absolved of my sins—sins such as lying, disobeying my parents and being mean to my brother. After doing something wrong I would feel very bad and pictured my soul as black. I tried so hard to be the perfect child so God would love me and bring me to heaven. I remember being terrified I would die with a mortal sin on my soul which would mean I would immediately go to Hell.

When I was in the third grade and was eight we moved to the ranch of my great uncle who had died and left the ranch to my dad and uncle. I went to a two-room country schoolhouse. Living in the country was peaceful, but I was very isolated from other kids so my mother became my best friend again. Although I had a horse, my grandfather was quite chauvinistic and the men would not let me go out riding on cattle drives. My dad never stood up for me and my eighty-nine year old aunt recently told me that I would cry and cry and ask why I could not go. She said that it made my mom furious. My six-year-old brother voiced the belief system quite clearly one day when he said, "Women belong in the kitchen and the bedroom." All of this made my mother even more protective of me. I became a very compliant child, partly out of fear that if I upset my mother I would have no one. My mother always rescued me from difficult situations. She did not want me hurt as she had been hurt.

After we moved to the ranch, to get to catechism, my brother and I were picked up by the nuns after school. The nuns had to drive thirty miles to get to our little church. Under their watchful eyes I became even more determined to be the perfect child. I remember the time my brother and I were singing "Don't Let the Stars Get in Your Eyes, Don't

Let the Moon Change Your Heart" and they told us that was a bad song and God wouldn't like it. (Thank goodness we weren't singing the songs of today; they would have had a heart attack.) My little brain struggled when each week I heard them gossiping about other nuns and couldn't quite reconcile that behavior with their getting upset with my brother and I for singing the pop song. My mother had taught me it was wrong to talk bad about other people, but she had never gotten upset when we had sung pop songs.

They told me once that they were praying I would become a nun and so I did feel affirmed in my attempts to be the perfect child. My prayers during this time were focused on asking God to help me stop wetting the bed. Apparently I had stopped when I was three but started wetting again at night at five (something was sure going on). This caused me great shame and anxiety. I could not have friends over or go to friend's houses. I even bargained with God that if he would stop me from wetting the bed I would become a nun when I grew up. These were heavy thoughts for a five-year-old.

I would build little altars at special times to the Blessed Virgin and other saints, but none of this worked so I concluded I still wasn't good enough. A little booklet I was given to study before each confession that outlined the sins under each commandment confirmed this. Under "Thou shall not kill" was listed "angry mean thoughts about another." Under each commandment I found something I did that was a sin in God's eyes. I continued to work on being perfect. This desire affected other areas of my life including my playtime. When I played jacks I was so afraid I would mess up that I would shake and freeze when trying to throw up the ball. At my first piano recital I completely froze and forgot everything. I can laugh about it now. The funny thing was that I ended on the right cord, the only correct keys I played. I was mortified and when I went to sit down my little brother didn't help when he said, "I don't remember hearing *that* song."

My perfectionism continued through adolescence. School was definitely the means through which I got my affirmation and I graduated from high school with an almost perfect straight A average. Of course the teachers loved me, but I had very few friends. I spent most of my teen years very depressed and crying a lot. I did have a romantic 'start' on the high school bus when a boy I thought was so cute started sitting with me. Every morning I was very excited to see him. After about three weeks the kids on the bus started teasing me saying, "Dae has a boyfriend." My already fragile self-esteem could not tolerate this so one morning when this boy sat by me I turned toward the window and completely ignored him—how hurtful that must have been. I blew him off when one of the things I wanted most was a special boyfriend. It seemed that I sabotaged my happiness at every turn that I made; always conflicted over what was the correct thing to do in the eyes of God.

Finally I was off to a big high school where I really felt overwhelmed with peer relationships. I was so shy and uneasy that I would not even say "hi" to peers I recognized in the hall. My escape was through academic performance. I studied constantly and worked to get straight A's to confirm my value.

Living in my family was great training for my future career as a psychotherapist as I was always trying to figure out the hidden agendas for each person and why the people in my family were the way they were. The dysfunctional nature of my household was fascinating to me. Although I was accepted to U. C. Berkeley after graduating from high school, my mother persuaded me to live at home while going to school, thus stifling my maturing process. I think she was afraid of losing me and was probably trying to protect me from the harsh world. So I went to Jr. College during the week and came home on weekends. My mother and father were having lots of problems in their marriage at this time.

During my first semester of college I started dating a Korean War veteran, Ron, who was five years older than I was. I had had a couple of other dates in college, but had not dated at all in high school as boys saw me as a "brain" and standoffish. I found out later Ron was dating a school teacher on Saturdays and me on Fridays because he did not want to get serious about anyone while he was in school. His strategy didn't work very well. He kept pursuing me, trying to figure me out. He decided he had to ask me to marry him because he could not study. I am not sure whether it was love or hormones. After dating a little over a year he had an engagement ring sitting on the snowman of my Christmas dance corsage. I was nineteen and certainly not ready for marriage. But my family was falling apart. My dad had decided, after twenty-one years of marriage, to divorce my mother. I think on some level I knew I had to separate from my mother in order to ever grow up.

I quit college and started working as a telephone operator. Ron and I were married six months later and then I worked to put my husband through school. Ron was accepted into Engineering School at U. C. Berkeley and I got a job at the Registrar's Office. I had to go to Berkeley to work before Ron started school and I was very scared and nervous. My first bus trip to work, I got on the bus, got to work and then proceeded to leave work and mistakenly catch the same bus in the same direction to go home. I knew in a few blocks I had blown it, but I sat, afraid to say anything and I rode to the end of the line. One and a half hours later I had to ask the driver how to get back to Berkeley from downtown Alameda. It is amazing to think I was so timid I could not say, "Driver I'm going the wrong way. I need to get off." The silliest thing is that I had to talk to him at the end of the line anyway. I was so afraid of looking stupid. This was a very critical time in my life. It was certainly a time I was going from a child to an adult.

Discovering "the guy in the sky" was a journey I began sixty-two years ago when I was barely five years old. My transformation from strict religiosity to spirituality has taken me nearly a lifetime. An epiphany can be a brilliant flash of insight that changes your life instantly or a slow dawning realization that may take years to impact your life. My epiphany was the latter process. As a result of it, here is what I know now:

I have discovered that finding God does not mean becoming more religious.

I have discovered that I don't have to look in church to find God.

I have discovered that the epiphanies I have had on this spiritual journey have brought me to the resting place where I stand today.

I have discovered the power of prayer, and that our prayers are not necessarily answered in the form we requested.

I have discovered that God loves me whether or not I am a perfect person.

I have discovered, and continue to discover God in the most unexpected ways.

I have discovered God has a purpose for our lives, and that what may seem a disaster at the time is used by God for good.

I have discovered that God communicates with me often about my purpose, but I must be aware. I must listen. I must see.

I have discovered that God does perform real miracles, even today. This realization is my most treasured epiphany and has encouraged me to trust in faith more often, therefore trusting Him.

With my husband going to school and me as the wage earner, we believed it would be wrong to bring a baby into our life, so we started using birth control. I felt tremendous guilt because I knew that in the eyes of my church this was murder. I confessed this sin and the priest would not absolve me of my sin unless I told him I would never do this again. I continued going to church, but every time I went I got headaches and felt worse when I left. *This was my first epiphany.* I decided at this time to stop going to church because I could not imagine that God wanted me to feel as miserable as I was feeling when I was seeking Him. *This was my first spiritual epiphany.* As a child I had been seeking absolute truth and my faith was based on fear. My journey would begin to seek truth through my own experience of God as a God of love.

My boss at U.C. Berkeley was very critical of me. He even criticized my check marks. After two years of working for him I was still feeling very anxious every day I went to work. He would come in at irregular times and by mid-morning I would start getting a stomach ache. I know all of you are thinking "Why in the world didn't she just quit and get a different job?" Remember I'm the one that could not tell the bus driver I was going the wrong way. Also one of my father's favorite sayings was "Don't be a quitter." (That little saying bit me more than once in my life.) It is hard to believe I didn't have enough confidence in who I was to get out, but my first epiphany had not a self-confident person made.

So I began praying to God that I would get sick. I prayed fervently everyday. I began experiencing joint pain which kept getting worse. The doctors discovered that I had a positive rheumatoid arthritis factor and of course stress will precipitate an attack. I was twenty years old and so crippled because of pain and stiffness that I could not walk up and down stairs and I would cry all night in my sleep because the pain was so intense. I then developed a fever of 104 and was admitted to the hospital. I was there almost two weeks with vacillating chills and fever. I had to be packed in ice when the fevers would start. As I was beginning to get better I had this dream in full color of Moses and the people of Israel wandering in the desert for forty years. God spoke to me in the dream and said, "You think you have it so bad—look at the trials these people had." I realized that God was telling me to stop feeling sorry for myself and figure out better ways to cope with life. I did get better, but was very anxious about going back to work. My vision had been affected and a very wise doctor who talked to me told me, "You should quit work and take some time off." Somehow he had surmised I could not handle the stress. I knew my emotional state had contributed to my illness. *I had certainly discovered the power of prayer.*

God led me to a book entitled "Prayer Can Change Your Life." Studying this book helped me really understand the power of prayer and how it could be used to help me manage my life in a more positive way. *I learned to turn my emotions of depression and anxiety over to God. I learned about surrender.* I learned that the only prayer that is always answered is "Thy will be done." Epiphanies are magical, but it can take years to integrate them into one's life so that real change occurs. I needed lots of practice through the years to learn the lessons I discovered. Life seems to give us many chances to practice those lessons we need to learn. I still need reminders today, and a friend gave me a little framed saying I keep handy and read daily "Good morning, this is God! I will be handling all your problems today. I will not need your help, so, have a good day."

My husband got his first job in Southern California. We had wanted to have a baby soon after he graduated so we had not been using birth control. The realization was dawning that for some reason I was not able to get pregnant. The vestiges of a punitive God remained with me and I felt that God was still punishing me for using birth control and abandoning my church. My husband and I applied for adoption and five months later our first child arrived home, a three month old little redhead. I was totally in love. He was a very high-need child and as with every step I took in life I seemed ill-prepared. My family was far away. I had no supports and again felt overwhelmed. I got sick when he was nine months old. It was the same chills and fever I had had each time I was under emotional stress. Because my mother had so adored her children she had never been able to say anything bad about being a mom. I thought children would just sit around in their cute clothes and do what ever you said. Wrong!! I was often depressed and distraught as a new mom.

My husband was transferred to Texas, even further from family. We adopted our second child, a little girl. The penicillin I was taking daily kept me from becoming sick physically, but the lack of ability to cope with life was still there. I felt God was absent and I felt dead spiritually. I was depressed and began drinking daily to deaden the pain. I began wishing I would die and one night I actually had a knife on my wrist ready to end the hurt. Somewhere a thought came to me, "This is a permanent solution that you can't take back." I also thought of my children. I adored them even though I did not know how to cope with being a mother.

We moved back to California after two years in Texas. A doctor I saw recommended I join a twelve-step program as I had begun using food to dull my pain. With the help of a sponsor and the serenity prayer I began to cope with life in healthier ways. I worked on trying to live one day at a time. Addiction of any kind is very painful. There is a cycle of pain, urges to use, giving in to the temptation, guilt, and depression and giving in again to ease the pain. My sponsor helped me through the difficult times and I was able to cope by relying on people God had put in my life rather than substances.

I found a church that taught about friends in the children's Sunday school. They taught that a friend is any one you walk up to and speak lovingly to. There was no judgement or condemnation in this church. I was looking for freedom from the overwhelming guilt I often felt in my life. At some point I had a realization that the people in this church were as rigid about their doctrine as I had been as a child and were traditionally religious based upon fear. I left this church and spent several years away from organized religion. This was another step away...

The spiritual growth I had experienced in the twelve-step program helped me have a personal relationship with God and helped me feel a sense of peace. Again life delivered me a challenge. My husband was transferred to Belgium. I was exited to get to see Europe, but soon found out the part of the company that my husband was with did not take care of us very well. We could not afford to live where the other Americans lived. I was living in the midst of the economy and trying to learn a new language, while my dear hubby got to work with people speaking English. Again I was very isolated. The children were having a hard time. Our youngest who was four had to go to Belgian preschool and cried every day because "nobody understands me." Our son was in American school but was not learning French fast enough to have playmates. I went through another period of depression. Unconsciously I know I was wishing again for this pain to end. I could not feel God beside me. I thought about jumping out the window of our sixth floor apartment, but couldn't do that because the window did not open. I was thwarted in another self-destructive plan, thank God. But I ended up having a terrible auto accident on the icy roads and I know that I was driving in such a way as to put myself at risk. Even when God seemed far away he was watching over me and I survived, though the car was almost totaled. Finally after two years we got to go back home. I was so excited.

I decided that if I could survive living in a foreign country I could do anything. Two years later we moved for the fourteenth time. Our children were now ten and twelve and I felt a need to find new meaning and purpose in my own life. I got an e-mail from God Himself. I rarely read the paper, but this one day I opened it to an article about a new bachelors program at California State University, Fullerton, called Human Services.

I had developed a fascination with psychology and the study of how we evolve to be the people we become. My intuition told me that God was leading me to this program. I got my Bachelor's and this program helped me understand myself better. It required therapy for oneself and through this I discovered a lot about my fears, and where they came from.

I was terrified of my own anger and realized I had used my husband to express my own anger these fifteen years. It made sense to me now why I was so fascinated with redheads. One therapist said to me you talk about your husband as if he is your little volcano you are so proud of. Wow! What an insight. I set to work learning about my own anger. Anger is often a repressed and suppressed feeling in an over-protected child. I felt a lot of rage about having been smothered and infantilized by my mother, but I also had tremendous fear about acknowledging it, for fear of abandonment. That buried rage had caused sickness and depression. So by learning to claim it, feel it, express it and let it go provided amazing healing. I did not share this with my mother, because I knew she had just tried to give me what she had never had and to express this would be too hurtful to her.

My beloved mother retired in 1978 after I had graduated and eleven months later she died of cancer of the pancreas. It was a terrible loss for me. I was so angry with God that he would take her just when she was going to be able to have some fun. I journaled a lot during this time and realized how much I had healed and how much my view of Him was changing. *I was no longer fearful of His condemnation or retaliation for my anger.* I did not even feel guilty. Life seemed so unfair, but then both of my parents had helped me realize God had a choice to make the world round or fair and He chose round. When crying for my mother in the terminal period of her illness I had prayed to Him to let her live, but as I had learned early, my will was not necessarily His.

I had taken a leave of absence from my job as Coordinator of The Early Parenting Program at the clinic (a program for children up to three years who were high risk for child abuse). I decided to go back to school and get my Master's in Social Work. It was truly a gift from God that my second field work assignment was at an adoption agency where I met my life-long adoption mentor, Sharon Roszia. It was perfect timing as my fifteen-year-old daughter was having tremendous difficulty with adoption issues. During this internship I learned all of the things I should have leaned seventeen years ago with our first adoption.

I learned how adoption affects birthparents, adoptive parents and adoptees. I had never really forgotten the mothers that had lost these two beautiful children I had raised; neither had my children. We had always been told that if adopted as babies, it would be as if you had actually given birth. But our daughter needed answers from her birthmother. "Why did you give me up? Who are you? Did I have another name? Do you think of me?"

This internship was the start of a wonderful career and I saw how God truly does use the difficult times in our lives for good. He had been preparing me for this job for the last seventeen years. I was able to give both of my children the permission to search to find those missing pieces to the puzzle that made them who they are. Although our son did not have a driving need to search, after he found his birthmother, Eleanor, he sounded different. When I remarked on this he said, "Well maybe I'm a little more complete."

I got my Master's in Social Work and began a twenty-five year career counseling birth parents, adoptive parents and adoptees. I had done much healing and felt much joy in my life but I still felt there was a spiritual piece missing. Oddly I still missed the pieces that religion added to a spiritual life—connecting with others who yearned for God and wanted to discover more about Him. I had been learning to pray by putting my prayers out and patiently waiting to see what answers God would provide. He led me to a large nondenominational community based church where I learned to worship through song and learned that we get mail constantly from God by picking up the Bible and reading it. This was a totally new discovery for me.

We had not been encouraged to study the Bible in my childhood church. As a priest I heard speaking during this time said, "We were told to beware letting you study the Bible because you know what happened when Luther did that."

A whole new world opened up to me spiritually. The Bible didn't say anything about mortal sin. I learned it said that none of us can be 'perfect' enough to get to heaven. I had found this out the hard way. Even the Bible said it. We could only go to heaven because of God's grace and forgiveness. God gave each of us special gifts for his purpose. I realized God had given me the gifts of compassion, healing and discernment. *I began to truly understand God's love for me was unconditional.* My faith was becoming a great joy in my life and my husband and I were baptized together.

I became a Titus Woman to the MOPS (Mothers of Preschoolers) group at our church. I describe the Titus Woman as someone who has been there and survived. Each meeting there were little boxes entitled "Dilemmas for Dae" with questions regarding problems with their preschoolers. I realized that God again was using one of the most painful years of my life for His good. I could truly empathize with this difficult time of a young woman's life. Each of these wonderful young women felt like a daughter to me.

I loved my work so much that Ron was afraid I would never retire so to help the process along he talked me into moving to Maui, Hawaii where our son had moved seventeen years ago. I agreed to give it a try. We moved in August of 2002. I was grieving the loss of my work and friends when at our family Christmas dinner God met me unexpectedly in the person of the woman who told me, "We may not be where we want to be, but we are where God wants us." So I began questioning; asking God to show me where He wanted me.

I had been having some stomach pains, but none of the medicine the doctor had given me had really helped. Another doctor had told me it didn't make sense that I felt the stomach pain when I worked out at the gym and he wanted me to have a stress test. I be-bopped in thinking I will do what he says, but this is a waste of time. The cardiologist wanted me to go to Oahu that week to have an angiogram. I was shocked. I had guests from the mainland and asked to wait until they left. The doctor said that I might not be around next week. God was there in the person of the friend that was visiting. This wonderful woman, who I had met twenty years earlier, had had two major breast cancer surgeries. She was a true survivor. I know God sent her to be with me at this time. She held me and comforted me. We prayed together, laughed and prayed together again before my surgery. I called the prayer team at our church as well as family and friends. I prayed a verse in the **Book of Proverbs:** *Trust in the Lord with all of your heart and lean not on your own understanding*

During the surgery I was awake and pictured all of the people praying for me. Our son and daughter-in-law had recently decided after thirteen years of marriage to have their first child. My prayer during my surgery was "God you know how much I want to be here to see this grandbaby." Well I guess you've figured out by now I did survive and they put a stint in my artery.

My first day back at church I walked in and the song being sung said, "I'm amazed at the way you love me, I'm amazed at the way you touch my life." God really spoke to me again when I got home and my son told me they had just discovered that they were going to have their first child in December. Wow, what a Christmas gift, and an answer to prayer.

I had been voluntarily counseling people at my church waiting for God to show me where He wanted to use me. Our pastor had also asked us to pray the prayer of Jabaez for thirty days. This is a prayer that asks God to expand your kingdom and your realm of influence. During this time I was also reading and studying *The Purpose Driven Life* by Rick Warren in order to understand where God wanted me to serve. I was counseling a wonderful young woman, named Jennifer. God used Jen in a mighty way. I called Oahu to try to get some support services for her. The person answering the phone ran to get Deanna Wallace who was supposed to have left two hours before. She told me I was an answer to her prayers, but she was also an answer to mine. *Suddenly I knew how God wanted me to serve. HOPE INC,* (Hope "In the Name of Christ") a faith based adoption agency, was born. We became licensed by the state of Hawaii in May 2004. Our passion was to find homes for older children in the foster care system whose only legal family was the State.

What you are is God's gift to you; what you do with yourself is your gift to God.

Danish proverb

My precious granddaughter, named Ohia before she was born, which means red tomato, red blood and is also the name of a Hawaiian tree with red blossoms, was born December 16, 2003. What a sense of humor God has that this little one was born with red hair. What a joy to have her growing up with us and to be able to see her every day.

After about nine months Ohia stopped gaining weight. The doctors performed all kinds of tests and could not find out what was wrong. She just seemed to have no interest in food. The games we all played to entice her were hilarious. Every time she saw food in a book she would mimic our yummmmmm, but a typical hungry baby, a voracious eater, she was not. Finally a geneticist on Oahu was the genius that called for the right test and Ohia was diagnosed with Velo-Cardio-Facial syndrome, a deletion of a piece of the twenty-second chromosome. It was thought that she had very minor symptoms.

I had just had her picture taken for the kids' birthdays when Ohia got sick and had diarrhea for over two weeks. The doctors told her mom to just keep her hydrated. Her mom got concerned because she wasn't getting better and was losing weight she could ill afford as she was already off the charts. She flew her to the children's hospital on Oahu. Her stomach was very bloated. They immediately began IV fluids and put her on antibiotics. It was later confirmed that she had a gastrointestinal infection, but God got her to the hospital just in time.

Ron and I left for a cruise to Alaska August 28, 2005. There were many prayers being offered up for Ohia's 'recovery. On September 3rd Ron and I boarded our ship and were two hours from sailing when we got a call from our son, Larry, sobbing. He said that if we wanted to see Ohia we had to come to Lucille Packard Children's Hospital in Palo Alto, as Ohia was being medi-vaced there. The doctors had discovered huge varises (blood-engorged veins) growing in her stomach and esophagus. The whole family flew to San Francisco. The doctors finally figured out that she was either born without a portal vein or it had clotted over. This vein takes blood from the digestive system to the liver. The doctors wanted to delay any surgery because she was so tiny. We found out later that they had never seen anything like this in a little one.

I had to leave to go back to Maui for a week. On my last night I was sleeping at the hospital with Jackie and Ohia and Jackie and I found blood in Ohia's diapers. We changed eighteen bloody diapers that night. In the morning Ohia threw up blood. The veins were breaking. The doctors did an emergency procedure to clot the veins. I flew home and two days later, as the prayer team at our church was at our home praying with us, Larry called. The varises had begun breaking and Ohia had thrown up a bowl full of blood. She had had seven blood transfusions. Everyone's prayers were going up from across the U.S. and far beyond—my cousin's son and his wife who are climbers were, *at almost that very point in time*, planting a Tibetan prayer flag with Ohia's picture on Mt. Everest.

I had always wondered when I read about the miracles in the Bible why I had not seen miracles in this day and age. We were all praying for a miracle. The doctors had decided they had to do surgery and on September 23, 2003, the day of Ohia's surgery, I was flying from Maui to San Francisco on a ticket I had *purchased over six months earlier*. What confirmation that is, about Who is in charge! I arrived at Stanford to see our little one resting comfortably. The doctors later told us they had almost lost her twice, but God above was watching over her. *Our miracle had happened.*

That Sunday Larry's birthmom and I attended a little Catholic Church near the hospital. We wanted to thank God together for the gift of Ohia's life. I told the priest I was a practicing Protestant and I was here to thank God for saving our granddaughter. I told him I would like to take communion. He welcomed me and told me he would be angry if I didn't. I had come full circle and I found God in the church of my childhood, but I had come back a different person. Six months later our little Ohia is running around laughing, playing hide-and-go-seek, and is at the three percent mark on the weight charts. What a joy to watch her eat. She can't get enough.

In 2006 *HOPE INC* received a state grant and God is continuing his miracles. God came to kick off our "Families for Waiting Keiki Program" in the form of a seventy-four-year-old black priest from the ghettos of Chicago. This priest had adopted four older boys and his story was truly inspiring.

God provided more healing, when in his presentation Father Clemmons said, "People who are worried about denomination are afraid of going to Hell and people that are concerned with spirituality have been to Hell and back."

I felt as if God was talking to me.

I am excitedly waiting to see the many more miracles God is going to perform. I have a new faith that enables me to handle what life sends and to wait and see how God will use it. So, who is the "Guy in the Sky?" He is the father I yearned for; the mother I lost too early. He is the birthmothers whose loss allowed me the gift of motherhood. He is the priests that brought me healing. He is the friends that have been there in times of need. He is the children we are finding families for. He is all of those wonderful friends, family and church flock that offered up prayers daily during our precious Ohia's illness. He is my Healer, my Comforter and my Guide. I see Him in all of the people that He has brought into my life. As I have relived my life through this writing I realize, in another epiphany, that He has always been there walking beside me ready to help. He, like my mother, has wrapped his arms around me, held me and hugged me. He has heard my every thought as a prayer, but I must look for Him, see Him and listen for His voice.

In presenting my story of struggles, discovery and growth, I realize I've left out the many joyful times I've spent with my beloved children and husband as well as dear friends, but that wasn't the story to be told. My hope is that any woman reading this who believes she is lost in a hopeless, black hole will feel a sense of hope that there is light at the end of the tunnel. I am thankful the Lord let me survive my Hell to reach this point in life. I can't imagine Heaven is much better. I am grateful each day to be able to wake and totally believe **Psalm 118:24;**

This is the day the Lord has made; let us rejoice and be glad in it.

***

Dedication

It is amazing the things God has done in my life since writing my story. *HOPE INC*, the adoption agency, has found permanent homes for twenty children. My husband and I became licensed so that we could be foster parents for some of the children. Our first foster child was a seventeen-year-old boy and the hearts of a family in California I had known for twenty years were opened to adopt this young man at eighteen to be part of their family. Our second foster child was a beautiful fourteen-year-old Hawaiian, Japanese, Caucasian girl who has become a permanent member of our family. I never dreamed that God might want us to be parents again. My story is dedicated to her and all of the children who have survived and thrived in a difficult world, and to the foster and adoptive parents who stand on the front lines supporting, nurturing, encouraging and healing the hearts and spirits of these Little Travelers.

CHAPTER TWENTY-FOUR
AN EPIPHA-MINI

CONTEXT

As we pulled into the parking lot of the ice cream shop one hot
afternoon we noticed the homeless man sitting on a folded fabric
remnant with his dog. The dog had water, but the sun was hot
and there was no shelter at the very corner of the entrance to the
parking lot where this man knew he would be noticed
by all who entered.

We got an extra milkshake and I took it over to him.
He looked up at me and said,
"Do you know how many of those I've gotten today, lady? This is
probably my fourth milkshake."
I was surprised to hear that remark, but said back to him,
"Well maybe your dog would like this one."
He said no, his dog was sick of them also.

I could not help but think how we all, sometimes, place ourselves
in the wrong context in life, expecting results to be different than
they are or ever could be.
Our expectations are unrealistic
given the circumstances with which we have chosen
to surround ourselves,
so we then see ourselves as a victim of the situation.

Wise people say that we *are defined* by what we think
constantly about;
I say that we also *become* a part of the context in which we choose to
surround ourselves.
If you are in the wrong context for your life's hopes and dreams,
think about changing your surroundings.

CHAPTER TWENTY-FIVE
VALIDATION
Lorelei Ann Hoxie

"Don't touch me! Nobody touches me!"

These were the first words I heard from him as he jerked around from the school's office counter and faced me with angry and defensive eyes that were years beyond his young age of twelve. As I removed my hand from his shoulder, I apologized in a soft, respectful, and assuring voice. I told him that I shouldn't have put my hand on his shoulder without his permission. This was the first day of school and I was the special education teacher. Chris (not his real name) was one of my many new students. With a caseload of forty-five middle school students, it was both a challenging and rewarding school year.

Chris was a very intelligent young man who had been diagnosed with a "borderline personality disorder" at a young age. He was integrated into his academic and special classes as much as possible. I was his case manager and even though he wasn't qualified to receive special academic services, my room was his home base.

Bang! Bang! Bang! We could hear him hitting and kicking the lockers as he came down the hall to our classroom. He would enter quickly, but quietly, and go directly to his carrel. A carrel is a small table, enclosed with tall sides and a tall front and is successfully utilized by students who are easily distracted and in need of privacy. There were several carrels situated in various areas in our small room and Chris had chosen the one in the far corner to be his and his alone. Even though he had a difficult time controlling his behavior in his regular classrooms, he knew he could choose to leave, come back to his carrel to have as much private and safe time as he needed in order to think about what had happened before talking to me. We would discuss what had caused the frustrating situation, his options, and what behavior he might choose the next time.

One day after school the school counselor brought our principal to my classroom. The counselor expressed his concern about Chris' carrel being enclosed with large sheets of black paper. He felt that this might be a sign of depression. I explained that since Chris' behavior was improving, he was able to spend longer periods of time in his classes; therefore, as requested, he had earned the privilege of covering his carrel with paper. I assured both the school counselor and the principal that this was his "safe place" and reminded them that, like my sons, all young boys like building tree houses and forts. This was also a special place for him since he and his mother had moved often and I assumed he seldom had a place he could call his own. I also reminded them of his improvements and called their attention to the sign posted at the entry to his carrel that read, "no admittance except Mrs.____ and Mrs.____." My paraprofessional and I were welcome, even though there was room for only one chair. He was sharing.

One of the reasons Chris was so angry was that he said he had "flunked kindergarten" due to his behavior. Our team agreed that if he could hold it together and not be expelled, he would be moved up to seventh grade for second semester. He signed his new "behavior modification" plan and strongly, verbally agreed to make a serious attempt to succeed. This was an enormous and rare opportunity for him, because he knew he should be a seventh grader and he often expressed anger at having to attend classes with younger peers. Chris had the skills to be academically successful, even though he had missed a great deal of schooling from being expelled in the past. He had a tremendous amount of support, not only from me, but also from his dedicated teachers, the school counselor, and the district psychologist, all of whom were willing to take the "extra steps" necessary to aid in Chris' success. To Chris' total satisfaction and delight, he became a seventh grader in January.

In addition, and significantly, Chris' mother told him that if he could finish the school year without being expelled, he would realize his seemingly impossible goal and dream of going to California and living with his father.

As the year's end was approaching, I learned from another student that Chris had moved out of the school district and away from our mountain area where he had lived and attended school. His mother was driving him up from the city every day—quite a commute. I talked to Chris and he said it was a long drive; about forty miles one way. We decided not to pursue any changes and allowed him to finish the school year with us, both honoring his achievements and admiring his mother for her dedication to her son.

The last day of school was a field day with lots of activities and freedom. Chris informed me that he did not want to attend field day because he might "lose it" and get into trouble. I agreed with him and told him that he had made a good choice.

He left early on his last day. As we stood outside the school waiting for his mom, I told him how proud I was of him and of the huge strides he had made in developing appropriate decision-making skills. I thought he was going to continue hugging me forever, a completely different scenario from the first day of school. Suddenly, he abruptly stepped back and with both a smile and a look of bewilderment on his face, he said, "This is the first year I have made it through the whole school year without being expelled."

I could tell that he was extremely proud of himself and I think we both felt that he had entered a new path. His mom came; she thanked me from the bottom of her heart and gave me a card with a lovely hand written message. We said our good-byes. I waved and watched as they drove away. I would never see him again.

...and then the day came when the risk to remain tight in a bud was more painful than the risk it took to blossom.

Anais Nin

Chris experienced success that school year because *we believed in him, focused on his strengths and empowered him* by allowing him to make decisions about his own life—and we guided him on his journey. He was respected as an individual and validated for who he was.

I could tell similar stories of the other forty-four students we had under our wings that year. And yes, I wonder where they are and how they are doing. As a teacher, I know how important it is to *validate the existence and importance of another human being,* especially our precious young people. Even though we are in their lives a short time, we can leave an imprint and make a positive difference in their lives and futures. They, ideally, can then continue on their new paths, making positive imprints on others. *"Validation" truly has a domino effect.*

***

Can one recognize an epiphany at the early age of eight? I think so. Even though I didn't know the word, I experienced one at this young age. I remember this early epiphany like it happened yesterday, even though it was fifty-eight years ago. There were three girls in our farm family and we were hoping for a baby brother. My sisters and I were sent to the neighbor's house for the night, as my Mother was going to give birth at home to our new sibling. Early the next morning, I heard my Father's excited voice and peeked around the corner and saw him sitting at the kitchen table. I dressed quickly, knowing that if I was ready, he would take me home with him. Sure enough, I got to go home with Daddy and meet my new brother.

I sat on the bed with my Mom and my baby brother as visitors came to greet our new little one. Because she thought I was wiggling too much and disturbing my Mother, the neighbor lady angrily told me to get off the bed. Without hesitation and in her kind voice, while softly stroking my arm, my Mother simply smiled in her accepting and loving way and said, "She's just fine." I'll never forget how unconditionally loved those simple little words made me feel.

We do not remember days; we remember moments.
Cesare Pavese

A forty-acre farm situated outside a small friendly town was an ideal environment for our growing and hard working family of five. Regardless of age, we all had our indoor and outdoor chores and were given a small allowance. Saturday would find us piling into the family car and driving five miles into town to shop for groceries, visit the mill to purchase feed for the animals, and spend our allowances, which consisted of pennies, nickels, dimes and even a quarter now and then. We would visit with neighbors and friends and my sisters and I would choose something special at the Five and Dime Store. Sometimes we would even save our money for a future purchase if we spotted something more expensive. It was a happy and glorious day of family sharing, celebration and renewal.

Our young years were filled with responsibility. We had to keep our bedrooms clean, dust other rooms in the house, help with the cooking, wash and dry the dishes, and fold and put away the clothes (we were too short to hang them on the line). As soon as we were tall enough and it was considered safe, Mom taught us how to iron and sew. She wanted us to participate in 4-H and Girl Scouts and so she started groups in both. I remember asking her to sew my 4-H apron because I thought she could do a better and faster job. As always, she let me know that I was doing a good job and that it was important for me to learn how to do things for myself.

Mom looked like a professional model—she was beautiful. She was tall, thin, had hazel eyes, brown hair and was full of energy; she loved to laugh and would do so at the drop of a hat. Having been an adopted, only child, she thrived at being surrounded by activity and with her determination and positive attitude thought she could achieve anything she desired and attempted. She was a professional seamstress who sewed for other women and herself, plus she also made all of our clothes and Halloween outfits. One day I was sitting on the living room floor watching her cut out a wedding dress with her new electric scissors—which she was very excited about having purchased. They were quite intriguing to me and when she went to check on something in another room, I decided to help her out. Needless to say, I didn't exactly follow the lines of the pattern pinned to the material and made quite a mess zigzagging around the fabric. When she returned, she simply thanked me for trying to help her and said that she was glad I wasn't hurt. She also told me that I needed to wait until I was a little older to use her electric scissors and that she would have to go to town and buy some more material. In my memory, Mom and Dad never gave us negative feedback or raised their voices at us. Regardless of how busy they were, they were extremely patient and took the necessary time to explain everything.

Daddy was gone during the day because, along with farming, he was a tool and die maker. Daddy was a tall, lean, handsome man with piercing blue eyes and brown wavy hair; he was kind and quiet but at the same time, had a great sense of humor. His mother had died shortly after his third sister was born, and since his father was an alcoholic, he became a caretaker at the early age of six. Daddy and his sisters spent time in an orphanage, and were then split up to live with relatives before returning home after his father remarried. It was entirely natural for him to be the strong and nurturing father he was to become after caring for his sisters and surviving a difficult childhood during the depression.

I was the family tomboy. I loved switching indoor chores for outdoor chores with my sisters. They preferred being inside, so I was able to spend most of my days happily outdoors. Feeding the animals wasn't really a chore in my eyes; it was pure fun! And even though those huge buckets of water were extremely heavy after pumping water in them and filling them to the very top, I could usually manage to pull, carry, and spill them to their destinations.

We had chickens, ducks, geese, rabbits, and pigs, all of a manageable size for young people. Collecting eggs from the chicken nests was such an exciting adventure, like participating in a daily Easter egg hunt. The best time of the year was when all the new baby animals were born. We were taught to be very quiet and not to touch the baby rabbits because the mothers would eat them if they smelled of human scent. Their nests were always so fluffy and beautiful, made of rabbit hair—such good mothers providing soft and safe homes for their babies to nourish and grow.

As the baby piglets were born, Mom and Dad would bring them in the house and put them in a large wash bucket on the kitchen table so the mother pig wouldn't roll over and squash them after birth. I remember how totally excited our fussy and proper Grandmother was at seeing the babies! She and Grandpa moved from the city to live with us on the farm after Grandpa became ill and bedridden. We all helped care for him. His bed was in the living room, along with the egg incubator, which he loved. My siblings and I wanted so badly to assist the baby chicks as they diligently worked at pecking out of their eggs, but we were informed that they needed to peck out on their own in order to gain strength and size for survival. Raising animals and administering the constant care necessary for their survival provided us with lessons in sharing, supporting, and living a meaningful life. They say that children learn by doing, and we mirrored the loving care of our parents as we mothered the animals.

The open, beautiful fields were our playground. When Mother would send me out to dispose of a container of rotten eggs, she would watch from the kitchen window as I threw them in the air and played Lindsey Clapsies—with a smile, she had told me that she was sure one would eventually land on my head. When the tomatoes were ready for harvest, I would simply overlook those huge, ugly, squishy green worms and wipe a plump, bright red, juicy looking tomato on my clothes and devour the whole thing. Digging under a potato plant was like an exciting treasure hunt because I never knew how many potatoes I would find. Daddy helped us build tree houses in all the trees that exhibited the correct branches. Mom favored the one over the pigpen as she thought it was safer. She figured that if we fell, we would fall into soft, mushy, mud—YUK! The ditches along the road were challenging when newly filled with rainwater. We had to decide where to jump over the deep water when taking a shortcut to play at our neighbor's house. We knew that deciding on the wrong crossing spot could lead to a disaster.

Shared family events were the center of our world. My Mother and Father were parents ahead of their time, understanding instinctively the concept of providing validation not to just their own children but others as well. They were incredible role models. After spending eight years on the farm, we moved to town so Mom could fulfill a dream of having her own clothing store. I planted flowers and vegetables in our yard. Our cleaning chores continued, along with checking with Mom to see what she wanted us to purchase and prepare for dinner, as there was always a complete, sit-down family meal. Mom and Dad started a baseball team for boys and girls—all children were welcome and all children played. When we were teenagers, they arranged for Saturday night dances in the town hall and on Main Street. Mom and Dad were active citizens. They stood for all good things and were loved by the townspeople and all our friends. They were responsible for many new and exciting family filled events in our small town.

In every possible way, our parents totally supported one another and their five children. Their ability to validate flowed well beyond our immediate family, like ripples in a pond, and I will always remember them as my most cherished teachers for how to live a meaningful life. By experiencing unconditional love, constant encouragement and validation throughout my upbringing, these traits became automatic for me to utilize in my daily family life and in my career.

Validation can be easily communicated through supportive eye contact, a reassuring and sincere smile, a gentle and caring touch or a nurturing gesture. It is a reciprocal act. As one validates another human being, one has an overwhelming feeling of being validated one's self. What goes around truly does come around!

Validation is free—it does not cost a thing and yet it is probably the most priceless gift we can give our children. Looking back, there is no doubt in my mind that our parents continually validated our importance from the time we were born—because that is what defined them. Validation is our greatest legacy to our children; one that we must tenderly and carefully cradle as we pass it on to future generations.

CHAPTER TWENTY-SIX
LISTEN AND IT WILL COME
Denise Diana Imansepahi

In spite of deliberately starting the year with no New Year's resolutions, 2007 was to be the year that would change my life unlike any other.

Although I was raised in a Lutheran family and was baptized and confirmed, I had rejected all organized religion long ago, believing that it was nothing more than man-made propaganda, designed by those in power as a way to control the masses. (Reading *The DaVinci Code* probably didn't help my cynical views any!)

I had never really understood the idea of spirituality at all.

On May 1, 2000, after five years of trepidation, I finally found the courage to face my fears about the state of my marriage and I moved out, beginning the twelve month process of splitting our lives in half.

The following summer I attended a self-help training program in California that had come strongly recommended by a dear friend. Although I went, looking for some strong therapy to help straighten out my head and my emotions, what surprisingly turned out to be the biggest find for me was a first-time connection to my spiritual self and something bigger that I eventually became comfortable calling The Light. This experience was like my baptism into the world of spirituality, as opposed to religion. This was no cult, and this is not what I would guess most people found there. Each of us found just what we most needed at that time and apparently what I needed then was an introduction to the fact that there were other ways of finding spirituality (Buddhism, Taoism, etc.) than those on the "Christian menu." *And I found myself.* For the first time ever, I understood the real meaning of the phrase "self-love."

Another wonderful benefit of this experience was meeting Tim. He was one of the facilitators of the program and I found him to be one of the wisest, most serene and loving people I'd ever encountered.

Once I returned home from this trip, having had my first touch with spirituality and a connection with my true self, I found my way to something called *A Course in Miracles*. This teaching of how to connect with the Light and Self felt so much gentler, palatable and authentic than any I had been exposed to before. And so it went for a time. I learned many life lessons such as, "There is no trying, there is just doing." When it comes to self-forgiveness and self-love, I learned that each day is a new chance to start over and that using the mantra of "Choose once again" really makes it easier to pick yourself up, brush yourself off and forgive yourself for not being perfect. *A Course in Miracles* helped me to heal many childhood hurts and family disagreements through understanding how to make a shift in my perception of the world around me.

Our Deepest Fear

Our deepest fear is not that we are inadequate.
Our deepest fear is that we are powerful beyond measure.
It is our Light, not our darkness that most frightens us.
We ask ourselves:
Who am I to be brilliant, gorgeous, talented, fabulous?
Actually, who are you not to be?
You are a child of God.
Your playing small does not serve the world.
There is nothing enlightened about shrinking so that other people
won't feel insecure around you.
We are all meant to shine, as children do.
We were born to make manifest the glory of God that is within us.
It is not just in some of us; it is in everyone.
And as we let our own Light shine, we unconsciously give others
the permission to do the same.
As we are liberated from our own fear, our presence automatically
liberates others.
Marianne Williamson from *A Return to Love: Reflections on the Principles of A Course in Miracles*

I met a wonderful man, Shawn, in December, 2001 and we began living together about nine months later. He had never been married before and had never been a parent before so, as you might imagine, we had a few bumps in the road learning how to mesh me, my children and him into one life. But on the whole, it went very well.

In December 2005, he asked me to marry him and I accepted. At first it was very exciting making the announcement to our friends and family and receiving their well wishes and excitement in return.

By the following August, however, the demands of daily life had smothered our short-lived excitement. I had become more and more disgruntled with my job over the years, working for an entrepreneur who couldn't delegate, but preferred to micro-manage every detail of his business. And it seemed that my fiancé's employer was always threatening another round of lay-offs (we had survived six lay-offs in four years). We were even in a rut with each other at home during our spare time, unable to answer the simple, recurring question, "What do you want to do tonight?" Instead, we were watching way too much TV and didn't have much of interest to say to each other at all.

Even the planning of our upcoming wedding had been affected by our recent doldrums. We had gone round and round about what kind of wedding we wanted to have and only after many months of discussion and changing our minds had we managed to set a date. When people asked me, "Are you excited about your upcoming wedding?" I had trouble mustering up much enthusiasm; instead I would comment on the numerous details, decisions and errands that were involved.

Since neither my fiancé nor I consider ourselves religious; we had struggled, specifically, with the decision of who would officiate our ceremony. We knew we didn't want an ordained clergyman or any traditionally religious influence in the wedding. After much discussion of people we knew that might be appropriate, I remembered my friend Tim from the training program six years ago. But how would I find him? I hadn't spoken with him in over five years! And I had heard that the organization no longer existed, having failed due to a lack of funding.

Well, I started by searching the phone listings in Sacramento, since that's where the training program had been. I placed a call to an old friend from the program, but didn't hear back from her. The only other thing I was able to remember that might be a clue was that Tim had been interested in going to work for another, similar organization. I found their website and sent an email asking if anyone there knew of him or how to get in touch with him and, if so, to let him know that I was looking for him.

Within three minutes I received an email from him! Not only had someone there known of him, but he was currently working for them full-time. What luck in remembering his association with that organization! It was so wonderful to talk with him again. He was the same loving, serene, sensitive person I had remembered him to be. He told me all about the new organization he was working with, how strongly he felt about the benefits of their program and how prestigious and legitimate it was. For a few moments I pondered the idea of signing up for this program, but then I dismissed the idea after learning about how much it would cost and that it was a ten day commitment.

After our wonderful phone conversation, he graciously and immediately agreed to perform our ceremony for us. I was so excited. It felt just perfect. "One wedding detail taken care of," I thought to myself.

Fast forward now, to January 2007. There were no New Year's resolutions, no goal-setting discussions for the year ahead. On the whole, we were both still in a terrible slump. Then, while unsuspectingly walking into my office one morning, I dislocated something in my back and proceeded to limp around for the better part of two weeks, generally feeling sorry for myself and spending way too much time thinking about the pain and wondering, "Will it every go away?"

After some gradual improvement in my injured back, I had a miserable, monotonous day at work. By late that afternoon, I was in terrible pain once again from sitting too much at my desk. So, in the spirit of feeling sorry for myself, I decided that I should go see my physician again, to see what his current assessment might be and, in my wallowing mood, to have someone to listen to me complain some more. I called his office and he wasn't available until the following morning. I agreed to the offer of an 8:30 a.m. appointment, figuring it was a great excuse to not have to be at work by 8:00 a.m. the next day.

For some strange reason, I decided to get on the scale that morning for the first time in a long time. I was thrilled when it said that I had somehow recently dropped about five pounds. (Part of what had been contributing to the overall unhappiness in my relationship with my fiancé was my serious disgust with myself over the fact that I was once again at my highest-ever weight. I was completely exhausted by this lifetime battle with my body.)

"Huh, that's a pleasant surprise," I thought. The idea that maybe NOT dwelling on this topic every waking minute might actually have done some good whispered through my mind.

As I lay on the examination table an hour later that morning with my leg stretched over and across my body in an attempt to loosen the muscles around my SI Joint, I complained to my physician, Gary, that I generally didn't have the patience for this kind of stretching. As he stood there next to me, applying pressure to my stretching, tight muscles, he peacefully responded with, "I do," and then continued to look blankly at the wall behind my head. He didn't mean it in a sarcastic or chastising way. He simply stated, with amazing calmness that "he did," without expecting any response from me, and continued to stretch my leg.

In an effort to get my mind off of the uncomfortable position he had me in, I changed the subject. "As long as I'm here," I said, "I'll take some of those nifty, little, magic, skinny pills on my way out, if you have any," hinting at my continuing frustration with the topic of my weight. We both chuckled and I continued, explaining that after years of dieting and binge exercise plans, I felt relatively educated on the topics of nutrition and health but that I knew my battle was a psychological one. I confessed that I continued to have the futile tantrum in my head about how unfair it was that some people could eat anything they wanted and their diet and exercise (or lack of both) had never even crossed paths with their self-esteem, so unlike my entire life! It just wasn't fair!

To this, Gary responded with an odd comment, "You know it's not random, don't you?"

I thought to myself, "What did he say?" I must have heard him wrong. "What is he talking about?" I sat stunned. I paused, trying to gather my thoughts and to understand. "What could he possibly mean by that?" my mind whirled.

In response, probably to my silence, he continued, "You realize, don't you, that you chose this struggle?"

Now my mind was really reeling, unprepared for this message. And then suddenly, my mind cleared and my paradigm shifted. He was no longer discussing medical terms and fitness tips!

"I think he's talking about something much beyond this medical office," I thought to myself.

And then, as the true message slid into my understanding, the tears started welling up in my eyes. The realizations started to take form in my mind. This was a struggle that I had chosen. My **SPIRIT** had selected this challenge to battle until such time as I faced it. This wasn't something that had happened **TO** me, victim that I am. I had chosen it! I had done this!

I felt a lifetime of sludge melt off of my shoulders and evaporate into thin air.

I remembered a book that I'd read some years back, and I asked, "Do you mean something like the story in *Jonathan Livingston Seagull?* You mean, my spirit won't move on to the next level of consciousness until I've conquered this seemingly inescapable curse? And that I have the power to actually choose this?" These thoughts had never occurred to me. He nodded gently and smiled, knowing the message had been communicated correctly.

He hugged me good-bye, as he always did. I'd known him for many years, and he'd been a friend during my divorce. I tried not to look at him as I left, hiding the tears that were just under the surface, threatening to overcome me like a deluge. As I left the office and reached my car, I allowed the sobs to escape.

"What just happened in there?" my mind asked.

I felt like my whole world had just been turned upside down, spun around a few times and sent through several time warps to where I had just landed, all during that very brief conversation. And every time I tried to explain it to myself, the question kept knocking at the edge of my awareness, trying to creep in: "Was I just speaking with God?"

"No, don't be ridiculous, Denise!" I would argue back immediately, terrified at the thought.

"That was just a wonderful man in there."

"Yes, but it seems that his words came from somewhere beyond this time and place, somewhere ancient and yet very present, somewhere bigger than this world, from something bigger than any of this."

The message that been delivered through this peace-filled, serene man felt like words that I'd been needing to hear for a very, very, long time. The relief that engulfed me felt like a washing away of a long,

long period of feeling stuck, powerless and directionless. A Light had penetrated that room that I hadn't seen in far too long.

And there, apparently, the Light had found me for a second time, in that place of deep self-loathing and sloth, and had spoken softly through Gary, to me, in the unlikely place of my physician's examination room.

The messages were simple, yet many:

"Just let go!"

"Surrender this fight up to the universe!"

"You have chosen this fight, it was no accident."

"Be gentle with yourself, don't fight yourself."

"Loving yourself is the only way to find happiness."

In order to truly appreciate why this moment was so huge for me, you have to understand the kind of person I am. Not only am I not a religious person, I am a very practical, grounded woman. I have always been very financially responsible, balancing my check book to the penny, contributing a dutiful 10% to my 401(k), etc. I was always a straight-A student, acquiring a business degree in finance. Creative endeavors have never felt good to me, being too loose, having no rules or guidelines and certainly no definitions as to "the right way to do it," which always leaves me feeling lost and clueless. I've always been very self-confidant in my professional life and I've approached all areas of my life very logically. I got married right out of college to someone I'd been with for four years. We made money, bought a house and furnished it, traveled, and then had two children, exactly on schedule, first a boy, then a girl. Perfect. I like things planned, predictable and tidy.

As I drove to work from Gary's office that morning, I realized that the tears were not only about the realization of my own power over my weight issues, but also about the pain and longing that had been hiding, undetected inside me over the recent years, squirreled away somewhere in the depths of my heart. The tears were for that connection to my Self, my Spirit, my Soul that I so desperately need in order to feel alive. I knew that I needed to recapture this for myself, and soon!

Even before I could take any action in this new direction, I was shoved right into it. I had barely sat down at my desk when the owner of the company came in, wanting to tell me about yet another decision I'd made that he disagreed with. I would have ordinarily become immediately defensive, refuting his opinion and creating yet another difficult, tense exchange with him. I had barely pulled myself together from the sobbing in the car, however, and having felt such a powerful connection with the love inside myself, I found that I was able to hear his criticisms in an unusually accepting way. I agreed with what he said, apologized for not having checked with him before going ahead and assured him that I would rectify the situation immediately. Wow! What a difference!

Later that very morning, I called Tim. I knew that one of the best ways to begin reconnecting with my Self was to get involved in doing things that had helped me find this part of myself to begin with. I knew immediately that I had to sign-up for the program that he had told me about. I signed up later that day, made all the arrangements for the time away from work and for the care of my children while I'd be gone. I also immediately contacted my instructor for *A Course in Miracles* and signed up for the very next session being offered.

Several other amazing things happened in my life shortly thereafter. It seemed that by simply *being open to the possibility of a connection with Spirit,* it manifested itself all around me. While talking on the phone to a friend of mine, she told me about a book that had been making headlines lately that talked about the Law of Attraction. Basically it says many of the same things I had learned at my training program; such as, the thoughts you hold in your mind attract like things to you from the universe. She had just received the book and video and had shared it with her sister. In just a few days, she couldn't believe the difference in her sister's reality that had been created by nothing more than putting a different intention into her thoughts and actions.

Just a few days after that, although I had been approached to participate in writing this book nearly a whole year before, the founding author mentioned that she was suddenly short a couple of chapters and wouldn't I reconsider participating? When she had approached me originally, I had not thought I had anything to contribute and had decided against it. Now suddenly, my whole life seemed to be filled with epiphanies! Of course I wanted to participate! And so things continued for some time.

But the biggest epiphany was still ahead for me.

The time for my trip to this second training program was approaching and I was torn between excitement and anxiety about all the difficult, personal, emotional work I would surely be facing when I arrived. If this experience was anything like the one I had done before, it would certainly be rigorous.

The day I was preparing to go to the airport, my supervisor called me into his office. We had been working for weeks on a new organizational structure at the company and I suspected that he wanted to talk to me about that. He proceeded to explain that, in spite of the fact that he and I had been working on this reorganization together for some time, he and the owner of the company had made a final decision without me. He informed me that the vast majority of my responsibilities were being taken away from me, that I would no longer supervise the team that had been mine for the last five years, and that I would be taking on lower level tasks and duties. I just stared at him, wondering, "Where in the recent years had I gone wrong and lost his support and trust? After all, he was the reason I had stayed at this company over the last five years! And now, here he was, betraying me? How could they do this to me, knowing that this is not what I want to do with my career? And, how am I supposed to look at it as though it is not a demotion?"

I left for the airport that day, torn up inside and crying, wondering why things had changed for me so suddenly. I was especially furious at their timing. How dare they intrude on what was supposed to be a ten day escape for me personally? I didn't want this soul-searching trip to be impacted by work-related issues! Damn them!

As the plane paused on the runway, waiting to take off, I debated the options in my head. I called my fiancé from my cell phone, explaining the events of the day and how upset I was. Rational, cool, logical Shawn that he is, of course, advised me to calm down before making any rash decisions. I knew before I called that this would be his response and I was prepared. I had already done the hardest work surrounding my next decision, and that was giving myself permission to have choices. I had already gone through the worst case scenario and decided that I needed to leave my job. If all else failed, I could live off of some of the money I had in my retirement accounts, if necessary. But I knew I could no longer stay at a job that was sucking the life out of me.

Knowing that he, himself, has a lot of fear around money issues, I headed-off his objections at the pass by asking him, "If I promise to meet all of my financial obligations in the same way that I have up to this point, could you be okay with my decision to quit my job?" He agreed.

But I promised myself that I would not act rashly in the heat of the moment. I did not call and quit that day. Instead, I made the deliberate decision to go on my trip, do a lot of difficult soul-searching work, asking for what I need in this life, and then and only then, while still in the best possible frame of mind, would I decide whether to quit or not.

Well, it was, indeed, a rigorous experience, attending this ten day process. I spent the time focused on my childhood and my parents, my negative, learned behaviors and most importantly, my vision for the life I want to create for myself from here forward. There were several instances when I experienced resistance to facing all this and when the fear of making decisions almost overwhelmed me, but I never wavered during my time away in my desire to quit my job. The most miraculous shifting of perspective that occurred, however, was that what had transpired at my job was not something to be angry about but, instead, something to celebrate. This was an amazing gift that I had apparently attracted to myself. Had this unpleasant, painful conversation not taken place with my supervisor before I left to attend this program, I would never have even thought to define my future outside of the parameters of working at that place, in that position, in that industry. Instead, while I sat, visualizing the life of my future, I was able to completely clear the slate of what I had to start with. I was able to free myself of the box representing my current job and I could now choose from so many more options than I had ever allowed myself before. By the time I headed home, I was at peace with my decision to quit, in spite of not necessarily having a plan for what I would do to support myself instead.

The miracles began to happen almost immediately.

I stopped in Sacramento on my way home to visit an old friend that weekend. She wanted to show me the new house that she and her husband had built since I'd last visited and I was eager to reconnect with her again. We had dinner, I spent the night and the next morning she and I went for a walk around her new neighborhood. While we strolled, watching the wild turkeys dart around, she pointed out her neighbors' nice, new houses. An amazing moment happened for me then as we stopped in front of one house, worth approximately $2.5 million in my estimation. She told me that although she didn't know their names, she knew that this particular house belonged to two people who both worked from home.

Now, if I asked my friend to remember which house it was or the details of that specific conversation, she probably would not be able to do it. For her, I'm sure, it was a very casual comment made on a morning walk around her neighborhood with a friend one day. However, for me, it opened up another whole realm of possibilities! Suddenly, not only could I see that I didn't have to work for my current employer anymore, but I could see that I didn't have to work for any employer anymore! Of course, it's obvious to most people that self-employment is always an option. But for the first time in my life, I was able to see that this could be a realistic possibility for me.

I returned to Denver that night, had a wonderful, warm reunion with my fiancé and then fell into bed, tossing and turning, visualizing how I might deliver the news the next day to my employer that I intended to quit.

Much to my surprise and relief, I arrived at work the next morning and found a card on my chair from my supervisor. His card expressed his apology for the way in which our last conversation had transpired and invited me to have coffee with him first thing that morning to discuss how he could be supportive of my professional future, either with this company or not. We went to coffee and I let him talk for a few minutes. He continued to try to persuade me that this new organizational structure was actually to my benefit. Then, I thanked him for his efforts and explained that I felt it was time for us to discuss a way for me to transition out of the firm. He was receptive and said he would take my request to the owner of the company. Part of my request was that I have a response by the end of the day with an agreement as to the terms of my separation. He seemed to think that was reasonable. I felt it was important due to the fact that I had put myself in a very vulnerable position and I wanted all of us to have closure on the discussion as soon as possible. Later that day, he informed me that they would not have a final decision by the end of the day, but that the owner of the company was reasonably open to the idea of working out a win-win agreement. I decided to take the afternoon off, feeling rather uncomfortable with the whole thing and letting thoughts of distrust and fear creep into my mind. All the while, I had been receiving advice from Shawn, my parents and close friends, recommending that I "stick it to them," take advantage of the fact that it was a very vulnerable week in the quarter for them to lose me, and to demand what I wanted.

Later that evening, my supervisor called and asked me to again meet for coffee. I agreed. When we met, he explained that if my position was to threaten them and to not return to work until I had an answer, then the owner of the company was prepared to let me leave immediately. I was shocked by this turn of events and I quickly started back-pedaling on my position. I backed-off of some of my demands and cited the fact that I was not speaking directly to the owner of the company as the reason for some of the miscommunication that had occurred. I explained that I thought that things that had been insinuated had been misunderstood. My supervisor was willing to help me get my negotiations back on track and we agreed that I should speak directly with the owner of the company myself to clear the air.

The next morning, I met with the owner of the company to try and work things out. I told him that I was sorry for any misunderstanding that had transpired up to this point and that I wanted to work out a win-win situation for both me and the company. In spite of the vulnerable position I was in, I was choosing to take "the high road" from here forward and I told him that he could completely trust me to continue on until such time as we reached an agreement about my transition. He agreed and asked if we could close the meeting with a hug!

It took them over a week to draft a formal agreement, but I was quite elated when it was presented to me. They had agreed to the vast majority of my requests.

I learned so many lessons from this experience that will live with me forever! I nearly made an awful mistake in this process by starting out coming from a place of fear, distrust and anger. Fortunately, I changed my approach quickly and, by coming from a place of love and trust instead, I was able to negotiate a five-month severance package from an employer that had previously only given severance packages of a few weeks. I would never before have believed it possible.

And I also learned that although friends and family can have the best of intentions, it is possible for them to become so wrapped-up in a situation, almost taking over ownership of it and making it their own, that they don't necessarily give the advice that is best for you. In this case, after I realized that I had nearly made a terrible mistake and had almost lost the possibility of any severance pay at all, I decided to not discuss it with anyone until after the final agreement had been reached. I deliberately did not return calls to my parents or my friends during the entire week while I was waiting for a decision. With Shawn, I simply stated that I thought it was best for both of us to let me handle it on my own. He, in all his wisdom, understood immediately and didn't mention it again until I came home that day with the news that they had granted me the package I had asked for.

And here I am, now just a few days into my severance period, busily setting out on the road of self-employment. I've set up my desk and have several possible clients ready to start as soon as I am. I don't have all my problems solved. I know that my future holds some days that will be better than others. I'm not sure how I'll navigate all the paths that lay ahead for me, but I have remembered yet again where happiness lies—if ever I should forget. *It lies within me. That's where I need to look.* I must look with loving eyes, not those of judgment, anger, and distrust; but with gentleness, compassion and love. And there it will be, connected to the bigger love that binds us all. Call it what you will, but I've touched it and it is out there. No, it is *IN* there. You need only quiet yourself and listen for it. It will come.

Waiting Until Spirit Is Heard

As my prayer becomes more attentive and inward
I had less and less to say.
I finally became completely silent.
I started to listen—
which is even further removed from speaking.
I first thought that praying entailed speaking.
I then learned that praying is hearing,
Not merely being silent.
This is how it is.
To pray does not mean to listen to one's self speaking.
Prayer involves becoming silent,
And being silent
And waiting until spirit is heard.
Soren Kierkegaard

CHAPTER TWENTY-TWO ENDNOTES
Endnotes

[1] An actual quote about Evergreen from the private billboard of Hamilton Farms along Interstate 5 – the college sold postcards of the photographed billboard, which sported a caricature of Uncle Sam, in its bookstore.

[2] Name changed out of respect for privacy.

[3] Name changed out of respect for privacy.

[4] The Stonewall Riots of 1969 are the widely accepted beginning of the modern Gay Rights movement. In 1994, New York City was host to "Stonewall 25," a week-long celebration and convergence of hundreds of thousands of Queer Men & Women, culminating in a huge march through the city.

[5] The oft-repeated joke, originated in the early 80s by comic Lea DeLaria (who incidentally made my weekend at a "womyn's" music festival when she told me I was cute), goes something like this... *Q: What does a lesbian bring on a second date? A: A U-Haul*

[6] hasbian (HAZ.bcc.un) *n.* A former lesbian who is now in a heterosexual relationship. [source: wordspy.com]

954836

Made in the USA